The Language of Technical Communication

A Practical Guide For Engineers, Technologists, and Technicians

Second Revised Edition

Preface to the Second Edition

The relatively short time period since the publication of the first edition has seen significant advances in the recognition of the importance of technical writing and in the movement toward a more scholarly approach to the subject. The power of the written and spoken word has of course always been recognized by an enlightened few who have supported and encouraged the instruction of technical writing for several decades. Yet the value of clear, concise writing in detailing project designs, in explaining research results and in obtaining grants is now more broadly recognized. Under the impetus of the Canadian Engineering Accreditation Board and some engineering advisory boards, technical writing is no longer regarded as a subject that students learn only through unguided practice. Most engineering departments and their students now realize that technical writing is a skill that needs to be taught by qualified teachers who discuss and explain the language principles and then guide the development of students' writing through practical assignments and exercises.

The first edition introduced the technique of using published examples of technical prose as the basis for explaining the principles of content, structure, organization and the language signals used by writers to guide their readers through the text. The discussion and examples demonstrate the principles of structured descriptive, problem-solving and argumentative technical writing, as well as the important concepts of technical style and tone. More importantly, perhaps, conciseness, precision, punctuation, and some common grammatical errors are all explained within a consistent overall framework. This enables students to understand and make sense of systems of language use rather than blindly following incomplete, inadequate or inappropriate rules.

This second edition builds on these strengths, providing additional material on computer, e-mail and Internet use and updated advice on editing techniques, which are changing rapidly as a result of advances in computer technology. As many students had experienced considerably difficulty in the transition from the essay-style writing in schools and early instruction in university, the early sections of the book have been strengthened by discussion on that subject. Recent publications on the use of acronyms and unrelated ("dangling") clauses have also led to improvements in related sections of the book. The indexes have also been improved to allow students to gain faster access to the checklists, terms and key topics discussed throughout the book. Minor changes to dates and times have also been made.

The second edition has benefited from the positive and helpful comments I have received from many students who have used the book over the last four years. I am also heavily indebted to Bob Hilderley and Susan Hannah of Quarry Press for their highly professional editorial, design and production work in publishing this edition.

Michael P. Jordan
Kingston Ontario Canada
August 2000

The Language of
Technical
Communication

A Practical Guide for Engineers, Technologists and Technicians

Second Revised Edition

MICHAEL P. JORDAN

Professional Engineer
PhD in Linguistics/English Language

Professor, Department of Mechanical Engineering,
Faculty of Applied Science
Research Associate, The Strathy Language Unit,
Department of English

Queen's University, Kingston, Ontario

For Eugene Winter, the pioneer of language-based instruction in technical writing.

ISBN 1-55082-277-2

Typeset and copyedited by
Jane Davenport.

Design by Susan Hannah.

Printed by AGMV Inc.,
Cap-Saint-Ignace, Québec.

Published by Quarry Press, Inc.,
P.O. Box 1061, Kingston,
Ontario K7L 4Y5.

Acknowledgements

This book is the culmination of 32 years of research and teaching at Queen's University, Ontario, Canada; the strong linguistic approach owes much to linguist Eugene Winter, and to linguists Michael Hoey and Peter Fries. Thanks to Queen's University and the Faculty of Applied Science for providing academic and financial support and to Neville Davies for his years of assistance in teaching and research. Thanks also to Queen's students Doug Savage, for extensive research and editorial advice during the early stages of the book, and Kristen Lamertz, Shaney Crawford and Adrienne Pratley for their input and effort. Thanks to Queen's student Jane Davenport, for editing and typesetting the final copy, and a special thanks to Bob Hilderley and Susan Hannah of Quarry Press for their expertise and professionalism in designing, producing and publishing the book.

Permissions

Thanks to the students, authors and editors who gave their permission to use the examples in the text. Contributors are listed here in alphabetical order.
Magazines and Journals: *American Society for Testing and Material, Canadian Aeronautical and Space Journal, Canadian Civil Engineer, Canadian Consulting Engineer, Canadian Journal of Chemical Engineering, Canadian Journal of Earth Sciences, Canadian Mining Journal, Canadian Institute of Mining Bulletin, Computing Canada, Engineering Dimensions, Engineering Fracture Mechanics, Geophysics International, Journal of Technical Writing and Communication, Key Engineering Materials, Machinery and Equipment MRO, Manuscript Review, Mujumdar, A. S., Ed., "Drying '89", Hemisphere Publishers, New York: 1989, Northern Miner, Nuclear Canadar, Proceedings of the Ist International Conference of Fluidized Technology, Pulp and Paper Canada, Queen's Applied Science Calendar, Queen's Quarterly.*
Queen's Students: E. Bacon. H. Iordanou, G. Logan, *Stat 865*, J. Fry and D. Yung, *Department of Computing and Electrical Engineering*; K. Haralamides and J. Howes, *Department of Mechanical Engineering*; G. Rumplar, *Department of Geological Sciences*; C. Seppala, *Department of Chemical Engineering*; B. Shaw, *Department of Chemical Engineering*; E. Turner, G. Narbonne and N. James, *Department of Geological Science.*

Table of Contents

Table of Contents

1   Chapter 1: **The Importance of Technical Communication**

     Background and Approach • Core Instruction and Practice • How the Book is Organized • The Learning Techniques • The Importance of Technical Writing • Practical Writing Situations

13   Chapter 2: **Understanding the Task and Preparation**

     Different Types of Process • Purpose and Readership • Topic Selection and Task Definition

31   Chapter 3: **Contents and a Sense of Order**

     Writing as a Reiterative Process • Organizing Your Work

47   Chapter 4: **Organizing and Signaling Material**

     Outlining • Signaling Your Structure

61   Chapter 5: **The Thread of Continuity (Description)**

     Basic Continuity • Using Separate Clauses • Descriptive Clauses • Connection by Association

93   Chapter 6: **Problem-Solution Structures**

     The Problem-Solving Philosophy • Complete Structures • Curtailed and Shorter Texts • Condensed Structures • Complex Problem-Solution Structures

113   Chapter 7: **Presenting a Credible Case**

     The Need to be Technically Convincing • Types of Evidence • Argument as Evidence • Special Structures • Types of Evaluative Writing

137   Chapter 8: **Technical Style**

     Review and Preview • The Concept of "Propriety" • Style • Important Factors Affecting Formality • Tone

161   Chapter 9: **Conciseness**

     Conciseness in Large Documents • Conciseness and Continuity • Special Structures • Other Techniques • Review: Style and Politeness

183   Chapter 10: **Punctuation**

     Approach and Major Errors • Mainly Commas • Colons, Semicolons, Dashes and Parentheses • Other Punctuation

211   Chapter 11: **Grammar, Word Use and Editing**

     Common Grammatical Errors • Word Choice and Use • Revising and Editing

239   Chapter 12: **Graphical Communication**

     The Importance of Graphical Communication • Graphs and Tables • Schematic Diagrams • Diagrammatic Representation • Maps and Photographs • Combining Text and Illustrations

267   Chapter 13: **Oral Presentation**

     General Principles • Informal Presentations • Formal Presentations • Answering Questions • Visual Aids

287   Chapter 14: **Technical Documents and Their Parts**

     Parts of Documents • Summaries and Abstracts • Technical Documents

305   Chapter 15: **Personal Communications**

     Electronic Mail • Letters • Resumes and Forms • Memoranda (Memos)

335   **Appendix A:** Information Retrieval

343   **Appendix B:** Describing People (Including 60 Ways of Avoiding Sexist Pronouns)

363   **Appendix C:** Conventions: Numbers, Symbols and Units (SI)

369   **Appendix D:** Conventions: Equations, Abbreviations and Consistency

375   **Appendix E:** Multiple-Choice Test Questions

385   **Appendix F:** Glossary of Terms

395   **Appendix G:** List of Checklists

399   **Subject Indexes**

411   **Special Indexes**

427   **Selected Bibliography**

Chapter 1:
The Importance of Technical Communication

This chapter introduces you to the subject of technical writing and to this book, including the learning and teaching techniques used here. It also explains the importance of technical communication to your career potential and your personal image as an educated person. The final section discusses practical writing situations you will become involved with in your educational program and your professional career.

Background And Approach
Attitudes
The Importance of
    Technical Writing
Literary and Linguistic Approaches
Essays and Reports

Core Instruction and Practice
Educational Needs
Contents and Approach
Uses of the Book

How The Book Is Organized
Modularity
Appendices and Indexes
Glossary of Terms
Bibliography

The Learning Techniques
Learning through Examples
Writing and Editing Exercises
Limitations of Spell Checkers
Review Questions

**The Importance of
    Technical Writing**
Career Potential
Personal Image

Practical Writing Situations
Topics and Readership
Writing in University and College
Technical Style

1

Background And Approach

Attitudes

Most of us entering careers in engineering, science or technology do so because we have an affinity to the practical and mathematical basis for such work. We like to know how things work, how to improve them, and how to make new things to meet needs we define. We are excited by the neatness of equations and methods of analysis that yield definite results. We are interested in the way we can prove theorems, and how we can demonstrate relationships by conducting experiments to verify established and new concepts.

Conversely many of us feel less comfortable with the more intangible aspects of life. We may be less able to understand or express opinions about art, movies or politics. We may not understand how — or even why! — people can discuss historical events or inter-personal relationships in great depth. Many technical students feel that years of study of drama, poetry and other literary works have done little to help them to write well.

Whether we choose a technical career because we like technical topics, or because we do *not* like other topics is often difficult to tell. Perhaps it is a little of both. But whatever the reason, most of us — perhaps subconsciously — choose a technical career partly in the expectation that we will not have to be too involved with language study or use.

The Importance of Technical Writing

It thus comes as a great surprise to many engineers, technologists and technicians that language is a vital part of their professional lives. Practicing engineers have been found to spend 1/4 of their time writing documents, and another 1/4 reading or editing documents written by others. Technical writing has also been ranked as the "most important" subject for technical staff in geological engineering and related subjects. More recently, Dr Garland Laliberte, newly-elected President of the Canadian Council for Professional Engineers, stated that ". . . the quality of communication skills is the deficiency most frequently mentioned by employers of recent graduates." In addition, a survey recently published by Professional Engineers of Ontario listed communications and publication as an area of considerable growth.

The message is clear. An ability to express yourself — not just adequately, but well — in written and spoken English (and with illustrations) will be an extremely important element of your professional life. However, given that 12 years or more of formal instruction in English may not have provided you with the skills you need for writing as a professional, how can we now remedy this?

Literary and Linguistic Approaches

Years of literary study may have failed to help you to become an effective technical writer because it is an indirect method. Its main aim is to enable you to understand and express well-considered views on various forms of literary expression. As a side effect, some students with an inherent ability in, and desire to learn about, language do develop a sound sense of style and expression. They are then able to apply that ability to their own written work.

Many technical students, however, have not made that huge jump. Perhaps largely through lack of interest, few have applied the general principles of literary analysis to the more practical tasks of describing and explaining technical information. Most of you will therefore benefit from a more direct approach.

The direct linguistic approach used here relies on the study of examples of the type of writing you will be producing in your professional careers. The examples will not all be in your own technical disciplines of course. But the style, clarity, conciseness and tone will be very similar to the forms of writing you will be expected to produce throughout your educational program and your professional life. In addition, you will actually be studying the ways writers communicate their technical information — not the individual writers, the protagonists, the settings, etc., which are appropriate for literary rather than linguistic analysis.

Essays and Reports

Perhaps the biggest difference between school writing and the writing of professional engineering is that the former is based on the essay, whereas the latter is based on the report. Essays are written in a flowing style with the argument being presented in a linear fashion to build up the overall message. They are written to be read in a linear fashion, from beginning to end, as the reader is lead logically through the discussion to the final conclusion. In contrast, reports are written for different readers, who often need to read only certain parts of the discussion — and not necessarily in the order presented in the document. Thus material is grouped clearly under headings, and summaries are provided to allow different readers to find information quickly and act on it.

Engineers do not write essays as part of their careers; they write, read and act on reports. The organization of material, the use of headings and sub-headings, the use of summaries, and the efficient no-nonsense writing style all make reports different from essays, and you will need to adapt your writing approach and style accordingly. In addition, reports often follow standard groupings of information, sometimes rely on the use of drawings to supplement the text, and are frequently presented orally by individuals or teams. This book will help you to collect and organize appropriate material, write it in a manner suitable for reading in professional engineering circumstances, and present it with supporting illustrations and orally.

Core Instruction and Practice

Educational Needs

From its infancy in Canada little more than 30 years ago, technical communication has grown to become a large and extremely important activity. It is now generally recognized that engineers, scientists and technologists cannot survive in today's competitive market without adequate written, graphical and oral communications skills. Engineering accreditation teams, faculty members in universities and colleges, and employers in industry and government are now demanding higher communication skills of their students and workers, and those who do not meet the requirements are being left behind in their career development.

Three levels of instruction have emerged from the Canadian debate concerning what and how technical communication should be taught:

(a) basic competence in written, oral and graphic comprehension, mainly for those whose first language is not English (usually as a pre-requisite for other English or writing instruction);

(b) core instruction and practice in the most important elements of written, graphic and oral communication; and

(c) more specialized instruction and practice relating to the special needs and documents of the many disciplines in engineering, science and technology (given in later years of study).

This book is designed to meet the central of these three needs. It includes instruction and practice in only the most essential elements of engineering communication, with emphasis on the written form. It provides you with a sound basis for understanding the language forms and structures in technical communication generally, leaving many of the specialized documents and techniques for later instruction.

The premise here is that once you can write, you can write anything. All you will need to do is to study and apply principles you learn here to special documents and communication needs related specifically to your discipline. This you can do in advanced writing courses relating to your speciality, or as on-the-job training when the need arises.

Contents and Approach

The essential questions then become: What do technical students *really* need to know about technical communication, and what must you be able to do? The answer provided here is that you must have a sound understanding of:

(a) how to plan and organize information to provide meaningful documents to meet readers' needs;

(b) how to express yourself clearly, properly, and concisely in descriptive, problem-solving and proposal-presenting forms of writing using appropriate technical style; and

(c) how to present your material concisely, accurately and properly in oral and graphic forms as well as in writing.

This book is a departure from other texts on the subject in its concentration on only those elements that are of vital importance to the achievement of these aims. It also differs from others texts in its approach to the study of written English. All principles explained are well founded in published language research, and you will learn how skilled writers write largely by studying how they do it — much like the way we all learned language in the first place. Examples used throughout the book are actual examples published recently in reputable Canadian technical magazines and journals, or by engineering students and faculty at Queen's University.

This is not a text of inviolable rules of effective writing. Instead, it introduces you to systems of cohesion, continuity and style that provide choices to writers. You will learn how to make intelligent decisions about language use based on the form of writing appropriate to your needs and in line with your own developing individual styles. This is a challenging approach — but then education, rather than training, always is.

The level of instruction of this book assumes that you can write grammatically acceptable sentences in English and can connect your ideas together into meaningful paragraphs. Access to a spell checker, dictionary and perhaps a handbook of English use or a related computer tool will also be useful. It is also assumed that you normally compose your written (and perhaps also your graphical) work on computers. You should note, however, that spell checkers have limited use and that some of the advice given by style checkers may be misleading or wrong.

Uses of this Book

This book is designed specifically as a communication and English language foundation course for all students of engineering, science and technology in universities and colleges. A wide range of technical subjects is included in the examples used here, demonstrating that the principles being discussed form a core of language use common to all forms on technical communication. Although the emphasis is clearly on technical writing, students in other professions (e.g. business, medicine, nursing, social work, law enforcement) will also find much here of direct relevance to their own communication needs.

One way of using this book is as the text for a course in basic technical communication. The chapters could be presented as fifteen or more lectures, although some of the material could be left for you to study on your own. For more advanced or better students much of this text could be a self-learning resource with students completing exercises and tests as necessary. Exercises in the book provide material for writing assignments for completion either during class discussions or work submitted for evaluation. Other review questions at the end of chapters could form the basis for a mid-term test and a final test or examination.

As an alternative, this book could form the basis of more advanced study and practice within the different disciplines. Used in this way, this text might form perhaps the first five or six weeks of a three-hour-a-week course with students proceeding through the material at a faster pace and being required to do more of the work outside the classroom. This instruction would then form a sound communication and language basis for later analysis and writing of reports, proposals, specifications, contracts and other technical documents related specifically to the needs of the disciplines involved. Used in this way, this text would be highly compatible with co-operative instruction between language and technical instructors.

How The Book Is Organized

Modularity

This book follows a natural sequence dealing with the overall process, contents and organization (*Chapters 1–4*), special structures and types of technical writing (*Chapters 5–7*), writing techniques (*Chapters 8–11*) and other principles (*Chapters 12–15*). However, many of the chapters are self-contained modules of instruction and practice, and this means you can omit some chapters or change the order without serious loss of understanding.

Some of the chapters provide extra depth to other chapters. For example, the principles of descriptive writing and the use of illustrations are useful in improving conciseness, a sound knowledge of punctuation will help you with elements of style and description, and concepts of preparation and propriety are useful in understanding oral presentations. However, each chapter will provide you with a sound understanding of the subject it covers, even if you have not studied related elements of technical communication.

Appendices and Indexes

Appendices include useful information which could not be fitted conveniently into the organization of the 15 chapters. The appendices cover methods of information retrieval, describing people (including avoiding sexist pronouns), and conventions — first of number and symbols, and then of equations and abbreviations. Other appendices include some test questions and a glossary of terms and a list of checklists.

In addition to the usual subject index right at the back, you will also find indexes of where you can find interesting language features in the examples cited throughout the book. Some special indexes will enable you to study the use of key connecting words in technical writing, such as *which*, *this*, *problem*, *solution*, *assessment* and *basis*. Other indexes will allow you to find many other language features in the examples — from punctuation marks to information structures and from signals of formality and informality to colloquial or metaphorical use.

Glossary of Terms

Appendix F is a Glossary of the Terms used throughout the book to explain the principles of effective technical communication. Definitions and examples of the terms are also provided there, together with the locations in the book where you can find explanations and discussion. You should refer to this appendix whenever you are uncertain about the meaning of a term used in the text.

Any worthwhile study requires the definition of special terms, and technical writing is no exception. By the time you have completed your course of study and practice using this book, you will be expected to know, for example, what *tautologies*, *acronyms*, and *outlines* are. You will also know what *existential 'there'* and *anticipatory 'it'* are — and when and where to use them.

The *glossary* will be an invaluable guide to you as you develop your knowledge of technical communication and its essential terms. Just as you cannot expect to learn much about electrical engineering without learning the meaning of *current*, *voltage*, *resistance* and *magnetic flux*, for example, you should not expect to understand technical communication without knowing and understanding its important concepts and terms.

Bibliography

A selected bibliography is provided for instructors and serious students and scholars of technical communication as the basis for more advanced study and practice. Many of these other published works include even more detailed bibliographies for scholars and instructors to examine the theoretical background for the work presented here.

The Learning Techniques

Learning through Examples

Much of what you will learn in this book is from the study of extracts of actual writing and graphical communications that express technical facts, explanations and views to technical readers. These extracts have been chosen to represent the most common structures, styles and methods used by skilled technical writers and editors. They also, in a small way, provide a representative collection of examples of Canadian technical prose, and they are thus suitable as a basis for more advanced study.

The technical topics of discussion in the examples are not important as we are studying only the *way* information is presented — not *what* is presented. If you find any technical subject in an example of special interest, you are encouraged to read the whole article. A reference is given for each example to enable you to do that, and you should be able to find the magazines in your library.

In addition to learning from the examples as they are included and discussed throughout the book, you can learn much more from them by using the special indexes at the end of the book. There, you will find all the features discussed in the book indexed for other occurrences in all the other examples. Thus, for example, although you will learn how (and how not) to use *which* in Chapter 5 with a few examples, you will find many other examples of its use listed in the index referring to many other examples in the text. This provides a useful basis for further self-study and improvement. It could also be used for more advanced study of special topics under the guidance of your instructor.

Writing and Editing Exercises

Suggestions are made throughout the book for writing exercises for you to do as essential practice in your development as an accomplished writer. In addition, it is assumed that you will be required to produce other written work as part of other courses in your technical specialty. Do not underestimate the importance of these exercises, as the more practice you can gain in writing, the better you will become. While at college or university, you should take every opportunity you can to write about your subject — or to write about almost anything — and to learn from the helpful comments given to you by skilled language instructors.

Some research exercises are also provided in some of the chapters. They encourage you to look in published sources for instances of the techniques being discussed and explained. You will develop a much deeper understanding of the principles being discussed if you complete these exercises, which are ideal for classroom discussion.

This book also includes many sentence-length and paragraph-length editing exercises. These are very useful for consolidating your understanding as you progress through the book. They will also be useful to you for revision purposes before a test or examination. Note that there is not always only one "answer" to the exercises; you must be guided by your instructor regarding what forms or expressions are acceptable or perhaps the "best" in a given sentence or paragraph.

Limitations of Spell Checkers

Unfortunately we cannot rely on our computers to write the work for us, or to make sure our readers understand what we are writing about. Spell-checkers are certainly useful in catching many of the silly mistakes we all make during the composition of a text, but they cannot tell us if we have used a wrong word ("mew developments" rather than "new developments," for example). You must therefore develop an ability to proofread your writing very carefully.

Style checkers also have their uses, but they often give quite misleading advice when you are writing for professionals. They will often suggest that you use short phrases and sentences, whereas that is often inappropriate for writing suitable for professional readers. Most of the exercises in this book have been "approved" by a spell checker and style checker; you must start with the assumption that this does *not* guarantee that the writing is correct and appropriate.

Review Questions

At the end of each chapter, you will find review questions based on the material presented in that chapter. If you have read and understood the contents of the chapter, you should have no difficulty in answering these questions. If you do have difficulty, re-read the relevant parts of the chapter, or ask your instructor for assistance. *Appendix E* is a random ordered list of multiple-choice questions, which you should be able to answer by the time you have completed your work with this book. Questions like these and the review questions at the end of chapters could well be included in tests or an examination for the course of instruction based on this book.

The review questions demonstrate that technical communication is an *examinable* subject — just like any other worthwhile study in college or university. You can be tested on your knowledge of the terminology and principles of effective communication and related language structures and techniques — as well as on your ability to write and edit technical documents.

The Importance of Technical Writing

Career Potential

The ability to communicate effectively will be very important to your career development. Those who cannot write tend to become marginalized and are not given positions of authority, where they will be expected to write or approve technical and management documents. No one wants a chief engineer or a manager who cannot express ideas clearly and in acceptable ways.

So if you want to be more than a laboratory worker whose work is written about and discussed by others, you must be able to discuss your own work yourself. While it may be possible to hide an inability to write by joining a group led by a reasonably literate colleague, it is often that colleague who gets the credit for the work — not those who may have actually done the work but who cannot explain it.

A brilliantly contrived invention is useless if no one can understand your explanation, and even an outstandingly good management suggestion will not even be examined if you cannot explain it clearly. In effect you will be judged on the basis of how others *perceive* your work rather than the work itself — and this means that communication is a vital part of your work and your career.

Personal Image

As a professional, you will be regarded by society (and your colleagues and superiors) as a knowledgeable, educated person, and because of this society has certain expectations of you. As technical professionals we are expected to know our subjects of course, and to produce technical work of a suitable quality. We are also expected to present our work in an ethical and professional way. The image of government, companies, politicians, the police, etc. would be tarnished if their communications were conveyed on scruffy bits of paper with dozens of spelling mistakes — or if they were so garbled we could hardly understand them. The same applies to your communications.

Your image as a professional will also be tarnished if you are unable to write clearly, concisely and grammatically. This means more than merely presenting your documents professionally, with an eye to pleasing layout and effective communication. It also means the writing itself must meet professional standards of clarity for the intended readers of your work. Your written communications must also be appropriately concise and be free of errors of organization, structure, grammar and punctuation. It must also be written in a style and tone appropriate for your readers and the type of document you are writing.

Practical Writing Situations

Topics and Readership

In the early years of college and university, the topics you will be given may be relatively simple, and the format of your writing may be defined for you (e.g. laboratory reports with defined headings). For these, you will be able to concentrate on the language rather than order and organization of your material. In later years, however, you will be expected to write reports or proposals either on a subject of your choice, or perhaps one you have chosen with your supervisor. For these, there will be a much greater need to select appropriate information and arrange it into acceptable structures — as well as writing and editing it.

When you graduate as a professional, most subjects will be defined for you by your supervisor, although the best professionals are always looking for opportunities to explain their work in reports and proposals. They will often suggest writing documents about new ideas, and they will then often define their own subject and aims. Reports in industry and government will have a defined purpose, and you will have to select and arrange your material to meet that need. The final-year technical report in university or college often simulates the working environment you will experience later.

The big difference between writing during your education and your later professional writing is that the former is written primarily for your instructor, whereas the latter is written for different readers — and often for several readers. A report explaining an idea from a new scientific instrument to your chief engineer would be vastly different for a report of the same instrument to the general public — or in a sales leaflet. The aims of the documents would be different, and both the technical level and the emphasis would reflect the purpose and readership of your writing.

Sometimes you will have mixed readers — some technical experts, but perhaps also managers, or accountants, or marketing executives. When this happens, aim your writing at the lowest technical level so that all readers can understand it. Then write additional sections (or appendices) for specialist readers. Your summary may take on special importance, as busy executives may decide only to read that and parts of your document they feel are relevant to them. Thus they may be impressed — or otherwise! — with the precision, clarity and conciseness of your summary and the conclusions and recommendations it contains.

Writing in University and College

In your early years, the laboratory reports you write have probably all been written a million times or more by other students over the decades. Your instructors know the material already. You are not imparting new information, but learning the scientific method of verification by experiment and producing the all-important documents that go with the procedure. Obviously writing in tests and examinations does not present new information to instructors. Instead you are demonstrating your knowledge of the subject. Thus for much of your early writing, you will not have to consider purpose and audience for your writing very much.

In later years, though, you will probably be writing technical proposals and reports about new projects and designs. For these, your documents will contain information that *is* new to your instructors. You will then have to pay more attention to deciding what to include and how to present the information. In your professional work in industry or government, all your writing will provide new information to your readers. An understanding of the purpose of your writing and who your readers are then becomes vital.

For all writing exercises in this book, the audience and purpose are given or implied by the instructions. You will be writing some texts for fellow students at your own educational level. Others will be aimed at a general audience of fellow professionals. When you correct or edit sentences, assume you are making the texts suitable for professionals in engineering, science or technology, unless the instructions say otherwise.

Technical Style

Technical writing is different from writing in the humanities and social sciences, and some of you may have to make significant changes in your style to reflect this. Perhaps most of your writing so far has been for book reviews, creative stories, literary analysis or personal accounts — probably all without a defined purpose or audience. You may have been told not to use headings, or to make sure your writing "flows," or to express your own views on a subject. These concepts may be less relevant to many of your technical writing tasks.

There are many technical styles. The styles of standards, specifications, instructions, patents and contracts are all quite distinct, and they are not discussed in this book on core language use. Instead we will be concentrating on the style of formal technical expression for fellow professionals — the sort of language you will be using in your reports and proposals throughout most of your professional life. We will also be discussing the less-formal styles used in letters, memoranda and e-mail.

Style also involves how you express your information in clauses, sentences and paragraphs. To help you to develop your own personal style within the general stylistic requirements of formal technical prose, you should note how the many writers of the examples in this book express facts, ideas and views. As you gain technical writing experience, you will develop a sense of appropriate language use and you will recognize the differences in tone and emphasis your choices make.

Review Questions

1. *Why do some technical students have difficulty with their technical writing?*

2. *What is the difference between the literary and the linguistic approach to teaching writing?*

3. *What are the three types of exercises offered in this book?*

4. *What are the limitations of spell checkers and style checkers?*

5. *Why is technical writing important for technical professionals?*

6. *Why are purpose and audience important in technical writing? How do they differ in industry and government compared with college or university?*

7. *What is technical style? What special technical documents have special styles?*

Chapter 2:
Understanding the Task and Preparation

In this chapter, you will be introduced to writing as usually a creative rather than a selective process and as a problem-solving activity rather than an analytical one. You will learn to recognize all written documents (and presentations and drawings) as solutions to defined tasks involving prior analysis of the purpose, readership and other requirements. You will also learn how to select, understand and define your technical and writing tasks before starting your detailed technical work and the planning and writing of your document.

Different Types of Process
Selection Processes
Creative Processes
Writing as a Creative Process
Problem-Solving and Evaluative Processes
Techniques of Composition

Purpose and Readership
Why Write?
Readership ("Audience")
Understanding Writing Tasks

Topic Selection and Task Definition
The Work and the Writing
Topic Selection
Defining Manageable Topics
Selecting and Defining a Specific Task
Writing a Task Identification

Different Types of Process

Selection Processes

If we are hungry we find something to eat. If we are desperate almost anything will do, but if we have time and can choose, we will consider the alternatives and make the selection that suits us best at the time.

Selection can be quite trivial — maybe between a Wendy's or a McDonald's hamburger, or between Pepsi or Coke. Others can be more important — which college or university to attend, for example, or where to accept your first permanent position. For large-scale purchasing in industry and government, the overall process could be very involved, including a detailed needs statement, a cost-benefit analysis, a request for quotations, detailed comparisons among possible alternatives, and the final selection.

For complex selections the options may first be "short-listed" to narrow down the alternatives before the final comparison and the selection. Other selections may become a two-way (reciprocal) process — for business partners, senior executives, for example — in which both parties are selecting and trying to be selected at the same time.

Selection may involve experienced-based decisions which the experts might find hard to justify (e.g. tea-tasting, art-buying, wine-tasting). Generals in war situations, master chess players, and perfume "noses", for example, often find it extremely difficult to explain the basis for many of their decisions. In contrast, other selections include defined and clearly expressed criteria as the basis for the decision.

Creative Processes

Creative processes are often more complex and difficult than selection processes. Rather than selecting a standard available product to meet a certain need, the decision-maker might instead decide to create (or have created) something special. Thus you might decide not to buy a "normal" hamburger at all, but instead buy the ingredients yourself and create your own special work of art. Harvey's customer selection of hamburger dressings and the selection of submarine dressings are somewhere between these two extremes.

It is much easier simply to buy a standard product, as creating something from scratch is more time consuming, costly and intellectually demanding — you have to think!!! However creation is a vital element in the development of solutions to new needs, and better solutions to old needs. As a technical professional, you will be learning to apply creative processes in the development of designs, analyses, or procedures to meet old or new needs.

Writing is one of those creative processes, and it is centrally important for a number of reasons. First, as it is the basis for all significant communications, it is a task that is common to students and professionals in all walks of life. Secondly, writing (and speech and drawings) are usually essential parts of any project — and indeed are often the sole basis for judging the effectiveness of your work. Thirdly, communication helps you to formulate concepts in your mind and to understand them more clearly. Finally, writing is often an account based on your thoughts and actions in completing a project. That is, the processes of investigation, invention, development and analysis are often very closely related to the process of writing about them. Because of this close connection between the writing and the thinking behind the practical work, an understanding of the creative writing process will help you to understand not only how to tackle any major writing task, but also how to tackle *any* creative task.

Exercise 2.1: Identifying Selective and Creative Processes

Identify the following needs as involving creative (C), one-way selective (OWS) or reciprocally selective (RS) process, or possibly a combination. Be prepared to justify your decisions. Where selection *or* creation would be possible, list the circumstances where each would be appropriate.

> (a) *landscaping for a new convention center*
> (b) *a business partner*
> (c) *a picnic table*
> (d) *computer software for club membership control*
> (e) *a complex home entertainment center for a new large house*
> (f) *a humanities/social sciences elective course*
> (g) *a sewage system for a new housing development*
> (h) *a nation for increased trade*
> (i) *a professor as a PhD supervisor*
> (j) *a meal at a wedding reception*
> (k) *a post-graduate program*
> (l) *a date for a formal dance*

Now think up other topics and discuss among yourselves and with your instructor what processes would be involved.

Writing as a Creative Process

Occasionally writing is a selection process. Students have been known to select from laboratory or analytical reports written by other students as the basis for their own submissions. Such practice is, of course, not permitted and could result in your being heavily penalized for plagiarism.

More acceptable is the use (or adaptation) of standard job applications or reply letters, although (unless your writing is really dreadful) that is not advisable as you then sound like scores of others doing the same thing. In business, however, standard letters are used frequently (for requesting payments, for acknowledging receipt of a letter, for rejecting job applicants, etc.) as this saves time and cost.

In industry, proposals are often partly made up of "boilerplate" pre-prepared sections, and many contracts and specifications contain standard legal clauses. Also the use of forms is standard (and indeed usually required) practice in real estate transactions, insurance documents, wills, court proceedings, and many business transactions.

Most writing in colleges and universities (and the most important writing in industry, business and government), however, is creative rather than selective. It is creative in the sense that, for each writing task, the writer must produce something original in wording and concept to meet a defined need for a specified readership. It is not creative in the sense of "creative writing" in a literary way, which means the writing of poems, short stories, novels and other fictional forms.

Exercise 2.2: Writing as Creative or Selective Processes

State whether the following documents would be creative (C), selective (S), or possibly either (E). Explain your decisions.

(a) *an essay exploring the psychological effects of AIDS*
(b) *a letter rejecting an application for a credit card*
(c) *a proposal for a company to provide tree-cutting services to a city*
(d) *a letter of application for a permanent position as a professional engineer*
(e) *a resume form*
(f) *a laboratory report explaining how you verified Boyle's Law*
(g) *a party invitation card*
(h) *a patent application*
(i) *definitions for "parking" and "stopping" for use in a city by-law*
(j) *an agenda for a monthly meeting*
(k) *a medical protocol explaining how the researcher intends to conduct a difficult experiment on a new drug*
(l) *an article for a student newspaper*
(m) *a memo sent to staff in a business asking them to indicate when they would like to take their vacations this year*
(n) *a proposal from a city to the International Olympic Committee seeking acceptance of their city as a venue for the olympic games*

Again think up your own examples and discuss them in class.

Problem-Solving and Evaluative Processes

Creative writing (in the sense used here) is always a problem-solving process because the end product (the report, the proposal, the article, or other document) is a tangible solution to a defined need to communicate. Whether you are asked to write a report describing a new solar-powered car, or one identifying the causes of an engineering disaster, the "solution" in both cases would be a document designed, created, written and edited to meet the needs of the assignment (the "problem"). However, what you write *about* may be a problem-solving process or an evaluative one, and it important that you are able to tell the difference.

As the solar-powered car is obviously a solution to a defined engineering problem, the problem-solving process you describe results (we hope) in something that overcomes a problem. Problem-solution types of writing are explained in *Chapter 6*.

In contrast, the analytical process about the disaster results in an assessment, hypothesis or understanding — the solving of an intellectual "problem" or a need to know something. This second type of writing involves evaluation, and the inclusion of adequate justification for your conclusions. Evaluative writing is explained in *Chapter 7*.

Techniques of Composition

The writing process described here explains how many writers progress from an early general requirement, through a detailed need analysis and content generation and organization, to the actual writing and later revision and editing. This is a sensible methodical approach, which is highly recommended for all large projects, and even for quite short writing tasks for those of you who have some difficulty in organizing your thoughts or in expressing them clearly.

However, you should not feel that *every* writing assignment must follow this process rigidly. For short writing tasks in particular, you should soon be able to produce reasonable writing with a minimum of preparation. Indeed you will be required to do so in examinations and in e-mail and memo messages in industry where time is limited. Depending on the importance of the task and the time available for it, you must decide for yourself what preliminary work is necessary to produce an acceptable piece of work.

Some writers can write an almost perfect finished version directly on their computers first time, and many journalists find this ability of great importance in meeting newspaper deadlines. Others use rough but detailed handwritten notes which they then convert into formal writing, while still others prefer to produce a rough computer draft (often very rough) to be polished later. More realistically, most of us use a number of approaches to help us compose our thoughts, using whatever method or combination is appropriate for the task at hand and our frame of mind at the time.

There is no "right" or "wrong" way to produce writing, and you should not be concerned unduly if your composition methods differ from those of your peers — as long as the end product is acceptable. That, after all, is what will be evaluated, not the way you produced it. However, knowledge of a formal procedure for producing original documents is a valuable asset, as you can always refer to it if you get stuck or find your work is not proceeding well. This procedure is discussed in this and the next two chapters.

Exercise 2.3: Writing about Process and Writing

(a) In a two-page comparative analysis to your writing instructor, explain the difference between the selective and the creative processes.

> *(b) In a 3–4 page essay to your instructor, explain the nature of writing as a creative problem-solving process while pointing out that some forms of writing are selective rather than creative.*

Purpose and Readership

Why Write?

Throughout your educational program, you will be required to produce many different types of writing for several courses. Although you will be writing for many instructors on several different subjects, the purposes of your writing will be quite similar. Many instructors may not actually tell *why* you are required to write about a subject (that is often taken for granted), but if asked they will usually explain the specific purposes of their assignments.

Important reasons for writing are that it forces you to think clearly, to organize your thoughts, and to articulate them clearly. You may think that you know a subject, but until you express your knowledge and ideas in words in formal written work, your understanding may lack precision and depth. As writing (including content generation and organization) clarifies your thoughts and actually helps you to think, it has become recognized as a powerful educational technique.

Knowledge and ideas in your head can only be assessed when you communicate them to someone else. For many subjects, it is essential that you learn to explain concepts to your instructors so that your mastery (or otherwise!) of the course material can be determined. This is what you do in examinations. If your writing is poor, you could well receive less credit than your knowledge warrants. Conversely, clearly expressed views usually earn higher grades as they demonstrate clear thinking and understanding. The same applies when you present your work orally, of course.

Many writing assignments are given, at least partially, to help you to improve your writing skills. Almost without exception, instructors recognize the value of clear writing, and many will help you to become better communicators — in speech and drawing as well as writing. You must realize, however, that your technical instructors' main tasks are to teach you their specialist subjects, and that they may not have the time, interest, or skilled background to help you with your writing as well. Even so your writing is bound to improve slowly simply through practice.

To help yourself to improve your communication skills, seek clarifications of any adverse comments about your writing (especially those like "muddled" or "unclear") and obtain the advice and help of a writing instructor or a tutor in a writing center if necessary. The work you do in following this book will supplement what you learn about writing in your other subjects, and will accelerate your learning and add considerably to its depth.

For writing assignments in the early years of your higher education, you are unlikely to be writing anything new to your instructors. One of the aims of this early writing is to introduce you to the ways that facts are presented and views are expressed in the subjects you will be studying. In science, for example, experimental laboratory reports introduce you to the scientific method of validation by experiment. As you become more skilled in the subjects you are studying, you will in later years (and especially for graduate work) be expected to present original ideas — including those your instructor may not have thought of. As a professional, all your written work will present information that is new to your readers.

Checklist 2.1: Aims of Educational Writing

✓ to encourage you to articulate your understanding and views of a subject and to clarify your thoughts

✓ as a means of evaluating your knowledge of a subject

✓ as a means of evaluating your ability to explain something or to express or demonstrate a point of view

✓ to show you how material is presented in a subject, perhaps in preparation for more original work in later years

---

Readership ("Audience")

A vital step in the understanding and planning of any communication task is to determine who your readers are. What, do you think, would be the result of an advertisement for air conditioners in Baffin Island? Or the reaction of Maclean's readers to a report on the laying of municipal sewage pipes? Readers would think it highly odd, to say the least, and could feel annoyed or even insulted. Such "communications" would betray the writer's lack of understanding of the readers' needs and interests, and would thus be doomed to failure. Effective communication can only be achieved when you match the topic of your writing with the needs and interests of your readers.

Exercise 2.4: Matching Topic and Readership

For the following topics and places of publication, identify and explain any mismatching of topic and readership. Also suggest what readerships the topics are suitable for and the types of publication they should be published in.

(a) beer commercials: during a Sesame Street program

(b) a detailed report on international nuclear proliferation: for a student newspaper

(c) a proposal to increase communications instruction for technical students: in a local newspaper

(d) hints on fishing brook trout: in an environmental magazine

(e) details of a new cathode ray oscilloscope: in a financial newspaper

(g) full details of an engineer's educational achievements and work experience: at the wedding dinner speech

(h) all the measured data of dioxin found at different points in a river: in a detailed report distributed door-to-door in the area concerned

(i) a scholarly exploration of current sexual morals and attitudes: in a leaflet enclosed in a pack of condoms

(j) a list of warnings about operating a chain saw: on a local radio show.

After you complete your higher education, your appreciation of readership (or your "audience" as it is often called) will become even more important. Then you will be writing for many different audiences, who all need to know different things about your work. The general public, technicians, marketing specialists, accountants, other experts in your subject, and many other groups may have an interest in your topic — and they will need to know different things about it. So your communications will be different depending on the needs, interests and background of your audience.

Realistic writing assignments that test your understanding of audience are difficult to create — and often even more difficult to evaluate. One way is to ask you to write your work for a specific magazine or journal in your specialty, but it may be asking too much to expect you to write publishable writing at this stage. Many instructors will not mention the subject. *They* are the audience; your task is to explain something for *them* to evaluate. Occasionally your instructor will stipulate a specific audience, and you must then follow the instructions.

A useful approach to writing to meet the needs of your audience is to imagine them being with you at all stages of the writing process. With "your reader over your shoulder" in this way, you should be constantly reminded that your task is to communicate a specific topic to a certain reader or group of readers. Several questions about your readers and their requirements are useful as general guidance in your writing.

Checklist 2.2: Audience Requirements — Some Useful Questions

✓ *Who are my readers? Will others receive copies?*

✓ *What do your readers know about this topic already?*

✓ *What do they really need to know about this topic?*

✓ *What are they likely to regard as irrelevant?*

✓ *What evidence or reasoning is likely to convince them?*

✓ *What tone and style are most appropriate for them?*

✓ *What will they be using the document for?*

✓ *What do I want them to know or to do?*

✓ *How will they be reading the document (in detail, a quick review before a meeting, etc.)?*

✓ *Do I need a summary, indexes, or checklists to help readers to grasp the main points or find specific information?*

In this book the writing tasks and many of the shorter exercises specify audiences to give you practice in writing for different groups of readers. For exercises and review questions that do not have specified audiences, assume that you are writing for your writing instructor or colleagues in your technical specialty.

Understanding Writing Tasks

You are now in a position to understand the requirements for any writing task — or in fact for any project for which a written or oral response is required. The task may be given to you specifically *as* a writing task or as a task to analyze, design, investigate, or propose something. In either case you have work to do and something to write, so you first need to understand the task before you start.

Many writing tasks and projects are presented to you in a rather vague way, with the expectation that you will think about the topic and decide on the appropriate requirements for yourself. You need to know whether you are describing something, or presenting a problem-solution report or proposal, or analyzing something — discussed in *Chapters 5, 6* and *7* in this book. Writing the wrong way about a topic would significantly reduce the effectiveness of your work.

You also need to know roughly how long the writing is to be (or how long your oral presentation will be), and perhaps whether illustrations might be useful and acceptable. You will need to know who your readers are, of course, and you should also know of any special requirements such as the need for a title page, summary, references or appendices. You also need to know whether the writing is to be presented formally or informally (using *I* , *we* etc.) and how you should present the work (just stapled with a title page, or perhaps dressed up in a binder with title page, contents, summary, etc.). All these need to be understood before you start your work.

Checklist 2.3: Requirements for Writing Tasks

✓ *the topic to be discussed with any special definition of the exact nature of the contents to be included or its emphasis*

✓ *the audience*

✓ *the type (or "genre") of document (description, proposal, evaluation)*

✓ *the approximate length*

✓ *the format (title page, contents page, summary, references, indexes, appendices, etc.)*

✓ *the style (informal, formal, passive voice reporting, etc.)*

✓ *any special requirements (diagrams, photographs, tables, indexes, acknowledgements, etc.)*

If you are unclear about any of these requirements for your work, you should seek clarification from your instructor.

For oral presentations, you need to know many of the above details and also the content, length and emphasis of your presentation. You will also need to know how large your audience is, the size and arrangement of the room for your talk, lighting and other equipment, and other features discussed in *Chapter 13*.

(a) *In a 500-word article for your student newspaper, justify the view that more writing assignments in different courses should have an audience other than your instructor. Explain the educational advantages of writing to different audiences.*

(b) *Write a 3–4 page article for a high school newspaper or a local newspaper about the importance of understanding purpose, audience and requirements before starting to plan your writing work. Although you will primarily be addressing students, bear in mind that your article might influence teachers too.*

(c) *In a 3-page letter to your dean, propose that instructors be encouraged to provide clearer instructions for writing tasks. Cite difficulties you or your peers may have encountered in earlier writing tasks because the instructions were incomplete or inadequate.*

Topic Selection and Task Definition

The Work and the Writing

Whether you are given or asked to select a technical topic for investigation, or asked to write a report or proposal on a given topic or one of your choice, these amount to the same thing. You are being asked to do some original work and then write about it to explain what you have done, discovered or created. The end result of any original work is a written document (often orally presented too), and the value of your work will be based on that document (and presentation).

By reading the document, readers will be able to judge the quality of your technical work and analytical abilities. Overall, you will be judged by the quality of your work (as perceived by your writing) and also your ability to explain it (the quality of the writing itself). As your writing is a summary of the main features of the work you have done, it represents your work and your technical abilities. It is therefore important to select your topic, and plan and write your document with great care.

Topic Selection

If you are given a well-defined topic, you will have to remain clearly within the terms of references given. However, you will often be asked to select your own topic (perhaps within a given area of work), and this extra degree of freedom presents a difficult yet potentially rewarding challenge.

The request for students to select their own topic is a useful educational technique used from early teaching (e.g. "Write an essay on a subject of your choice.") right through to PhD and post-doctoral research, in which the student/researcher often has great latitude in selecting a research topic. The selection of the topic should be seen not as an annoying preliminary, but as an important test of your ability. If you choose an inappropriate subject, or if you keep changing your mind during the work, you will waste valuable time. Careful selection and planning should avoid drastic changes to your technical aims.

Be guided by the instructions you have received. If topics have been suggested, look them over carefully and try to find one that interests you, that you think you can do well, and that you feel will be personally rewarding. If, however, you are given only general guidelines as to the sort of project to work on (usually later in your education, when more is expected of you), you will need to think more deeply. Here are a few suggestions of ways of defining a situation which could yield an acceptable topic.

Checklist 2.4: Techniques for Finding a Suitable Topic

✓ *ask your instructor or peers if they have any general or specific suggestions*

✓ *ask students from previous years or a tutor for suggestions*

✓ *find some previous work in which you can discern some unsolved or incomplete task (authors often indicate this in their conclusions)*

> ✓ *find a situation in which you can identify a problem (including an intellectual need to know or understand something) that needs to be studied*
>
> ✓ *find a situation which you feel deserves detailed study and analysis*

You might learn about your topic through reading related literature (see your librarian), discussions with instructors and peers, or reading technical magazines. Alternatively you might hear about a suitable topic on television or in a newspaper, or through personal contact as, for example, in summer employment. Upper year students who have completed similar tasks in previous years can be a useful resource. So are graduate work and final year theses, which may be available in your department.

Defining Manageable Topics

Your initial topic selection might be quite vague, or you may have been given a vague topic deliberately to make you think about the topic and select a defined task. The vague, general topic first needs to be understood clearly and then reduced to a clearly-stated aim or set of aims for your work. To understand the relationship between a vague topic or situation and a specific task, we need to examine different levels of hierarchy.

If, for example, a government decided it needed to improve the nation's transportation facilities, this would be a broad policy decision. They might decide to improve major inter-city road connections, or to provide more airport facilities — or a combination, of course. Whatever they decide is their solution (or partial solution) to their policy decision, but it is also a directed aim for provincial or regional administrators. They in turn would direct their technical staff to find ways of implementing the aims at provincial or regional level. Finally planners, contractors and engineers would need to write specific proposals to meet the defined regional needs at local levels.

So it is with writing. You as a single worker — or even a small team — cannot hope to solve the larger overall problems in the time you have available. You can only be expected to contribute toward their solution. If you are faced with a subject that is too large or too general, you must select a manageable task within that subject before you can hope to find something that you (or your team) are able to do well. By completing a lower-level aim thoroughly, you will succeed in making a significant contribution to the understanding of the wider task. However, as a brief description of the wider task will become a useful part of your introduction, you should seek to gain some understanding of it at this early stage of your work.

As an example of defining a manageable situation, you could start with the broad topic of "transportation", decide to deal with safety, and then with safety and car-driving, and then drinking and driving. You could decide to concentrate on any of several topics e.g.:

(a) *details of laws in different jurisdictions*
(b) *the statistics relating to drunk driving before and after legislation*
(c) *examples of the human suffering involved*
(d) *organizations promoting alcohol-free driving*
(e) *designated driver programs*
(f) *mechanisms for preventing drunk drivers from entering or starting a car*
(g) *penalties for drunk driving*
(h) *defining and testing "drunkenness" and its relation to blood alcohol level*
(i) *recommendations for changes to the law*

Exercise 2.6: Using Levels of Hierarchy

For the following topics, choose successively lower levels in the hierarchy until you reach a level suitable for writing a proposal for a design or research project.

(a) *home sanitation — killing animals/insects . . .*
(b) *illnesses — cancer — causes of skin cancer . . .*
(c) *computers — internet uses . . .*
(d) *garbage — disposal. . .*
(e) *energy efficiency — reduced use in homes . . .*

Now think up your own general topics and see how many "branches" and "sub-branches" of specific topics you can generate. Draw them out like the roots of a tree to show the relationships and hierarchies between the different topics you generate. Try to come up with some interesting design or research tasks you feel would make a significant contribution to a concern or problem in society.

Selecting and Defining a Specific Task

Having a manageable topic is just the beginning. You now have to determine a specific task that will meet the objectives of your manageable situation. If, for example, you had decided to propose a new way of preventing drunk drivers from entering or starting a car, you might wish to design and propose one of the following solutions:

(a) *a device that would prevent a driver from entering a car unless a low-level breath were first registered*
(b) *an alcohol-sensing monitor in the car that would sound an alarm or disable the car*
(c) *a mechanism that would test a driver's reaction speed, or cognitive or speaking ability and prevent the car from starting in the case of a test failure*
(d) *a complex time-limit sequence for starting the car*

You should be able to think of others to add to this list. From all the possible tasks about a topic, you will have to decide on the specific task and the emphasis you will give it in your work before you are ready to proceed. Many factors enter into this stage of planning, and this also involves some preliminary technical work. Here are questions you should ask and answer in selecting and identifying a specific task:

Checklist 2.5: Questions for Task Selection and Specification

✓ *Do you understand the hierarchical level at which you will be working?*

✓ *Have you an understanding of the levels above and below your level (as input for your introduction)?*

✓ *What questions will your work address or answer, or what intellectual or practical need will your work meet, or what problems will you be trying to solve?*

✓ *Are there any related questions or issues you have decided not to address (again often suitable for your introduction)?*

✓ *Will your planned work meet the needs you have identified?*

✓ *Is the selected work significant and original enough to make a valuable contribution to an understanding of the subject or a resolution of the problems?*

✓ *Have you the knowledge and expertise (and if appropriate the resources) you will need to complete the work in the time you have available?*

✓ *Does the project interest you?*

✓ *Does the project match the intended audience and meet all the requirements for the work?*

Writing a Task Identification

For large projects, some instructors and departments may ask you to write a task identification (perhaps with an outline of your proposed work) before you proceed. They do this to make sure you are taking on a worthwhile, significant and workable topic the instructor feels you can complete well and in time. A task identification also allows instructors to make useful practical suggestions about your proposed work before you waste time doing work that is insignificant, irrelevant or perhaps has already been done. Your task identification should also indicate that you have done all the essential preliminary work for the project, and that you understand the subject sufficiently to start.

Task identification becomes very important when you are working as a member of a team, as it is vital that all of you clearly understand (and agree on) what you are seeking to achieve. For graduate work, task identifications are usually required by your supervisor and/or your steering committee — again for the reasons given above. At all levels, make sure you understand any comments your instructor makes about your task identification, and seek clarification if necessary. Follow any suggestions carefully as these give skilled and knowledgeable guidance.

In writing your task definition (also called a "project proposal"), answer all the questions you have asked yourself in specifying and selecting your project. But do not dwell too much on topics at higher levels of the hierarchy — especially if your readers already know about it. If, for example, you are proposing a method of growing mushrooms near horse stables using soiled straw or wood chips, there is no need to establish that half the world is starving as a basis for your analysis. The obvious commercial and environmental issues are reason enough. So omit (or mention only in passing) any wider issues already known by your readers, and concentrate on the specific issues you will be analyzing.

Checklist 2.6: Contents for Task Identification

✓ *Answer all relevant questions in Checklist 2.5.*

✓ *Explain any previous work that seeks to achieve a purpose similar to the one you have chosen, together with any unresolved issues or questions.*

✓ *Explain your proposed research approach, indicating what you hope to achieve at specified times for large projects.*

✓ *Itemize any equipment or other facilities you will need.*

✓ *Explain any major difficulties you foresee in your work, and discuss how you will approach them.*

✓ *Provide a provisional list of references if appropriate.*

All this work in selecting and identifying a specific task is important not just because it helps you to decide on a suitable project, but also because it gives you a sound understanding of your technical objectives. Once you have completed the analysis involved with these checklists, you should be in a good position to undertake any serious study or design project to meet the needs of your technical instructors.

The preliminary analysis involved with the checklists in this chapter is also an extremely valuable basis for your introduction, which will largely deal with the background information you have unearthed. Many students have great difficulty in writing introductions, often because they have failed to understand clearly what they are doing technically — and why. If you have completed the work recommended here for task selection and identification, you should have much less difficulty in writing your introduction.

Checklist 2.7: Writing Preliminaries

✓ *Make sure you understand all requirements set for the work and the writing (audience, genre, length, format, style) — see Checklist 2.3.*

✓ *Select a suitable topic and a manageable topic for your work — see Checklists 2.4 and 2.5.*

✓ *Select a suitable specific task and write a task definition — see Checklist 2.6.*

Exercise 2.7: Writing About Topic Selection

(a) *Using your own examples, explain the concept of hierarchies to instructors in your subject of specialization. Discuss how this concept helps you to understand where parts of the subject fit within the wider area of study. Your discussion should be about three pages.*

(b) *In preparation for a 20-minute speech you will give to new graduate students about the importance of topic selection and task identification, prepare a one-page summary of your talk and the notes you will use for five or six overhead displays.*

(c) *Repeat (b) for an audience of high school students entering your college or university.*

(d) *Perhaps working in groups, work through the checklists in this chapter with subjects of your own choosing.*

(e) *Write a task definition for one or two of the topics you have analyzed, including enough information for a technical instructor to be able to provide meaningful advice to help you with your work.*

Review Questions

1. *What are selective and creative processes?*

2. *What are reciprocal selective processes?*

3. *Is writing a selective or a creative process? Explain.*

4. *What is the difference between problem-solving and evaluative projects?*

5. *Is the writing of a document a problem-solving or an evaluative process?*

6. *What are the reasons for making you write in college and university?*

7. *Why is an understanding of readership important?*

8. *What should you know before starting to plan a large writing project?*

9. *What is the educational benefit of asking you to select your own topic?*

10. *Where are you likely to find information leading to your discovery of a suitable situation for your project?*

11. *How does an understanding of hierarchies help us to arrive at manageable topics and projects?*

12. *What is the difference between a manageable topic and a specific task?*

13. *What is a task identification, what information does it include, and what is it used for?*

14. *What is the process used for preliminary work for a project?*

Chapter 3:
Contents and a Sense of Order

In this chapter you will learn how to generate suitable contents for your writing and how to organize your thoughts to create structured writing. The relationship between contents and structure is an important feature of this chapter. You will also learn how to signal your structure to readers through the table of contents, the introduction, headings and structural indicators within the text itself.

Writing as a Reiterative Process
Content, Order and the Writing Process
Structure as an Aid to Content Generation

Organizing Your Work
Content and Description
Division and Contents
Dividing by Characteristic
Unavoidable Overlaps
Undesirable Overlaps
Subdivision and Order
Natural Orders

Writing as a Reiterative Process

Content, Order and the Writing Process

The writing of a significant document is a process in which the writer decides on a topic and specific task, determines contents, organizes the material, produces a first draft, revises and edits it, and presents it as a communication. Like all creative processes (e.g. design, innovation, learning), writing is not, however, simply a matter of starting at the beginning and proceeding to the end. You will often need to re-examine your objectives as your work proceeds. The planning of writing also involves finding out what you need to say and in what order you want to say it. The two are closely related, and this is explained in this chapter.

It would be a mistake to simply regard writing as a means of typing into your computer ideas that you have already formulated in your head and in a sequence you have already determined. Usually the planning and the writing are vital parts of the formulation of your ideas and how they are structured — and this involves almost constant reiteration between the general thoughts in your head (and your notes and outline) and the results of your emerging efforts to articulate them clearly. The thoughts and notes form the basis for your writing, but it is the writing itself that enables these thoughts to take shape and to become exact clearly-communicated statements.

It is thus unrealistic to expect to complete a complex writing task in a simple fashion: determine the purpose and readership, generate contents, organize the work, and then write and edit it. Instead you must expect to have to reconsider your purpose, your overall message and also its structure as the planning and writing progress — and as your understanding of the subject becomes clearer.

Structure as an Aid to Content Generation

The contents, planning and writing are connected in another way. Some understanding of the type of writing you are engaged in not only helps you to structure your writing, but also helps you to decide the contents. Experienced writers can often decide what they want to say in general terms before arranging the material, but writers with less experience often need to think in the opposite direction. Faced with a given writing task, they seek a "standardized" structure which, they hope, will help them to know what to include as well as how to organize the material. The standard way of arranging laboratory reports (using headings of Objective, Apparatus, Method, Results and Analysis) is a clear example of how order and contents go hand in hand.

This and the next four chapters provide practical advice and guidance in both content generation and how it can be organized. Here are some examples of how knowledge of writing structure helps to generate useful contents.

Checklist 3.1: Relating Structure to Contents (Examples)

✓ *A student is asked to write an analysis explaining a particular point of view (e.g. that air pollution has caused irreparable damage to the earth). This is a "thesis-backing" type of structure, in which a clear statement is supported by evidence and reasoning. The writer needs to identify different types of air pollution (carbon dioxide, acid rain, ozone, etc.). Clear supporting evidence needs to be obtained if the thesis is to be clearly demonstrated for some or all of these types. Perhaps arguments that give an opposite point of view need to be expressed and countered. That is, the information to be included in the analysis is largely determined by the structure of the writing and vice versa.*

✓ *A writer seeking to compare one type of piston engine to another (e.g. reciprocating and rotating) would adopt a "comparison/contrast" structure, in which details of the two types would be determined and used as the basis for the comparison.*

✓ *A writer with the task of explaining features of a technical measuring instrument (e.g. a micrometer) would recognize the need for a "descriptive" structure, and would therefore seek information answering questions such as "What is it?," "What does it do?," "How does it work?," "What does it look like?," "How is it used?," "What range does it measure?" and "How accurately does it measure?."*

✓ *A writer preparing a proposal for a new device to reduce drunk driving would recognize that the structure is essentially one dealing with a problem and its solution, and would therefore collect information answering the questions "What is the situation?," "What is the problem or need?," "What is the proposed solution?" and "How well will the solution work?."*

✓ *A writer who needs to explain how something was invented (aircraft, computers) or to write a biography of a famous scientist or engineer would probably choose a "narrative" structure, in which events are described in a time-oriented sequence. This sequence should help the writer to generate suitable contents for different periods of time.*

These examples indicate some typical overall structures and contents of documents — also called the "macro-structures." An understanding of structure will also help you to organize smaller parts of the macro-structure into recognized patterns. For example, description is almost always part of the "solution" category of problem-solution texts, thesis-backing patterns are often part of comparisons, narratives often include descriptions or problem-solution patterns, and problem-solution patterns are often found in descriptions. That is, although the overall macro-structure of a document may be essentially one of the main types of organization, it may contain "micro-structures" organized by other patterns. So whatever type of writing you are engaged in at any one time, you will need to understand *all* types of organization to help you to generate contents for the details and the order of the lower levels of your writing.

Exercise 3.1: *Writing about the Writing Process*

(a) *Explain, in about two pages to high school students, the nature of the writing process and the need for reiteration. Use an informal style (using "you" and "your" where appropriate).*

(b) *Using your own examples, explain to peers who have not read the previous section how a knowledge of structure helps writers to know what sort of content to include in a piece of writing. Again take about two pages, but this time use a more formal style.*

(c) *In a formal 3-4 page explanation to your writing instructor, describe the main macro-structures used in your area of specialization. Also, identify and explain the need for the micro-structures used.*

(d) *Prepare an illustration, a half-page summary and point-form notes to accompany a talk you will give to high school students about macro-structures and micro-structures in writing. Use examples they will be familiar with.*

Exercise 3.2: *Structure and Contents*

For each of the following topics, select the most appropriate structure (description, problem-solution, evaluation, narrative) and write brief notes on likely contents for the audience and purpose specified.

(a) *a better mouse trap (brief article for* Popular Mechanics*)*

(b) *your reasons for liking your favorite course (an article in a student newspaper)*

(c) *the room, apartment or house you live in (a pen pal who has not seen your accommodation)*

(d) *the major events and achievements of your life (notes for the chairperson of a meeting at which you will be introduced as a speaker)*

(e) *the components of an incandescent light bulb (a description to Grade 9 science students)*

(f) *learning about non-fictional writing and learning about literary writing (an article in your student newspaper explaining the relative importance and differences)*

(g) your resume (for summer or permanent job application)

(h) a newly-discovered beetle (an entry in an encyclopedia)

Organizing Your Work

Content and Description

To simplify the teaching and learning of the complex subjects of content and organization, the discussion in the remainder of this chapter concentrates on descriptive structures, leaving organizations for other structures until *Chapters 6 and 7*. *Chapter 5* deals with the patterns and types of continuity found in descriptive writing — and as the thread of continuity in *all* forms of writing.

In description, we provide details about the topic being described, and for each topic there is an extremely large, but finite, number of features that could be included. When writing descriptions, you need to decide what items of information to include and what to exclude — a decision based on the needs of your readers and your purpose in writing. For example the description of a person varies considerably depending on the reason for the description.

Checklist 3.2: Typical Contents for Describing People (Examples)

✓ **for a job application:**
academic achievements, age, experience, personality, interests, aims, ambitions

✓ **for police records:**
sex, age, racial origin, height, weight, color of eyes and hair, peculiar features, clothes last seen wearing, fingerprints

✓ **for a passport:**
facial appearance (photograph), age, sex, profession, height, weight, distinguishing features

✓ **for an academic resume:**
academic qualifications, subject specialty, publications, honors and awards, teaching experience, administrative experience, grants

✓ **for a dating service:**
sex, age, sexual orientation, interests, hobbies, marital status, children, profession, financial position, smoking/drinking habits

---

Although it is possible to produce a detailed checklist about any topic you need to describe, the information you choose to include — and the order in which you present it — will depend greatly on the purpose of your communication (and thus the needs of your readers). For some purposes, certain types of information are vital, other information may be marginal, and still other information may be irrelevant for the purpose of the communication. As examples of the last category, age, sex, and racial origin should be irrelevant to a description of an author of an article in a scholarly journal.

The decision as to what to include in a description should not be a haphazard affair. Here is a procedure to help you generate a preliminary list of relevent contents for descriptive writing.

Checklist 3.3: Initial Selection of Contents for Description

✓ *Identify the topic you need to describe, the purpose of your writing and the needs of your readers.*

✓ *Write down all the features of the topic as they come to mind — in random order. (This is called "brainstorming" and is usually best done in small groups.) Write them in specific terms if you can (e.g. committee composition six including past president as ex-officio member), but general terms will do at this stage (e.g. committee composition).*

✓ *From the list you have made, select items of information that you judge to be vital for the purpose of your writing and the needs of your readers.*

✓ *Select other material that is of marginal or possible relevance if there is space in your description.*

✓ *Make the general information specific by finding out the necessary details, and seeking any other important information you have missed.*

Exercise 3.3: Analyzing and Writing about Description

(a) Make a collection of short biographies (found as details about authors in journals, or personalities in alumni magazines), and then:
  (i) determine the types of information usually included,
  (ii) determine the types of information sometimes included, and
  (iii) determine the types of information not normally included.

(b) Write a report to your writing instructor on your findings from (a) above, providing lists of useful and not useful information for the purpose(s) you have studied. Explain why some types of information appear vital, others appear useful but not essential, and still others irrelevant. The length of your report will depend on the depth and *scope of your research — from a two-page summary to a PhD thesis! Check with your instructor.*

(c) *Using your own examples, explain "description" in terms of the typical information present and the questions they answer about the topic. Write to peers who have not studied this subject. The length will be two to five pages, depending on the depth of your study and the number of examples you use.*

(d) *In a half-page summary for your writing instructor, explain the term "relevance" in terms of the purpose of descriptive writing and the needs of your readers.*

Exercise 3.4: Generating Contents for Descriptions

Generate contents for the following descriptions for the specified purposes and audiences. This can be done individually or as a group.

(a) *an incandescent light bulb for an illustrated book on common electrical components for primary school students*

(b) *main features of personal computers for an illustrated book on recent electronic equipment for first-year college and university students*

(c) *any of the following for a high school CD-ROM description of important technical instruments: voltmeters (ac, dc, electrostatic, or multi-purpose), calipers, sound meters, water pressure meters, gas meters, humidity meters, thermometers, carburetors, pH meters, tachometers, speedometers, frequency meters, micrometers, balance weight scales, sonic depth finders, ammeters (in-circuit or clamp), fluid flow meters, light intensity meters, wattmeters, gas chromatographs, electrical resistance meters, spectrometers, ultrasonic detectors, stroboscopes, microwave meters, potentiometers*

(d) *do the same for any of the following important technical equipment or components: silicon chips, hard rock core splitters, electrical machines (ac or dc), internal combustion engines, traffic light controllers, fluid pumps, bearings (ball, roller or tapered), concrete, autopilots, pneumatic drills, elevators, cranes*

(e) *do the same for any of the following common household tools and appliances: electric drills, electric saws (jig or Skil), CD players, modems, televisions, microwaves, telephones, dimmer switches, fluorescent lights, refrigerators, humidifiers, dehumidifiers, telephone answering machines*

(f) *do the same for your own topics and purposes of description*

Note: Do *not* analyze just one manufacturer's model — provide appropriate information for the whole class you are studying.

Your search for appropriate contents does not end here. Remember that, after you have divided your work into groups of information and selected an order for your writing, you may realize you need other information to complete your description.

Division and Contents

You now need to group your work into appropriate sections, determined primarily by the subject matter of your work. Division of descriptive material can be achieved in a number of ways, as we now see.

Checklist 3.4: Methods of Dividing Descriptive work

✓ **by geographical location**
e.g.: oil deposits, rivers and other natural features; geographical subjects such as climate, agriculture and wildlife

✓ **by function**
e.g.: the human body in terms of respiration, circulation, and digestion; electrical networks in terms of generation, transmission and distribution; a manufacturing plant in terms of its functions

✓ **by component**
e.g.: any document in terms of its chapters, most manufactured products in terms of their parts

✓ **by characteristic**
e.g.: achievements, abilities and personal features of people; current in terms of alternating and direct; bacteria in terms of contagion methods

✓ **by time**
e.g.: historical accounts and sequenced events of all types

✓ **by type or model**
e.g.: for cars, computers, VCR players, televisions

Dividing by Characteristic

Perhaps the most important way of dividing details about a topic is by using characteristics. We can divide details about aircraft by their size and shape, carrying capacity, purpose (military, civil), navigational aids used, etc., and thus a detailed account of aircraft can be arranged in some sort of orderly fashion. The key to division of information and subsequent organization of the writing is in the recognition of important groups of features about the topic. Here are some more examples.

Checklist 3.5: Features for Division of Information (Examples)

✓ **apples:** *type, color, size, taste, sweetness, suitability for cooking, storage features, insect resistance, growing areas, yield, market acceptance*

✓ **students:** *age, sex, racial origin, religion, educational background, languages spoken, height, weight, parental background, academic interests, sporting and athletic interests, hobbies, academic ability*

✓ **cars:** *manufacturer, country of manufacture, year, model and type, color, size, shape (sedan, sports, wagon), performance, fuel economy, engine capacity, number of cylinders, turning circle, price, service record, hauling capacity*

Exercise 3.5: Recognizing Characteristics as a Basis for Division

Make a list of features for the following topics, and underline the features that you feel are the most important (i.e. the ones you would probably want to use as the basis for division of the information about each topic).

(a) televisions
(b) birds
(c) voltmeters
(d) cancers
(e) telephones
(f) modems

Note that all these topics are plural and you are dividing information about them according to the main features shared by different sub-groups of each topic. When you are describing a *specific* topic (e.g. a Panasonic KX-P1091 computer printer), you still follow the above procedure for *all* similar printers so that you have the main categories of information that need to be included in your description. Such descriptions involve explicit or implicit comparisons of features of the topic you are describing with the same features of similar topics.

You now have a sound basis for dividing the information about any topic you are describing. Remember, however, that not all genres of writing (e.g. problem-solution, thesis-backing) are divided in this way.

Once you have divided your descriptive work into sections, you have another opportunity to improve the contents you intend to include. Perhaps a complete section is missing, or some items of information could be added within the sections. Conversely you may now find that information you had previously thought important is no longer needed or can be added briefly to a more vital group of information. You may find that some information does not conveniently fit into the categories you have established. These overlapping categories are discussed next.

Exercise 3.6: Dividing Descriptive Detail

For the topics listed in *Exercise 3.5*, divide the contents into appropriate sections and re-examine the contents for each description. If you have some less-important items of information that cannot easily be placed within one of your categories, you might consider a section labeled "Other Features" or "Other Functions."

Unavoidable Overlaps

Often one particular feature of your topic will be of greatest importance, and you will then decide to make your initial division based on that feature. Examples are: students by female and male, aircraft by military and civil, trees by conifer and deciduous, birds by water birds and others, and beverages by alcoholic and non-alcoholic. There can be more than two major groups in such divisions, as in cars by sedan, sports and station wagons; and cancers by lung, prostate, breast, skin, etc.

All the types of topic you are describing (or all the features of a specific singular thing) cannot always be conveniently grouped into such divisions of information. Where would we place tamaracks, for example (conifers that loose their needles in winter) or convertible cars (sedan-sports)? Some overlapping may be unavoidable — and ironically often quite useful.

If, for example, you are classifying herbs, you will find that some are used for their leaves, some for their berries, some for their seeds, and some for their roots. But some have overlapping functions — coriander leaves and seeds, for example. Rather than ignoring such instances (which would be intellectually dishonest), you should openly acknowledge their existence, and ideally use them as effective transition examples between the groups.

Here is how one author identified an unavoidable overlap:

3.1

There are two categories that are often used to describe solar devices, active and passive. The distinction between the two isn't always clear-cut. In general, passive devices are self-contained, self-regulated and self-energized. On the other hand, a solar heating plant that requires an electrically-driven water pump is an active device. But there are solar heating plants that function without external energy sources. Are they active or passive?
— *Queen's Quarterly*, Winter 1984, P775

The writer admits that all solar devices cannot be neatly classified into the two main groups, but this becomes an interesting subject to discuss — not something to avoid or hide. It also becomes ideal transition material between the active and the passive types.

Exercise 3.7: Identifying Unavoidable Overlaps

For the following topics and identified major categories of division, identify the unavoidable overlaps.

(a) *human sexuality: homosexual — heterosexual*
(b) *wildlife: mammals — birds — reptiles*
(c) *animal eating methods: herbivore — carnivore*
(e) *types of life: flora — fauna*
(f) *forms of precipitation: snow — rain*
(h) *technical studies: engineering — science*
(i) *vegetation: useful — weeds*

Now think of your own topics that exhibit unavoidable overlap.

Undesirable Overlaps

Poor thinking and division of your work can lead to undesirable overlaps in your work. An acceptable division of vegetables might be

vegetables: root crops
leafy vegetables
other

with the "other" category including tomatoes, cauliflowers, garlic and peppers, and with beets and onions as clear examples of acceptable overlap between root and leafy vegetables (we eat both). We could further sub-divide these categories as the basis for a well-organized description of types of vegetables.
   However we could not use

vegetables: root crops
onions
tomatoes
leafy vegetables
zucchinis

as an acceptable basis for division of this topic, as these categories are on different levels of the hierarchy.
   Nor could we use

vegetables: root crops
vegetables used for feeding cattle
carrots
vegetables used for cooking
broccoli

as the basis for division because this time the division has been made by function (cooking, feeding cattle) as well as by type (root crops) and also specific examples (carrots, broccoli). Obviously some root crops are used for cooking, so which category do we put them in? The creation of overlap by division at different levels of the hierarchy or by different functions (or any other characteristic) is undesirable and can lead to poorly organized writing.

Exercise 3.8: Avoiding Undesirable Overlaps

For the following topics and major divisions, identify and explain instances of undesirable overlap and make changes to improve the structure. Also identify any unavoidable overlaps you notice.

(a) *vegetables: green vegetables, peas, beans, onions, canned vegetables, salad vegetables*

(b) *types of writing: literature, novels, description, articles, non-fictional writing, letters*

(c) *domesticated animals: agricultural animals, goats, pets, animals that are ridden, rabbits, donkeys, siamese cats*

(d) *meals: snacks, stews, hamburgers, five-course dinners, nutritional meals, meals with eggs and cheese, vegetarian meals, soups and salads, breakfasts*

(e) *boats: canoes, manually powered boats, rowing boats, flying boats, ocean liners, inflatable boats, paddle boats*

(f) *subjects of study: business, law, psychology, medicine, biology, anatomy, nursing, political science, electrical engineering, physics, economics, science*

(g) *hats: hats used in sports, safety helmets, sun hats, mortar boards, hats used for ornament, toques, riding helmets*

(h) *personal motion: walking, cycling, motor-assisted motion, skiing, in-line skating, traveling by car, swimming, snowmobiling, motion in or on water, parachuting, taking a bus*

(i) *colors: red, bright, crimson, navy blue, white, pink, black, gaudy, turquoise*

(j) *drinks: lemonade, beer, sherry, water, pop, brandy, non-alcoholic beverages, milk, martini, tea, fruit drinks, gin*

Now think of your own subjects and divide the contents in appropriate ways to avoid undesirable overlaps.

Subdivision and Order

The principles you have learned in this section apply equally well at all levels of writing: whether you are dividing your major topic into smaller parts, or dividing one of the smaller parts into still smaller sub-divisions. Re-examine the topics in the last few exercises and recognize the different levels of hierarchy, how sub-topics are sub-divided, how these can be further sub-divided, and so on.

Once you have decided on your major subdivisions, you can determine the order of your material. If you were describing hats by function, would you start with ornament, or protection, or sports uses, for example? The answer to this question is largely a matter of which you feel your readers need to know most — or what you feel should be communicated first. Another factor could be the unavoidable overlaps, as these can be used to connect sections together.

Natural Orders

Sometimes the order of presentation can be almost arbitrary, but on other occasions the order can be very important and you could be criticized for inappropriate sequence. The first thing to look for in deciding sequence is whether the subject naturally leads you to a certain order or presentation. The description of a river, for example, will almost certainly have a geographical sequence (from origin to the sea), and the description of your college or university will probably be based hierarchically (senate, faculties, departments, groups).

Checklist 3.6: Natural Orders as the Basis for Sequence

✓ **chronological:** *according to time sequence, or reverse chronology as in your experience in a resume*

✓ **spatially:** *from north to south, inside to outside, etc.*

✓ **sequentially:** *from start to finish, input to output, etc.*

✓ **size or shape:** *largest to smallest, circular-elliptical-rectangular, etc.*

✓ **by hierarchy:** *most general or dominant to least general or dominant, or vice versa*

✓ **by complexity:** *least to most complex, or vice versa*

✓ **by convention:** *alphabetically, left-to-right, red-to-blue (in a rainbow)*

✓ **by importance:** *whatever the natural order, you might decide to place very important information first and least important information last*

Exercise 3.9: Recognizing Natural Orders

For the following topics, determine which natural order or orders would be suitable for the sequence of material.

(a) *the solar system*
(b) *a list of students in the class*
(c) *a procedure for installing an answering machine*
(d) *ranks in the army*
(e) *bird eggs*
(f) *the Tour de France bicycle marathon*
(g) *a dinner menu*
(h) *a store "map" in a multi-storey shopping mall*
(j) *safety and use of a chain saw*

Exercise 3.10: Writing about Organized Descriptions

For a readership and level of formality specified by yourself or your instructor, write a two-to three-page discussion on the following topics. Include your own examples.

(a) *Describe the effects of audience and purpose on the contents for descriptions.*
(b) *Explain how writers divide descriptive work.*
(c) *Explain unavoidable and undesirable overlaps in descriptive organization.*
(d) *How do writers arrange their divided material into suitable orders?*

If your subject matter cannot easily be arranged in a natural sequence, you must use other criteria to determine the order of your writing. Here is a list of possibilities.

Checklist 3.7: Arranging your Material

✓ *Use a natural order if possible (see* Checklist 3.6).

✓ *Place important matters first, and perhaps repeat them very briefly at the end. "Important" here means what your readers need to know first, e.g. safety instructions before starting a procedure.*

✓ *If possible, arrange material to ensure a transition between sections of your writing by using unavoidable overlaps and placing closely-related topics next to each other.*

✓ In difficult cases, try to use a natural order for the main sequence and build other items around this. Even then you may find that very complex topics cannot be fully organized into a clear sequence; you may have to "force" a structure onto your writing to make it work reasonably well.

✓ If the order really is arbitrary (and that is very rare), don't try to justify the sequence — just indicate what you have chosen to do.

Review Questions

1. What is meant by the writing process being reiterative?

2. How can the structure of a document help you understand typical contents?

3. Why can there be quite different descriptions for the same thing?

4. What are major methods of dividing technical descriptions?

5. How can we compare the description of a group of things (e.g. all moving coil voltmeters) with the description of a special type of thing (e.g. a Panasonic KX-P1080i printer)?

6. What are unavoidable overlaps? How can we take advantage of them?

7. What are undesirable overlaps? How can we avoid them?

8. What are the natural orders for descriptive information?

Chapter 4:
Organizing and Signaling Material

In this chapter you will learn to prepare an "outline" for your planned work to help you to write your document. You will also learn how to obtain advice about your work, and to work with others who are writing a large document with you. You will also learn how and where to signal the contents and sequence of your information to meet your needs.

Outlining
Do You Need to Plan Your Writing?
The Outline and its Use
The Genre and Your Outline
Outline Structures
Advantages of Outlines
Master Document Control

Signaling Your Structure
Using the Table of Contents
Using Headings
Creative Headings
Structure Signals in Introductions
Structure Signals for Major Sections
Structure Signals Throughout the Text

Outlining

Do You Need to Plan Your Writing?

For short documents, there is rarely any need to plan your writing first. You simply think of what you want to write, and then write it. You might need to re-arrange things once you have written your first draft, but that can easily be done on your computer. Even for some quite lengthy documents, you might not need to plan the work in any detail because you may have to follow a standard set of headings with expected types of information under each heading. Laboratory reports are examples of this.

However, for lengthy documents where the structure has not been determined, you will need to plan your work before you start to write. An experienced technical writer would never embark on a such a writing task without at least first having made a list of likely contents and the order in which they might appear. This is called an "outline" of the planned document, and the preparation of an outline is often an important step in the writing process.

Checklist 4.1: Factors Affecting the Need for an Outline

✓ *the extent to which you are required to follow standard headings and sequence*

✓ *the length of the document*

✓ *the complexity of the information to be included*

✓ *whether you need approval at this planning stage*

✓ *whether you are or will be working with co-writers*

✓ *your personal way of planning and writing a document*

The Outline and its Use

For some writers, the "outline" may be little more than a few scruffy notes and indications of sequence and grouping of information. For others, it is an organized list of headings indicating the planned contents, grouping and order — in fact a "Table of Contents" of how they see the final document. The type and extent of your outline will depend on the factors in *Checklist 4.1*, including your personal preferences for planning and organization at the early stages of the writing process.

Some writers do not start their writing until they have developed a very good understanding of the subject, and they are then able to plan their document with reasonable accuracy. Others, however, recognize that only the writing itself will enable them to understand the subject sufficiently to explain it well — and they choose to prepare a rough initial outline, and then to improve it as the writing progresses.

However well you feel you know the subject you are about to write about, you should recognize that no outline will be a perfect plan of your work. You must be flexible in your attitude toward your outline, and change it as your writing develops. Inevitably you will find you know more than you thought about some subjects, and less about others. Your headings, order, depth of treatment and continuity between the sections of your document may all need to be adapted to the reality of the actual writing. Although your outline guides your writing, change it while you are writing until it becomes your final Table of Contents.

The Genre and Your Outline

Chapter 3 discusses the relationship between the type, or genre, of writing and the structure of the document. We saw there that there are many natural orders for descriptive material, and clearly any of these could form the basis for an outline of a detailed description. Once you have decided on the major items of information to be included and have selected an appropriate overall order, you should be able to arrange the information within the larger group of information, and so create a two- or three-level outline of your planned work.

If, however, you find your report or proposal is a problem-solution document, the major sections of your outline will follow the four-part problem-solution structure. You will need to include elements of the situation, problem, solution and evaluation under suitable headings to group your planned material. See *Chapter 6* for a detailed example of a problem-solution outline.

Similarly, if your document is to be essentially basis-assessment, or comparison, or narrative (see *Chapter 7*), your outline will largely reflect your need for a structure that follows such a pattern. With a clear understanding of the overall informational pattern in mind, you should be able to create a useful outline including and relating all important elements of the information you need to include.

Outline Structures

Your computer software will offer you three or four different outline systems with as many as nine levels. You should, at this time, become familiar with outline facilities provided by your software. If you have not used these facilities before, go to *Outline* in your *Help* file and follow the directions given. As these functions can be a little complex, you might wish to observe the *Outlining a New or Existing Document* demo if you have one.

Typical outlining facilities on computers are the "paragraph," "outline" and "legal" (or "decimal") systems, with other systems and a make-it-yourself system is often available also.

Checklist 4.2.: Typical Outlining Systems for Eight Levels

✓ *"Paragraph "*   *1. a. I. (1) (a) (i) 1) a)*

✓ *"Outline"*   *I. A. 1. (a) (1) (a) 1) a)*

✓ *"Legal" or "decimal"*   *1. 1. 1. 1. 1. 1. 1. 1*

Each level may be indented five spaces (one tab) in both the outline and the actual document. By writing your document according to the selected outline, you can ensure that your outline and actual document structure coincide exactly. Of course you do not have to use one of these systems at all if you use indentation or capitalization or bold type to distinguish the levels. See how this is done in the prefatory material, and throughout the rest of this book.

In practice you will rarely need to use more than three levels unless you are writing an extremely large or complicated document. In spite of its length and depth of treatment, this book usually has only three levels (chapters, sections and subsections) with a few exceptions (e.g. in Chapter 15 and Appendix A).

Creating an Outline

Once you have collected sufficient material for your document, you should be able to start to create an outline. A formal outline will look very much like a table of contents, and in fact it is a planned or proposed table of contents — the way you envisage your document when you have finished it.

Make your headings as descriptive as possible so that you, your colleagues and your supervisor all know what you intend to include under each heading. Some writers add notes separated by dashes under each heading to create an "expanded" outline, but other writers are unable (or feel it inappropriate) to plan to that level of detail. Arrange your material in an acceptable overall order appropriate for the genre and information you expect to include. Then break down the information within each major level into sections and perhaps subsections, again ensuring a suitable sequence at these levels too. Ideally your sequence should enable you to provide sensible transitions between the parts of your document.

Here is a sample outline for an article describing a new high speed transport system. Note how the description for new system is based on the known "Maglev" equipment.

A New High-Speed Surface Transportation System

Introduction
Existing Magnetic Levitation System
New High Speed Train
Advantages and Implementation

Magnetic Levitation Transportation
Conventional Induction Maglevs
Principles of Linear Induction
History and Development
Applications
Limitations

High Speed Surface Transport
Separating Lift and Drive
Maintaining Rail Gap
Drive System
Capital Cost Advantage

Performance
Testing Procedures
Speed Data
Efficiency Limitations
Capital and Running Costs

Planned Applications
Short-Distance Use
Speed and Cost Factors
Planned Track Near Yokohama
Trials in Germany

Make sure you divide information into at least two parts — not one. A partial outline of

4. **Applications**
   4.1 Uses for Electrostatic Measurement

5. **Calibration**

would leave readers wondering what, if anything, is to be included under the *Applications* heading. Also, a reference to *Section 4* could refer to all of that section (including 4.1), or just to information under 4 itself.

Make sure that information on related topics appears in the same section or subsection, and that information only occurs in one place. Try to give roughly equal "weight" (length and depth of treatment) to the different topics on the same level to provide some "balance" to the depth of treatment for each topic. If there is too much material for one topic, split it into two or three to achieve a better balance

Try to indicate what you will write in the *Introduction* section. Subsections dealing with *Earlier Research, Literature Review, Related Design Problems, Research Procedures, Definition of Terms,* and *Scope and Purpose* are much clearer than the almost meaningless *Background* or *General*. A clear understanding of information to be included in the introduction is invaluable to all members of a technical team, especially the supervisor.

Advantages of Outlines

There are many advantages to outlines — not just the obvious ones of helping yourself to plan and organize your thoughts and material, but also informing those in your writing team and receiving approval and useful guidance from your supervisor.

Checklist 4.3: Advantages of an Outline

✓ *It makes you understand the genre of writing you need to meet the purpose of your writing and the needs of your readers.*

✓ *It forces you to organize your thoughts and the material you expect to include in the document into bundles of material related to each other.*

✓ *It helps you to realize what information you still need to obtain in order to make a complete document on your chosen topic.*

✓ *It enables you to arrange groups of material in acceptable sequences.*

✓ *It helps you to think about how you will provide transitions between subsections and sections.*

✓ *It provides the basis for your creation of meaningful headings to represent the information under those headings.*

✓ *It enables you to write some sections later in the document first if that information is available.*

✓ *It allows all members of a team to contribute to the planning and organization of the final document.*

✓ *It then informs all members of the team of the contents, structure and order of the whole document — and keeps them informed as the outline changes to reflect the actual writing.*

✓ *It enables the team leader to allocate sections and subsections of work to members of the team, and to monitor and control the work of each member and the project as a whole.*

✓ *It allows the writer(s) to receive initial advice and approval from a supervisor*

For the topics you analyzed in *Chapter 3* (or any other topic), prepare outlines to two or three levels.

Master Document Control

For long documents — or when several of you are writing different parts — you should use your computer's *Master Document* control facility. Selection of this facility automatically provides you with the *Outline* commands, and allows you to label each major section (or chapter) as part of your overall document. This in turn allows you to add, re-organize or delete parts of your total document, and the computer will make appropriate changes as you do this.

The *Master Document* control facility is ideal for revising and editing large multi-section documents. It allows several authors to unite their contributions almost as separate documents, with the group leader monitoring the progress of the work and re-organizing it to create an effective overall document. This facility will create a Table of Contents for you from the headings in the body of the text.

Signaling Your Structure

Using the Table of Contents

Dividing your material and arranging it in a suitable order are only part of your task: you have to tell your readers too. For large documents, the obvious place to do this is the "Table of Contents," placed immediately after your title page. The contents list is really an outline of your document after you have finished writing it, and it indicates the contents, divisions, sequencing and page numbers of the sections of your document. See *Page 290* for a sample.

For extremely complex topics, you could have major sections or chapters and divide these into smaller parts with a contents list for each section or chapter. An abbreviated (including chapter headings) *and* detailed (including chapter sub-sections) Table of Contents can often be useful. Note how this has been done in this book. For very large documents, you could even separate chapters — or groups of chapters — with colored index cards as "tabs" to help readers find information. Very large documents may contain several separate volumes.

This book uses three levels. You might care at this stage to review how the book is divided into chapters, how each chapter is divided into three or four major sections, and how these sections are again divided into smaller parts. The main contents list and each chapter contents list contain details of the sections within the chapters and the parts within each section. Note how the headings used in the text are exactly the same as those indicated in the contents list — your computer will do this for you if you use the outline or master document facility.

Note also the different "weights" of the headings to indicate the different "levels" of writing, i.e. the use of large bold sans-serif letters for sections and smaller bold serif letters for the parts within the sections. With other documents, you could use numbering and/or lettering systems (see your computer software) to indicate these weights and levels.

Using Headings

For some technical articles, headings may be stylistically unacceptable and some instructors may not wish you to use them. If you are allowed to use headings, find out if standard headings are commonly used for this sort of writing, or whether you are free to make up your own. If you are writing a paper or article for a newspaper, magazine or journal, you can find out the stylistic requirements for headings simply by looking through a few issues of the publication. If in doubt, ask the editor.

Almost all technical documents do use headings. They are extremely useful ways of indicating your structure to your readers, and they also help readers to find information more quickly. For some writing tasks, headings may be required, and you may have to use standard headings, such as:

Checklist 4.4: Some Systems of Standard Headings

✓ Introduction	✓ Aims	✓ Need
Background	Apparatus	Analysis
Method	Set up	Problem Details
Solution	Method	Selected Solution
Data	Results	Analysis
Analysis		Other Solutions
Conclusions		

These sorts of headings are useful for writers with little practice writing functional documents, and they also help readers to find certain types of information quickly. However, when the project task is more original than the experimental detail often found in such reports, you will do better by using more creative headings.

Creative Headings

Standard or conventional headings are highly suitable for technical reports where the work follows a predictable pattern. They are rather vague, however, for other purposes. The more specific and creative you can be with your headings, the more informative they will become — and thus the more useful they will be for your readers. Creative headings are usually longer than the conventional ones, but the extra few words are often well worth including. Below the original creative headings are given with standard and general reductions.

Checklist 4.5: Conventional, General and Creative Headings

✓ Standard	✓ General	✓ Creative
Introduction	Introduction	The Struggle Against Inflation
Body	One Strategy	A Losing Strategy
Conclusion	Policy	The Policy Dilemma
	Disinflation	Disinflation Won't Work
	Other Policies	Other Ineffectual Policies
	Another Strategy	A Winning Strategy
	Success	Requirements for Success
	Conclusion	Transitional Methods

—*Example 4.1*: Queen's Quarterly, Spring 1983, P1-15

The headings of the original creative headings give readers a much clearer picture of the contents and structure of the writing, and they also help readers to find detail they may have read earlier and wish to re-read. For some documents, the initial section has no heading at all, as it is obviously an introduction. Again follow the standard practice of the publication you are writing for, or the preference of your instructor.

The same principle of using informative headings applies to document titles too. Try to make them as informative as possible — even if that means having quite a long title, or perhaps using a sub-title or a brief abstract on the title page to expand on the main title. See Page 288 for further detail.

Structure Signals in Introductions

Your work may need an "abstract," which tells readers what is in the document, or a "summary," which summarizes its main points — or sometimes both. If so, write these using the same sequence you use in the main body of your document, as this helps readers to understand the sequence of your writing.

Many writers include a brief paragraph at the end of their introductions in "abstract" style overtly saying what is in the document and in what order. This is a very useful technique — especially if you are not using headings. Here is how one writer explained the structure of a research proposal.

4.2

```
The layout of the document is as follows: Section 2 is dedicated to a brief review of the analysis techniques required for working with multivariate linear dynamic systems and also presents critical background information relevant to the proposed research contributions. The third section contains a process description and a literature review for an industrial process which has been largely overlooked in terms of multivariate analysis and modelling - the thermo-mechanical pulping process. The planned research contributions are outlined in section 4, and section 5 completes the body of the proposal with a tentative schedule for completion of the proposed research topics and a plan for field testing.
                    —PhD Thesis Proposal,
                      C. Seppala, Chemical
                              Engineering
```

Structure Signals For Major Sections

It is also often useful — especially in very large documents — to explain to readers the structure of your major sections of your document. Here is an example:

2. Methods of Analysis and Background Information

4.3

```
In this section, background information relevant to proposed research into multivariate linear dynamic systems will be provided. The general structural representations of multivariate systems will be presented in section 2.1, followed by brief reviews of three well known model classes for characterizing multivariate systems: multiple time series analysis
```

```
(2.2), state space repre-      in section 2.5. Finally, an
sentations (2.3), and mul-     overview of some powerful
tivariate spectral analysis    time series analysis tech-
(2.4). Previous research       niques developed in econo-
carried out on the dynamic     metrics will be presented
analysis of variance for       in section 2.6.
multi-input single-output                         —ibid
systems will be discussed
```

The editors of this example also left additional white space between the major sections of the article; others sometimes use asterisks for the same purpose, or indicate major sections with initial large bold lettering.

Structure Signals Throughout the Text

When you are using headings it is often useful to introduce the topics you will discuss first, in the order in which they will appear:

Splice Loading

4.4
```
There are three categories     double-shear splice.
of fuselage skin splice:          — Canadian Aeronautical
the single-shear lap                    and Space Journal,
splice, the single-shear              Dec 1994, P15
sult splice, and the
```

Whether you are using headings or not, clear transitions between what you have just discussed and what you are about to discuss can be extremely useful:

4.5
```
Having explained how the       gy can be used to meet
receipt of solar energy can    human needs.
be measured, I shall now          — Queen's Quarterly,
examine how the solar ener-           Winter 1984, P775
```

Checklist 4.6: Structure Signaling Devices

✓ *the contents list*

✓ *major dividers (colored tabs, dividers, chapters and separate binders)*

✓ *other dividers (white space, asterisks, initial bold letters)*

✓ *the abstract or summary*

✓ *discussion at the end of introductions*

✓ *discussion between major sections*

✓ *discussion and transitions throughout the text*

Research Task

Examine large documents in your technical specialty. Note the use of titles, abstracts, headings and other methods used by authors to signal document structure.

Review Questions

1. *When would you, and when would you not, prepare an outline?*

2. *What factors affect the need for an outline?*

3. *What is an outline, and what alternative do some writers use?*

4. *What is the connection between the genre of your document and its outline?*

5. *What are the three major outlining structures, and what letters/numbers do they use?*

6. *What is meant by "levels" of a document?*

7. *Why is it inappropriate to "divide" material in an outline with only one sub-section?*

8. *What do "weight" and "balance" mean in document organization?*

9. *What is the difficulty with words such as "Introduction," "Background," and "General" in outlines (and in documents too)?*

10. *What are the advantages of outlines?*

11. *What computer facilities are available for outlining and Master Document control?*

12. *Where could you signal your document structure to readers?*

13. *What are standard, general and creative headings? What are their advantages and disadvantages?*

14. *What can you do to make a title clearer?*

15. *What do abstracts and summaries do?*

Chapter 5:
The Thread Of Continuity
(Description)

In this chapter you will learn how to use the system that achieves continuity in writing, including connection between sentences, connection linking clauses of sentences (including lists), and more advanced methods of achieving connection through association of technical topics. As description relies entirely on this system of continuity in language, you will also understand and become able to use all the techniques skilled writers use in describing technical items and systems.

Basic Continuity
General Principles
Re-entry and Repetition
Generic Nouns
Naming and Acronyms
Substitution

Using Separate Clauses
Relative Clauses
Clausal Ellipsis
Writing and Punctuating Lists
Correcting Faulty Parallel Structures

Descriptive Clauses
-ing Clauses
-ed Clauses
Verbless Clauses (Including Appositions)
The Three Positions

Connection by Association
The Use of Associations
Using Perspective Connection

Basic Continuity

General Principles

The language of technical description is connected entirely by "re-entering" established topics and sub-topics into the text. In this way more information is provided about these topics until the description is complete. There is no "Introduction," "Body" or "Conclusion" in the accepted sense of the words; the description is simply an organized collection of information about the topic being described.

In addition, this principle of topic connection is central to *all* forms of technical writing, as it is this which provides the thread of continuity in any text. Problem-solution, evaluative and comparative forms of writing have other types of connection in addition to continuity, but there will *always* also be patterns of "descriptive" continuity throughout these other types. Thus mastery of continuity methods and practices is a key element in all forms of technical writing.

This chapter shows you how to achieve continuity between, as well as within, sentences and paragraphs. It also demonstrates: the use of clauses dominated by *which*, *that*, and other connecting words; how to connect two clauses by "omitting" (or "eliding") the subject; and how to compose, organize and punctuate simple and complex lists. You will also be introduced to other clauses skilled writers use to make their writing more mature and concise, and you will also be shown some of the more complex techniques used by experienced technical writers and editors.

Re-entry and Repetition

Quite simply the basic idea of description and continuity is that the writer first establishes a topic and then re-enters it in successive sentences and clauses until the description is complete. This can be illustrated as:

Figure 5.1: Basic Re-entry Pattern

This basic re-entry pattern is easiest to see in advertising, where the copywriter (the person writing the "copy" or text for the advertisement) often uses the clearest and most pronounced form of re-entry: full repetition.

5.1 GEOTEMRIII Multi-Coil System

Geoterrex is pleased to announce the availability of GEOTEMRIII, a multi-coil time-domain airborne electromagnetic (AEM) system. The new system is the result of several years of multi-coil bird and receiver design, development and testing. This enhancement to the wide-

```
ly used single-component          bird and next-generation dig-
GEOTEMR system provides a         ital receiver of the GEOTEM-
powerful new tool to the          RIII system are designed to
exploration and resource          collect two additional compo-
evaluation community. GEOTEM-     nents, the vertical (z) and
RIII is the first commercial-     the horizontal lateral (y).
ly available multi-coil time-        — Canadian Mining Journal,
domain AEM system intended                          Feb 1995, P16
primarily for mineral explor-
ation. . . . The new towed
```

The topic of description is clearly GEOTEMRIII, which is re-entered by its name three times in this short passage. This repetition is ideal for advertisements (and perhaps circus ring announcers), but would be unsuitable for most technical descriptions. Instead we use other methods to re-enter the topic in successive sentences.

Instead of repeating the whole of a topic or name (called "full repetition"), writers often repeat only part of the topic. This makes the writing less emphatic or "marked," as we see in:

5.2
```
Domtar will invest $245          the program include
million in a program to          improved operating capabil-
update its northern              ity, environmental compli-
bleached softwood kraft          ance, cost reductions, more
(NBSK) pulp mill in Lebel-       consistent product quality
sur-Quevillon, QC. The mod-      and approximately 30 000
ernization program will          tonnes increased capacity.
include multiple in-plant          —Pulp and Paper Canada, May
modifications, a cogenera-                             1995, P7
tion plant and a new
boiler. . . . Benefits of
```

The topic, introduced at the end of the first sentence, is *a program to update its northern bleached softwood kraft (NBSK) pulp mill in Lebel-sur-Quevillon*. As this is clearly far too long to re-enter by full repetition, the writer chose the partial repetition *The ... program* instead in two successive sentences. Further information about the program is given by the addition of *modernization*.

Generic Nouns and Synonyms

A re-entry method that is similar to partial repetition is the use of a general or "generic" noun. For partial repetition part of the topic is included in the re-entry. For generic nouns, however, the noun used for re-entry is *not* part of the topic:

5.3
```
Plans have been announced        free. The project marks the
to install a treatment sys-      first mill-scale develop-
tem to help Avenor's             ment under . . .
Thunder Bay, ON, newsprint          — Pulp and Paper Canada,
mill to become effluent-                            May 1995, P7
```

Use of the partial repetition *The system* here would have imparted a narrower meaning than the writer had intended, as it was the installation of the system that is the topic to be re-entered. So the generic noun *The project* is used instead.

In effect, the generic nouns used for re-entry purposes are "synonyms" for the topics they are re-entering — they say the same thing using another word. We see the use of a synonym even more clearly in the following example:

5.4

> The third major traffic management system around Metro Toronto monitors and controls the approximately 1700 traffic signals in the city. The *lights* are co-ordinated to reduce stops and delays.
> — *Engineering Dimensions*, Nov/Dec 1994, P25

The topic (*the approximately 1700 traffic signals*) is re-entered using the synonym *lights*.

Generic nouns and synonyms are extremely useful methods of re-entering a topic. Typical nouns used in this way are *machine, instrument, material, compound, device, tool* and *product*; in context these are not vague or they re-enter a previous specific topic.

Naming and Acronyms

As we saw in *Example 5.1*, we often give names or code numbers to designs or inventions. This helps us to identify them and also makes it easier for us to refer to them in speech and writing. (We do the same for people, of course.) Once we have named something we can use the name as a re-entry device:

5.5

> Geotech reported a new development in integrated airborne multiparameter geophysical survey systems, the HUMMINGBIRD. . . . The basic HUMMINGBIRD consists of a small ``strap-down'' console comprising an IBM compatible 486 PC, data acquisition HDD, and plug-in processor boards.
> — *Canadian Mining Journal*, Feb 1995, P54

This example, as well as illustrating the use of naming and re-entry by the use of the name, also contains three acronyms: IBM, PC and HDD. Use of acronyms in this way is acceptable only when we are sure our readers know what they mean. It would be unnecessary to use, for example, "International Business Machines" instead of the well-known acronym IBM; in fact it would have been insulting to professional readers to include both (i.e. "International Business Machines (IBM)"), as that would imply that we thought our readers did not know that.

In general use in Canada, RCMP, NATO, USA and other acronyms are so well known we rarely need to use the full version. Similarly in all technical disciplines there are established acronyms (*ac, dc* and *rms* in electrical work, for example), which are usually used without definition. If you are not sure whether your readers know an acronym (or if only *some* of your readers know it), write the acronym first and place the full version in parentheses immediately after it.

Sometimes we might wish to introduce our own acronym, as this permits easy and concise re-entry later:

5.6

Data production is where data is first captured, and occurs in a variety of production systems. These systems are often referred to as on-line transaction processing systems (OLTP). OLTP systems are optimized for storing large volumes of data gathered one record at a time. Examples of OLTP systems are order entry systems, invoicing and general ledger systems. Unfortunately, the data gathered and stored in OLTP systems is not very accessible to end users.

— *Computing Canada*,
June 1995, P26

Note that the writer excluded *systems* from the acronym here, and so had to repeat that word with each re-entry of the acronym: a five-letter acronym (OLTPS) would have avoided the need to repeat *systems*. For plural acronyms the simple addition of an *s* is better than *'s* (which is used for possession) although both are acceptable. When you need an indefinite article before the acronym, use *a* if the start of the acronym sounds like a consonant (*a NATO project*) and *an* if it sounds like a vowel (e.g. *an NRT detector*). The use of *a* before *SCSI* in Example 69 indicates that the writer was not aware that *SCSI* is usually read as *"scuzzy."* If you need to use a lot of acronyms in a large document, include a "List of Acronyms" with their meanings at the front of your document. If you include it at the back instead, you *must* indicate that you have done this on your Contents page.

Research Tasks

1. Study examples of technical writing for yourself, noting occurrences of the re-entry devices discussed so far. Collect any examples you have difficulty in understanding and bring them to class for discussion.

2. Study examples of technical advertising. Note how the names of the company and their products are often given prominence.

3. Note where and how acronyms, generic nouns and synonyms are used in the writing you are studying.

For each of these tasks — or for others selected by yourself or your instructor — be prepared to write analyses based on the examples you have found. Follow the style of this book by using key examples to illustrate the conclusions you reach. As an alternative, prepare an oral presentation using overheads of your examples.

Writing Tasks

1. For a real or imagined product, write an advertisement for publication in a technical magazine.

2. Now rewrite the advertisement, making it suitable for inclusion in a "New Products" section of a technical magazine.

3. Do the same for your own company (give it a name) and a service you want to offer (e.g. window cleaning, snow shovelling, painting).

Substitution

Another way of re-entering a topic is substitution (or "pronouns" if you like). As in technical writing we are usually discussing inanimate things, the main substitute words are *It* for singular topics and *They* for plurals. A simple example is:

> **5.7** Rustrak has introduced the Ranger II Harmonic Power Logger. The 1250 Series records harmonics with respect to time rather than via summary readings, so isolating the factors causing harmonic distortion is simplified. *It* records simultaneously volts, amps, true power and harmonic distortion to provide maximum information on all phases.
> — *Machinery and Equipment MRO*, Sep 1994, P6–7

The topic is given in the first sentence and re-entered by a series number in the second. Substitution is used to re-enter the topic into the final sentence.

Here is an example using the substitute *They*. It also shows the use of two already-defined acronyms and a newly-defined one:

> **5.8** Invehicle route guidance systems use AVI, GIS and sometimes global positioning systems (GPS) . . . to help drivers find destinations in unfamiliar locales and avoid areas of congestion. *They* can provide step-by-step instructions on how to reach one's destination.
> — *Engineering Dimensions*, Nov/Dec 1994, P26

It is important to note that *They* re-enters the *subject* of the sentence, not other plural topics later in the sentence (*GPS, destinations, areas of congestion*). Likewise, in *Example 5.7 It* re-enters the subject of description (*The 1250 Series*) not the other singular topic (*maximum information*), which comes later in the sentence.

If we need to re-enter the immediately preceding topic into the next sentence, we use *These* for plurals and *This* for singular topics. This is not an absolute rule, but a strong tendency. Here is such an example:

5.9

Ainsworth has announced that it is stocking the Legend Plus Controller from Red Lion Controls. *This* is a full-featured count controller for process, batch or totalizing applications.

— Machinery and Equipment MRO, Sep 1994, P13

This re-enters the immediately preceding topic (*the Legend Plus Controller*). As *They, It, These, This* and other substitutes re-enter the whole noun phrase (not just a single noun), it is more accurate to call them "substitutes" rather than "pronouns."

These substitute words are also sometimes used in front of a noun, often a generic noun e.g. *This* machine. Writers also use "embracing substitutes" (e.g. *All* for several or *Both* for two) and "partitive substitutes" to indicate specific partition (e.g. *10%, half*), general partition (e.g. *most, a few, some*) and partition by characteristic (e.g. *the new drills we bought last week*).

Exercise 5.1: Using Appropriate Re-entry Techniques

Make each of the following less marked (less emphatic) and more concise by using more appropriate re-entry methods.

(a) *Final approval has been given for the ABB-CE System Reactor. The ABB-CE System Reactor is rated at 1,350 MW.*

(b) *According to Steve Probyn, president of the Independent Power Producers Society of Ontario, it is important to recognize that renewable energy sources are viable. Steve Probyn says his Toronto firm has financed $800 million of projects since 1987.*

(c) *Falconbridge is examining four bar and metal possibilities near Timmins. Falconbridge began working on the Kam Kotia mine in 1992. The former Kam Kotia mine produced 6 million tons of copper-zinc ore until the mine was closed in 1992.*

(d) *The University of British Columbia recently decided to use metal halide rather than high-pressure sodium lighting. It had been expected that the choice would be based on observations and assessments by University of British Columbia professors, students and staff.*

(e) *High-Sense Geophysics Ltd. has developed a high sensitivity magnetometer system, the MSM-MK II. The high-sensitivity magnetometer system is coupled with a sensor and can be rapidly installed in a variety of helicopters.*

(f) *Material from a fifth drill hole is currently being assayed in the laboratory. The material from this drill hole extends the strike length of the deposit for over 800 m.*

(g) *The data gathered and stored in OLTP systems is not very accessible to end users. The lack of accessibility does not constitute a design error in OLTP systems. Rather, the lack of accessibility highlights that the OLTP systems were not designed to allow data gatherd by the OLTP systems to be assessed by end users.*

(h) *The French goverment authorized the restoration of the 1,240 MW Superphoenix fast breeder reactor located at Creys-Malville on August 3. This 1,240 MW Superphoenix fast breeder reactor has been shut down for the last four years.*

(i) *"Our other interesting, but much smaller, projects, will be carried by our partners," Exall President Stephen Roman told shareholders of the Exall corporation. The Exall President said he is counting on placer diamonds and gold from the Mazaruni River project to provide the necessary cash flow.*

(j) *The Enerpac WalkPac battery-powered hydraulic pump weighs 18 lb. The Enerpac WalkPac provides power for cutting, bending, crimping, lifting and other high pressure applications.*

Research Tasks

1. Analyze the use of all the re-entry techniques in examples of descriptions in "Product News" sections of technical magazines. Note how the substitutes are used, and bring interesting examples to class for discussion.

2. Prepare an analysis of the use of re-entry methods in "Product News" technical writing, using examples you have found. The length and depth of your work could be almost anything — check with your instructor.

3. Repeat 1. and 2. for other forms of technical writing (advertising, text books, general articles, scholarly papers, abstracts/summaries), and compare your findings.

Using Separate Clauses

Relative Clauses

Instead of using the substitute *This* in Example 5.9, we could have used , *which* and continued with the sentence. That is, both *This* and *which* re-enter the immediately preceding topic. Your choice of a separate sentence or a single one depends on the length and complexity of the information in both clauses. It will also depend on your audience and the style you wish to use. The clause you create using *which* is called a "relative" clause, and *which* is called a "relative substitute" or "relative pronoun."

Thus we find relative clauses at the ends of sentences, providing information about a recently introduced topic, as in:

5.10
From West Instruments comes the 6100 Series 1/16 DIN Universal I/O Process Controller, *which* uses the West pre-tune and adaptive tuning algorithms.
— *Machinery and Equipment MRO*, Sep 1994, P17

Relative clauses are particularly handy devices because we can also use them between the subject of a sentence and the main verb. Note the re-entries in the following:

5.11
RMS instruments now offers in its HDS series for magnetic recording, a 500 Mbyte hard drive together with either a 60, 150 or 525 Mbyte tape drive depending on users' requirements. The recording system, *which* uses an SCSI interface, provides the option of simultaneous recording to tape and hard disk.
— *Canadian Mining Journal*, Feb 1995, PS-7

The generic noun *system* re-enters the previous topic (*a 500 Mbyte drive . . . requirements*) into a new sentence. Two items of information are then presented about this topic: first in the relative clause, and then in the main part of the sentence:

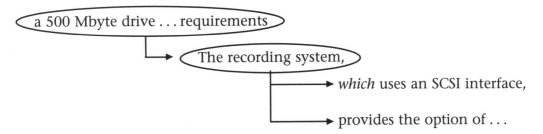

Figure 5.2: Re-entry with Relative Clause

Other relative clauses occur with places (using *where*), times (using *when*) and people (using *who*). The distinction is often useful. What does *which* re-enter in the following example?

5.12
Helge Eklund, CEO of Sodracell, *which* produces over a million tonnes per year (t/y) of TCF market kraft in direct competition to many Canadian producers, delivered a controversial keynote address.
— *Pulp and Paper Canada*, May 1995, P13

The relative clause provides information about the company *Sodracell*, whereas the main clause is about the speaker *Helge Eklund*. We know this because *which* re-enters things into the text, while *who* re-enters people.

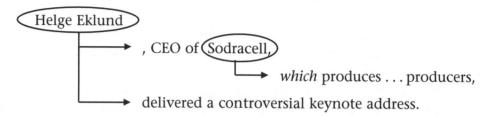

Figure 5.3: Re-entering Things and People

Writers place the *less* important information in the relative clause and the *more* important information in the main clause.

Note that these relative clauses have commas around them, indicating that they are providing incidental ("non-restrictive") information. When relative clauses are "restrictive" (i.e. they define, limit or restrict the meaning of the topic they re-enter), you must *not* place commas around them. A sound test is to try the word "incidentally" after the relative substitute (*which, who, when* or *where*). If the meaning of "incidentally" is compatible with the meaning of the clause, the clause must then be separated from the rest of the sentence with commas.

Relative clauses for people, places and times are signaled by *who, where*, and *when* for both restrictive and non-restrictive clauses. However, for things we can use *which* or *that* for restrictive clauses, but only *which* for non-restrictive clauses. For restrictive clauses *that* has a more direct and less formal tone than *which*, and is more usual in technical writing than writing in the social sciences and the humanities. Some technical writers follow the rule of using *which* for all non-restrictive clauses and *that* for all restrictive clauses. This is not a bad general rule, but try not to impose it on other writers when you are editing.

Exercise 5.2: Using Relative Clauses

For each of the following, use a relative clause for the *less* important information to create a single sentence. Punctuate your sentences correctly. Note the positions (at the end of the sentence, or between the subject and main verb) of your relative clauses.

(a) *Light, in its interaction with matter, behaves as though it is composed of many individual bodies called photons. These photons have particle-like properties such as energy and momentum.*

(b) *Paramax Electronics Inc. came into being in 1983. It was recently awarded the contract to design the defensive systems in the Canadian patrol frigates.*

(c) *Turbo boost pressure normally flows from the intake manifold to the injection pump. It is at the injection pump that the pressure moves a metering valve to increase fuel flow.*

(d) *A fixed steel beam is used to support this soft polyolefin absorber, and the absorber collapses and distributes the load when the car bumper is hit.*

(e) *The system has been tried out in the construction of irrigation systems. It was developed in Valencia.*

Clausal Ellipsis

When we have two statements to make about the same topic, we can put them together in a single sentence and omit (or "elide") the topic in the second clause; this is called "ellipsis." Here is an example containing two such ellipses:

5.13
```
The on-board navigation        The system is applicable to
computer reads the planned     both helicopter and fixed-
flying surface,                wing surveys, and___is most
and___advises the pilot, in    advantageous in very steep
real-time, of the current      topography.
deviation from the planned     — Canadian Mining Journal,
survey altitude and the                       Feb 1995, PS7
planned rate of climb or
descent for the location.
```

The long underlining indicates where the writer has deliberately elided the subject. In both of these sentences, the topic is the same for each clause. The re-entry by ellipsis achieves the connection in a less marked and more concise way than using repetition, a generic noun, or substitution. Clausal ellipsis allows us to provide two items of information *on the same level of importance*, whereas relative clauses lessen the importance of the information they contain.

Several types of ellipsis are possible. Here is an example where the subject and the verb are elided:

5.14
```
Tubules have micritic walls              and N. James,
1-2 m thick and___inner diam-   Department of Geological
eters of 5 to 11 m.                     Sciences, 1995
   — E. Turner, G. Narbonne
```

In this example, the subject and verb *Tubules have* are elided in the second clause, a technique which is more appropriate here than, say, substitution: "Tubules have micritic walls. They also have inner diameters of 5 to 11 m."

Ellipsis is an extremely useful technique, especially when the topic is quite long. Here we see it being used with a long subject and *but* to show a surprise:

5.15
```
The sudden appearance of       reflect some environmental
abundant well-calcified        change that permitted the
cyanobacteria near the         expansion of a previously
Precambrian-Cambrian bound-    limited biota.
ary is not a true evolu-
tionary event, but may                            — ibid
```

Exercise 5.3: Using Clausal Ellipsis

Use clausal ellipsis to improve the conciseness and lower the emphasis of the following.

(a) *Bruce Fleming, formerly of PAPRICAN, made a spirited attempt at defending us. However, he was disallowed by the chair.*

(b) *Sandra Jean Simpson joined the Toronto law firm of Fraser and Beatty in 1975. From 1986-1988, Ms Simpson was with the legal services section of the Federal Bureau of Competition Policy.*

(c) *In 1862, the Beaver was commissioned into the British navy as a survey vessel and, for the next seven years, this ship transported the crews charting more than a thousand miles of coastline. But by 1874, the Beaver was past her prime, and the vessel was sold repeatedly to a variety of owners. On July 25, 1888, the Beaver ran aground at the entrance to Vancouver Harbor. She was abandoned to the pounding seas and souvenir hunters.*

Writing and Punctuating Lists

We can simply extend this understanding into lists of any number of items:

5.16

```
Base and precious metals       deposited by reducing
have been leached from sul-    agents in Upper Devonian
phides hosted in basal         sandstones and brecciated
redbed sandstones,___car-      limestones overlying the
ried by oxidizing, saline      Precambrian basement.
brines along major regional     — Canadian Mining Journal,
fault systems and ___re-                    Feb 1995, P11
```

The subject and part of the verb (*Base and precious metals have been*) are elided in the second and third branches of the list. The part that is elided is called the "root" of the list (or the ellipsis).

This sort of list is called a "continuing list" because the branches of the list are an essential part of the sentence — it could *not* stop at the end of the root, i.e. after *have been*. For these lists a colon (**never** a semicolon) *may* be added if you feel the length and/or complexity of the sentence justifies it. We see the optional colon used in:

5.17

```
Fibreprep supplied most of     two Gyroclean high-density,
the process equipment          light and heavy centrifugal
including: two Lamort          cleaners and 0.008-in.
pulpers, three Lamort holed    slotted fine screens.
coarse screens, four            — Pulp and Paper Canada,
Veticel flotation cells,                    May 1995, P10
```

The colon tells readers that a long and/or complex list is coming and it indicates where the root is — often useful information for complex lists. However, the colon is not essential grammatically; *you* must decide whether or not one is helpful to your readers.

Other types of lists, called "introduced" lists, *must* have a colon (**never** a semicolon) to introduce it. An example is:

5.18
```
The following advantages      edges of the magnetic bod-
are reported: 1) it contains  ies so the analytic sig-
high wavenumber informa-      nalis independent of mag-
tion, similar to the verti-   netic latitude.
cal derivative,               — Canadian Mining Journal,
2) the peaks are over the               Feb 1995, P57
```

We know this is an introduced list because

Checklist 5.1: Criteria for Obligatory Colon Before a List

✓ *the branches of the list are __not__ essential for the completion of the introductory statement (which could have been a separate sentence), and*

✓ *we naturally ask "What are they?" at the end of the introduction.*

Both of these criteria always work for introduced lists, so they are easy to recognize. The colon is necessary for introduced lists, whatever its length, i.e. it is a *grammatical* requirement. For continuing lists the colon is only included if you decide it helps your readers to know there is a list coming and that this is where it starts. For short, informal introduced lists, some writers use a comma instead of the colon (see the last sentence of *Example 5.1*).

Note in these examples that the comma before the final branch of the list is optional; include it if you like, or if it helps to clarify the meaning. Note also how numbers, letters and separate lines make the structure of the list clearer or more marked. You can also use bullets or dashes with separate lines for each item of the list. By definition, introduced lists can be expressed as separate sentences:

5.19
```
Jean-Raymond Boulle points   ocean shipping feasible to
out that a mine at Voisey    any part of the world. And
Bay would have several       fourth, and very important-
advantages. First, it        ly, a mine would bring much
appears that it will be a     needed jobs to a province
big project. Second, the     where unemployment hovers
deposit lies close to the    around the 20% mark, Boulle
surface and should be read-  remarked.
ily mineable by open pit     — Canadian Mining Journal,
methods. Third, the discov-            Feb 1995, P9
ery is located only 10 km
from tidewater, making
```

The topic *a mine at Voisey Bay* is re-entered in various ways into the four branches of the "list" of four sentences after the introduction by a full sentence.

If the branches of continuing or introduced lists become very long and/or complex, writers often use semi-colons to mark the boundaries of the list without the overt marking of numbers, letters, etc. This is especially useful when one or more of the branches includes a comma, as it is then often unclear where the boundaries between the branches are. Here is an example of that technique:

5.20

```
The three areas of this
partnership approach
include Operation Stop
Leak, which identifies
hydraulic, chemical, and
air leaks; the MERIT
Program, which offers free
training on how to avoid
problems before they occur;
```
```
and the Consolidate and
Save Program, offering
advice to reduce logistical
and inventory costs by
standardizing on fewer
adhesives and sealants.
    — Machinery and Equipment
          MRO, Sep 1994, P16
```

The semi-colons help us to understand the structure of this list, which includes three branches, each with its own non-restrictive clause indicated by the commas. The numbering of items within the text (e.g. The *three* areas) can also help readers. Although the final *comma* of a list is usually optional, the final *semicolon* of a complex list is required. You *must* include the final *; and*.

Do *not* use semicolons in quite short and simple lists unless you want them to be very marked, for example if you are introducing topics to come in a section of your report. There is of course less need for semicolons if you are using separate lines, numbers, letters, bullets, etc. as these tell readers where the branches of the list are. Also do not use a colon in front of a continuing list unless it really helps readers.

Exercise 5.4: Punctuating Lists

For each of the following lists: (a) decide whether it is a continuing list (C) or an introduced list (I), (b) find the root, and (c) make any necessary changes to the punctuation. Note how you can use different systems of punctuation to give different effects for different purposes in a document.

(a) *There are three types of heat transfer; conduction, convection, and radiation.*

(b) *The watchwords on the benefit front are on the surface paradoxical "control" and "flexibility."*

(c) *It is safe to say that extensive switched image and video systems will become widely available through fiber optic systems personal i.e. independent of location communications through cellular radio systems will become ubiquitous electronic procurement payment and information systems provided on demand will be commonplace and long distance transmission will become cheaper.*

(d) So far the courts have defined three categories change in remuneration geographical change and demotion.

(e) Outstanding opportunities exist for engineers to work in a multi-disciplinary environment and apply their analytical skills in the following six areas fuel design and analysis licencing probabilistic risk assessment physics safety analysis and thermohydraulics.

Correcting Faulty Parallel Structures

A problem for clausal ellipsis, lists, and other structures is what is called "faulty parallel structure." This means that the branches of the sentence are not parallel, and that one or more of the branches does not make sense. In simple clausal ellipsis, it is very difficult to make this mistake, as your options only affect emphasis and conciseness. However, when you want to use combinations such as *either . . . or, not only . . . but also,* and *both . . . and* you have to be more careful. If, for example, you wrote:

> "In noise control, we are concerned with both a dynamic energy source and with the path the energy takes."

the parallel structure would be faulty. We can see this by drawing the parallel structures:

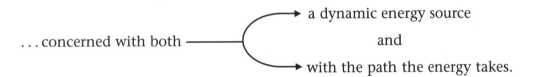

Figure 5.4: Faulty Parallel Structure Diagram

Obviously the second branch does not make sense. To correct it, we could (a) remove the second *with,* or (b) interchange the positions of *both* and the first *with.* Draw the diagrams to verify this. The more you put into the root, the more concise and less marked your sentence becomes.

For lists, we have to ensure that *all* branches are parallel. Thus in

> "The coating should be thin and light in weight, should have some self-healing characteristics, and not adversely affect the substrate."

the three branches are not parallel. We could take the root as being after the first *should* and delete the second *should,* although the two positives and one negative are not ideally parallel. Instead, we might add a third *should* before *not* — or we might opt to use a separate sentence: "It should also not affect the substrate."

Exercise 5.5: Correcting Faulty Parallel Structures

Suggest one or more ways of correcting the following faulty parallel structures. If you have a problem, draw the structural diagram and work it out.

(a) *Tidal power is of interest not only to Canada and the USA, but it is of interest to Russia too.*

(b) *For this model, there is no hot water hook up, no cost for heating water, and simpler to operate.*

(c) *Omissions may be either due to the response to the questionnaire or to insufficient knowledge.*

(d) *Telephone switching technology will enable office switchboards to handle telephone information, computer information and even cope with video information.*

(e) *Professional engineers would be wise to remember the following: they cannot afford to compromise design standards to satisfy clients, they must look beyond the client to the end user of all they design, and reasonable judgment in the exercise of their duties must be exercised.*

Research Tasks

1. Find examples of relative clauses, clausal ellipsis and lists in technical writing, and note their structure and punctuation. Bring interesting examples to class for discussion.

2. Write a more detailed analysis of clausal ellipsis and lists in technical writing using some of the examples you have found.

3. Present your material orally, using selected examples to illustrate your findings.

Writing Tasks

1. Find out about various instruments, tools, machines, equipment, etc. in your area of interest. See *Chapter 3* and the end of this chapter for some suggestions. Write a brief description of one or more of these for students in your year who are not in your own speciality.

2. Note how, in your own writing, you use the re-entry devices discussed in this chapter so far.

Descriptive Clauses

-ing Clauses

You may have noticed that *Example 5.20* contained two non-restrictive relative clauses in the first two branches of the list. However, rather than use the same structures again for the third branch, the writer chose to write *, offering* instead of *, which offers*. The clause *offering . . . sealants* is called an *-ing* clause because it is dominated by the -ing form of the verb. As it is non-restrictive, the comma is used.

Writers use -ing clauses as an alternative to relative clauses to provide variety in their writing — and to remove the many *which*'s that inexperienced writers often use. For example, the sentence

> "The metacarpal heads, which fit into shallow cavities at the base of the proximal phalanges, are approximately spherical in shape."

can be converted into

> "The metacarpal heads, fitting into shallow cavities at the bases of the proximal phalanges, are approximately spherical in shape."

using an -ing clause instead.

As this is a non-restrictive clause that tells us more about the subject of the sentence, we can move the -ing clause to the front of the sentence if we like — something we cannot do with relative clauses. Here is such an example:

```
5.21   Weighing just 2-1/2 lb,      tery packs.
       these hand-held instruments    — Machinery and Equipment
       have no heavy external bat-          MRO, Sep 1994, P7
```

As restrictive clauses can *not* be used in this first position, we can use this as another test of whether a clause is restrictive or not. It is usual to add the comma after such non-restrictive clauses that start the sentence. Like relative clauses, -ing clauses contain less important information.

Exercise 5.6: Creating -ing Clauses and Changing Position

Rewrite each of the following using -ing clauses. See whether you can then change their positions in the sentences.

> (a) *The high normal contact forces, which average 120 grams, are provided by the pre-loaded leaf-type stainless-steel contacts.*
>
> (b) *The transmitters are arranged in chains, and each chain contains three or more transmitters placed 1000 km apart.*

(c) *The SCR power controllers feature zero-crossover firing of the SCR's to eliminate generation of RF interference. They are designed for use with transformerless loads and where line spikes in the power plant system have to be maintained.*

(d) *The miniature transmitter is swallowed by the patient before surgery. The transmitter contains a sensitive transducer.*

(e) *The electrodes consist of strips of aluminum foil attached to a strip of adhesive tape. These electrodes are connected to a signal generator and detector circuit.*

-ed Clauses

We can also convert relative clauses into clauses dominated by the "-ed" form of the verb:

> **5.22** This report, released to the public on May 27, recommended a further reduction to just 20 Bq/L in five years time.
> — *Nuclear Canada*, Jul/Aug 1994, P5

The relative clause counterpart is, "which was released . . . ." As the tense (*was*) is not needed, we can use an -ed clause instead, which is briefer and adds variety. We have the added advantage of being able to move the -ed clause to the start of the sentence if we like. Here is an example:

> **5.23** Founded in 1974 by three engineers, Geophysics GPR International Inc. now has about 50 employees . . .
> — *Canadian Consulting Engineer*, Jan/Feb 1995, P18

Although -ed forms of the verb are also known as "past participles," the term "-ed" is used here because -ed clauses are tenseless (time is not included in the verb form). Another reason is that -ed forms are used for the present ("is presented") and future tenses ("will be analyzed") as well as the past. Unfortunately the -ed forms of irregular verbs do not end in -ed! Examples are *given, found, made, known, shown,* and *said.* We still call clauses dominated by these forms -ed clauses.

Exercise 5.7: Creating -ed Clauses and Changing Position

Convert the following relative clauses into -ed clauses, and see if you can change their positions. Watch out for irregular forms.

(a) *Miniature radio transmitters are swallowed by patients like pills. They are helping doctors understand an illness that costs industry* *more than $100 million per year.*

(b) Jose Luis Masera was arrested on October 1994. Last month he was transferred to a military hospital with head injuries.

(c) The four-conductor cable is known as "spiral four." It is polythene insulated, is well balanced electrically, and weighs less and is more rugged than the rubber-insulated counterpart.

(d) This star is located in the vicinity of Cygnus, and is as bright at 2 microns as Vega.

(e) The part was cut to size. It was then mounted on the DC-9 nacelle.

Verbless Clauses

A third type of clause you can create instead of using relative clauses is not dominated by any verb form at all — and is thus called a "verbless clause." These are often dominated by an adjective or a preposition, but not always. Here is an example where the verbless clause is used at the start of the sentence:

5.24	An accurate and user-friendly instrument, the Elcotrol Navovip portable digital power analyzer is	used for the control of electrical systems. — *Machinery and Equipment MRO*, Sep 1994, P7

The verbless clause is followed by the usual comma to indicate where it ends and the subject of the sentence begins.

For *Example 5.24*, we could have used a relative clause instead:

"The Elcotrol Navovip portable digital power analyzer, *which* is an accurate and user friendly instrument, is used for the control of electrical systems."

However, the verbless clause in initial position is more concise, and is arguably better style.

A special type of verbless clause, called an "appositive," names or identifies the topic, and is identical with the topic. For example, in "The capital of British Columbia, Victoria, is . . . ," Victoria is the appositive. We can always place the topic and appositive in the other order if we like: "Victoria, the capital of British Columbia, is . . . ."

Exercise 5.8: Creating Verbless Clauses (Including Appositions)

Use verbless clauses to improve the following.

(a) The Canadian Chamber of Commerce is a voluntary national federation of community and business leaders. It is dedicated to good citizenship, good government, and a strong and vital economy.

(b) *The mixture, which is now a bubbly sort of liquid, is heated through a heat exchanger.*

(c) *The group was chaired by David S. Scott, who at present is a Professor of Mechanical Engineering at the University of Toronto.*

(d) *The bacteria is a product of Flow Laboratories, Inc. of Inglewood, which is located in California. The bacteria is purchased as a dry powder of bacterial spores. (Use two verbless clauses!)*

(e) *Valcanus II is an 837 000 gallon capacity ocean incineration vessel. It is capable of thermally destroying highly toxic wastes anywhere in the world. It was launched in November in Emden, which is in East Germany. (Use three verbless clauses!!)*

The Three Positions

Although relative clauses can only be at the end of the sentence or between the subject and the main verb, -ed, -ing and verbless clauses can also appear at the start of the sentence. Here is an example that provides a review of the three positions:

5.25

A two-year project to design and develop a computer system to analyze statistics of the mineral industry has resulted in the release of the most comprehensive report ever produced by the Ministry of Natural Resources.

Manag*ed* by the Ministry's mineral statistics section, the computer system, call*ed* the Video Census, has just produced its first publication, entitl*ed* the 1981 Ontario Mineral Score.

— *Engineering Dimensions*

The subject of the second sentence (*the computer system*) re-enters the previous topic (*a computer system . . . industry*) by partial repetition. The three -ed clauses, in the three positions in the sentence, provide information about the system and about the first publication:

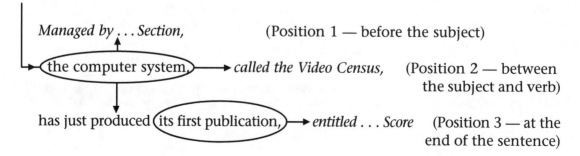

Managed by . . . Section,   (Position 1 — before the subject)

the computer system,   → *called the Video Census,*   (Position 2 — between the subject and verb)

has just produced its first publication,   → *entitled . . . Score*   (Position 3 — at the end of the sentence)

Figure 5.5: The Three Positions for Descriptive Clauses

Restrictive and Non-Restrictive Clauses

Relative clauses, -ing clauses, -ed clauses and verbless clauses can all be restrictive or non-restrictive. So can "to-infinitive" clauses and prepositional groups. Restrictive clauses restrict, modify or limit the meaning of the topic they follow, and cannot be in first position in the sentence. They must *not* be separated by commas from the topic they restrict.

Checklist 5.2: Types of Restrictive and Non-Restrictive Clauses

An example of a restrictive clause is given first, followed by an example of a non-restrictive clause.

✓ *Relative Clauses*
   A skin test which *tells in less than an hour whether or not a woman is pregnant has been announced.*

   Most of the problems facing Wells and his liberals, who *hold 33 of the legislature's 52 seats, are beyond their control.*

✓ *-ed Clauses*
   A survey conducted *by the Gallup Poll last summer indicated that one in four Americans believe in ghosts.*

   This product, manufactured *by Dupont of Kingston, has proved exceptionally hard-wearing.*

✓ *-ing Clauses*
   A satellite passing *through the belt is subject to bursts of gamma rays.*

   These meteorites, traveling *at a speed of 10 kilometers a second relative to earth, could cause enormous damage on impact.*

✓ *Verbless Clauses*
   All rents due *in accordance with the rental agreement must be paid on or before the due date.*

   These balcony planters, available *in three lengths and two colours, incorporate a special drainage system.*

✓ *To-infinitive Clauses*
   A proposal to *identify sexual harassment as grounds for refusing a license has been introduced in the legislature.*

   Spanish Conversation I, to *cover basic principles over nine hours of instruction and practice, will commence on February 11.*

> ✓ *Prepositional Groups*
> *The mirror* on *the wall* in *the den needs to be replaced.*
>
> *The Maple Leafs,* in *the Stanley Cup finals for the first time in sixteen years, have high hopes of winning the cup this year.*

Research Tasks

1. Find all sorts of non-restrictive descriptive clauses in the three positions defined above from various forms of technical writing. Note how different writers use these techniques.
2. Prepare an analysis of the use of non-restrictive descriptive clauses based on some of the examples you have found.

3. Present your work orally, using a few key examples as overheads.

Connecting by Association

The Use of Associations

Imagine you had just written:

5.26
```
This hand-held instrument        battery-powered unit.
combines a dual channel 50         — Machinery and Equipment
MHz digital storage oscil-              MRO, Sep 1994, P7
loscope and a 3 2/3 true-
rms multimeter in a rugged,
```

and now wanted to say that it had certain features, which you would then list. One possibility is to write:

"The instrument has certain features, which include ...,"

but an experienced writer would instead write:

5.27
```
Features include one-button      ing functions.
measure menu, continuous            — 5.26 continued
automatic setups and graph-
```

There are four ways of expressing information that is associated with a topic: rather than being direct about it:

Checklist 5.3: Ways of Expressing Associated Information

✓ *separate clause:* "*The instrument has certain features, which include . . .*"

✓ *post-triggered association:* "*Features of the instrument include . . .*"

✓ *pre-triggered association:* "*The instrument's [or Its] features include . . .*"

✓ *untriggered association:* "*Features include . . .*"

The topic of description (*the instrument*) is called the "trigger," and the new subtopic is *features*. We can place the reference to the trigger after the new subtopic (post-triggered), or before the new subtopic (pre-triggered) — or not mention the trigger at all (untriggered). As untriggered associations are more concise, we try to use them whenever we can:

5.28 C.M.D. spent a lot of time finding out and satisfying what the partners wanted in a recycled pump. . . . Prior to startup, *the 35 produc-tion employees* received extensive training to ensure any problems that arose could be solved quickly.
— *Pulp and Paper Canada*, May 1995, P12

As there is no need to say that the production employees are at C.M.D., the untriggered version is used here.

When some reference to the main topic is felt necessary, pre-triggering is a compromise between the untriggered and post-triggered versions:

5.29 PEO members have an ethical duty to preserve their employer's intellectual property that goes beyond what's expected of other employees. *The associa-tion's Code of Ethics* requires professional engi-neers to:
— act as faithful agents or trustees
— *Engineering Dimensions*, Nov/Dec, 1994, P19

Here *The Code of Ethics* would not have provided the necessary continuity, so a pre-triggered association is used with the generic noun *association*.

When the main topic needs to be clarified, post-triggering may be necessary. This occurs when the topic is a long way back in the text, or if there are two possible topics, or if the topic is not very clear:

5.30 The first to study this were Miller & Musgrave (1956) for the case of cubic Nickel. *The excellent diagrams and comprehensive nature of their paper* make it extremely useful.
— G. Rumpker, Department of Geological Sciences, 1995, P 760

Triggering of *their paper* is needed here to achieve clarity.

Exercise 5.9: Using Associations

For the following examples, convert the underlined sentence into an association as subject of a sentence , e.g. *"Tests have been made on the instrument's vibration resistance. These are detailed in Appendix C."* becomes "Vibration resistance tests are detailed in Appendix C."

(a) *A new combination tool resulted from this activity. It has several advantages over previous wire-wrapping tools in that it cuts the wire, skins it, and wraps the connection.*

(b) *There is a need for such resolution. This is greatest when signals occur only once, for then large as well as small signals must be captured in a single occurrence.*

(c) *This weakness has a cause. This is the presence of flaws or cracks in the solid, especially at the surface.*

(d) *The compressed asbestos-free gasketing material operates at up to 400 degrees celcius. It has a wide range of applications. These include flange connection and cross-over piping connection.*

(e) *This design is a high-accuracy instrument capable of measuring any electrical value critical to analyzing demand and consumption on both balanced and unbalanced systems. It has wide measuring capabilities. These include RMS voltage and current, W, VA, Wh, power factor and frequency.*

Perspective Connection

Associations provide connection between one noun phrase and another. Perspective connection provides connection between a noun phrase and a whole clause or sentence. Here is an example:

5.31 Preliminary metallurgical testwork has been done at Lakefield Research and is encouraging. . . . Tests on cobalt recovery were also underway.
— *Canadian Mining Journal*, Feb 1995, P9

The final sentence is an untriggered perspective meaning that tests on cobalt recovery are underway *at Lakefield Research*.

For example, in a geologic report, the sentence "Coal seams are common." does not mean that coal seams are common (!); and the sentence "Amber is abundant." does not mean that amber is abundant (!!). These sentences mean, in their context, that coal seams are common and amber is abundant *in the specific location being studied*. That is, they take on a specific meaning (or "perspective") by being part of a larger text.

The sentence "Coal seams are common." is an untriggered perspective connection, and "Coal seams are common in this location." is a triggered perspective connection. We can recognize statements like "Batteries are included" and "There are three output sockets." as being untriggered perspectives.

This form of connection forms the central core of technical abstracts, in which the meaning of *in this paper* is inherent in almost every sentence. (See *Page 297*.)

Exercise 5.10: Using Perspective Connections

For each of the following, identify the perspective connection and convert it to an untriggered form.

(a) *The V-ring seal is made in Nitrile or Viton. A 12-page selection guide is available for this product.*

(b) *The OL-195 catalog contains photographs, technical specifications and dimensioned drawings for the stainless stell air cylinders. Additional options, such as extra rod extensions and heavy springs, are also described in the catalog describing the product.*

(c) *This paper demonstrates three regimes of air-core vortex formation that exist for the free draining of liquids with angular momentum. The influence of Froude number on air-core vortex formation is also discussed in this paper.*

Research Tasks

1. Find examples of associations (post-, pre- and untriggered) and perspective connections (triggered and untriggered). Note how writers use these techniques in technical writing.

2. Write an analysis of the use of associations in a chosen branch of technical writing using some of the examples you have found.

3. Present your findings orally using some of your examples as the basis for your conclusions.

Checklist 5.4: Methods of Re-entering the Topic

✓ *repetition - full*
    - partial

✓ *generic nouns*

✓ *synonyms*

✓ *naming and acronyms*

✓ *substitution*

✓ *relative clauses*

✓ *clausal ellipsis*

✓ *lists*

✓ *descriptive clauses — -ing clauses*
    -ed clauses
    verbless clauses (and apposition)

✓ *associations*

✓ *perspectives*

Writing Task: Writing from Notes

Based on all, but only, the information given in the following notes, write full-sentence versions using a variety of re-entry techniques. The notes are in a reasonable order for your final written version, but make minor changes if you really need to. For each exercise the title given is the main topic, but you might decide to provide a more informative title for your writing.

1. **MVG Soil Sampling Tube**
   tube sampler has 30 cm tube — tube will take a 25 cm core of soil — can be used for sampling of soils for agricultural purposes — also for compaction sampling — can also be used for soil survey work — all parts made of steel — steel heat treated for longer wear — all parts plated with cadmium — comes complete with tube type carrying case.

2. **CanWest Global Communications Corporation**
   provides television services in Ontario — strengthened its share in its broadcasting unit — a Winnipeg-based company — now entered into agreement with Peli Ventures Inc. — a Manitoba corporation — Global would acquire 41 per cent of shares of Can West Broadcasting Ltd. — shares currently owned by Peli Ventures — purchase would raise Global interest in Broadcasting to 70.7 per cent — previously 66.6 per cent — purchase price $2.3 million — paid

through issue of 134,321 voting shares to Peli — transaction subject to regulatory approval.

3. **Housing Conference for Vancouver**

Canada is global leader in energy efficiency — also in environmentally responsible housing — Canada will host conference on the latter topic — will be world's largest — planned for Vancouver — will be next month — called Innovative Housing — central gathering of experts — will come from around the world — will exchange information — also will see new developments in environmental housing — subject of vital importance — housing affects environment for its whole life cycle — starts with construction — housing must impact in a minimal way — conference will offer plenary sessions — also tours and demonstration houses — all houses against the Vancouver backdrop — includes ocean, forest and mountain scenery.

4. **New Tear Tester**

made by Adamel Ltd. — accurately determines tear resistance of paper and light cardboard — also for textiles and other sheet materials — operates on a constant tear length — provides direct readout of force measurement — appears on a liquid crystal display — display is highly visible — tester has a main feature — this is a pendulum — pendulum tests samples — pendulum also supplies data absorbed by tear — pendulum designed to receive certain masses — masses are 400, 800, 1,600, 3,200 and 6,400 centi-Newton — abbreviated as CN — allow five force scales to be measured — tester has a control panel — panel displays selected scale — also shows number of sheets used for test — tester also has an interface board — can be connected to tester — gives even greater efficiency.

5. **Labrador Tea**

also known as Hudson's Bay tea, swamp tea and bog tea — official name *Ledum palustre L.* — has thin stems — straggly evergreen shrub — grows 0.5 to 2.0 m high — has leaves — leaves are crowded near ends of twigs — leaves short—stemmed and elliptical — have rounded to pointed tips — upper surface leathery in appearance — underside densely woolly — young leaves point upward — light green — have white fuzz underneath — mature leaves turn down — become dark brown or reddish-brown — fuzz underneath deep-rust color — flowers white and attractive — grow in dense round-topped clusters — ripen into brown oval capsules — entire plant has sweet aroma — also spicy — very noticeable when walking through patch of bushes — actually two species — *palustre L.* described here — *groenlandicum L.* grows taller — has broader leaves — *palustre L.* and *groenlandicum L.* suitable for making tea.

Open-ended Writing Tasks

This section provides lists of things, people, places and events you could write about; the topics are not always specific, so you may have to choose to write about a special type or model. The lists are by no means exhaustive, and you are encouraged to think up your own topic to write about. You will probably find your writing task more interesting if you select a specific rather than a general topic, as then you can make your work original by providing information you are aware of or you discover during your research. For any of these writing tasks, make sure you clearly define your audience before you start.

Things to Write About

In writing your accounts of things, you may need to describe and explain component parts of your topic and how they work together to achieve the device's design function (what it is designed to do). It is also often useful to explain how the thing works and what you have to do to make it work. You may need to obtain manufacturers' details (from brochures) for some of the complex topics. Also many topics have several variations, which you might want to discuss. Note that a diagram could be extremely useful for many of these topics.

computer	venetian blind	radio
printer	can opener	CD player
stapler	grapefruit knife	loudspeaker
pen	cooking thermometer	earphones
pencil/eraser	rotary hand whisk	CD ROM player
binder	bottle cork remover	television
three-hole punch	potato masher	cassette player
hair curler	brace and bit	electric drill
hair dryer	workstand	jack hammer
toaster	screwdriver set	jig saw
electric iron	adjustable pipe wrench	rotary saw
electric toothbrush	chisel	sander
blender	vice grips	lathe
incandescent light bulb	rotary tape	shop vac
carrots	wheat	whales
cauliflowers	herbs	beavers
garlic	maple trees	caribou
melons	pines	salmon
lettuce	mosses	bears
tomatoes	fungi	Canada geese
beans	kelp	mosquitoes
cars	skis	chess set
aircraft	squash rackets	bridge counter
yachts	tennis nets	playing cards
helicopters	hockey pucks	Trivial Pursuit
snowploughs	baseballs	Monopoly
submarines	basketballs	bingo
snowmobiles	footballs	dart set

CHAPTER FIVE: THE THREAD OF CONTINUITY (DESCRIPTION)   89

People to Write About

When you are writing about people, explain who they are, what they do and what their importance is. Their age, sex, occupation, achievements, interests, and hopes might also be relevant information to include. When you are writing about groups, their common heritage, culture, activities, beliefs, language and attitudes could be important items of information to include in your discussion. See *Appendix B* for advice on how to describe people.

an engineer	a scientist	a teacher
your best friend	the Prime Minister	your doctor
sister or brother	the Governor General	sports person
parents	your premier	sports coach
grandparents	your Lieutenant General	a vocalist
teacher/instructor	your mayor or reeve	a priest
your pet	your councillor	a writer

Inuits	Canadians	Jews
Canada's first nations	Americans	Christians
Aztecs	Mexicans	Muslims
Laplanders	Europeans	Sikhs
Maoris	Chinese	Zoroastrians
Aborigines	Japanese	Hindus
Boers	Australians	Agnostics
Zulus	Russians	Mormons

You can find other people or groups of people to write about by reading your local or regional newspapers.

Places to Write About

When you are writing about places, explain where they are and discuss important or unique features, landmarks or cities.

Canada	Prince Edward Island	Toronto
The Prairies	Vancouver Island	Montreal
The Maritimes	Lake Winnipeg	Vancouver
The Yukon	Great Slave Lake	Calgary
The North-West Territories	The Laurentians	Halifax
The Great Lakes	The Bay of Fundy	Winnipeg
The Rocky Mountains	Labrador	Saskatoon

your college	North America	the Arctic
your town/city	Central America	the Caribbean
your province	Europe	the Antarctic
your church	Asia	the Pacific
your house	Australasia	the Mediterranean
your shopping center	Africa	the Balkans
your sports center	South America	the Middle East

Events to Write About

When you are writing about events, explain what happened, who was involved, and when and how it happened. Also try to explain why things happened the way they did or comment on the importance of the event.

a party	a hike	a mud slide
a dance	a ski trip	a flood
a picnic	a bus tour	a war or rebellion
a trip	a snowmobile ride	a sports event
a vacation	an aircraft flight	a sale
a special occasion	a boat trip	a fire
a presentation	a skating event	an earthquake

You can find out about specific technical events by reading technical magazines and journals.

Review Questions

1. *What is the difference between full and partial repetition? When are they used?*

2. *What is the difference between re-entry by generic noun and partial repetition?*

3. *When should we, and when should we not, define acronyms? When should we make a list of acronyms, and where should we place it?*

4. *What is the difference between* This *and* It*?*

5. *What is the connection between the use of* This *and relative clauses?*

6. *What is clausal ellipsis? What is the connection between clausal ellipsis and lists?*

7. *What is the difference between continuing and introduced lists? How are they punctuated differently?*

8. *Under what circumstances could we use a semicolon to introduce a list?*

9. *When and how would we use semicolons in a list?*

10. *How else can we separate the branches of a list?*

11. *What is the connection between relative clauses and -ing clauses?*

What is the difference between these as far as position in the sentence is concerned?

12. *What is the connection between relative clauses and -ed clauses? What is their positional difference?*

13. *How do irregular verbs complicate -ed clauses?*

14. *What are verbless clauses, and what is their connection with relative clauses?*

15. *What is apposition?*

16. *What are restrictive and non-restrictive clauses? How are they different?*

17. *What are associations and why are they used?*

18. *What are the three forms of associations?*

19. *What are perspectives and why are they used?*

20. *In what form of writing are perspectives most noticeable?*

21. *What are the two forms of perspectives?*

Chapter 6:
Problem-Solution Structures

As engineering is a problem-solution activity, many technical documents follow a problem-solution structure. This chapter explains the basic four-part structure typical of many problem-solution texts and discusses many important variations. The patterns of communication discussed here are shown to apply equally well to very short texts (of two or three words) and also to extremely large documents.

The Problem Solving Philosophy
Solving Problems in Engineering
Solving Problems in Science
The Technical Work and Related
    Documents

Complete Structures
Description and Problem-Solution
    Texts
The Basic Four-Part Structure
Proposals and Design Reports
Outlines for Problem-Solution
    Documents
Outlining Exercise: An Example

Curtailed and Shorter Texts
Excluding Informational Elements
Problem-Solution-Evaluation Texts
Basic Problem-Solution Texts
Purpose-Means Texts
Purpose-Means-Evaluation
    Structures

Condensed Structures
Very Short Texts
Problem-Solution Summaries
Problem-Solution Titles

**Complex Problem-Solution
Structures**

The Problem-Solving Philosophy

Solving Problems in Engineering

Engineering is often defined as the application of scientific principles for the betterment of humankind, and many engineering schools prefer the title "Applied Science" to that of "Engineering" to stress their objective. Engineering involves solving problems in a wide sense, including overcoming difficulties, meeting established needs, and improving existing techniques and designs. More importantly, perhaps, engineers go about their task of problem-solving in a recognized sequence, and undertake recognized tasks in the process. The writing that describes their work follows this sequence and includes the information about the tasks performed during the process.

A "design methodology" has been established that seeks to explain the complex series of steps of any problem-solving procedure. This procedure starts with the recognition of an area of concern and proceeds until satisfactory resolution of a problem or need is achieved. Numerous books deal with this subject from a design perspective, and the principles described there are fully consistent with this present explanation of the related written work.

Because of the complex nature of the series of steps in engineering design and problem solving, analysts use different numbers of steps to describe the work. They also often use different labels to describe these steps. The overall principle, however, is common to all:

Checklist 6.1: The Four-Part Problem-Solution Structure

✓ *understanding the situation*　　　　　　　　**"SITUATION"**

✓ *recognizing and defining the problem*　　　　**"PROBLEM"**

✓ *creating, analyzing and refining a solution*　　**"SOLUTION"**

✓ *evaluating and testing the solution*　　　　　**"EVALUATION"**

We will be using this as our initial model for texts that describe problem-solution activities. It is, of course, rather a crude model, but it is a useful starting point in understanding these texts.

Solving Problems in Science

The problem-solving nature of science is a little different although just as apparent. The scientist's aim is to discover principles that describe how and why things happen in nature the way they do, and then to seek to explain phenomena in terms of these established principles. To do this scientists investigate natural "situations" and find answers to things they previously did not know or understand.

Thus, in science, the "situation" is an area of nature selected for study, and the "problem" is something we do not fully understand — a "need-to-know" problem, if you like. The "solution" is an explanation for the observed occurrences consistent with an overall framework of understanding (or "theory"). The "evaluation" is an assessment of how well the explanation actually describes and explains the observations. Thus the overall four-part structure of "Situation-Problem-Situation-Evaluation" is also an adequate initial model for describing many scientific documents.

The Technical Work and Related Documents

Many engineering and scientific documents follow the problem-solution structure simply because this describes what the workers did (both their analysis and their actions) throughout a problem-solving procedure. That is, a report of the thought-action process of a team of engineers during a problem-solution procedure must itself follow a problem-solution structure and order. Also a proposal must include the analysis of the situation, the problem being addressed, the proposed solution, and its evaluation.

Such a problem-solution thought-action process can be found as *Exercise 9.1* in this book. That letter is written in a verbose manner to suit the needs of that exercise. However, you should still be able to see that it follows the thoughts of the writer and the things the writer did in understanding and solving a problem, and in designing and using the solution. The letter is a representation of the thoughts and actions of the writer, and because the thought-action pattern follows the problem-solution pattern, the writing that describes it must also follow that pattern.

We need to start with the premise that anything that has ever been designed or devised to solve a problem or meet a need is a "solution" to that problem or need. If you look around you right now (unless you are on remote island!), you are almost bound to find dozens or even scores of items that have been designed to meet needs in society. These are all "solutions" to those needs. When we write about them, we can either describe them (see *Chapter 5*), or we can place the description as the "solution" component of a problem-solution text.

Complete Structures

Description and Problem-Solution Texts

When a type of product is well established, there is no need to explain the problem it is designed to solve; all we have to do is describe its features. Thus, for example, description is probably appropriate for a new electrostatic voltmeter, a new mouse trap, a new computer disk, a new car, etc. Our task is to describe the main elements of the new product, perhaps with some comparison between it and earlier types or models.

Example 6.1 explains how a bulletin describes a new multi-amp circuit breaker. As the need is not new (and does not therefore have to be justified), the text describes the bulletin and the circuit breaker. The "problems" it solves are included as its applications — not as overtly signaled problems.

6.1 Bulletin MS-2 describes the MULTI-AMP Model MS-2 Circuit Breaker and Motor Overload Relay Test Set used to verify proper motor overload protection and eliminate nuisance tripping.
Model MS-2 incorporates a variable high-current output and appropriate control circuitry and instrumentation to test thermal, magnetic or solid-state motor overload relays, molded-case circuit breakers and ground-fault trip devices.
— *Machinery and Equipment MRO*, Apr 1994, P42

When, however, you have designed or created a solution to a *new* problem — and that, after all, is the more challenging and rewarding task — then you will need to introduce, explain and justify the problem clearly before discussing your solution. You will then be using the problem-solution structure:

6.2 Oily compressed air condensate can be expensive to dispose of. Literature from Van Air Systems describes how the Envirosaver oil-water separator isolates the oil, thus reducing disposal costs. The brochure covers features of the separator, plus operation, applications, standard equipment and accessories, and includes a sizing chart.
Machinery and Equipment MRO, Apr 1995, P8

In this example, the problem is first introduced as the *expensive* disposal of oily condensate. Only then is the literature describing the new produce introduced. The final clause of the first sentence (*thus reducing disposal costs*) explains how the new product is a partial solution to the established problem. The final sentence provides further descriptive information about the literature and the product it describes.

Note that description is still an important element of the problem-solution structure. As the "solution" is a product designed to meet specific needs, you will need to describe it as the "solution" element of the overall structure.

The Basic Four-Part Structure

Although there are many variations of the overall problem-solution structure, it is useful to start with the four-part structure "situation-problem-solution-evaluation" discussed earlier. Even with minimal information included in each of the four parts, this structure provides a satisfyingly complete account, or "story" of events, as we see in:

> **6.3** **Time:** 0625 hours. **Type of Target:** Enemy Dispatch Rider. **Number of Rounds Fired:** Five. **Result:** Made Dispatch Rider Accelerate.
>
> — Anonymous Report from *Artillery Post*, Normandy, France, 1944

We are provided with some background information ("situation"), the "problem" with the implicit objective of killing the dispatch rider, the attempted solution, and evaluation of the attempt (its failure to achieve the objective). Although, of course, much more could be added to each of these four categories of information, this skeleton document does provide us with an informationally complete account of the important events.

As texts become larger, each of the four elements will contain more information, especially the description of the solution. Here is a slightly larger text.

6.4 Maximizing Bearing Life

> Today's bearings are intrinsically reliable machinery components. *Nevertheless* some bearings *fail* before their design service life. Of these failures, 16% have been attributed to *in*correct installation and a further 36% to *in*adequate lubrication. In other words, the *problem* is human *error*. Bearing mounting and dismounting using equipment *un*fit for the purpose often results in premature bearing *failure*. *To overcome this* and ensure trouble-free operation, SKF has developed a range of products designed to ease the tasks of mounting and maintenance, minimize the risk of failure, and so reduce downtime.
> Among these tools are . . .
> — *Machinery and Equipment MRO, Apr 1995, P6*

The situation is given in the first sentence, with the problem being introduced and explained in the remainder of the paragraph and the next sentence. Details of the solution and information on which readers can evaluate it are provided in the remainder of the text.

It is important to note the language signals the writer used to help readers to recognize the structure of the text. *Nevertheless* (and *However, But, In spite of this*, etc.) mediates between two types of information (situation-problem, good and bad evaluation, try-failure, etc.); here *Nevertheless* mediates between the situation and the problem, i.e. it tells readers that the situation is finished and the problem is about to start.

There are several signals of problem in *Example 6.4:* the prefixes *in* (2) and *un*, and the words *fail, failure, error* and of course *problem*. The solution is introduced by *To overcome this*, where *this* re-enters the problem just discussed. Clear signaling of the parts of the structure and the transitions between them is an important element in the clear expression of all forms of technical communication.

Proposals and Design Reports

You should have no difficulty in extrapolating the principles explained here to understand the structure of very large documents based on the four-part structure. One difference is that the four parts, especially solution and evaluation, are likely to be more clearly distinguishable in large documents because the four parts will each be much larger. In addition, headings are more likely to be used, and these may also signal transitions between the major types of information.

Proposals are essentially problem-solution texts. In a "solicited" proposal, a company asks another company to propose a solution to a problem they have. The proposal will consist of general background or introductory material as the "situation," an analysis of the problem and needs as the "problem," the proposed design or plan as the "solution," and an assessment of its value or merits as the "evaluation."

For "unsolicited" proposals, the problem has not been presented, and so the writer has to introduce a problem or need and also convince the reader that the problem does indeed need to be solved. However, the overall structure of the text is the same. As many advertisements are a form of unsolicited proposal, they illustrate the structure of these documents in microcosm:

6.5

```
As someone who has a small
business to run, you never
know what you'll have to do
next.
At a moment's notice, you
may need to be a designer,
accountant, marketing man-
ager, engineer, or adminis-
trator.
That's why you'll want to
look at a helpful tool that
can keep up with you every
step of the way.
It's the Apple Macintosh
computer. The computer that
lets you choose from more
then 3,500 different soft-
ware programs, including
programs that enable you to
create sophisticated 2-D
and 3-D designs, solve com-
plex mathematical equa-
tions, access comprehensive
databases, keep things on
schedule, on budget, and
run a business.
In fact, there's almost no
business task that the
Macintosh computer won't
make quicker, simpler, and
more efficient.
  — Engineering Dimensions,
        Mar/Apr 1992, P32
```

The copywriter did not have a specific problem or need to solve here, and so had to express the problem in quite general terms. The computer is then presented as the solution to the readers' needs, and is evaluated as being an extremely useful tool for owners of small businesses.

Similarly reports describing new designs follow the four-part problem-solution structure. The situation, or introduction, provides details of the related work and designs and the overall situation within which the problem is perceived. The problem includes not just what the problem is, but also the causes, importance and extent of the problems together with details of partial solutions, failures and problems with earlier solutions. The solution describes your design in sufficient detail for your readers, and the evaluation provides an assessment of how well it overcomes the problem, together with other features worthy of note.

Outlines for Problem-Solution Documents

We are now able to recognize types of information that typically occur in the four major sections of problem-solution texts:

Checklist 6.2: Typical Information for Problem-Solution Texts

✓ **Situation**
- *background information*
- *earlier related work*
- *earlier partial solutions or failures*
- *definition of an area of interest*

✓ **Problem**
- *the actual problem or need*
- *the cause(s) of the problem*
- *the extent or seriousness of the problem*
- *related problems and their evaluation*

✓ **Solution**
- *description of the solution*
- *how it works*

✓ **Evaluation**
- *how well it overcomes the problem (often the result)*
- *its other features and advantages*
- *its limitations and defects*
- *its other potential applications*
- *recommended further development*

Outlining Exercise: An Example

Based on this grouping of information, we can now plan the possible contents and sequence of almost any problem-solution text. Assume the following outlining task:

> "Deaths among elderly people involving electric blankets have been increasing over the last few years, and the government sent a six-point safety checklist to all elderly people last year. This appears to have had some effect, but the deaths are still unacceptably high, and the government is planning to revise and reissue the plan this year. Prepare an outline for a detailed report on this subject."

This will clearly be a problem-solution document, which will report on the situation, identify the problem, and propose solutions. Considerable background data will be needed, and the problem will need to be analyzed in some detail. The existing and other possible solutions will need to be discussed and evaluated. Here is a possible working outline for this task:

Title

INTRODUCTION

General Material

Purpose

Brief Overview

Document Structure

Previous work

Earlier Reports

Related Analyses

Discussion of Standards

Solutions in Other Jurisdictions

Background Analysis

Larger Elderly Population

Greater Need to Keep Warm

Increasing Heating Costs

Less Able in Emergencies

Causes of Deaths (*fire, electrocution*)

PROBLEM

Extent

Numbers Involved

Comparison and Trend with Previous Years

Ages of Victims

Types of Homes (*owned, supervised*)

Other Factors (*illness, infirmity*)

Causes

Blankets

Faults (*by manufacturer and type*)

Age

Instructions (*comprehensible, readable*)

Use

Overheating due to Doubling and Extra Blankets

Malpractice with Electrical Connections

Incontinence and Leaking Water Bottles

Other

SOLUTIONS

New Six-point Plan

Previous Plan used last Year

Authorship

Contents (*see Appendix*)

Circulation

Differences from Last Year

Need to Improve Standards

Need to Improve Instructions

Clarity and Illustrations

Warnings

Using Solutions from Other Jurisdictions

EVALUATION
  Possible Results from Last Year
  Anticipated Results this Year
  Need for a Permanent Solution
  Final Recommendations

APPENDICES
  Six-point Plan Last Year
  New Plan for this Year
  Related Standards
  Details of Statistics

Exercise 6.1: Planning Problem-Solution Documents

Any problem-solution topic can be handled in this way to provide a sound basis for the contents and organization of the document. Here are some examples you can use:

  (a) acid rain in North America or Europe
  (b) zebra mussels
  (c) highway accidents
  (d) boating accidents
  (e) tuition fees
  (f) the ozone layer
  (g) fruit flies
  (h) adult illiteracy
  (i) web page pornography
  (j) cancer
  (k) sexist pronouns
  (l) the Canadian Football League
  (m) writing standards among technical students
  (n) youth unemployment
  (o) the national debt
  (p) classroom sizes
  (q) AIDS
  (r) world population
  (s) demands for water
  (t) overcrowding in cities

That is, whenever there is a problem, the document analyzing it and providing or suggesting solutions will be a problem-solution text. You should now be able to understand the types of information that you will need to include in such documents — and also the sequence in which to place them.

Curtailed and Shorter Texts

Excluding Informational Elements

Although the full four-part problem-solution structure is extremely common in long and short texts, there are occasions when this is curtailed, leaving fewer than four elements for the structure. These occasions are:

Checklist 6.3: Reasons for Curtailing the Four-Part Structure

✓ *Writers may omit certain elements of the structure if they think readers already know the information, or if the information is obvious from the other details provided in the document. Situation and Evaluation are most often omitted, but the problem may also be left out in some circumstances.*

✓ *The work described in the document may be stopped prior to successful completion. Some conditions when this occurs are: when no serious problem is identified, when the problem becomes unsolvable (or not worth the effort or expense), or when the project runs out of funding or has been beaten by a better solution by a competitor. For all these conditions, only those elements that have been determined or resolved can be included in the report.*

✓ *The work may still be in progress, and the progress report can obviously only contain the elements that have been dealt with at that stage in the work.*

Problem-Solution-Evaluation Texts

An extremely common structure occurs when the situation is either clearly obvious from the later discussion, or is so general it need not be mentioned. In these instances, we have just three parts to the structure:

6.6 Another Philips Lighting Solution

The Problem: When chicks are young they need more light and heat but as they get older the same lighting level contributes to stress, panic and even death.

The Light Solution: Philips Lighting converted Mr Kallagi's incandescent system to twin Philips T8 fluorescent lamps with Advance Mark VII dimmable electronic ballasts. Over the six week life of the birds, lighting levels gradually dim to 20% of their original levels.

```
The result is a lower          Kallagi will save over
stress level for the chick-    $6,000 a year in energy
ens and that means healthi-    costs across his four
er, fatter birds with a        barns.
lower mortality rate. And          — Engineering Dimensions,
as an extra bonus, Mr                   Nov/Dec 1994, P2
```

As this example obviously applies to all situations where chickens are being raised, that does not need to be mentioned. Although both problem and solution are clearly signaled by the headings, the last two sentences are evaluation rather than solution. We know this because they tell us how well the system works rather than describing the system and how it works (description of solution). Evaluation here is signaled by *The result.*

Basic Problem-Solution Texts

The basic structure Problem-Solution is a special case of the more general four-part structure. In this basic structure the situation is a general unstated one and the evaluation is unnecessary because the solution obviously *is* a solution, and this does not need to be stated. Here is a clear example:

6.7
```
Problem: How to measure        want to measure. Then
close tolerances in a con-     remove it and use your
fined, hard to-get-at          calipers to measure your
space.                         mould made by the
Solution: Use some             Plasticine or Duxseal.
Plasticine or Duxseal.             Machinery and Equipment,
Press it into the space you             MRO, Sep 1994, P37
```

Full and curtailed problem-solution structures are often found as parts of larger texts, where they might be used as part of an overall description or other organization of material. Here is an example of a curtailed two-part problem-solution text that is part of a larger document:

6.8
```
The problem was that the       built that removes much of
fineness of the grind in       the finer material, yet
the mill produced a tail       retains the benefits of
that was too fine to make a    high-density fill.
mechanically stable back-          Canadian Mining Journal,
fill material.                              Oct 1994, P19
So a plant was designed and
```

The problem is signaled by *The problem* and *too*; the solution is signaled by *So.*

Purpose-Means Texts

A close synonym to the problem-solution informational pair is purpose-means. The connection is that, faced with a *problem*, it may be our *purpose* to solve it.

The *solution* to the problem is the *means* of achieving our purpose:

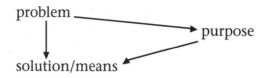

Figure 6.1: Problem-Solution and Purpose-Means

This connection can easily be seen in *Example 6.7*, which could have been expressed as:

> **Purpose:** To measure close tolerances in a confined hard-to-get-at space.
> **Means:** Use some Plasticine or Duxseal. Press it into the space you want to measure. Then remove it and use your calipers to measure the mould made by the Plasticine or Duxseal.

Understanding how purpose-means structures are essentially problem-solution structures helps us to recognize many more of these structures within the organization of sentences. Purpose-means pairs are clearly signaled within the sentence:

Checklist 6.4: Typical Purpose-Means Signaling within Sentences

✓ To *measure close tolerances in a confined space, press Plasticine into the space and measure the mould made.*

✓ *Measure close tolerances in a confined place* by *pressing Plasticine into the space and measuring the mould made.*

✓ *Press Plasticine into a confined space and measure the mould made* to *measure close tolerances.*

✓ By *pressing Plasticine into a confined space and measuring the mould made, you can measure close tolerances in confined spaces.*

That is, the binary pair of purpose-means (or means-purpose) is typically indicated by *to* (*in order to* if you like, though that is rarely necessary) for the purpose and *by ... ing* (or *through ... ing* or *by means of*) for the means. Between sentences and paragraphs this structural connection is made by using synonyms of purpose (*goal, aim, objective,* etc.) or of means (*way, method, how,* etc.).

Purpose-Means-Evaluation Structures

As purpose-means and problem-solution mean virtually the same thing, we often see clearly structured texts of purpose-means-evaluation that are much like the problem-solution-evaluation structures discussed earlier. Here is an extract of a purpose-means-evaluation text.

6.9 Canada's Anik Satellites

Purpose: *To* provide telecommunications coverage for all of Canada (including the far north) and most of the continental United States. All of Canada's major television networks use the satellite channels to broadcast their signals across the country.
The Anik satellites are also used *to* provide voice, data and image transmission services to the business, educational and government sectors.
How: Because satellites in geostationary orbit are always in the same position relative to earth, ground antennae can be in constant communication with a satellite without needing to be adjusted. Signals can thus be sent to a satellite from one ground antenna and instantly retransmitted to another ground antenna at a different location on Earth.
Amplifiers on board satellites are powered by electricity generated from solar energy. Satellites are kept ''on station'' using hydrazine-powered thrusters. Usually the life of the satellite is determined by the amount of hydrazine fuel the spacecraft can hold.
Results: Because Satellite signals reach across the country, virtually any kind of information can be sent to the satellite from one location and received all over the country instantly. Thus, world events can be seen on TV screens in living rooms across Canada within minutes, a Stanley Cup hockey game can be seen live by all Canadians, . . .

> *Engineering Dimensions,*
> Sep/Oct 1992, P31

Condensed Structures

Very Short Texts

Once you can recognize problem-solution and purpose-means patterns in sentences, you will be able to recognize many very short texts as containing one or more of the four major elements. For example "Steep Hill" is a problem, whereas "Go Slow" is a solution, and "Mind the Gap" is a solution-problem text. Sentences such as "Deposit $1 to receive peanuts." are clearly means-purpose (solution-problem). Note that for these very short texts — and summaries and titles discussed next — the order of the four parts will probably *not* follow the natural time-sequenced order found in longer texts. When we include two or more parts of the four-part structure in one or two sentences, we create a "condensed" structure.

Some statements or short texts (e.g. "No Smoking") might be a problem to some people but a solution to the needs of others. These have to be recognized as having a simultaneous dual role. Such structures are at the center of many arguments, fights, and disputes, which can only be analyzed in this way. These "interactive" problems are defined as solutions for one person or group that simultaneously create a problem to another person or group. Fortunately, these sorts of problems do not occur frequently in technical writing.

Exercise 6.2: Recognizing Problem-Solution Structures

Identify the components of information in the following examples:

(a) *Mud on Road.*

(b) *Johnson Street closed at Toronto Street. Use Union Street.*

(c) *Kill Your Speed.*

(d) *ALONE? Meet new friends of the opposite sex. Join Countrywide Introductions.*

(e) *Fields are laying off more workers. Not enough orders.*

(f) *Place a few coffee beans in the microwave for a few seconds next time you make instant coffee for guests. The smell will make them think they are getting the real thing.*

(g) *Beet juice stains can be removed by soaking them in ice tea.*

(h) *Car owners are requested, in their own interest, not to park in this location.*

(i) *An alcohol counselor has been hired by the school board to combat growing alcoholism.*

(j) *Disconnect the electrical supply to this unit before opening this inspection cover.*

Problem-Solution Summaries

The summary of a four-part problem-solution text is still a four-part problem-solution text. That is, the secret to writing summaries for these sorts of documents is first to recognize the major informational elements of the text, and then to include all of them, though in much briefer form, in your summary.

Many texts — especially informal reports — start with a summary of the longer text in the first sentence or two. This is seen in:

6.10 An on-line drill monitoring system developed by Aquila Mining Systems Ltd. of Montreal is helping New Brunswick Coal Ltd. to improve productivity and cut costs. This ''smart'' computerized drilling system was developed under a Mineral Development Agreement between CANMET and New Brunswick Coal. *By* providing information on the exact location of softer rocks, the on-line drill monitoring system has reduced the need for explosives for efficient blasting, resulting in improved muck pile fragmentation. As for the problem of coal being

> mixed with waste rock, the drill's performance variables are monitored to identify rock types based on their response to various parameters. The *result:* significantly less of the valuable coal is being wasted.
> — Canadian Institute of Mining Bulletin, May 1995, P9

The first sentence summarizes the more detailed information given in the second paragraph. It contains all four elements of the structure: the situation is the coal mining operation of New Brunswick Coal, the problems are high costs and low productivity, the solution is the use of the new on-line drill monitoring system, and the evaluation is that this is reducing costs and improving productivity.

For larger texts larger summaries may be needed, but here is an effective brief situation-problem-solution summary used to start a lengthy article:

6.11
> Although engineers have always been faced with conflict of interest situations, serious problems have been rare. *However,* as society becomes more litigious and as issues become more entwined, the *problem* of conflict of interest is increasing for the professions generally, including engineers. As professionals, engineers must be aware of what constitutes conflicts of interest and how to avoid them.
> — *Engineering Dimensions*, Jul/Aug 1995, P3

This well-structured and clearly-signaled summary provides a sound initial basis of understanding for readers about to read the full details in the article that follows.

Problem-Solution Titles

A possible title for *Example 6.10* is:

> "On-line Monitoring System Cuts Costs at New Brunswick Coal"

and in this we can see the four major elements of the problem-solution structure. These occur in the following order: solution (*On-line Monitoring System*), evaluation (*Cuts*), problem (*Costs*) and situation (*at New Brunswick Coal*).

This is the "active" form, in which the active voice (*Cuts*) is used. The counterpart "passive" form is equally possible:

> "Costs at New Brunswick Coal Cut by On-Line Monitoring System."

using the passive verb form (is) *Cut*. For this title, the order is problem-situation-evaluation-solution.

Titles such as these present highly condensed information. They are excellent summaries because they contain information representing all four elements of the four-part problem-solution structure.

Exercise 6.3: Analyzing Problem-Solution Titles

For each of the following, identify the four types of information and the order of presentation. Also identify whether it is an "active" or "passive" form. Then rewrite it in the other form, and again identify the four parts and the order of presentation.

(a) *Peening Process Prevents Intergranular Corrosion of Stainless Steels.*
(b) *Inaccessible Gasket in Aircraft Engine Sealed by Plastic.*
(c) *Operating Debt at Harfords Eliminated by Layoffs.*
(d) *Food Ferry Brings Relief to Famine in Somalia.*
(e) *New Home Computer Demand Met by Windows 2000.*

Writing Task: Writing a Proposal

Write a four-part problem-solution document proposing suitable changes to the "degree day" definition currently used by the Canadian Department of the Environment. The proposal should be suitable for publication in a general interest technical magazine read by engineering and scientific personnel of all specialities. Here are some details you will need.

1. Current method: take high and low temperature readings between midnight of one day and midnight of the following day, average them, take the average from 18°C, and you have the "degree day" — a measure of the degree of heating needed for that day.

2. Degree days are added for the days to arrive at a measure of the amount of heating needed in homes, offices, etc. during a given period — used by oil delivery companies to assess fuel needs — also a basis for heating efficiency calculations and climate change assessments.

3. Because hours of daylight are fewer than hours of darkness during winter, and temperature highs and lows relate to light and dark times, single readings are a poor basis for an "average" temperature — worse the farther north you go.

4. The method is still the same if the daytime temperature goes above 18°C. Is that reasonable? There can be no negative degree days, of course.

5. What about wind? Wind can get into cracks and can significantly affect fuel consumption. And what about sunlight, which also has a significant effect?

6. Is 18°C an acceptable level to use? Should it not be different at night? But how should we define "night" for this purpose? What about the different heating needs during the day and at weekends?

The present method is not that bad as a rough approximation, and it has the advantage of simplicity, but suggest something you think would provide a more accurate measure, and justify it. You will need to explain the present situation, of course, and also explain the problems with the present system. Include a four-part title.

Complex Problem-Solution Structures

Because problem-solution texts follow and describe the complex thoughts and actions of engineers and scientists as they do their work, these texts often must include many complexities in addition to the basic types of information discussed so far.

Here are some of these other complexities:

> ### Checklist 6.5: Some Complexities of Problem-Solution Texts
>
> ✓ *The situation may have been redefined to yield a problem definition within the capability (or cost, or time) of the workers.*
>
> ✓ *Several problems may need to be discussed, and there may be analysis to determine which are more important or more easily resolvable.*
>
> ✓ *The cause(s) of a problem may not have been known or may be unclear, and there may therefore be explanations of the work done to determine the cause(s).*
>
> ✓ *Several possible solutions (or variations) may have been considered, and the report may need to include pros and cons of each, leading to a decision to refine and develop the most promising.*
>
> ✓ *Before the final design is implemented, it may have to be tested and evaluated mathematically, by model, or other means to determine possible weaknesses that may then have to be removed or accepted.*
>
> ✓ *Even after implementation, the final solution may need to be tested and evaluated further, resulting in additional sections of information for the report.*

There are other complications too. In fact, the report usually has to be as complex as the thought/action patterns it describes. This means that problem-solution patterns are potentially extremely numerous if not theoretically infinite in their variety. Only the major simple patterns often found in technical reports and proposals have been discussed here. However, you should have developed enough understanding of the principles to understand more complex structures.

Writing Task: Writing a Report

The information given in note form below is all you will need to write a technical report using a complex problem-solution pattern. There is a summary/situation, a problem, a solution in general terms, and three (or four) solutions with some evaluation, and a final evaluation. First organize the information into an acceptable order, then write the report using full sentences and appropriate paragraphing. Finally add a four-part title in "active" or "passive" form. Your report is to be written for publication in a general technical magazine.

1. Foster Miller Ltd to design system burning fuel mixed with air — generates steam by direct contact with water — both steam and combustion gases could be injected farther into the reservoir — avoids problems of atmospheric pollution.

2. Third contract — World Energy Systems developing down-hole system generator — would produce steam by mixing and burning hydrogen and oxygen — do this at bottom of well.

3. Injecting steam into oil reservoir so far limited to wells less than 750 m deep — reason: at greater depths losses through drill pipe greater — losses so great steam's efficiency reduced.

4. The DoE plans to select technique with best potential — will then conduct field trials — these to be in 2002.

5. Another Rockwell proposal being studied — use of electric heater at bottom of well — this will produce steam there.

6. Solution to problem may be to generate steam at or near bottom of well — DoE now awarding three research contracts — purpose: investigate methods of doing this.

7. Rocketdyne Division of Rockwell International working on a similar idea — steam generated in "down-hole" heat exchangers — not by direct contact as with Foster Miller's idea — exhaust gases vented to atmosphere avoids possibility of "plugging" reservoir with particles generated during fuel combustion.

8. New methods of extracting more oil from conventional wells by the "steam drive" process — to be investigated — to be done by US companies — contracts just awarded by American Department of Energy.

Writing Task: Writing an Article

Write an article of interest to fellow technical professionals based on the information given below. First re-arrange the numbered chunks of information into the four parts of the problem-solution structure, and then write the article using full sentences.

1. Milkiway President and CEO is Hung Vu — discussed the need to protect an electronic network from hackers — likened it to protecting a house from burglary.

2. Internet security business is proving good for young businesses — those like Milkiway — they turned a profit in their first year — also grew from 4 to 17 employees.

3. Vu said there are two types of securities for the Internet — first is access — Black Hole provides this — then there is transactional security — like Brink's armoured truck on information highway — Milkiway is developing product called Waterfall — will solve second type.

4. Some 38 companies will be at "Technology in Government Week" — a show at the Congress Centre in Ottawa — Canada's largest public sector high-tech exhibition.

5. Vu envisioned Black Hole 5 years ago — said information world is harder to protect than real world — not dealing with tangibles — dealing with intellectual conflict — a mind game — you need a lot of sophistication and experience.

6. Government looking at internet as a way of saving money on information dissemination — Black Hole is Milkiway's security system — placed between private network servers and internet — acts like a bouncer at a bar — checks ID — allows access only to those authorized.

7. Milkiway Networks Corporation one of companies at exhibition — produce network security systems — hope to promote their product there — feel government internet activities could provide a market for their expertise — so have decided to participate.

8. Most communications systems currently unsecured — skilled hackers have no trouble hacking into unsecured systems from internet — important confidential information must be protected — unwise and dangerous to do otherwise.

Review Questions

1. *Why are problem-solving activities important in engineering?*

2. *What are the differences between problem-solving activities in engineering and science?*

3. *What is the connection between problem-solution structures in documents and problem-solution activities in engineering and science?*

4. *What are the four major elements of the problem-solution structure, and what do they mean?*

5. *How does the problem-solution structure apply to proposals? Explain.*

6. *What types of information might be found for each of the four parts of the four-part structure?*

7. *What are the reasons that some parts of the four-part structure might be omitted?*

8. *What is the connection between problem-solution and purpose-means?*

9. *How are purpose-means and means-purpose pairs typically signaled (a) within the sentence, and (b) between sentences?*

10. *What are "condensed" structures?*

11. *What are "interactive" problems? Give examples and explain.*

12. *What is the structure of summaries of problem-solving texts? Why?*

13. *How are four-part titles constructed a) in the active voice and b) in the passive voice*

Chapter 7:
Presenting a Credible Case

In this chapter you will learn what constitutes credible basis or evidence for your technical conclusions and opinions, and how you can present it to convince your readers. Methods of argument are discussed together with a pattern of information that presents and then counters the views of others. Different types of evaluative writing are also explained.

The Need To Be Technically Convincing
Technical and Mathematical Proof
Less-Definite Proofs
Evaluative Writing and its Elements
The Definiteness of the Conclusion

Types of Evidence
Levels of "Proof"
Strong and Weak Forms of Evidence
Experimental and Other Facts
Facts and Figures
Expert Testimony and Authoritative Publications
Personal Credibility and References
Weaker Forms of Evidence

"Argument" as Evidence
The Need for Argument
Giving Examples
Using Analogies and Hypothetical Argument
Comparisons
Recognizing Problems with Competing Views

Special Structures
Pros and Cons
Rebuttal with Basis
Concession-Rebuttal

Types of Evaluative Writing

The Need To Be Technically Convincing

Technical and Mathematical Proof

At this stage in your technical career, you are probably more attuned to the idea of technical "proof" than you are to presenting a view that you cannot demonstrate fully. Your training in science has perhaps largely been based on the concept of experimentation. You have probably verified established principles such as Ohm's Law and Charles' Law by defining your aim, setting up suitable apparatus, conducting a methodical procedure, measuring and tabulating quantities, and drawing conclusions based on these results. You thus proved that these and other laws of physics were indeed true.

You learned two other important things. First, you learned how to use the method of experimentation as a sound basis for demonstrating how things work. Second, you should have realized that scientific "fact" is always subject to the ultimate test of experimentation. Your conclusions must be such that others can conduct the same experiment, based on the details you provide in your report, and reach the same conclusions.

You are also well aware of the procedure of mathematical proof, moving from self-evident premises to complex mathematical theorems and relationships using established geometric and mathematical principles. Here again you have become able to "prove" that something was true, declaring QED (*quad erat demonstrandum* — what was to be proved has been proved) when you had proved the theorem or relationship you had set out to prove. There could be no doubt or counter-argument to such proofs; they are established truths which others must agree with after following the procedure in your analysis.

Less-Definite Proofs

The principles you learned in following experimental and mathematical proofs form essential background for any technical career. They also provide training of value in many — arguably all — specialities outside engineering and science. However, we must now recognize that there are other types of evidence that are used to convince readers of the validity or appropriateness of conclusions and decisions. There are also forms of "argument," which are yet other methods of justifying a decision.

Your recent and future searches for suitable employment present you with a clear example of the need to present a case. You cannot "prove," in the experimental or mathematical sense, that you are suitable for a particular position. Nor can you demonstrate without any doubt that you are the best candidate for that work. You have to use other forms of "evidence" to convince someone of your suitability and, implicitly, your advantages over other applicants.

So it will be in many other aspects of your professional career. You may need to convince a chief engineer that your technical idea is worth spending time and money developing. Or your company may be proposing to do work in a solicited or unsolicited proposal. Or you may need to argue that a theory or engineering concept or relationship is true. Or you may wish to convince other technical people to buy and use your company's products or services. Or you may need to present a convincing report on the causes of an accident or disaster.

Thus the work of technical professionals, though solidly grounded in experimental and mathematical forms of proof, will often also depend significantly on other ways of presenting a credible case. You will learn how to do this in this chapter.

Evaluative Writing and its Elements

You learned about descriptive writing in *Chapter 5* and problem-solution structures in *Chapter 6*. The forms of writing discussed in this chapter — those that present a credible case — are called "evaluative" forms. Evaluative writing depends on your ability to reach valid conclusions and to present them in a convincing way. Being convincing means finding and presenting adequate evidence or basis for your conclusions.

In writing evaluative documents you will need to gather and present relevant facts of course, and often these will be derived from experiments or mathematical calculations. However, you will also have to make sound judgments based on these fact, often assessing how "good" or "bad" something is. You will also need to present these judgments clearly with adequate justification. Thus evaluation usually has two elements:

Checklist 7.1: Two Elements of Evaluation

✓ *Assessment: the decision, judgment, conclusion, recommendation, selection, or assessment made*

✓ *Basis: the basis, grounds, evidence, argument, or reasoning that supports the assessment*

In consumer advertising, it is possible to convince people to buy something based on vague impressions without providing meaningful reasons for making that choice. In technical documents, however, you will have to go beyond impressionistic values (what you or others might "feel" is right or wrong — or the "best" — without basis or reasoning). You will need to provide substantive information or argument that will lead readers to accept your judgment.

The Definiteness of the Conclusion

It is often possible to reach definite conclusions based on experimental and mathematical work. For these (such as the verification of Boyle's law or Pythagoras' theorem), it would be inappropriate to indicate that there is any doubt. You have proved them to be true beyond any doubt, and of course you must clearly state that. Most original and practical work, however, might not be quite so definite.

For the more mathematical disciplines, it is often possible to be quite or very definite, but in the earth sciences in particular, many technical conclusions can only be tentative. For example meteorologists can never be certain of the direction a hurricane will take. When you are not sure, you must report the degree of certainty you are able to achieve. See *Chapter 11* for a list of signals of doubt or "hypotheticality."

Clear signaling of a tentative conclusion is seen in:

7.1

The granitic vein that intruded the Rexon's Cove greenschist-facies mylonite zone at 1113+6 (S46, Fig. 8) is less than 3 km from the western end of the Gilbert Bay Pluton, dated at 1132+7 Ma (Gower et al., 1991). This *supports* the *suggestion* that the granitic vein, and indeed much of the discordant granitic veining observed in the northeastern part of the GRB, *may be* related to the Gilbert Bay Pluton (Gower et al., 1987; Hanmer and Scott, 1990).
— *Canadian Journal of Earth Sciences,*
30, 1993, P1467

The first sentence is definite though not fully defined because of the use of *less than*. This information is then used as supporting evidence (note the use of *supports* rather than the definite *demonstrates*) for an earlier *suggestion*, which is again only a tentative conclusion signaled by *may be*.

Types of Evidence

Levels of "Proof"

We must first recognize that different assessments need different levels of "proof" or basis. The only proof necessary to demonstrate that someone is guilty of illegal parking is the signed form from an authorized meter inspector. However, for a conviction for armed robbery of a store by a masked person, we might need a complex array of evidence such as:

Checklist 7.2: Possible Evidence for Armed Robbery of a Store

✓ *an eye-witness account of the height and build of the attacker*

✓ *the testimony of the store owner regarding the attacker's voice*

✓ *burnt rubber from the attacker's car tires matching that on the suspect's car*

✓ *the finding of considerable amounts of unaccounted-for cash (like that stolen from the store) on the suspect's premises*

> ✓ *footprints in dust outside the store probably matching those made by a pair of sneakers owned by the suspect.*

Even then, is this sufficient evidence to convict someone of the crime? Only a judge or jury can decide given their assessment of all the available evidence, including the definiteness of each element and the credibility of the witnesses. For murder trials, of course, the level of proof must be "beyond a reasonable doubt"; whether the evidence is sufficient to justify such a level of certainty must be determined by a jury. For civil litigation, the level of proof is at a lower "preponderence of evidence."

So it is with technical assessments. The decision to paint local fire extinguishers red and orange rather than red and green might depend on the availability of paint or simply personal preference. It does not really matter. In contrast, the decision regarding the final design of a bridge would depend on computer-aided design and mathematical analyses, wind tunnel and load tests, and cost estimates for the material, installation and maintenance. The assessment would be a much more rigorous and serious activity, and the report and recommendation would involve many chapters of detail supported by demonstrable data and evidence. Thus the more important and costly the project, the more necessary it becomes to provide higher levels of "proof" or certainty.

You as a writer must decide how much basis is needed for your assessment. Should you feel that the basis only weakly demonstrates your conclusion, you may wish to seek further evidence or try to obtain supporting basis through experimentation, reference to other work, or other means to make your case more convincing. If your conclusions are still only weakly demonstrated by your evidence, you may have to change your conclusions — or at least indicate the level of doubt you still have.

Strong and Weak Forms of Evidence

In the armed robbery discussed earlier, the suspect could probably have been convicted solely on a fresh fingerprint on the drawer of the till, or two or three clear eye-witness accounts if the suspect had not worn a mask. These would have been "strong" forms of evidence, which almost on their own are sufficient proof. Other forms of evidence are "weaker," however. The rubber from the tires would match many tires, the shape and build would match many other people, the footprints would match others too, and the voice matching is subjective and rather dubious evidence. Even the money does not, of itself, demonstrate the guilt of the suspect.

When you have strong evidence for a point of view, that may be all you need to communicate. When, however, the individual elements of your basis are weaker forms of evidence, you will have to rely on the combination of these elements to justify your decision. In presenting your evidence, you should take into account that it is what *your readers* will feel is strong or weak evidence that matters; they are the ones you have to convince.

Obviously strong forms of evidence are preferred when they are available.

But weaker forms can still be useful in supporting other types of evidence. In deciding what forms of evidence to seek and to include in your writing, you first need to understand what forms of evidence you can use.

Experimental and Other Facts

Strong forms of evidence are those that lead inevitably to the conclusion you have reached. Simple experimental and mathematical procedures are clear examples, as these are usually facts and figures that provide sufficient proof on their own. For example, a well-documented procedure to determine the relationship between voltage across and current flowing through a resistor is sufficient proof of Ohm's law. Other workers can repeat your experiment and come to the same conclusion, and thus this proves your conclusion beyond any doubt. Similarly, mathematical calculations based on sound initial data and principles will usually provide undeniably sound results.

In practice, outside the classroom where we need to demonstrate established laws and principles, experimentation is still a significant means of demonstrating a conclusion:

> **7.2** The application of AFT improves all calending operations enhancing product quality and contributing to the evolution of new value added grades.
> A number of recent applications show how AFT has been applied and the results achieved.
> — *Pulp and Paper Canada*, May 1995, P54/58)

The four recent applications presented after this introduction — together with measured data, tables and graphs — provide sound basis for the stated conclusion.

Observations recorded by yourself or other competent individuals are also acceptable forms of basis, as we saw in the first sentence of *Example 7.1*. Such observations are often recorded as photographs and included in the document to provide permanent graphic evidence of the observations. It is for this reason that photographs or video films are often included with many investigative reports.

Facts about the design or concept you are recommending provide sound basis for your decision, as long as these facts are favorable. What something can do, how well it works, and even its cost, weight or appearance could be useful information to include as basis for an assessment in favor of an instrument, for example. However, you may feel ethically constrained to include any relevant *negative* information too, as this provides a balanced account. *Chapter 5* will help you to know what sort of information to include in any description that also includes an assessment based on the details provided. In many descriptions, the information provided enables readers to form conclusions regarding the value and usefulness of the topic being described, i.e. the description is the basis for their assessment.

Facts and Figures

General statements about what how well something works provide some weak evidence, but it becomes a much more convincing basis when you can quote exact figures. Usually the figures themselves are indisputable and can only be countered by claiming that they are not relevant or do not represent the whole picture. Often a single figure is sufficient as basis for a general statement:

> **73** Russian commercial power reactors showed noticeable improvement in safe operations during 1993. Operators recorded a total of 154 deviations from normal power operation, reduced considerably from the 1992 total of 199 deviations.
> — *Nuclear Canada*, Nov/Dec 1994, P3

although sometimes several sets of data are required:

> **74** National Mining Week is intended to focus the attention of all Canadians on the importance of this technologically advanced industry. Mining is an essential component of Canada's economy. Canadians should be aware that our mining industry directly employs 330 000 people and is the mainstay of employment in some 115 communities. Canadians also need to know that mining provides approximately 15% of total Canadian exports, contributing nearly $12 billion of our trade balance. In addition, Canadians should know that mining accounts for over 4% of Canada's total production of goods and services.
> — *Canadian Institute of Mining Bulletin*, May 1995, P7

Any one of these figures on its own might not provide a very convincing basis for the assessment in the second sentence. Combined, however, they provide an acceptable level of proof.

Statistical evidence is often also quite strong evidence. Its advantage is that the level of certainty of the conclusion (e.g. 95%) is mathematically linked to the margin of error (e.g. within 3%) for a given sample size. Reporting statistics provides a clear example of the importance of the need to include the level of doubt in your conclusion. For a bigger sample (better evidence) the degree of certainty of the conclusion increases for a given margin of error. The overall credibility of statistical data may also be affected by such factors as the reliability of the individual data or opinions, the representativeness of the sample, and any perceived bias.

Expert Testimony and Authoritative Publications

Frequently facts and figures alone may be insufficient to establish a conclusion. This may happen when the conclusion is a general one (which figures may not be able to prove), or when skilled judgment is required in interpreting the data. The following example shows two other forms of evidence often used in such circumstances: expert testimony and reference to an established code of practice.

7.5

A professional Engineer appeared as an expert witness (Expert 1) on behalf of the Association. He had specifically reviewed the masonry piers. The drawings were submitted to the city in December 1988 and the Code for the masonry walls which was applied to the drawings was CAN3-S304-M78, hereinafter referred to as M78.

His opinion about the wall on grid line ''A'' was that the main supporting masonry piers were less than required by the empirical design method specified in M78. This code states that walls may not be higher than 18 times their nominal thickness, and the length of piers in such walls shall not be less than three times their nominal thickness and that if these rules are not met, an engineering analysis is mandatory.

— *Engineering Dimensions*, Gazette, Nov/Dec 1994, P1

As the nominal thickness (and therefore whether the design meets the code) may be a matter for skilled interpretation, an expert witness was asked to present a knowledgeable opinion. The assessment of the appropriateness of the design is based on this judgment as it applies to relevant parts of the appropriate code.

Evidence for your point of view can be given by citing supporting details and views published in other authoritative publications such as encyclopedias, books, journal papers, magazine articles, codes, specifications, standards and technical reports. The extent of the evidence they provide is determined by the scholarly level of the publication and author(s), the relevance of the information cited or summarized, and the claims made together with their degrees of certainty.

Personal Credibility and References

Occasionally the writer needs to establish personal credibility as an expert to give weight to information given and opinions expressed. This is done in:

7.6

I read, with concern, your new article in the January/February 1992 issue, ''Disband Lending Agencies: Probe International,'' p.14 in which the international environmental group condemns engineering projects in the developing world. I have lived in the Third World for a decade and

> recently retired as direc-
> tor of telecommunications
> for the Canadian
> International Development
> Agency (CIDA), so I feel
> qualified to comment.
> — *Engineering Dimensions*,
>   Mar/April 1992, P6

The comments that follow will be taken much more seriously now the writer has established personal credibility.

The views of experts can be expressed through reference to or summarization of information in published works. Such inclusion of details of the work of others is not just a matter of recognition of earlier work, or even simply a way of avoiding discussion of established concepts. It can also lend credibility to your own argument:

7.7
> In a dual impeller agitat-
> ed, gas liquid system,
> Abrardi et al. (1990) iden-
> tified several hydrodynamic
> regimes. Different behav-
> iour was observed for vari-
> ous turbines as far as
> flooding, loading and com-
> plete dispersion behaviours
> were concerned.
> — Nocentini et al.,1988,
>   *Canadian Journal of*
>   *Chemical Engineering*,
>   June 1995, P275

Rather than simply stating that the different regimes and different behaviors occur, the writer provides credibility for these statements through reference to published papers by other researchers. Such references also acknowledge the work of others.

If, through reference to publications, you are able to demonstrate that your conclusions are in line with (or at least do not contradict) established theory or the assessments of experts, then that will provide supporting evidence for your views. Such evidence is used in:

7.8
> In addition, the sulphur to
> molybdenum ratio increased
> molybdenum loading. This
> suggests that, as the
> molybdenum loading was
> increased, more Mo having
> bulk properties was avail-
> able for sulphidation. This
> explanation is consistent
> with the observations of
> LoJacono et al. (1973) and
> is further supported by
> previous kinetic data which
> showed that the 15%
> Mo/Al_2O_3 catalyst behaved
> in a manner similar to that
> of pure crystalline MoS_2
> (Mulligan and Berk, 1992).
> — *Canadian Journal of*
>   *Chemical Engineering*,
>   Jun 1995, P353

If, on the other hand, you find your views *conflict* with those of others, you will need to provide much more evidence for your conclusions. You will still have to discuss the contrary views. You also need to explain why the other conclusions are not correct for or relevant to the work you are doing.

Weaker Forms of Evidence

Other forms of evidence are often included when the view being expressed is not vital — or perhaps if no better evidence is available. Although the opinion of anyone on the street about the reason for Canada's recent downturn in manufacturing may not be worth recording, the opinion of an important figure in manufacturing *is* worth noting:

> **7.9** Jack MacMillan, president and CEO, PPG Canada Inc., said low productivity is partially to blame for Canada's manufacturing downturn.
> — *Canadian Mining Journal*, Dec 1994, P14

Although some further support for this assessment would be useful, a weak form of credibility is created simply by virtue of the position of the person expressing it. As long as the person is knowledgeable about the subject being assessed, and we can assume there is no personal bias, most readers would be inclined to accept such an assessment.

When you are writing a document, *you* have some credibility, and so you do not have to demonstrate the validity of every statement you make, especially if it is well known or will be readily accepted. If you are sure that information is common knowledge, you can state that — as a weak form of evidence. Both of these types of evidence occur in:

> **7.10** Often a constant factor is used to relate the speed of the feeding system to the oven dry (OD) pulp mass flow. However, *it is well known that* this factor is not constant because of continual changes in chip properties such as density and moisture content.
> — *Pulp and Paper Canada*, May 1995, P31

The author presumably knows that the statement in the first sentence is true, and does not have to justify it. The second sentence is prefaced with *it is well known that* to indicate that this is common knowledge.

Some writers (and speakers) overuse such signals. Examples are *Everyone knows that, It is obvious that, I assure you that, No proof is needed to establish that, You would be a fool to question the fact that*. Such forms of "credibility by insistence" are inappropriate for any serious writing or speaking task. They are not likely to convince discerning readers or listeners.

Exercise 7.1: Deciding on Types of Evidence

What sorts of evidence would you expect as basis for the following conclusions? Write notes and discuss you views in class.

(a) "Pain Relief in just one Tablet" (consumer advertisement)
(b) a formula for measuring the flow of water in a given river (a report

to a conservation authority)

(c) a prediction of the weather for a city three days from now (a meteorological report)

(d) an accusation that a patent claim is a plagiarized version of an earlier report (a court case)

(e) a conclusion that nickel (or any other natural deposit) exists in exploitable quantities in a surveyed area (a proposal to start a new mine)

(f) a claim that a new computer software is as user friendly as a well-established competitor (an article in a computer magazine)

(g) a conclusion that a small new battery-driven car could be useful for city driving (a leaflet for potential customers)

(h) justification for government spending cuts to colleges and universities (an oral presentation to students and instructors)

(i) a conclusion that a bridge design will meet all expected loads and conditions of nature (an engineering report)

(j) a decision to grant a technical certificate or degree (calendar regulations)

"Argument" as Evidence

The Need for Argument

The basis for some judgments may be hard to understand or to articulate. Selections by wine tasters, art critics, and perfume "noses," and decisions made by generals in battle, master chess players, or hockey coaches perhaps cannot all be explained in terms we can understand. For these, we have to trust the experience and developed evaluative sense of the experts. Your own views on personal preferences (of friends, movies, career choices, etc.) may similarly be hard to explain or justify to others, or even to yourself.

In our professional lives, however, we should always seek to present strong facts-and-figures evidence as the basis for definite conclusions whenever possible. Failing that, we need to present other forms of strong evidence if it is available. Unfortunately, many of the important conclusions we reach and decisions we make cannot be demonstrated in quantitative terms, and we must then resort to other forms of justification. We may have to use examples, analogies, comparisons and other forms of "argument" to present a credible case.

Giving Examples

A general conclusion can often be adequately supported by citing examples. While even one or two can often provide quite compelling support for an assessment, three or four relevant examples can provide very strong evidence indeed. The claim of uniqueness in a Canadian context is well justified in this way in:

7.11

The Ontario government recently decided to apply the concept of the public-private partnership on its new Highway 407 project. Almost everything about this project *is unique in a Canadian context*. Its scale, the introduction of tolling and the way the highway is being developed established it as a *milestone* in Canadian infrastructure development. The 407 is, in fact, the *largest* road construction project in Ontario in more than 30 years; it was in the planning stages even before that.

At a cost of $1 billion, the 69-kilometre, multi-lane urban toll highway is also the *largest* single civil-engineering contract tendered in Canadian history. Once completed near the end of 1998, it will become Canada's and one of the world's *first* all-electronic toll highways, have created an estimated 20,000 new jobs, and be the *first* major infrastructure project in Canada to be developed through an innovative public-private sector partnership.

— *Engineering Dimensions*, Nov/Dec 1994, P30

The claimed uniqueness in the Canadian context is justified with several examples of unique features of the project. These are all clearly signaled by the superlatives (*largest*) and the words *milestone* and *first*.

Examples can often answer the question "What are they?" about the introductory assessment. When the assessment and basis are quite short, the assessment can be the root of an introduced list and the examples are the elements of the list. When, however, the information becomes too large to fit into even a long list, separate sentences are used:

7.12

There are indications that exploration strategies are beginning to change as a direct result of new developments in geophysical technology. *First*, rapid advances in GPS navigation technology have made it possible to determine a survey platform's position in 3-dimensional space in real-time with sub-metre accuracy. *Second*, further miniaturization of geophysical survey instrumentation has made it possible to install lightweight systems in any type of aircraft/ helicopter, i.e. so-called ``available aircraft.'' *Third*, the systems are now so automated that a geophysical operator is not required — the pilot is

```
the operator. All of these          rapidly, and at a reduced
have led to the possibility          line km cost.
of carrying out airborne               — Canadian Mining Journal,
surveys with the detail of             Feb 1995, P52 of supplement
ground surveys, much more
```

The assessment is formally stated using existential *there*, and readers will naturally ask "What are the indications?." These are then given in the next three sentences, with clear signaling of *First*, *Second* and *Third*. An elaboration of the assessment is then given in the final sentence, again clearly based on the examples cited in the central three sentences.

Examples are used extensively in this book not only as illustrations that show you how technical language works, but also as a form of "proof" that the statements being made are valid. You are invited to seek your own examples on any subject discussed here — and to form your own conclusions based on the evidence you find. The research tasks encourage you to do that.

Using Analogies and Hypothetical Argument

You may have noticed how the hypothetical case of an armed robbery was used earlier in this chapter to explain the use of strong and weak evidence and the concept of adequate proof. The claim was then made: "So it is with technical assessments." This is a form of argument using analogy, i.e. explaining how something similar works and then claiming that the main topic always operates in much the same way. We are, in fact, asking readers to understand a generality based on one example they understand — and then to realize that the subject under study will also operate this way because it too operates according to that generality.

Two analogies support the recommendation (an assessment) in the following:

7.13
```
The information highway          access to content.''
will be a failure unless         Other bits of technology
the issue of content is          have come and gone while
addressed, says the presi-       some have almost existed as
dent and chief executive         the ''living dead,'' most
officer of MediaLinx             notable video conferencing,
Interactive Inc. . . .           he said.
''Not that long ago, Beta        To prevent that from hap-
and VHS battled it out and       pening to the information
Beta was clearly the supe-       highway, providing content
rior technology. It (Beta)       must be made a priority,
lost the battle,'' he says.      Klinkhammer said.
''It lost the battle                — Computing Canada,
because of content and              Jun 1995, P14
```

The speaker uses the demise of beta technology and the underuse of video conferencing as analogies when discussing the information highway. The claim is that lack of content and access to content caused these two failures, and that it could cause weakness in or failure of the information highway too if the problem is not remedied.

A special form of analogy is the use of a hypothetical (made-up) scenario as basis for an assessment. Here are extracts from such a form of argument:

7.14 It is our belief that a better choice might be to use the transfer-screw speed to control the motor load. One reason for not using the plate gap is best illustrated with the following scenario: . . . .
Let us assume that the density of the incoming chips increases, meaning that B increases. This will in turn cause the motor load to increase.
If plate gap is being used to control the motor load, the gap will increase in order to bring the motor load back down to its original level. However, as can be seen from the above equation, this will result in a decrease in the specific energy.
The motivation for considering the use of transfer-screw speed to control motor load can be illustrated with the same scenario: Assume as above that the density of the incoming chips increases which in turn causes the motor load to increase. If the transfer-screw speed is used, . . . this control scheme may have a better chance of maintaining a constant specific energy.
— *Pulp and Paper Canada*,
May 1995, P32

The assessment (or belief) is given in the first sentence, and considerable hypothetical argument is offered as basis. This is in the form of an assumed set of circumstances (a scenario) within which the performances of the two competing methods are assessed and compared. The better performance of the transfer-screw method under these assumptions then forms the basis for the selection recommended in the first sentence.

Comparisons

Evidence in *Example 7.14* is provided by a form of comparison as well as hypothetical argument. The writers compare the performances of two methods of motor load control, and find that one is better; this becomes the basis for the recommendation to use the transfer-screw method. Comparison is also seen as the basis for a recommendation in:

7.15 For travel in the Quebec City–Windsor corridor, Transport 2000 advocates the use of electric trains. ''Unlike automobile and air travel, rail has the capacity for expansion by upgrading existing infrastructure without consuming a lot of land,'' Evans said.
— *Engineering Dimensions*,
Mar / Apr 1992, P10

This comparison of one attribute of three competing methods of transportation is used as basis for the decision to advocate the rail system for this application. Of course a more thorough analysis would have to involve comparison of many other attributes such as capital and running costs, time, safety, and environmental considerations.

Comparisons can often be quite simple, sometimes meeting the reader's expectation for information given in the assessment:

7.16

> The case of a kiss singularity differs significantly from that of a conical point, *because* the group velocities on the two quasi-shear sheets are regular at a point of tangential touching *whereas* they are singular at a conical point.
> — *Geophysics International*, 118, 1994, P760

Details of the significant difference are given as basis for the statement that they *are* different. The basis is signaled by *because* and the transition between the two conditions is indicated by *whereas*.

Recognizing Problems with Competing Views

Often an important way to demonstrate a point of view is to identify problems with something you are comparing something else with. In *Example 7.15*, we saw how the need for more land must accompany the expansion of automobile and air travel. As it is claimed this problem does not exist for upgrading rail capacity, we have evidence to support the conclusion that the use of electric trains should be increased.

Thus in seeking to justify your positive conclusion of one view or product, one method is to recognize problems or deficiencies with other competing views or products. If what your are advocating does not have these problems or deficiencies, you will have established a form of evidence for its acceptance.

Checklist 7.3: Types of Evidence

✓ *experimental evidence*

✓ *mathematical calculations*

✓ *facts and figures*

✓ *observations and facts*

✓ *expert testimony*

✓ *reference to authoritative publications*

✓ *references to work in technical papers*

✓ *personal credibility*

✓ *claiming known information ("It is well known that . . . ")*

✓ *examples*

✓ *analogies*

✓ *hypothetical argument*

✓ *comparisons*

✓ *recognizing problems with competing views*

Research Tasks

Find examples of the use of all forms of evidence as basis for establishing a conclusion, opinion or decision. Note what sorts of evidence are used most for certain types of technical writing. Based on examples you have found, prepare a report and/or presentation elaborating on any interesting aspect of basis and assessment. Check with your instructor regarding length and depth.

Writing Task: Presenting a Credible Case

Using one or more of the following statements as a base, define a position you feel comfortable defending. Then prepare an outline including all the sorts of evidence you would include in a report to a specified audience of your choice. Finally gather the evidence you need and write the report.

1. Many technical students had little practice in schools with writing related to their chosen professions, and there should be more instruction and practice in such writing in schools.

2. The depletion of the ozone layer is becoming a serious problem, and more must be done to reverse it.

3. Government cutbacks in higher education are reducing accessibility and lowering standards. These in turn will reduce Canada's ability to compete on a global market.

4. With creative curriculum changes and more integrated learning in an independent center, engineering schools could improve undergraduate education and save money.

5. Engineering is a more demanding program of education than arts programs.

Special Structures

Pros and Cons

If there are limitations or disadvantages with something you are proposing or recommending, you should include that information as well as the advantages. While you may not be compelled to do that when you are presenting yourself as a candidate for a position with a company (!), you are ethically bound to be honest in all forms of technical communication. This often means including the negative information (the "cons") as well as the information supporting your assessment (the "pros"). Note how this is done in:

7.16

In comparison to an INS, a GPS attitude measuring receiver has many *advantages*, including being relatively small, light and inexpensive, not requiring a long settling time, and not being degraded by high altitude. *However*, GPS also has *disadvantages*, such as a susceptibility to loss of signal and a much lower data rate.
— *Canadian Aeronautical and Space Journal*, 41(1), P13

Note how *However* is used to mediate between the advantages and the disadvantages. Writers signal such transitions very clearly.

Frequently the pros and the cons can take up several paragraphs each, and the structure of large documents can be organized around such blocks of information. Here are extracts from a larger example in which the writer provides negative elements of information to balance the positive information used as the basis for the assessment:

7.17

The profile linear anti-friction technology has gained recent popularity . . . .Rail technology offers *advantages* in service life for accessible or inconvenient maintenance situations, assuming non-harsh operating conditions and stresses. *Also*, rail technology usually entails a lower base-to-mounting surface height for applications requiring compactness.
On the downside, rail systems require precision machining . . . .

Also, using rails in harsh operating conditions requires that special sealing bellows or covers be considered. . . .
Once installed, maintenance options are *limited* . . . .
Some recent product developments in machining have overcome this limitation somewhat, but more importantly, the longer service life of rail technology can sometimes offset the maintenance inconvenience.
— *Machinery and Equipment MRO*, Sep 1994, P15

The reasons for the popularity are given, but so are the drawbacks, this time signaled by *On the downside*. Note how *Also* is used twice to indicate continuity of first the positive and then the negative aspects of rail design. For larger documents, the headings may be the transition signals of continuity and contrast.

Rebuttal with Basis

You may find you disagree with someone else's view on a topic and feel you need to correct the impression given to readers. To do this, you first need to state the view, then "deny" that is it correct, and finally provide basis for your view that the original opinion in wrong. This three-part structure, "statement-denial-basis," is common in letters to the editor, and can be found in many forms of evaluative writing. The structure is clearly seen in:

7.18

You state that the average starting salary in Great Britain is $38,000, while Canadian graduate engineers can start at $33,000. This statement is *wrong*. On average, starting salaries in the United Kingdom are less than they are in Canada; our associate company in England typically pays graduates about $25,000.
— *Engineering Dimensions*, May/June 1992, P8

The three parts of the structure form the three sentences. As we see here, the basis for denying the validity of the original statement is also a "correction" of the statement, i.e. it says what *is* true.

The correction here consists of actual facts and figures, which provide good evidence. Another way of rebutting a point of view or recommendation is by claiming (and justifying) that there is a flaw in the thinking. This is seen in the following statement-denial-basis structure:

7.19

The ACES report is concerned about a minimal risk to human health, in isolation and out of context. It is *not a good* prescription for public policy. The recommendations of the ACES report ''A Standard for Tritium'' should be *rejected*.
The ACES recommendations are fundamentally *flawed*, first *because* the main conclusion rests on a *dubious* extrapolation of the relevant scientific data. Scientific *evidence*, casting *doubt* on the empirical and theoretical *basis* for this extrapolation, has accumulated. The risk to the people of Ontario from tritium in drinking water is known to be undetectably small, and that will continue to be the case if no change is made. This would be serious enough if it was the document's only *fault*. Regulation entails social and economic costs, and the government ought to ensure that the benefits

clearly exceed the costs.
There must be clear *evidence* that a problem
exists, that intervention
is justified, and that regulation is the best alternative open to government.
``A Standard for Tritium''
fails on all accounts.
— *Nuclear Canada*,
Jul/Aug 1994, P3

The recommendations are attacked because of an alleged *flaw* in the reasoning and then because of a failure to provide adequate basis (reasoning) to justify the recommended government action. The clear signaling of this example is worth noting.

Writing Task: Statement-Denial-Basis/Correction

Using the three-part structure "statement-denial-basis/ correction," write letters to the editor of a newspaper or magazine of your choice rebutting the following views or decisions. Add any other specific information you need. Counter any basis given for the assessment you are challenging and also make sure you provide adequate basis for your point of view.

1. The Minister of Education's decision to increase tuition fees by 20% announced in today's news.

2. A claim by Computers Inc. in a news release published last month entitled "Error-Free Writing Now,"claiming that current spell checkers ensure error-free writing.

3. A report published today entitled "Fair Language Standards" by your International Students Society proposing that technical students whose first language is not English should not have to meet the minimum writing standards in English required of those whose first language is English. (Or do this using French instead of English.)

4. A suggestion in your today's student newspaper by your electrical engineering department that instruction in engineering drawing no longer be required of all technical students on the basis that computers are now used for all drawings.

5. A proposal by your Housing Committee that, within three years, all students must remain in residences throughout their time at your college or university.

6. A letter in your local paper last week from a "Men's Liberation Movement" stating that (a) we should no longer have to avoid sexist pronouns because it is too difficult to do well, or (b) that all women's sports teams should be abolished in keeping with the principle of equality.

7. A claim made in an interview on TV news last night by your provincial school boards that schools in your province give technical students detailed and adequate instruction and practice in technical communication.

8. A motion for the next Senate meeting that "Frosh week be abolished."

9. A proposal just released by your food services operator to convert all outlets to Tim Horton's.

10. A claim by one of your professors that she is now teaching only "easy" material because she needs to obtain good student evaluations — and therefore that student evaluations should be abolished.

Now find other views you disagree with, and write letters for them that rebut the claims or suggestions made.

Concession-Rebuttal

When you are presenting your argument, you may need to concede some points that counter your point of view. When you do, you will then need to rebut these points by explaining why they do not invalidate your thesis — perhaps because they are irrelevant or are a weak form of evidence. A useful structure for concession-rebuttal is to use signals such as *Admittedly*, *Granted*, or *True* (*O. K.* or *Sure* for speech) to indicate the concession, and *However*, *Nonetheless* or *But* to indicate the transition from concession to rebuttal. Alternatively the structure can be signaled by *Although* or *Despite*:

7.20

```
For several catalysts . . .
the performance . . . was
remarkably similar to that
of a two-stage reactor with
interstage addition of oxy-
gen . . . Although these
results indicated that
there was no benefit to be
gained, in terms of overall
reactor performance, from
staging the oxygen addi-
tion, they are important
```
```
because they imply that a
large-scale reactor could
conceivably be operated
with staged oxygen addition
(an inherently safer oper-
ating mode) without perfor-
mance loss.
        — Canadian Journal of
        Chemical Engineering,
            June 1995, P335
```

The concession occurs in the subordinate clause dominated by *Although*, the rebuttal is the main clause (*they are important*) and the reason (or basis) for the rebuttal is signaled by and follows *because*.

Writing Task

Take a completed letter from the previous exercise and argue for the *opposite* of that presented in the letter. Counter the arguments presented by detecting weaknesses in the evidence offered, and by presenting evidence for your view. Concede and rebut at least one point against your claim.

Types of Evaluative Writing

You have presumably been introduced to writing in which you "compare and contrast" two things, ideas, or concepts. In this form of writing, you note features that are in common and those that are different. Significant information in common is needed for there to be a meaningful discussion of differences. The pattern of the document is usually similarities-differences, with clear signaling between the two elements.

Another form of evaluative writing you are no doubt aware of is the structure thesis-support, which of course is the assessment-basis we have been discussing in this chapter. In this form of writing readers expect a clear thesis (or claim, or decision) followed by whatever support, basis, evidence, etc. is needed to convince them of the validity of the thesis.

Less well known is the type of evaluative writing which explores a subject with the aim of providing enlightenment and understanding without the writer reaching a definite conclusion or thesis. In this type of writing, different views are usually discussed, analyzed and compared in thoughtful reflection of the subject as a whole.

Another structure is the narrative, in which information is presented in time-oriented sequence. Within the elements of information, however, problem-solution and descriptive detail will inevitably occur to reflect the aims and plans of those involved in the account: their plans, problems and solutions, and also the results of their actions.

Checklist 7.4: Types of Evaluative Writing

✓ *Comparative: you compare and contrast the details, advantages and advantages of two or more topics or proposals*

✓ *Thesis: you demonstrate that a defined thesis or hypothesis is valid, perhaps with some exceptions to or refinements of the thesis as originally stated*

✓ *Exploratory: you discuss the details and significance of the topic, exploring and analyzing different aspects to provide greater understanding and enlightenment*

✓ *Narrative: you organize your work in a time-oriented sequence, including descriptive and problem-solution material as necessary*

Exercise 7.2: Recognizing Types of Evaluative Writing

For the following communication tasks, state whether they would be comparison (C), thesis type (T), exploratory type (E) or narrative type (N) — or perhaps some combination. Explain your choices; expect some difference of viewpoint for some of these topics.

(a) a presentation you will give to high school students explaining the benefits of a higher education

(b) a written course evaluation

(c) an analysis of user-friendly aspects of Macintosh and Windows 2000 software

(d) the results/conclusion sections of a laboratory report

(e) an account of Alexander Graham Bell's design of the telephone

(f) a proposal to undertake design work for a major project

(g) a decision on, and justification of, the award of a technical scholarship

(h) a book review

(i) a student society submission to the Board of Trustees regarding increases in tuition fees

(j) an analysis of burning and burying garbage

(k) a discussion of technical career options

(l) a report on the appropriateness of the proportions of visible minorities in different technical departments in your college or university

(m) the procedure section of a laboratory report

(n) an analysis of the growing problem of garbage disposal in your area

(o) a discussion on recent advances in computer technology and communications systems

(p) advice to students on how to start their own summer businesses

(q) the president's annual address to the faculty and student body of your institution

Now think of other types of evaluative communication and decide the most appropriate structure for them.

Review Questions

1. What are the values of learning the experimental method during your technical training?

2. What does QED stand for and what does it mean? Why is it an important concept in technical evidence?

3. What sorts of topics cannot be "proved" in an experimental or mathematical sense.

4. What are the two elements of evaluation? Give synonyms for each element.

5. What are typical signals of doubt or hypotheticality? In which technical disciplines are hypotheticals most important? Why?

6. What is meant by "levels" of proof? Explain using legal and technical examples.

7. What factors determine the level of proof? Give examples.

8. What is meant by "strong" and "weak" forms of evidence? Give examples of each.

9. What can you do if you find your evidence only weakly establishes your view?

10. Why do figures usually present strong evidence?

11. Why is statistical evidence a prime example of the importance of reporting the degree of doubt?

12. What factors do or might affect the usefulness of statistical evidence?

13. How can observations become a form of evidence? Why are photographs useful in this context?

14. What is meant by an "expert witness"?

15. What is personal credibility, and how is this related to expert status?

16. What methods can be used to include the views of experts?

17. Why would we want to refer to work published elsewhere? Give three reasons.

18. How can a person's job or profession affect the strength of evidence?

19. What is "credibility by insistence"? When is it, and when is it not, acceptable to use signals such as "It is well known that"?

20. What are some of the occasions when there may be little or no articulable basis for an opinion or decision?

21. How can an example provide credibility? What is the connection between introduced lists and examples?

22. How can analogies be used to provide evidence for a point of view?

23. What is a hypothetical argument, and how might it be used to provide support for an opinion?

24. How can comparisons be used to provide evidence?

25. What are the forms of evidence used in technical documents?

26. Why do we often have to include disadvantages as well as advantages?

27. What are typical signals of the transition between advantages and disadvantages? What is a typical signal indicating continuity?

28. What is the three-part structure used to report and rebut an opinion? Where is it typically used?

29. What is meant by concession and rebuttal and how is that structure signaled?

30. What are the different types of evaluative writing?

Chapter 8
Technical Style

In this chapter you will learn about the need to express your information in ways appropriate to the purpose of your communication and type of document you are producing. You will also learn to recognize — and to write in — many different technical styles, and to identify the many factors affecting both formality and informality in technical writing. This chapter also explains the importance of tone in your writing and how different tones are appropriate for different communication purposes.

Review and Preview

The Concept of "Propriety"
Meaning and Principles
Propriety in Speech
Propriety in Writing
Styles for Special Documents
Elements of Propriety

Style
Definitions
Formal Technical Styles
Informal Technical Styles

Important Factors Affecting Formality
Intransitives, Passives and Actives
Word Choice
Punctuation and Emphasis

Tone
The Importance of Tone
Aggressive and Weak Tones
The Friendly "You" Tone
Tone in Correspondence

Review and Preview

After the introduction in *Chapter 1*, you have primarily been studying contents, structure and continuity in technical writing. *Chapters 2*, *3* and *4* concentrated first on typical contents for technical descriptions and documents generally, and then on how to organize, outline and signal the structure of that material. *Chapter 5* explained how skilled technical writers connect their technical facts and ideas together within a systematic network of material, thus achieving continuity in their writing. *Chapters 6* and *7* dealt with the contents and structure first of problem-solution texts, and then of evaluative writing.

What you communicate, and the order and continuity of your written expression, are obviously of vital importance. However, probably of equal importance is *how* you communicate your material — using an appropriate style and acceptable levels of conciseness, punctuation, grammar and other writing conventions. These are the subject of the next four chapters.

This chapter deals with propriety, style, formality and tone, and *Chapter 9* explains the principles of conciseness. All forms of punctuation relevant to technical writing are discussed in *Chapter 10*. Finally *Chapter 11* deals with common grammatical errors, word choice, and principles of revision and editing. *Chapters 12–15* discuss graphical and oral communication, document parts and presentation, and correspondence.

The Concept of "Propriety"

Meaning and Principles

Propriety means behaving in an acceptable manner, within established norms of behavior. We do not always behave in the same way, of course; it all depends on the situation we are in. The way we dress, for example, is highly dependent on the circumstances at the time. Clearly you would not wear jeans, a sweater and a baseball cap to a formal dance or an interview; or a swim suit to an evening in a pub; or a formal suit or dress to classes. Instead you wear clothing suitable for the occasion.

Note that there is nothing inherently "wrong" with items of clothing or a complete attire. They can only be judged to be appropriate or otherwise in the situation within which they are used. A swim suit, a formal dress or suit, a baseball cap, revealing nightwear, jeans and sweater, etc. are all appropriate in given circumstances. It is only if they are used in unsuitable situations or surroundings that we have to conclude that they constitute a breach of propriety. An example of impropriety in dress would be the wearing of large jewelry, heavy perfume or aftershave, or nose rings for a job interview.

Obviously there are degrees of impropriety. There is a range of clothing suitable for attending classes. Look around you and take note of the accepted "norm" in our culture, and of the differences individuals display within that norm. We may not have consciously considered what that norm is, or what it should be, but we are all aware of it. Most of us dress to be reasonably in accordance with this norm. We are also aware that the norm changes with the weather throughout the year — and perhaps also from year to year. There are also significantly different norms of dress in cultures throughout the world.

However, as long as we do not go beyond what others feel is appropriate dress in a given situation, we all feel we have the freedom to dress as we see fit. That is we can express our individual personalities within the confines of an ill-defined but nevertheless very real set of limits. Although we can dress any way we like in any situation (within bounds of decency and related laws of course), most of us prefer to dress in a "normal" way for any situation — so that others do not think we are weird!

Propriety in Speech

The principles of propriety apply equally well to speech. We speak differently to pets and babies than we do to adults; we also use a different tone and expression (as well as words) when speaking to our friends, members of our family, and loved ones. An informal discussion with a group of classmates would again be different, and so would a formal presentation to professors and students. As a professional, you will be expected to talk with, and to, many different people and groups in many different circumstances. These will all require you to present your work and ideas in manners appropriate to those circumstances.

Again, however, you have the freedom to express yourself in your own style within the accepted limits of the requirements of the speech situation. Especially in speech, you have great scope to present yourself and your personality through the way you present your message and the manner of your presentation. As long as you remain reasonably within the accepted norms for the type of speaking you are engaged in, such personal variation (of speech, variation, tone, manner and delivery) is to be encouraged.

Propriety in Writing

There are many types of technical document, which have all evolved to meet specific communicative needs. Because of this, they have also evolved different forms or "styles" of expression. Some are more obvious than others. For example, the style you would normally use for e-mail to a friend would be inappropriate for a formal report or a letter applying for a permanent position with an organization. Also the style you find in the advertising of technical products and services would not be suitable for the text of a formal report for your instructors — or your chief engineer in industry. Our writing must be suitable for the document, and therefore also suitable for the aims and circumstances appropriate for that document.

Once again, though, there is ample room for personal self expression within those established norms, although far less in formal legal documents and much more in informal writing (e.g. e-mail and memos). English provides us with a rich variety of ways of expressing ourselves, and you should actively seek to develop your own personal "style" of writing. As long as your method of expression is within the bounds of the stylistic requirements for the type of document you are writing, your work will be stylistically acceptable.

Styles for Special Documents

Some technical documents have very special styles, and when you are writing these you must adhere to the conventional styles used for them. Here are some of the more important technical documents and their styles.

Checklist 8.1: Special Styles for Technical Documents

✓ **Abstracts** (as opposed to summaries) tell readers what is in the document and therefore have two linguistic forms: (a) the document, author or related topic as subject of the sentence, and/or (b) use of the present passive (e.g. is analyzed (in this paper)).

✓ **Instructions** use the imperative mood, clear step-by-step instructions, and separate labeling of steps with use of appropriate diagrams.

✓ **Patents** are written in a special legal style with absolute technical clarity and very clear reference within the text and illustrations.

✓ **Specifications** use one of three possible styles: (a) the instruction style, (b) the "standards" or legal style, or (c) simply a list of topics and the required materials or technical requirements.

✓ **Standards** (also contracts and many other legal documents) list requirements using the formal "shall" form of expression for legal insistence.

In addition, some documents require very precise, clear commands or instructions, while other require a friendly rather than a formal tone. If your writing does not meet such basic requirements of style and tone, that would be a serious breach of propriety.

Elements of Propriety

There is more to the broad concept of "propriety" than simply using a style appropriate for the document your are writing. If you fail to meet other presentation requirements, your writing can fail badly.

Checklist 8.2: Elements of Propriety

✓ being within the established norms of expression for the circumstances of the communication and the type of document your are writing

> ✓ *the tone of your writing (i.e. whether you appear weak and assertive, or are being too dogmatic or bullying, or are presenting the material in a friendly or a formal manner)*
>
> ✓ *professional etiquette (i.e. whether you are observing the accepted codes of behavior for technical professionals and professionals generally)*

All of these elements of propriety must be observed at all times if you are to produce an effective technical communication.

Exercise 8.1: A Sense of Propriety

For each of the following examples, first decide whether there is any breach of propriety by (a) improper style for the document or circumstance (S), (b) inappropriate tone (T), or (c) unsuitable etiquette (E). Then suggest how you might improve the communications. You should expect some difference in opinion about some of these examples, and how they should be corrected. Note that context is often vital in considering propriety; writing that might be suitable for one context might be totally unacceptable in another.

> (a) *I have had extensive experience in your sort of business and so I am sure I can make major savings in your administrative control system if you give me the chance.*
> **Context:** *Student seeking permanent employment after two year's summer experience in related work.*
>
> (b) *I realize this is a poorly written report, but I just did not have time to do a good one. There is so much other work I have to do, and I hope you will take this into account.*
> **Context:** *A note accompanying an end-of-course report.*
>
> (c) *All work ought to be of a reasonably high level of workmanship.*
> **Context:** *A clause in an engineering contract.*
>
> (d) *I most gratefully accept your invitation, and you have my every assurance that I will co-operate with you fully in effecting successful execution of this matter.*
> **Context:** *Best man writing to the bride's parents.*
>
> (e) *We stuck the electric plug in the hole and got the machine going.*
> **Context:** *Part of a procedure for a laboratory report.*
>
> (f) *"Haven't you done that list yet? I need it, so you'd better drop everything else and get it done."*
> **Context:** *Opening remark to a colleague of equal status.*
>
> (g) *I stopped at the red traffic lights beaming brilliantly into the oppressive darkness of the night. The lights cast a myriad ripples from the wet surface of the road.*

Context: Part of an accident report for insurance and legal purposes.

(h) *I feel there is something I should tell you at this stage in my application, and this is that I wear spectacles. Based on my rather limited experience of workplace environments, however, I venture to suggest that this would not be a seriously adverse factor in my employment with you.*

Context: Part of a letter for summer employment.

(i) *The writer conversed with Jackson and Ryder about this matter, and they expressed the opinion that their work would not be seriously affected by their relocating their place of work to the new building.*

Context: Part of a memo to an immediate supervisor.

(j) *Perhaps your organization would be good enough to provide us with delivery of these items as soon as you are able to do so.*

Context: Response to the Delivery Required *part of a purchasing contract.*

Style

Definitions

We have already seen the word "style" used in two or three different ways, and we need to clarify its meanings before proceeding. Unfortunately, perhaps, "style" has many different meanings:

Checklist 8.3: Some Meanings of Style in Writing

✓ *the manner of presentation appropriate for different documents (instruction style, list style, "shall" legal style, etc.)*

✓ *as a more general indication of a form of writing (e.g. legal writing, advertising or "sales" writing, technical writing, poster prose, literary style)*

✓ *as an indication of the personal expression of individuals, also known as "idiolect"*

✓ *the degree of formality or informality of a document (e.g. formal style)*

✓ *as programmed "formats" (e.g. for letters and memos) for repetitive use on computers*

Formal Technical Styles

Although we tend to talk of "formal technical writing" as if it were a single well-defined style, there is in fact a broad range of styles that can be called "formal." These range from the styles found in very formal technical legal documents through formal technical papers published in professional journals, to quite formal technical reports and proposals. You always have to decide on (or find out) the level of formality appropriate for the type of writing your are producing.

Here is an example of technical legal writing:

8.1
```
The building official for the town gave evidence on behalf of the Association which confirmed that the town had concerns with respect to the wood beams supporting the first floor joists and glulam window arches shown on the first drawings, which were submitted to the town in January 1990. Investigation by the town revealed over-stressing by at least 250% for the central wood beam and as much as 150% for the wood beams framing the glulam window arches at the second floor. The engineer submitted a further three sets of revised drawings to the town before the building department considered them acceptable enough to issue a permit.
   — Engineering Dimensions,
     Mar/Apr 1992, P3 Gazette
```

There are many indications of formal style in this example:

(a) the one single paragraph,
(b) the long complex sentences,
(b) the use of technical terms and the clarity of technical detail,
(c) the use of "reporting" rather than "reported" speech,
(d) the anonymity of *the town* and *the building department* and the use of *The building official* and *the engineer* rather than their names, and
(e) the use of the passive voice in *were submitted*.

You should also note the *absence* of indications of informality. Some of these are the opposite of those stated above (for paragraphs, sentences, reporting, naming, etc.). Others are the lack of contractions, colloquialism, metaphors, quotations, dashes and other signals of informality. These are discussed later in this chapter.

Other indications of formal technical prose are found in the following example from a technical paper:

8.2
```
In recent years concerns have been raised regarding the potential hazardous nature of the waste (Nieto, 1989). These concerns have arisen because of the fact that toxic metals, such as lead, could leach out into the groundwater. This has
```

resulted in ASR being clas- | with more stringent govern-
sified as a regulated waste | ment regulations and public
in a certain number of | pressure for recycling,
regions in North America. | have made landfilling an
In the meantime, declining | increasingly unsatisfactory
landfill capacity and dif- | disposal option for ASR.
ficulties in obtaining per- | — *Canadian Journal of*
mits for new landfill sites | *Chemical Engineering,*
have created a major prob- | Jun 95, P357
lem for the shredding
industry (Repa and Sheets,
1992). These factors, along

The formal references to other published work, the clear cohesion with *These concerns*, *This*, and *These factors*, use of the acronym *ASR*, and the assessment-basis and cause-effect relations are additional factors compatible with a formal technical writing style. The long subjects in the last two sentences are also a feature of formal technical writing; the subject of the first sentence (*concerns . . . regarding the potential hazardous nature of the waste*) is also very long, but has been "split" by the passive verb form *have been raised*. The large paragraph, long sentences and technical vocabulary and subject matter are factors shared with those in *Example 8.1*.

Note that such writing, although the expected form of expression for formal technical writing, is not accepted by style checkers. Ask your own style checker what it thinks of these examples. You will probably be given advice to reduce sentence length, reduce the length and complexity of noun phrases, and perhaps other suggestions to make the writing more "readable." If you were to follow such advice, however, you would be making the writing unsuitable for its intended purpose and readers.

Writing Task

Rewrite *Examples 8.1* and *8.2* in a much less formal style, using shorter sentences and paragraphs and generally making the writing "easier" to understand. Make up any information you might need (about those involved, for example) in making your versions conform to the needs of an interesting general-interest article.

Checklist 8.4: Signals of Formal Technical Writing

✓ *long paragraphs*

✓ *long and complex sentences*

✓ *some long subjects*

✓ *some use of the passive voice*

✓ *clear signals of cohesion between sentences (using strong connectors)*

✓ *use of problem/solution, purpose/means, assessment/basis, and cause/effect relations*

✓ *formal citations of published work*

✓ *technical vocabulary and subject matter*

✓ *precise details provided as necessary*

✓ *euphemisms and political correctness (see later discussion)*

✓ *the* absence *of signals that indicate an informal style (see* Checklist 8.5)

Informal Technical Styles

Following the gradation from very formal to very informal, we can recognize that texts we might loosely regard as "informal" also cover a broad range of styles. At the more formal end, they merge with formal texts in a category we might regard as "semi-formal." Such texts, which we find as informative technical articles in magazines, contain some indications of formal writing and perhaps also some indications of informal writing. Here is an example of this style of writing:

> **8.3** Similarly, APEO has recently begun to examine whether our admissions process is fair, consistent, and meets the needs in 1992 and beyond. This issue is currently under study by a top-notch committee, which is anxious to receive input from any interested parties.
>
> Technically, we are being challenged by the best engineers of other countries to make more out of less (or in the instance of environmental issues, less out of less). Will we be up to the challenge? Can we continue to adapt to changing times?
>
> I believe that we can and we must, although it will take all of us working together to continue the transition — from university professors researching new techniques and theories, to practising engineers applying those theories to develop new processes and solutions.
>
> —*Engineering Dimensions*, May/Jun 1992, P3

The technical level of this extract is lower than in the formal texts, although the vocabulary is clearly intended for highly educated readers. The paragraphs are shorter, though they still contain meaningful groupings of information. The sentences are quite complex — especially the last one.

On the other hand, there are also signs of informality in this text. The use of *we*, *our* and *us* personify the text, and the two rhetorical questions make the text more dramatic and forceful. The loose parallel structure in the first sentence, the colloquial use of *top-notch*, and the faintly humorous parenthetical insertion in the second paragraph all add to the informality — as does the dash.

Lower on the scale of informality are informal journalistic articles providing information and perhaps also expressing the writer's views. Here is an example of such a style:

8.4

The Bank of Montreal invested $50 million in the construction of its opulent Institute for Learning, a glass-encased structure in Markham, Ont. that opened 18 months ago.
Matt Barrett, the bank's charismatic chairman and chief executive officer, describes it as an ``incubator of new ideas, an opportunity for all employees.''

It's not your typical training facility.
A 150-room hotel is situated on the premises. There's an exercise room, swimming pool, a gymnasium, social centre, a tuck shop and even a licensed lounge with fireplace and pool tables.

— *Computing Canada*,
June 1995, P1

In this style paragraphs rarely have more than one sentence, although the sentences can still be quite long. The subjects of the sentences, however, are very simple. The use of direct quotations and naming of the source of the information are distinct features of this style, and the writer injects personal subjective assessments by the use of *opulent*, *charismatic* and *even*. Contractions of *It's* and *There's* are also typical of this style, although the possessive form *bank's* is not a signal of informal style.

Other signals of informality are discussed in the next section of this chapter. However, we have already seen enough indicators of informal style to create a checklist.

Checklists 8.5: Signals of Informal Technical Writing

✓ *short paragraphs — often containing only one sentence*

✓ *simple subjects for sentences*

✓ *personal involvement of the writer, reader and those involved in the account including the use of personal pronouns — known as the "You"-tone (see later)*

✓ *inclusion of writer assessments*

✓ *rhetorical questions*

✓ *contractions*

✓ *word choice including colloquialisms, metaphors, similes and particle verbs (see Checklist 8.9)*

✓ *considerable use of quotations*

✓ *dashes and exclamation marks*

✓ *relaxation of some grammatical rules (including sentence fragments)*

✓ *use of weak conjoiners (e.g.* and, but, or) *as sentence starters*

✓ *the* absence *of signals that indicate a formal style (see Checklist 8.4)*

In e-mail commun-e-cations to friends, we often deliberately have fun with language and are not so concerned with following the accepted rules of grammar and usage. Letters and memos written to those we do not know on familiar terms can be fairly formal, but other letters and memos can be very informal — often as brief handwritten notes. Notes or e-mail messages to friends and co-workers are usually extremely informal, with a great deal of assumed shared knowledge:

8.5
```
<Thanks for your e. I'll dig up the details and get
<back to you in a day or so when I surface for air..
```
                    — personal e-mail message, 1995

As e-mail responses reply to known material (which is often re-copied with the return), replies can be very brief. The use of the contraction *I'll* and the abbreviation *e* for e-mail message is typical of such r-e-plies, as are the metaphorical and colloquial uses of *dig up*, *get back*, and *surface for air*.

Writing Tasks

1. Perhaps working in groups, create a director-e of as many words as you can using *e* as part of new abbreviations for discussing e-mail messages. Also work out all the ways you could use *e* as a verb and a noun. Then write a "fun" article for a magazine of your choice — or for the internet — explaining the new words and how they can be used.

2. Rewrite *Examples 8.3 — 8.4* in a more formal style.

Important Factors Affecting Formality

Intransitives, Passives and Actives

When we describe something and say what it is or has or does, there is no direct object and the verb is known as "intransitive." Typical intransitive verbs in technical writing are *be*, *have*, *occur* and *happen*. Intransitive verbs are seen in:

8.6 The analog Nova-Scrobe AB and digital Nova-Strobe DB stroboscopes *are* available with either high-performance internal rechargeable batteries or with an AC power cord. Weighing just 2 1/2 lb, these hand-held instruments *have* no heavy external battery packs.
— *Machinery and Equipment MRO*, Sep 94, P7

Most verbs, however, are "transitive," i.e. they *do* take direct objects, and transitive verbs can be in the "passive" or the "active" voice. The passive voice says what is or was done to something, and is typical of many forms of technical writing, especially experimental reports:

8.7 Before analysis, samples *were wetted* thoroughly with de-ionizing water and *viewed* through a 10X planachromat HD objective with transmitted light in Koehler illumination (10X final magnification). A green filter *was used* to enhance contrast of the ink particles.
— *Pulp and Paper Canada*, May 1995, P6)

This examples has three instances of the passive voice in the past tense, known simply as the "past passive." When we are writing about general things, the present passive *is used*:

8.8 The latitude employers have in managing their employees *is changed* by the introduction of a collective agreement. Management decisions, which *can be made* without consultation in a non-unionized environment, *may be challenged* through grievance and arbitration procedures. When management decisions *are reversed* in this way, managers may begin to doubt their right to manage.
— *Engineering Dimensions*, Mar/Apr 1995, P26)

When the writing does not say who or what did the action, it is called an "agentless" passive, as in the second and fourth instances of passives in *Examples 8.8*. However, when who or what did the action is added (usually with *by* or *through*), it is called an "agentive" passive, as in the first and third passives in *Example 8.8*. The second clause of the last sentence is in the "active" voice, as it says who did what to whom.

Checklist 8.6: Summary of Transitivity Statements

✓ *Intransitives (e.g. "The meter has a 1-10 V output.") have no direct object.*

✓ *Agentless Passives (e.g. "The output was measured.") say what was done but not who did it.*

✓ *Agentive Passives (e.g. "The output was measured by our research assistant.") say what was done and then who did it.*

✓ *Actives (e.g. "Our research assistant measured the output.") say who did something and then what was done.*

For most formal technical documents, we tend to use intransitives and agentless passives. This is because it does not matter who did things — only what was done, i.e. we are reporting repeatable procedures, and who did them is not important. Sometimes we may not know — or have not bothered to find out — who did something, as again that may not matter. Again the agentless passive is ideal for such circumstances.

When we want to emphasize *who* did something, we use the agentive passive (e.g. "It was done *by me*.") or another emphatic structure such as ("It was our supervisor who removed the samples."). On the other hand, if we are explaining what someone has done and that person is the subject of the writing, then the active voice is ideal. Thus for much formal writing, where we are discussing things, we often use more passives than actives. For less formal writing, when we may be discussing people as well as things, we often use more actives than passives. Actives are used extensively in letters, memos and e-mail messages; for these the passive voice could appear stilted and too formal.

It is possible to "hide" who did something or who has made a decision by using the agentless passive. Thus we might write "The decision has been made to . . ." rather than "I have decided to" if we wish to obscure the agent. When you see writing in the passive voice which could easily have been in the active voice, you might wonder whether the writer is deliberately (and perhaps unethically) trying to avoid stating the agent. On the other hand there are legitimate reasons for excluding the agent.

Checklist 8.7: Reasons for Excluding the Agent

✓ *we do not know who the agent is*

✓ *the agent is unimportant*

> ✓ *we do not wish to state who the agent is*

There are connections between the use of the active and passive voices and the level of formality.

Checklist 8.8: Connections Between Voice and Formality

✓ *Informal (Active): "Our research team tested the N3 hose to 1 million impulse cycles."*

✓ *Formal (Agentless Passive): "The N3 hose was tested to 1 million impulse cycles."*

✓ *Formal — stressed agent (Agentive Passive): "The N3 hose was tested to 1 million impulse cycles by our research team."*

Word Choice

Our choice of words in any writing task must reflect the level of formality we are seeking to achieve. We use longer, more complex words in formal writing:

> 8.9 Before proceeding with the three resolutions that have been received for presentation at the meeting, the President advised members present that resolutions at the Annual General Meeting are expressions of the meeting's opinion, for the guidance of Council in its decision process. Should a resolution be passed at the meeting, it would be referred to the Executive Committee and Council for further study and consideration.
>
> —*Engineering Dimensions*,
> Mar/Apr 1992, P1

Note the use of *proceeding*, the many *-ion* words (*resolution, presentation, expression, opinion, decision* and *consideration*), and *Should* followed by the subjunctive *be passed*. These are all compatible with a very formal style. In this example, the writer uses a combination of intransitive, active and passive verb forms to present the message.

In informal writing — and in many forms of speech — word choice can be a clear indicator of informality. The use of subjective adjectives or nouns (e.g. *beauty*), colloquial expressions (e.g. *a catch-22 situation*), and metaphors (e.g. *in the spotlight* meaning being closely examined) and similes (which overtly say what something is *like*) are typical examples of how words affect informality.

Another word-choice signal of informality is the use of two- or three-word verbs instead of a single verb. For such verbs the second word (e.g. *up* in *throw up* meaning *vomit*) is not a preposition as it is inseparable in meaning from the main verb form. Nothing is being thrown up in a positional sense. The second part of such verbs is called a "particle" and the verbs are called "particle verbs." Similarly in *move on* meaning *continue*, *on* is not a preposition meaning on something; it is a particle, inseparable in meaning from the main verb form. Some two- and three-word verbs (e.g. *get on with*) may not have clear formal counterparts. Particle verbs are found in informal writing and in speech.

The selection of connecting words between sentences also affects formality: weak conjoiners (*And, But, Or* and *So*) are used to start sentences and paragraphs only in informal writing. For formal prose, we use the strong connectors (e.g. *In addition, However, Alternatively, Therefore*) instead.

Exercise 8.1: Editing Informal Word Choices

For each of the following, identify the type of word choice that indicates informality: subjective words (S), colloquialisms (C), metaphors (M) and similes (Si), particle verbs (P) and weak connectors as sentence starters (W). Then rewrite each text to make it more formal. Note that there is nothing "wrong" with these texts as they are. They do, however, make ideal samples as an exercise in recognizing informal word choice and choosing more formal alternatives.

(a) *Although establishing any new business is difficult, the beauty of a career in arbitration and mediation is that it is ideally suited to development first as a sideline.*
— *Example 8.10:* Engineering Dimensions, *Mar/Apr 1992, P25)*

(b) *It's the best way to ensure that we, as a profession and as individuals, take our share of the leadership necessary to tackle the problems we all face. But we are in a catch-22 situation.*
— *Example 8.11:* Canadian Consulting Engineer, *Jan/Feb 1995, P38*

(c) *Several Ontario schools are also gearing up to deliver engineering curricula remotely, including the universities of Toronto and Waterloo, and McMaster University.*
— *Example 8.12:* Engineering Dimensions, *Jul/Aug 1995, P28*

(d) *As an integral part of the building envelope, windows have long been in the spotlight where heat loss is concerned.*
— *Example 8.13:* Canadian Consulting Engineer, *Jan/Feb 1995, P26*

(e) *But use of inert gases alone is not enough to achieve truly high performance, so it is imperative that new window technologies be combined.*
— *Example 8.14:* Canadian Consulting Engineer, *Jan/Feb 1995, P27*

(f) *It's time for Canadian industry to accept the challenge of technology and grab the opportunity that it offers.*
— *Example 8.15:* Pulp and Paper Canada, *Apr 1995, P19*

(g) *However the mill hung in there, the smaller capital projects had a better than expected effect and the economic turnaround meant prosperity.*
— *Example 8.16:* Pulp and Paper Canada, *Apr 1995, P10*

(h) *If a designer is starting from scratch, it would be useful to consult the energy-rating standard.*
— *Example 8.17:* Canadian Consulting Engineer, *Jan/Feb 1995, P27*

(i) *Start up went off without a hitch.*
— *Example 8.18:* Pulp and Paper Canada, *Apr 1995, P10*

(j) *Canada's transport industry is cleaning up its act.*
— *Example 8.19:* Engineering Dimensions, *Mar/Apr 1992, P10*

(k) *Arguments about whether ECF or TCF is the more environmentally friendly process are like arguing about how many angels can stand on the head of a pin.*
— *Example 8.20:* Pulp and Paper Canada, *May 1995, P13*

(l) *The push to put renewable energy sources on the power map may seem somewhat quixotic to some, but those in the independent power industry believe it's just a matter of time before the wisdom of wind farm and solar water heaters gains an edge over heavily subsidized nuclear plants and non-renewable technologies.*
— *Example 8.21:* Canadian Consulting Engineer, *Jan/Feb 1995, P22*

Checklist 8.9: Types of Word Choice Creating Informality

✓ *subjective adjectives and nouns*

✓ *colloquial words and expressions*

✓ *metaphors and similes*

✓ *particle verbs*

✓ *weak connectors as sentence starters*

✓ *crudities and swear words*

Crude words and swear words are, of course, an indication not only of informal style but of a crude character too. They are not acceptable in the communications of a professional person. The opposite, known as "euphemisms," are used in formal writing to make unpleasant statements more palatable. Thus we might write that a worker "Perhaps lacks the intellectual ability necessary for this task." instead of rather crude "This worker is a blithering idiot" or is "as thick as two short planks." The words "restrooms" and "conveniencies" are euphemisms of course.

Political correctness is a recent form of euphemism. It is kinder (although of course longer) to write about a "person with a mobility handicap" instead of a "cripple." Because of this it is now "politically correct" to use more acceptable terms. As an example it is now politically correct to refer to a someone as a "person with a disability" rather than a "disabled person," and to use "mentally challenged" instead of "mentally retarded."

However, you can go too far with political correctness. Rather than saying a "short, fat, bald, old man," we might (jokingly, of course) refer to him as a "height-deprived, well-built, follically-challenged, experienced gentleman." An appropriate balance is needed.

Punctuation and Emphasis

The exclamation mark, although rarely used in technical writing, provides emphasis and often adds a note of surprise or incredulity (see overleaf). Dashes are much more common. They are used to separate incidental information from the rest of the sentence. In this role, they provide more emphasis than commas:

8.22

```
To establish credibility     for the first few occa-
and a track record in medi-  sions.
ation, it may be necessary        — Engineering Dimensions,
to offer services for a                  Mar/Apr 1992, P25
nominal fee — even gratis —
```

Dashes are also used to give emphasis to a final statement of a sentence:

8.23

```
''We don't consciously make  information.''
a bad environmental choice        — Canadian Consulting
— it may be a                             Engineer,
combination of lack of               Jan/Feb 1995, P28
information and mis-
```

As we see in this example, the apostrophe used to create contractions contributes to an informal style — and is the normal form in speech. Here is an example with several signals of informality and emphasis:

8.24

```
Wright added that the cli-   ond. ''What we need is the
mate for innovation is not   will and the climate to
as good as it must be to     implement our research and
make use of all that's hap-  technology activities.''
pening. It's a case of            — Pulp and Paper Canada,
reluctance of some of your             Apr 1995, P23
industry to be first, but
everyone wanting to be sec-
```

The *climate* is a metaphor of course, and there are two contractions. Emphasis is provided by the structure "What we need is" instead of the normal "We need."

Another structure used for emphasis is the rhetoric question, in which we first ask a question and then, usually, answer it:

8.25
What is Paprican looking for? As would be expected, one of the driving forces is the whole range of questions surrounding the environment. This includes eliminating some process chemicals that cause environmental concerns.
— *Pulp and Paper Canada*, Apr 1995, P22

Emphasis is also provided "orthographically" i.e., by the appearance of the text. Before the days of the computer, writers might deliberately write or type a word and strike it out, giving the impression that they have thought about the choice. Some writers might use, for example, "Dear Customer" and then strike it out in pen and use your name. This gives the impression they have consciously changed the level of personal connection. A similar effect can still be achieved by striking out in print, although it is now clearly deliberate:

Engineers m~~ust~~ w~~ill~~ *can* communicate!

— Title, *Canadian Consulting Engineer*, Jul/Aug, 1995, P25

The writer uses large type, strike outs, bold face, an exclamation mark and italics to provide emphasis for this title. Italics are the usual way of providing emphasis for single words, although underlining and bold type are also used. Note the importance of the emphasis in:

8.26
So if you want the right of appeal, say so in your contract. More important, if you **don't** want right of appeal, even on questions of law, you **must** spell this out in the contract.
— *Engineering Dimensions*, May/Jun 1995, P25

We can recognize a range of emphasis, from the usual unemphatic form to extreme levels of emphasis:

Checklist 8.10: Range of Emphasis for "cannot"

✓ *can't*	*normal form for speech*
✓ *cannot*	*normal form for writing*
✓ *can not*	*some emphasis on not*

✓ can not	*more emphasis on not*
✓ can NOT	*even more emphasis on not*
✓ I emphasize that we can **NOT**	*extreme emphasis on not*

Tone

The Importance of Tone

There is more to effective technical communication than contents, structure, and style. You must also give the right "tone" to your writing. What this means is that you must appear, through your writing, to be a responsible, trustworthy professional person — not someone who has little self confidence, or who is a bully, or has a domineering nature, or who has no understanding of or appreciation for the feelings of others.

You will often be writing to people who are senior to you in your organization — and also to those who will be your junior. Obviously the tone will be a little different. The tone will also change depending on many factors relating to the communication, such as the urgency and importance of the matter discussed, what authority you have, and your degree of personal involvement.

The tone of your writing can also indicate whether your are being friendly or "distant," whether you are being aggressive or pleading, or whether you are upset, annoyed or angry. It is not wrong to display your emotions sometimes of course — as long you know that is what you are doing and you have assessed what effect it might have on your readers.

You must, of course, always be polite in all forms of communication — a matter discussed more in *Chapter 9*. This may mean you will have to consider the effects your communication will have on those receiving it, and on those you send copies to. It may also mean that your writing is a little longer than you might think really necessary.

Aggressive and Weak Tones

There may be times to be quite aggressive and very assertive in your speech and writing. That is not wrong as long as you are not always aggressive! You may have to make something very clear to someone, and the tone you use will help to convey the importance of the matter. When you feel very strongly about a subject, your tone should reflect that. Note the quite aggressive tone in the following:

8.27

```
I find Becker's statement       look at old yearbooks, I
that some of today's engi-      see such events as Lady
neering students are            Godiva rides, where naked
''lacking in social             women were paraded through
graces'' offensive. When I      campus on horseback.
```

> How could such disgraceful acts have occurred when the students were being taught ``society's diverse val- ues'' by arts and humanities courses?
> — *Engineering Dimensions*, Mar/Apr 1992, P8

The words *offensive* and *disgraceful* are powerful words that help to set the assertive tone being used here. On the other hand you must not sound like a wimp — someone who has no self confidence and who you would not trust with an importance task. Note how the writer combines intransitives (*find* and *occurred*), actives (*look at* and *see*) and agentless passives (*were paraded* and *were being taught*) effectively in this extract.

The Friendly "You" Tone

Many documents convey a friendly, personal tone in which the writer uses the personal pronoun *you* to refer to readers, and often also *I* or *we* for reference to the writer or organization publishing the text. This tone is very clear in many technical advertisements:

8.28

> If *you* sometimes think that international competition has *you* caught between a rock and a hard place, *you* should be exploring the National Research Council. *We* can help *you* develop the technology or engineer the new products that will give *you* the competitive edge *you* need.
> — *Canadian Mining Journal*, Dec 1994, P10

Many communications are effective partly because they appeal directly to readers in this way, and because they recognize the needs or problems of readers and suggest or provide solutions to them. When your writing is giving help or advice to readers, you should consider using this tone. Note how the "You" tone is used in the previous sentence — and extensively throughout this book. Here is an example of the "You" tone and the imperative mood being used in a fairly informal article:

8.29

> If you can't resolve the dispute yourself, think of creative ways of seeking a solution. Is there and industry leader both parties respect who could give his or her opinion on who is right? Once you've exhausted all the avenues for resolving the dispute directly, you may need an independent third party to bring both sides together.
> — *Canadian Consulting Engineer*, Mar/Apr 1992, P24

Tone in Correspondence

Tone is very important in all forms of correspondence, and it is discussed more in *Chapter 15*. Here is a memo written for a person on a higher level in the organization than the writer. However, the writer has special responsibilities for, and concerns about, health and safety issues. Thus the tone of the memo is quite definite and assertive, while still being polite to and respectful of the recipient. Note how personal pronouns are used sparingly and effectively at different points in the memo.

Memorandum

To: Janice Freeman, P Eng, Manager, Calibration Division
From: Jan Novotnik, Health and Safety Department
Date: September 14,
Re: Monthly Health and Safety Inspection of your Department

I completed my monthly health and safety inspection of your department this morning. Several points need your attention.

The door to the trichloroethylene cleaning room was open, allowing fumes to escape into the general testing areas; this door should be kept closed at all times when not in use. Also in that room the "No Smoking" sign is missing, and there is evidence that workers have been using the room for smoking. As noted in Health and Safety Procedure CD.14, the trike room is to be used only to place and retrieve components in the baths for cleaning — no one is to stay in the room for more than a few seconds at a time.

Although most of your fire extinguishers have been checked regularly each month, the one near the entrance to the potentiometer calibration room has not been checked for 3 months. That extinguisher is also poorly located, as it is partially hidden from view when the door is left open. Relocation should solve both problems.

I found connecting cables reaching across the space between Row 6 and the new (temporary?) Row 7 to provide power for Row 7. As this is a tripping hazard, permanent wiring is needed if you propose to continue using Row 7.

When timed Watt-Hour calibrations are being conducted at finely-controlled fixed wattages, the calibrators are seated in the corridor at the ends of the rows. Those walking past the calibrators disturb their concentration, and the positioning of the calibrators partially blocks the corridors. This difficulty has been noted in earlier reports. I suggest you either:
(a) re-arrange the calibration stations so that they are within the spaces between the rows, or
(b) see if a reliable automatic wattage control mechanism can be designed to meet the rigid requirements of the Ministry inspectors.

Perhaps we could discuss this problem at the next company health and safety meeting.

1. Find examples (short articles or extracts) of informal writing in technical magazines of your choice. Then identify the signals of informal prose. Finally rewrite them in a more formal style.

2. Find some interesting technical advertisements, and rewrite them to make them suitable for newsworthy descriptions such as "New Product News" or as interesting general articles. (These are published free by many technical journals, as long as the writing is not overtly "selling" a product or service, so remove the "You" tone.) Write your material as "Press Releases" for the technical press to use.

3. Find examples (probably short extracts) of formal technical writing. Then identify the signals of formality. Finally rewrite them in a less formal style, making up individuals and other circumstances if necessary.

4. Find some brief informal articles or descriptions of new products, and rewrite them as very informal advertisements, using the "You" tone.

Review Questions

1. What is "propriety"? Explain how it applies to (a) dress, (b) table-manners, and (c) behavior on a first date.

2. How is propriety in dress affected by (a) the weather, (b) different cultures throughout the world, and (c) the passage of time?

3. How does propriety apply to (a) speech and (b) writing?

4. What is the affect of propriety on personal style?

5. What are some special styles for some technical documents?

6. What are the elements of propriety?

7. What does "style" in technical writing mean?

8. What is meant by a "range of styles" in formal technical writing? Give examples of documents or types of writing to illustrate your answer.

9. What are the signals of formal technical writing?

10. What is meant by a "semi-formal" style?

11. What is meant by a "range of styles" in informal technical writing? Give examples of documents or types of writing to illustrate your answer.

12. What are the signals of informal technical writing?

13. What are the main stylistic features of e-mail messages?

14. What are "intransitive" verbs and when are they used?

15. What is the "passive" voice? What are present passives and past passives and when are they used?

16. What are agentless and agentive passives and when are they used?

17. Under what circumstances would we choose not to include an agent?

18. What is the connection between formality and the use of the passive or active?

19. What are typical word choices that indicate (a) a formal style and (b) an informal style?

20. What are colloquialisms? Give examples. How do they affect formality?

22. What are subjective nouns and adjectives? Give examples. How do they affect formality?

23. What are metaphors and similes? Give examples. When are they used?

24. What are particle verbs and when are they used? Give examples and explain why the particle is not called a "preposition."

25. How does the choice of sentence connectors affect formality?

26. When should professionals use crudities and swear words? Do not give examples!

27. What are "euphemisms" and when and why are they used? Give examples.

28. How is political correctness related to euphemisms? Give examples of political correctness and explain their use and problems.

29. What punctuation marks often indicate informality? Give examples of their use.

30. *What is a "rhetorical question"? How does it create informality?*

31. *What are "orthographic" methods of achieving emphasis?*

32. *What is meant by "tone" in technical writing? What sorts of tones can be conveyed?*

33. *What is the "You" tone? How is this tone related to the use of personal pronouns?*

34. *Where is the "You" tone most important, and where is it inappropriate?*

35. *What is the role of the "You" tone in semi-formal memos?*

Chapter 9:
Conciseness

A key element of technical writing is that it should be concise. In this chapter you will learn the major elements that create verbosity (the opposite of conciseness) and how to avoid them.

Conciseness in Large Documents

Conciseness and Continuity
Basic Continuity Devices
Combining Clauses and Sentences
Using Associations and Perspectives

Special Structures
Existential 'There'
Anticipatory 'It'

Other Methods
Tautologies and Pairing
Wordy Phrases
General Words
Expanded Verb Structures
Expanded Modifiers
Combining Sentences

Review: Politeness and Style
Applying the Methods
Politeness Strategies
Style
Final Note

Conciseness in Large Documents

We can take for granted that a brief report or proposal is better than a much longer one if they are equally clear and contain the same relevant information. No one wants to read through verbiage to get at the message — we all have better things to do. So it is important that all your technical writing is relevant to your task and as brief as possible. This section deals with general factors in large documents that can lead to verbosity (or lack of conciseness). Most of the remainder of the chapter deals with the many smaller elements of verbosity which, combined, can adversely affect the conciseness of your writing. The final section explains how you should consider style, politeness, audience and other factors in deciding how concise to make your writing.

By far the biggest single factor causing verbosity is the inclusion of large amounts of irrelevant material. If you are describing a new highly efficient wood stove for third world countries, there is no need for detailed discussion about how half the world is starving and how scarce wood is in many countries. Cover these briefly in the introduction if you have to and concentrate on the technical description and its evaluation. Similarly, if you are explaining the use of computers in language research, there is no need for a detailed account of the evolution of computers. That is largely irrelevant. Often huge sections, or even chapters, can be removed from a draft report or proposal if the writer has failed to understand the audience and the purpose of the document.

Likewise, you should not include large amounts of information already known to your readers. What is the point? True, you might occasionally need to summarize known information as a basis for the new material you are about to present. But keep that information very brief, and acknowledge that you know your readers already know it — with signals like "As you know . . . " or "It is generally accepted that . . . "

A third category of verbose information at the document level is repeated material. Again there are occasions when you will need to refer to information you have already discussed, but again acknowledge that and keep it very brief. References to earlier discussion can be quite general (e.g. *as mentioned earlier*) or can be specific references to discussion in an identified section — this is where numbered sections and subsections are particularly useful.

Finally, a great deal of writing can often be avoided by using illustrations, tables, graphs, etc. A picture may not really be worth a thousand words, but sometimes it can save several hundred — and it can also achieve more effective communication. Graphical communication does not have to be separate from the writing. Writers often combine writing and illustrations to give the best — and most concise — form of communication.

Checklist 9.1: Material to Avoid to Achieve Conciseness

✓ *information that is not relevant to the needs of your readers and the purpose of your document*

✓ *large amounts of information your readers already know*

> ✓ *unnecessary repetition of information you have already provided*
>
> ✓ *inappropriate use of words when illustrations or tables would be better.*

Exercise 9.1: Making a Letter More Concise

The following letter to the editor of *Popular Science* was written by a first-year engineering student. Note how all four parts of *Checklist 9.1* contribute to the verbosity, then make the writing more concise and add paragraphing. Attach a drawing and refer to it in your text.

Dear Editor:

I would like to relate to you my story about an experience I had over the last weekend. I had an interesting problem which I solved in a unique way. I thought you might like to publish this letter to help other readers of your magazine who might encounter a similar problem. It was Saturday morning when I decided that I would make myself a stand for my computer, printer, modem and other stuff, which I had recently purchased from the campus book store. All of us in engineering now have to buy our own computers. To make the stand, I first had to cut a 4 X 8 ft, 1/2 in. ply board lengthwise on my neighbor's table saw. The first problem I encountered was that I needed something adjacent to the table to support the board as it came off the table after being cut. The solution seemed simple enough. This was my use of a saw horse, which is a triangular trestle with a flat top. I placed this on the other side of the table containing the table saw and sawed some of the length of the wood. But then I found the saw horse was too low. This was another problem, which I decided to solve by adding a 3 ft length of 2 X 4 in. wood onto the top of the saw horse to raise its altitude to that of the table saw table. So I nailed it to the top of the saw horse. This is where the real problem was encountered. The piece of wood I was cutting kept sticking against the top of the wood I had attached to the top of the saw horse, causing a great deal of friction. This friction caused the piece of wood I was cutting to vibrate. It was so bad it caused a bad cut and even knocked the saw horse over onto the ground. After further examination, I discovered that the friction had caused the cut to be jagged. As I was pondering the situation, I noticed my friend rolling out some dough with a rolling pin, and an idea came to me. I "borrowed" the rolling pin and found another one and attached them onto a frame using dowel pins. I then clamped the assembly onto the original saw horse after I had first removed the 2 X 4 in. piece of wood that I had previously attached to the top of it. I made sure that the height of the new clamp device on the saw horse was the same as the table containing the table saw. This was to avoid the first problem I had had. I tried it out and it worked well. As I cut the wood, it moved out over the rollers , and I was able to achieve a really good straight cut. I thought your readers might be interested in knowing about my invention, and so I am bringing it to your attention.

Conciseness and Continuity

Basic Continuity Devices

The techniques used to achieve continuity in a text (*Chapter 5*) are a sound basis for understanding several important aspects of verbosity — and how to remove them. Clearly partial repetition is more concise than full repetition, and the use of generic nouns, acronyms and substitution can be even more concise. Where appropriate, statements can be combined using ellipsis or lists to achieve even greater levels of conciseness.

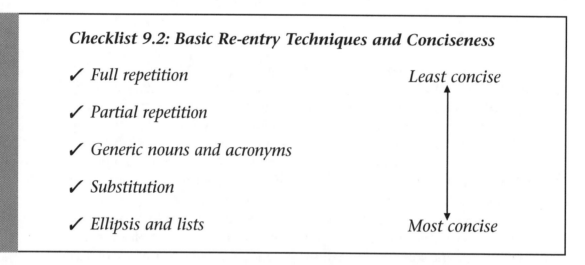

Checklist 9.2: Basic Re-entry Techniques and Conciseness

✓ *Full repetition*   *Least concise*

✓ *Partial repetition*

✓ *Generic nouns and acronyms*

✓ *Substitution*

✓ *Ellipsis and lists*   *Most concise*

See *Exercises 5.1 — 5.4* for practice in using basic re-entry, substitution, clausal ellipsis and lists to improve the conciseness of your writing.

Combining Clauses and Sentences

Just as we can achieve greater conciseness by using substitution, ellipsis and lists, we can also use relative, -ed, -ing and verbless clauses to make our writing more concise — and also more mature. Remember that we can often remove *which* plus the following form of the verb *to be*. By converting relative clauses to -ed, -ing and verbless clauses in this way, we remove the often too repetitive *which* from our writing, as well as making it more concise. This also adds variety to our style, especially as the new clauses can be moved to the front of the sentence if we like. Here are examples of how to convert from relative clauses to -ed, -ing, and verbless clauses.

Checklist 9.3: Condensing Relative Clauses

✓ *Our printer, which was manufactured by Hewlett Packard, produces high quality prints.*

> *Our printer, manufactured by Hewlett Packard, makes high quality prints.*
>
> ✓ *This design, which relies on work by last year's team, results in a superior product.*
>
> *This design, relying on work by last year's team, results in a superior product.*
>
> ✓ *MS3-C steel rods, which are available in three standard diameters, are ideal for many applications.*
>
> *MSC-3 steel rods, available in three standard diameters, are ideal for many applications.*

Using -ed, -ing and verbless clauses allows us to write two or more statements in a much more concise way. See *Exercises 5.6 — 5.8* for the use of descriptive clauses to improve both style and conciseness.

Using Associations and Perspectives

Instead of writing "The car has a turning circle.," which is insulting to technical readers, as it is so obvious, we can use a post-triggered association ("The turning circle of the car is . . . "). Or we can use a pre-triggered ("The car's turning circle is . . . ") or untriggered form ("The turning circle is . . . ") to make the writing even more concise. As another example "Tests were made on the vibration resistance of the instrument." can be converted into the much more concise — and mature — "Vibration resistance tests . . . ." Thus by using associations, we can make our writing more concise and appropriate for technical readers.

Similarly, we can use untriggered perspective connections to improve conciseness. See *Exercises 5.9* and *5.10* for the use of associations and perspectives to improve both style and conciseness.

Special Structures

Existential 'There'

One type of *there* indicates place (in that place, or over there), and another is used as a soothing, pacifying statement ("There, there, dear."). A third type is known as "existential" *there* because it announces the existence of something in a formal way. A well-known use is as an introduction for children's stories (*"There* was once a slimy, green frog . . ."). In technical writing existential *there* is also used to announce something:

9.1 *There* are two main types of mesoscopic framework components, descriptively called dendriform and lamelliform elements.
— E. Turner, G. Narbonne and N. James, Department of Geological Sciences, 1995

This formal announcement of the two types is appropriate because it establishes the types first, and is followed by details about each type later in the text. Existential *there* is ideal for such communication needs.

However, many writers over-use existential *there*, often using it as a sort of throat clearing device while they are thinking what to write next. Used in this way, existential *there* is verbose, repetitive and poor technical style. So you should avoid existential *there* unless it is serving a useful purpose. Examples of its verbose use and improvements are:

Checklist 9.4: Examples or Verbosity with Existential 'There'

✓ **Verbose Use**	✓ **Improvement**
There are many people who disagree with the government's policy on tuition fees.	Many people disagree with the government's policy on tuition fees.
There are two letters of support and these are included.	Two letters of support are included.
There is a fault in the d.c. amplifier. This is causing the output to vary.	A fault in the d.c. amplifier is causing the output to vary.

Note how the existential *there* makes the introductory statement quite dramatic. If you want to give that effect, then use existential *there* — but not very often. Other uses of existential *there* are:

Checklist 9.5: Some Uses of Existential 'there'

✓ *formal announcement (see* Example 9.1)

✓ *existence as untriggered perspective (see* Chapter 5*):*
There was very little discussion.
— *Example 9.2*: Pulp and Paper Canada, *May 1995, P1*

✓ *unemphatic introduction:*
The authors point out that there is still a large step from TCF to TEF bleach plant, and an even larger one to the TEF mill.
— *Example 9.3*: Pulp and Paper Canada, *May 95, P15*

Exercise 9.2: Removing Existential 'there'

Remove existential *there* from the following:

a) *There are typical construction applications including uses in water tanks, pumps and water haulage equipment.*

(b) *There are three voltage scales: 0.1, 1 and 10 V.*

(c) *There is also a discussion included in this report concerning reliability and safety factors.*

(d) *There are four different methods used, and these are shown in Figure 4.*

(e) *Surrounding the pump there is a case. This has been molded to conform to the user's hip. There is also a strap so that the pump can be worn while the worker is performing a task.*

Note the differences between "There are three ways of doing this:" and "Three ways of doing this are:." The first is an introduced list and therefore *must* be followed by a colon (or a separate sentence), whereas the second is a continuing list, and therefore *may* be followed by a colon. Also the first states that there are *only* three ways, whereas the second implies there are other ways and we are only mentioning three of them. "*The* three ways . . . " would make the second version mean the same as the first.

Anticipatory 'It'

In sentences such as "It is hard to predict the results.," *It* "anticipates" the last four words in the sentence and *hard* evaluates them. This sort of *it* is called an "anticipatory" *it*. Such sentences are often extremely useful, especially when the part being anticipated is quite long. However, some writers use anticipatory *it* too much, creating verbosity. Typical verbose introductions are "It is noted that . . . ," "It can be seen that . . . " and "It should be emphasized that." You can often delete the whole introductory phrase. Often a simple connector can be used instead of an anticipatory *it* phrase. For example instead of "At this stage in the discussion *it* can be concluded from the data presented earlier that . . . " we can use *Thus* or *Therefore*, which mean the same thing.

Occasionally it may be important to emphasize something. When it is by all means use anticipatory *it* to say so. There are many other uses for anticipatory *it*. Here are the most important:

> ### Checklist 9.6: Some Uses of Anticipatory 'It'
>
> ✓ *to signal probability:*
> *Therefore, it seems likely that the ore is of magmatic origin.*
> — *Example 9.4:* Canadian Mining Journal, *Feb 1995, P8*

✓ to indicate uncertainty:
At this time, it is unclear how the decommissioning of the site will be financed.
— Example 9.5: Nuclear Canada, *Jul/Aug, 1994, P1*

✓ to indicate basis and conclusion:
It is clear from examining Figures 12 and 13 of Aitken (1988) that the "laminae," "septa," and "walls" are themselves threads.
— Example 9.6: E. Turner, G. Narbonne and N. James, *Department of Geological Sciences, 1995*

Exercise 9.3: Removing Anticipatory 'It'

Remove anticipatory *it* from the following sentences only where its use cannot be justified. Justify the use of the others.

(a) It should be noted that thirteen types of coals were used for this study.

(b) In light of these observations it can be concluded at this point in the discussion that claims were staked with the hope of finding ore deposits.

(c) It was observed that the rms output voltage oscillated at 2.3 V once every 3.4 s.

(d) It was reported to me by Ms Jones during a telephone conversation that our proposal had been approved.

(e) It is worth noting that further progress in this line of enquiry, it is believed, is not likely to prove fruitful.

Other Techniques

Tautologies and Pairing

Some writers have the unfortunate habit of saying the same thing twice in consecutive words, known as "tautologies." If, for example, we write "past history," the *past* is redundant because all history involves the past. We could, of course, use "ancient history," or "recent history," or "Canadian history," as these add something new in the adjective.

Checklist 9.7: Examples of Tautologies

✓ Tautology	✓ Possible improvement
attached together	attached
collaborate together	collaborate
essential pre-requisite	pre-requisite
vital essentials	essentials
ohms of resistance	ohms
watts of power	watts
sufficient enough	sufficient

In context you might find uses for some of these to provide emphasis (e.g. *absolutely essential*), to provide clarification (e.g. *attached together* — not to something else), or to provide information (*ohms of resistance*) when writing to readers who are unfamiliar with the subject. Otherwise you should avoid tautologies.

Occasional inclusions of tautologies will probably not make much difference to the conciseness of your writing, but their constant use will certainly make a significant difference. More importantly, perhaps, some of your readers will be more attuned to this form of verbosity than any other — and they will jump on your "errors" with great glee, and think you are poorly educated.

Related to tautologies are redundant pairs of words that mean the same thing. This is extremely common in legal writing, e.g. *aid and abet, break and enter* (the "break" means break the plane at the threshold of the premises, and is the same as "enter"), *all and every, cease and desist*. In technical writing, we often find *produce and manufacture, determine and calculate, adjust and modify*, etc. where, in their contexts, one of the words is unnecessary. Remove these too.

Exercise 9.4: Removing Tautologies and Unnecessary Pairings

Remove the tautologies and unnecessary pairing in the following. Justify any you decide to leave in.

(a) *If recycling is legally required by law, it will become less popular.*

(b) *High-sensitivity airborne surveys were, for the most part, primarily used for the exploration for diamonds.*

(c) *This technique is ideal for the production and manufacture of micro-circuits.*

(d) *It is absolutely vital that senior managers of this company understand the past history of our organization and structure.*

(e) A resistor having 10 ohms of resistance was used for this purpose.

Wordy Phrases

When writers try to be pompous or to impress their readers with what they think is an eloquent style, they sometimes use unnecessarily wordy phrases such as:

Checklist 9.8: Examples of Wordy Phrases

✓ Wordy phrases	✓ Possible improvement
in the event that	*if*
in view of the fact that	*because, as, since*
conditional on the occurrence that	*when*
prior to the time of	*before or until*
subsequent to	*after*
in the case of	*for*
in the order of	*about*
at some time in the near future	*soon*

Note, however, that there may be differences between the longer and shorter forms in context. For example *in the event that* indicates an unlikely event (which could be emphasized by *in the unlikely event that*), whereas *if* does not have that meaning. Also note that some of the wordy phrases can form the basis for very useful structures, such as *in view of the possibility that* or *in view of the surprising fact that*, demonstrating again that the wordy phrases often have slightly different meanings than the shorter versions in context. So use shorter forms whenever they are suitable, and only use the longer versions when you need to express something slightly different. The longer forms are more formal.

Exercise 9.5: Removing Wordy Phrases

Use shorter forms for the following sentences. Then see if you can recognize how some of the meanings of the longer form might be justifiable to indicate special meanings.

(a) In view of the fact that your application was late, we could not consider it.

(b) *In the case of very limp porous materials, fluid models still apply even in the event that the materials are bonded to a plate.*

(c) *Prior to the time of the arrival of these components, we will continue to use the older type and make appropriate adjustments.*

(d) *The unsolicited takeover bid is perhaps likely to be accepted by the board at some time in the immediate future.*

(e) *However such an acceptance will be conditional on the occurrence of an increase in the bid in the order of 10%.*

General Words

It is often possible to delete certain general words that contribute nothing to the message. Here are some examples:

Checklist 9.9: Examples of Verbose General Words	
✓ *General Words*	✓ *Possible Improvement*
costs the sum of	costs
fined in the amount of	fined
in the city of Kingston	in Kingston
in the year 1998	in 1998
in the country of Australia	in Australia
for a period of 5 years	for 5 years

Such wording is used in legal writing, e.g. "in the City of Kingston, in the County of Frontenac, in the Province of Ontario" instead of simply "Kingston, Frontenac County, Ontario." Lawyers and accountants often use such phrases, which arguably play a role in being consistent stylistically with very formal announcements or decrees. In most technical writing, however, the phrases are generally inadvisable, although they are used in complex titles for technical papers.

An important exception is the avoidance of ambiguity. Readers might be a little perplexed with "in 2000" because the new century is still quite new; the longer form may be more appropriate. Also "the city of Quebec" may be needed to avoid confusion between the city and the province.

Exercise 9.6: Removing General Words

Remove the unnecessary general words in the following. Retain any useful ones.

(a) The mine is located in the Northern forests of the Province of Quebec.

(b) COMPASS monitors the traffic flow along the transportation route Highway 401 west of the City of Toronto.

(c) A large increase in uranium will be needed by the year 2020 to meet projected needs for nuclear power generation.

(d) The wattmeter reading was observed continuously for a period of time equal to 15 minutes.

(e) The author Day (1991) reported that the gases H, N, and O were used for this analysis.

Expanded Verb Structures

Another possible source of verbosity is the use of expanded verb structures (e.g. *make a study of*) when a shorter form (e.g. *study*) is just as clear. Here are other examples:

Checklist 9.10: Examples of Expanded Verb Structures

✓ Expanded Verb Structures	✓ Possible Improvement
make an examination of	examine
take out a patent on	patent
provide information	inform
hold a discussion on	discuss
have a preference for	prefer
take a measurement of	measure
conduct an investigation into	investigate
effect an improvement on	improve
give consideration to	consider

However, again the longer form may prove useful as the basis for a special meaning you wish to express. We may wish to write *took out an interesting patent on*, or *have a special preference for* rather than the shorter forms. As most formal technical writing is in the passive voice, we can see the usefulness of the longer forms in the passive, e.g. *an examination was made, measurements were taken, an investigation was conducted*, and *consideration will be given to*.

Another use of the expanded verb structures is in abstracts, which tell readers what is in the document. We may not wish to use the shorter forms for *This report evaluates* or *This proposal concludes that* as documents are inanimate objects, incapable of such human activities as evaluating or concluding. So instead we can use the longer forms *This report includes an evaluation*, and *This proposal presents the conclusion that*. (See *Page 298*.)

Exercise 9.7: Converting Expanded Verb Structures

Convert the expanded verb structures in the following examples into shorter forms. Then think of possible uses of the longer forms.

(a) *The company made a decision to take out a patent on the idea after conducting an investigation of its marketability.*

(b) *The committee held a discussion on whether to give consideration to the additional information submitted.*

(c) *The engineering team made an examination of the competitive products as the basis for effecting improvements in our own products.*

(d) *Students are asked to provide information to their advisors regarding whether or not they have a special preference for a particular scheduling of their laboratory sessions.*

(e) *In making an application to file an appeal, Barlow and Felhabur were following the wishes of their clients.*

Expanded Modifiers

It is often possible to change post-modifying restrictive clauses into pre-modifying adjectives or adverbs (e.g. changing "items that were damaged" into "damaged items" using the adjective *damaged*, and changing "without any undue difficulty" into the adverb *easily*). Here are other examples:

Checklist 9.11: Examples of Expanded Modifiers

✓ Post-modification	✓ Adjective or adverb
the model designed last year	*last year's model*
extinguisher used to fight fires	*fire extinguisher*

the resistors having a 5 Watt capacity	*the 5-Watt resistors*
within a reasonable period of time	*quickly*
without any noticeable variation	*smoothly*
at a high level of efficiency	*efficiently*

There is a practical limit to this technique, however. If you wrote "A $1.5 million tinned-goods, computer-operated, pushbutton, theft-proof supermarket . . . " readers may have some difficulty digesting all the information you have crammed into this subject. A sensible compromise is needed.

Exercise 9.8: Using Pre-Modifiers or Adverbs

Make the following more concise by converting the post-modifications into pre-modifiers or adverbs. Note any subtle changes of meaning.

(a) *This step must be made within a reasonable span of time or else the glue will set.*

(b) *A 60,000-tonne-per-day operation should yield 139,000 tons of copper on an annual basis.*

(c) *It has been claimed that grass units that have been grown hydroponically produce animal feed at about half the cost of units that have been produced conventionally.*

(d) *Plants of the type that can be eaten by humans are not the only ones that have proved adaptable to environments that contain no soil.*

(e) *Since sounds at the low end of the owl's spectrum yield clues to azimuth and sounds that are produced at the high end of the spectrum yield clues to elevation, the owl can produce enough sound information to locate its prey.*

Combining Sentences

A significant way for many writers to improve their conciseness is to combine ideas into longer sentences while still retaining the required connection between the statements. If you find yourself using *Therefore, However, Moreover* and other such connectors rather a lot in quite short sentences, you should consider combining your sentences more if you are writing to fellow professionals. One way of doing this is to use subordinators (e.g. *although, in addition to, because of*) if the information in the subordinate clause is known or would be readily accepted by your readers:

9.7 *Despite* its wide array of properties, Exall Resources has narrowed its focus to two key assets: the Mazaruni River gold-diamond project in Guyana and the large Santo Tomas copper-gold mine in Mexico's Sinaloa state.
— *The Northern Miner,* Jul 10, 1995, P1

As readers either know that Exall has a wide array of properties, or would readily accept that assertion without question, the subordinate clause is ideal — and more concise than using two sentences. If you stated a fact that is well known to your readers as a separate sentence without an acknowledging *of course*, it could of course be insulting to them. Subordination acknowledges the "knownness" of information in a mature and concise way.

Checklist 9.12: Comparing Three Types of Connection

✓ subordinators	✓ connectors	✓ conjunctions
although, in spite of, despite	however, nevertheless	but, yet
whereas	however, nevertheless	but, yet
in addition to, as well as	in addition, moreover, also, indeed	and
because, since, as	therefore, thus, hence	so, and so

The connectors differ from the conjunctions in that they can occur in many different places in the sentence, whereas the conjunctions always occur at the start of their clause or sentence. Another important difference is that connectors require strong punctuation (a semicolon or a period), whereas the conjunctions usually occur with a comma or no punctuation.

Another way of avoiding too many heavy connectors (*however, moreover, therefore,* for example) is to use *but, and* and *so* instead — especially for "plain" writing to the general public. A further method of achieving conciseness is simply to combine two statements, as shown by:

Separate Sentences
Another approach might be to go high-tech. This could be achieved by providing video packages for enhanced learning.

Single Sentence
Another approach might be to go high-tech by providing video packages for enhanced learning.

Although some computer style checkers may try to convince you to write using short sentences, use longer ones if you wish your writing to be appropriate for educated readers — or if you wish to make your writing more concise.

Exercise 9.9: Combining Sentences

Make the following more concise by combining the sentences.

> (a) *The police had several objectives. One of these objectives was to ensure that the settlement of the Canadian west was not marked with the excessive violence so familiar on the American frontier.*
>
> (b) *Storm windows partially solve the problem. They do this by emitting light while reducing heat reduction losses.*
>
> (c) *The program will terminate. This will happen when the regulation has been officially amended.*
>
> (d) *Dr. Shahami has established himself as a leading authority on the role of lactobacilli in human nutrition. He has achieved this leading status by leading research projects throughout the world and publishing over 150 papers.*
>
> (e) *We save you time and money. We do this by eliminating duplication of your efforts.*

Politeness and Style

Applying the Methods

In your understandable desire to be concise in your writing, it may be all too easy for you to adopt an unbending attitude toward what is verbose. A little knowledge of conciseness can lead you to apply the methods discussed in this chapter without enough thought, and that could harm your writing. Your writing is *too* concise if you remove useful information. If, for example, you changed "Brenda Sullivan, a company located in Vancouver, . . . " to "Brenda Sullivan, of Toronto, . . . ," you would have left out the important information that it is company, not a person, we are discussing.

Also none of the methods provided in this chapter should be accepted as *always* indicating verbosity, and acceptable uses for the possibly verbose structures have been noted for each method. You must develop an understanding of how and where to use existential *there*, anticipatory *it*, expanded verb structures, and all the other methods, rather than simply not using them at all. You would be doing yourself and your readers a great disservice if you decided not to use the methods discussed in this chapter just because some writers use them repetitively and in a verbose manner.

There is also a valid argument in favor of extending the writing on some occasions. Where the concept you are explaining is particularly complex, you will need to help your readers to assimilate the information. This may involve more repetition, examples and explanation than would be needed if you were explaining a simpler concept. Your audience is also important, as you may need to be less concise to readers unfamiliar with the subject of your writing. The level of verbosity you include in any particular writing task should be a conscious choice, and not the result of arbitrary rule-following.

It is even more important to adopt a liberal approach when you are editing someone else's writing. There are few absolutes in conciseness, and it would be a pity if you destroyed someone's pleasant, though slightly verbose, style in the name of conciseness. However, you should correct significant instances of verbosity, and inform the writer of recurring weaknesses in the writing.

Politeness Strategies

You should also be aware that conciseness is only one of many factors to consider in your writing. No one with normal social perceptions would go to a secretary, thrust a page of writing on the desk, and say *"Type — now!."* That would be extremely concise, of course, and the message would be extremely clear, but it would be an inappropriate communication because it would be impolite. Instead, we might say something like "I wonder if you would type this for me as soon as you can?" or "Do you think you'll be able to type this in the next hour or so?" Yes, it is much more verbose — but it is also much more effective as a communication because it is polite.

In all personal communications — in speech and writing — you need to consider politeness, especially when you are making requests. A friendly tone and consideration of the personal feelings of those you deal with can be much more important than conciseness in many letters, memos and e-mail communications.

Exercise 9.10: Being Polite

For each of the following, identify the causes of impoliteness and suggest how to eliminate them. Note that you may have to make the examples *less* concise to achieve an acceptable level of politeness.

(a) *"Haven't you done that list yet? I need it so you had better drop everything and get it done."*
    Context: *A request for a co-worker of equal status.*

(b) *I have had extensive experience with your type of business, so I am sure I can make many improvements to your company if you let me.*
    Context: *Part of a letter of application for summer employment.*

(c) *As you have supported this organization for many years, please sell all the enclosed lottery tickets and send us the proceeds no later than March 27.*
    Context: *A complete letter.*

(d) *Sign the attached form as course instructor.*
   Context: A complete note from a student to an instructor asking for exemption from the instructor's course.

(e) *This is a mess. Rewrite it by tomorrow.*
   Context: *A note from an instructor attached to an uncorrected technical proposal.*

Style

There may initially be a tension between your developing personal style and conciseness in your writing. You will need to develop a feel for what is acceptable and appropriate in a given piece of writing, and learn to trade off conciseness with legitimate ways of self expression. Be especially careful with the personal style of the writer when you are editing someone else's writing.

Style is also affected by the type of document you are writing. Formal technical reports and proposals rarely contain much verbosity, but letters, memos, and e-mail communications may contain more because of the need for politeness and because of the less formal nature of the writing.

Oral reporting is *much* more verbose than any form of writing. In this form of communication, conciseness is rarely cause for concern unless there is considerable repetition of information. Bear this in mind if you write a text to be read orally; concise written explanations are not really suitable for oral presentations because they are usually too concise! You may need to make the writing less concise to make it suitable for reading aloud.

A further factor in considering style and conciseness is that you need to adopt a less concise writing style for younger readers or for those struggling to understand a difficult topic. The less concise "Plain Style" of writing is suitable for such readers — but not for fellow professionals.

Final Note

The major methods of achieving conciseness in your writing have been discussed in this chapter. However, it is not a complete list, and you may find others that will help you to be more concise when you need to.

From this chapter, you should have gained a sense of what to look for in making writing more concise. You should also have become aware of some of the pitfalls you can fall into if you unthinkingly accept the advice of style checkers. Many of the techniques discussed here are noted by style checkers as being inappropriate in writing. That is not always so, and you must develop an ability to make intelligent decisions about whether, when and how to use all of the techniques explained in this chapter.

Checklist 9.13: Methods of Achieving Conciseness

✓ *basic continuity devices*   - *substitution*
                                     - *generic nouns*
                                     - *acronyms*

		- ellipsis
		- lists
✓	*combining clauses and sentences*	- -ed clauses
		- -ing clauses
		- verbless clauses
✓	*associations*	- their use
		- deleting the trigger
		- using perspectives
✓	*special structures*	- existential 'there'
		- anticipatory 'it'
✓	*other methods*	- tautologies and pairing
		- wordy phrases
		- general words
		- expanded verb structures
		- expanded modifiers
		- combining sentences

Exercise 9.11: General Sentence Exercises

Improve the conciseness of each of the following:

(a) *There is a current hypothesis, and this is that the hydrocarbons that have just been mentioned have been largely and primarily derived from gums and saps of plants that grow on land.*

(b) *It was several years ago that Steven Browning, who was a young inexperienced scientist from the country of New Zealand, was rushed at great speed to the emergency unit of a hospital that is located in the city of Quebec.*

(c) *Fatigue is also a contributory factor that leads to the occurrence of accidents. We know this because a worker who is tired is more apt to suffer a back injury. This happens because workers who are tired pay less attention to their work than do other workers who are not so tired.*

(d) *This book is rooted in a long and detailed study by the author of past medical history in the subject, and the book has been improved and strengthened by the vast and considerable experience of the author of the book.*

(e) *The college will avoid separating the humanities from the sciences. This will be done by using and employing team teaching. Another technique they will adopt to achieve their goal is to insist on collaboration between teachers of different subjects.*

Exercise 9.12: Short Text Exercises

The following passages are complete texts intended as general informative articles to technical professionals of all specialities. Add titles and make them more concise.

(a) *Tejinder Dhillion, which is a company located within the boundaries of Toronto, has taken out a patent for a completely unique soldering pen which is used during the production and manufacture of microcircuits. This unique invention consists of several parts, having an inner core on the inside of the device. It also has a heating element, and there is additionally an outer space outside the heating element which holds the soldering metal used for the soldering of microcircuits. The solder becomes molten when it is heated, and it is allowed to pass through to the microcircuits when the point of the pen is depressed, such action being accomplished when the pen is pressed down onto the microcircuit.* Note: Add an illustration.

(b) *There is a pushbutton supermarket located in Tokyo which is run and operated by a computer which cost $1.5 million. There is still a manager to manage the enterprise and two checkout girls to do the actual checking out, but everything else in the store is automated so that no other labor is necessary. It works quite simply. The customer makes her selection from about 2,500 items that are for sale and which are displayed behind transparent panels so that the customer can see the products but she cannot touch them or remove them from the panels. She inserts a small plastic card in a slot, and then presses a button to make her selection. After some whirring, buzzing and beeping, her selection pops out of the machine and she puts it in her cart and continues to make further selections in the same way. When the customer has finished her shopping, she goes to one of the checkout counters and feeds her card into the computer, which then lists and itemizes the products which she has selected, and calculates the final amount for the customer to pay before she leaves. The store used to employ 20 girls at 10 cash registers to effect the checkout calculation and procedure. Now, at this time, two girls can handle up to 400 customers per day without any undue difficulty. Another point to consider is that the loss due to shoplifting in the store has been reduced from $830,000 to nil because the customer*

cannot obtain any product unless and until she has inserted her plastic card in the appropriate slot and made the selection, and then the purchase is irrevocably registered on her card, and she has to pay for the product which she has selected as she leaves the store.
Notes: Indicate paragraph breaks and remove all sexist language.

(c) *Polychlorinated biphenels have been reported to be found in small amounts in carbonless paper, which is known as NCR (short for No Carbon Required). This type of paper (NCR) is gaining widespread acceptance in offices today. The reason for this gain in acceptability is that NCR eliminates the need for carbon, which as you probably know, is rather messy. It should be noted that there have been no specific problems which have been directly attributable to the use of carbonless paper. However, I should point out that polychlorinated biphenels have been suspected as a possible cause of bronchitis and liver cancer, which are undesirable afflictions. In addition to this possibility, an allergic reaction by some people to chlorinated biphenels is also possible. Generally speaking, employees who happen to be using NCR paper should be advised to wash their hands thoroughly, and to do this after handling the paper. This course of action would ensure that no possible polychlorinated biphenels are transmitted or conveyed to other parts of the body through contact with hands that have been contaminated with chlorinated biphenels.*

Review Questions

1. *Why should we be concise in our writing?*

2. *What are the four major contributors to verbose writing in large documents?*

3. *Under what circumstances would you include information your readers already know?*

4. *How would you signal information that is included earlier in the text?*

5. *Explain how re-entry methods can be used to improve conciseness.*

6. *How can associations improve conciseness? Why is the untriggered form often better?*

7. *How does the connection between relative clauses and the other descriptive clauses help us to improve conciseness?*

8. What is existential 'there,' what is its major use, and how can it contribute to verbosity?

9. What is anticipatory 'it', what are its uses, and how can it contribute to verbosity?

10. What are "tautologies"? How might they occasionally be justifiable? What is "pairing" and how does it contribute to verbosity?

11. Give examples of wordy phrases that contribute to verbosity. How might they be justifiable in some contexts?

12. Give examples of general words that contribute to verbosity. How might they be justifiable in some contexts?

13. What are expanded verb structures, and how do they contribute to verbosity? How might they be justifiable in some contexts?

14. How can adjectives and adverbs be used to improve the conciseness of your writing?

15. When should we use subordination and how does it improve conciseness?

16. How can we often combine sentences to reduce verbosity?

17. What is the connection between conciseness and politeness?

18. What is the connection between conciseness and personal style, the style of different documents and the needs of readers?

Chapter 10:
Punctuation

In this chapter you will learn how to punctuate any technical text. Emphasis is placed on punctuation (or the lack of it) that is unarguably wrong in given conditions in the writing. You will learn to recognize and correct such errors. You will also learn when punctuation is optional, and what differences are created when punctuation is, and is not, used in such circumstances. The many uses of the comma take up most of this chapter, but you will also learn how and when to use the colon, semicolon, apostrophe, hyphen and other punctuation marks.

Approach and Major Errors
Introduction
An Initial Premise
Comma Splice
Run-on Sentences

Mainly Commas
Punctuating Non-Restrictive
    Clauses
Other "Asides"
Punctuating 'However' and Other
    Connectors
Commas after Introductory Clauses
Commas with Clausal Connection
Commas before Final Effects
Commas with Lists

**Colons, Semicolons, Dashes and
    Parentheses**
Colons
Semicolons
Dashes
Parentheses

Other Punctuation
Punctuating With Quotations
Using Apostrophes
Hyphens
Other Punctuation Marks

Approach and Major Errors

Introduction

Although you may not have realized it, you should have learned a great deal about punctuation from the earlier discussion in this book. The explanation of restrictive and non-restrictive clauses in *Chapter 5*, for example, is useful background for understanding an important use of the comma. Also in that chapter, the discussion of the types and structure of lists could not avoid the related matter of how they are punctuated. Punctuation was also discussed in *Chapter 9* as a factor affecting the formality of writing. In addition, simply by reading the examples provided, you should have developed some understanding of good punctuation in technical writing.

This chapter builds on the earlier discussion to provide you with a sound knowledge of punctuation, and an ability to use it well in both writing and editing. An ability to use punctuation well is especially important as style checkers give little or no guidance in this important subject. The primary aim of this chapter is to enable you to punctuate without making errors in your writing — or anyone else's. The secondary aim is to provide you with the basis for developing your ability to punctuate with great skill to convey your desired degree of continuity, emphasis, and tone.

Punctuating effectively is an art as well as a science. Although there are many instances where punctuation can be said to be "right" or "wrong," punctuation is often more a matter of emphasis and personal style. It is important that you can recognize the difference, so that you avoid making unnecessary punctuation changes to other people's writing when you are editing. If the original punctuation is acceptable (though not perhaps the way you would choose to punctuate it), you should leave it the way it is. However, you *must* correct punctuation *errors* when you are editing.

Punctuation is often unobtrusive, assisting the reader to follow the sense of the writing with ease without being consciously aware that the writing *is* punctuated at all. But that is not always so. Punctuation can be used in many powerful ways: to stop the reader abruptly at an important point, to raise in prominence certain words or phrases, or to show relationships between ideas clearly. To punctuate effectively, you will have to learn how to use *all* the punctuation marks, and know the effects they have on your writing.

An Initial Premise

First, though, we need to start with an important premise: that we do not use punctuation unless we need to. A significant proportion of sentences in technical writing contain no punctuation at all other than the period and capital letter to indicate a new sentence. Here is an example containing three medium-length sentences that demonstrate this principle:

10.1

```
The value of B has been        as gravel and sand with
experimentally calibrated       various soil densities in
for various soil types such     the tank embedded
```

with the probe. The soil is subjected to a steady flow by keeping the water heads constant at the upstream and downstream sides for measuring Vs. The value is less than 1 when the perme-

ability of the soil such as sand is smaller than that of glass beads in the chamber.
—*Canadian Civil Engineer,*
May 1995, P4

Checklist 10.1: General Rules for Not Punctuating

✓ *only add punctuation to indicate a significant structural change or special meaning in the sentence*

✓ *never split the subject of a sentence from its verb with a single comma*

✓ *never split a main verb from its object with a comma*

Comma Splice

A "comma splice" is created when two independent clauses are spliced together with a comma, as in:

> "About half of the country's five million engineers are engineering graduates, the other half hold degrees in disciplines ranging from languages to the sciences."

These two statements do not "depend" on each other grammatically — they are independent clauses. Because of this, we cannot splice them together with the comma as shown. There are four ways of correcting this error:

Checklist 10.2: Ways of Correcting the Comma Splice

✓ *Use a new sentence:*
   . . . are engineering graduates. The other half . . .

✓ *Use a semi-colon:*
   "About half of the country's five million engineers are engineering graduates; the other half hold degrees in disciplines ranging from languages to the sciences."
— *Example 10.2:* Canadian Consulting Engineer, *Jan/Feb 1995, P12*

✓ *Use a subordinator at the start of the sentence:*
   "Although half the country's . . ."

✓ *or between the clauses*
   " . . . are engineering graduates, whereas the other half . . ."

✓ *add a conjunction — with or without the comma — between the clauses:*
"... are engineering graduates, but *the other half..."*

Notes: 1. These paraphrases have slightly different meanings.
2. Not all these methods can be used to connect all comma splices.

Exercise 10.1: Correcting Comma Splices

For each of the following, show several ways of correcting the comma splice. For each method note differences in meaning and emphasis.

(a) *The material properties and dimensions are listed in Table 1, the frequency range of interest is 0 — 500 Hz.*

(b) *The problem with tritium is toxicity not its radioactivity, as a result, ACERS encountered a number of difficulties interpreting current radiation protection standards.*

(c) *AutoCAD LT is descended from AutoCAD, therefore it uses the same file format so drawings can be exchanged in both directions.*

(d) *The Sinai workshop was closed peacefully in the 1980s, however, the Golan Heights workshop is still in operation.*

(e) *They offered to establish appropriate professional guidelines, their enforcement process would support the procedures*

The comma splice is particularly common with connectors (*however, therefore, moreover,* etc.) as writers often incorrectly treat them as conjunctions (*so, but, and,* etc.). The special problems of punctuating the connectors is discussed later in this chapter.

Run-on Sentences

Run-on sentences occur when writers keep adding clause upon clause to a sentence, often stringing them together with commas:

"Tech Ltd. has problems on several fronts, which we know from a systems review of employment practices which would indicate that breakfast meetings exclude employees, primarily female, who have drop-off responsibilities for young children, and further investigation would also reveal that two wheelchair-bound engineers cannot see the notices."

While, unlike the comma splice, there is nothing *grammatically* wrong with this sentence, it is extremely difficult to follow. The cause of the difficulty is that three separate statements have been "run-on" into one:

10.3

Tech Ltd. has problems on several fronts. A systems review of employment practices would indicate that breakfast meetings exclude employees, primarily female, who have drop-off responsibilities for young children. Further investigation would also reveal that two wheelchair-bound engineers cannot see the notices.

— *Engineering Dimensions*, May/June 1995, P19

Exercise 10.2: Correcting Run-on Sentences

(a) *All models measure DC and AC voltage, diode test, continuity and resistance, and include circuit protection and are supplied with a heavy-duty holster with test probe holders and tilt stand, battery, test leads, and instruction manual.*

(b) *The 1240 MW reactor, which has been shut down for the past four years, was shut down because of contamination in its sodium coolant and its operating licence expired last year after the French nuclear regulatory authority raised concerns about the plant's ability to resist sodium fires.*

(c) *Ultrafunnel offers a large 25 m diameter "target" for pouring waste material into drums that eliminate overspills commonly associated with smaller conical-shaped funnels because its unique channeled surface diffuse splashing and allows filters, paint cans, buckets and bottles to drain passively.*

(d) *A two-day Total Self Management Success Development Series seminar is offered by H.E.Huhn Consulting Services as a holistic workshop limited to 25 participants and including the High Five approach to effective sales covering such topics as setting goals, planning and successful selling skills.*

(e) *A new Toronto high school with a science- and technology-focused, socially-conscious curriculum will open its doors to 230 students this fall and is named The Ursula Franklin Academy for Dr Ursula Franklin, professor emeritus, metallurgy and materials science, University of Toronto, who helped design its curriculum.*

Mainly Commas

Punctuating Non-Restrictive Clauses

We saw in *Chapter 5* that writers indicate incidental, or "non-restrictive," clauses with commas to show that they *are* incidental. This applies to all forms of non-restrictive clause: relative clauses, -ing clauses, -ed clauses, and verbless clauses. Commas are usually used for these clauses:

10.4 The most recent IVHS America annual meeting, held in Atlanta in April 1994, was attended by over 3000 registrants from around the world.
— *Engineering Dimensions*, Nov/Dec, 1994, P27

but dashes provide a little more emphasis:

10.5 . . . but the advantages of HPS in terms of efficacy - the amount of light pro- duced per watt of energy consumed - are unquestion- able.
— *Canadian Consulting Engineer*, Jan/Feb, 1995, P19

and parentheses lower the emphasis slightly:

10.6 The micro-hardness test (Vickers or Knoop) has long been a popular method . . . .
— *Canadian Aeronautical and Space Journal*, Dec 1994, P163

Such clauses at the start of the sentence are *always* non-restrictive and most writers indicate this with a comma at the end of the clause:

10.7 Available from Uni-flex, Todo-matic self-sealing couplings feature spill- free connection and discon- nection . . . .
— *Machinery and Equipment MRO*, April 1995, P32

Non-restrictive clauses at the end of the sentence are also indicated as being non-restrictive by a comma:

10.8 The second initiative aimed at the trucking industry is under way at border cross- ings in the Windsor/Detroit area and the Niagara fron- tier, *where* systems are being investigated to apply AVI technologies to speed trucks or commuter vehicles . . . .
— *Engineering Dimensions*, Nov/Dec, P26

Note that the subject of this sentence contains a *restrictive* -ed clause (aim*ed* at the trucking industry). This restrictive clause restricts, defines and limits the meaning of the subject and therefore *must **not** be separated by punctuation.*

Exercise 10.3: Punctuating Non-Restrictive Clauses

For each of the following add punctuation only if it is necessary. Justify your decisions.

(a) *Gold production for 1995 the second full year of operation is expected to be 30,000 oz.*

(b) *Weighing only 2.6 kg the SN-5 clampmeter operating on the principle of a current transformer provides readings of 0-10 or 0-100 A depending on the range selection.*

(c) *The inviscid solver used in this work was the BGK model which is a two-dimensional solver extended for use in three dimensions.*

(d) *Designed to transport workers and light loads quickly and safely around industrial facilities the Norped model CP-3 Utili-Trike uses three robust pneumatic wheels all connected to the drive system.*

(e) *Together with his design team the Chief Engineer ensures that the product always meets the stringent quality requirements which are designated ISO 9001/EN 29001.*

Other "Asides"

Non-restrictive clauses can be regarded as being "asides" from the main information in the sentence, their punctuation indicating that they contain non-essential information. Other "asides" provide information about the connection between sentences (e.g. *however*), emphasis (e.g. *of course*), level of importance (e.g. *by the way*), time (e.g. *last year*), writer assessment (e.g. *hopefully*), indication of a problem (e.g. *unfortunately*), time (e.g. *initially*), and many other essential meanings.

In technical writing, we usually place these indicators at the start of the sentence, because it is there that they are most prominent. No punctuation is needed with them, but a comma creates a momentary pause and thus makes them a little more prominent:

10.9

```
They will also allow the
AECB to issue orders to
amend licences to require
persons with responsibility
for mining activities to
fulfil their decommission-
ing obligations.
```

```
However, the AECB has indi-
cated that it will not pre-
scribe specific approaches
or methods for financial
assurances.
            — Nuclear Canada,
              July/Aug 1994, P1
```

The separate paragraph and placement of *However* at the start of the sentence (rather than before or after *indicated*) makes the signal of contrast prominent. The comma adds a little to this emphasis.

Similarly, when such asides are included somewhere inside the sentence, no punctuation is needed:

10.10

```
The primary function of the
flowmeter is therefore to
measure Vm . . .
```

```
— Canadian Civil Engineer,
              May 1995, P1
```

but adding the commas makes the signal more noticeable and powerful:

10.11

Several features, *however*,
suggest that the cellular
crust structure may represent the calcified thallus
of a metaphyte.

— E. Turner, G. Narbonne,
N. James, Department of
Geological Sciences, 1995

Punctuating 'However' and Other Connectors

This brings us to the question of how we use punctuation with the strong "connectors" (e.g., *however*, *therefore*, *moreover*). We have just seen that, unlike the
conjunctions (*but*, *so*, *and*, etc.), they are "mobile" within the sentence. In any
of the positions in which they can be placed, connectors do not have to be
punctuated, but may be if you want to make them more prominent.

The more important issue is punctuation in front of the connectors when
they *are* at the start of the sentence (or clause). In this case, connectors *must*
have punctuation stronger than a comma, whereas *and*, *but*, etc. can have no
punctuation, or a comma (or a semicolon or period in informal writing).
Usually writers start a new sentence:

10.12

There are provisions for
bleaching following the
disc filters. *However*,
Beaulieu explained that the
bleaching tower is used

more for high-density storage.
—*Pulp and Paper Canada*, May
1995, P10

although the semi-colon is occasionally used:

10.13

The experimental results
from 18 different specimens
confirmed the stress/strain
distributions calculated by
the NASTRANTM FE code; *however*, every specimen found

. . . failed prematurely. .
. .

— *Canadian Aeronautical
and Space Journal*, Dec
1994, P159

The main point to remember is that when the connector starts its sentence or
clause, it needs something stronger than a comma before it. Otherwise you
would create a comma splice.

Exercise 10.4: Punctuating 'However' (and Other Connectors)

Correct the punctuation in the following:

(a) *It is not possible to compare life annuities with other options however, some calculations suggest that life annuities are not so bad.*

(b) *It is difficult in an article such as this to go into all the fine points,
however we are preparing a detailed brochure on the policy.*

(c) *Typical absorbers include gypsum board partitions, wood panelling and windows, however, since the absorption coefficient depends on mass, size and rigidity, it is difficult to forecast how a panel will operate in practice.*

(d) *The interest on actual tool performance is keen what industry want; however are reliable estimates of the critical speed region.*

(e) *One method is to carry out a trial and error solution technique, this is, however inefficient.*

Commas after Introductory Clauses

Many clauses are used to start a sentence other than the non-restrictive clauses and other "asides" discussed earlier. Some usually have a comma after them and others often do not. Introductory clauses that usually have a comma after them are those that provide information about the purpose, means, cause, effect, basis, assessment, contrast and surprise — with the corresponding information coming in the main clause after the comma. These meanings are often signaled by the subordinators (e.g. *Based on, In order to* (or simply *To*), *By . . . ing, Since, Because, Although*).

As we saw in *Chapter 6*, a common type of information at the start of a sentence is "purpose," which is followed by the "means" of achieving it in the main clause:

10.14

```
To expedite these negotia-    1996.
tions, the province has        — Canadian Mining Journal,
withdrawn some areas in and              Feb 1995, P9
around Inuit settlements
from staking until July 1,
```

A relation of surprise is signaled by *Although* in:

10.15

```
Although no legislation       — Engineering Dimensions,
codifies it, employees have           Nov/Dec 1994, P19
a common law obligation to
protect their employer's
confidential information.
```

A comma at the end of the subordinate clause helps readers to know where the subordinate clause ends and the main clause begins. When, however, the subordinate clause is placed at the end of the sentence, we know where it begins because the subordinator tells us that. A comma there is therefore less necessary:

10.16

```
Bealieu hopes to increase     lower.
the rail shipments because     — Pulp and Paper Canada,
transportation costs are               May 1995, P10
```

although still possible:

10.17 Nobody seemed to consider that it was worth defending chlorine, *although* data presented from the Bahia Sul mill in Brazil showed | the discharges of effluent were within the EPA's proposed Cluster rule . . .
— *Pulp and Paper Canada*, May 1995, P13

Other clauses at the start of the sentence indicate time, conditions or circumstances. Many writers do not place a comma after these clauses, but others do:

10.18 During the development stages of these new materials, there is a need to quickly characterize their properties . . . | — *Canadian Aeronautical and Space Journal*, Dec 1994, P163

If the introductory clause is long or complex, or if it could be misleading without the comma, you should put one in, as in:

"When the piston closes the exhaust valve in the lifting stroke the air cushion obeys a known physical law." (student writing)

A comma after *stroke* is needed to prevent the initial confusion that the time clause ends after *closes*. Better still, you could change the clauses around to prevent any confusion.

Commas with Clausal Connections

When we connect two clauses together eliding ("missing out") the subject, it is called "clausal ellipsis". If the clauses are short and we connect them with *and*, most writers do *not* add a comma:

10.19 The company has drifted through the dacite to the zones on four levels *and* is developing several shrinkage stopes between levels, | spaced 60 metres apart.
— *Canadian Mining Journal*, Feb 1995, P15

When a comma is included, some emphasis is added to the separation of the clauses:

10.20 The next part of the program analyses the data, *and* allows graphical viewing of the results. | — K. Haralampides, Department of Mechanical Engineering, 1995

When, however, the two clauses are connected with *but*, there is more need for a pause and a comma is more usual:

10.21

> The diameter of the resul-
> tant rod can be several
> times that of the thread or
> tubule enclosed, *but* is
> variable along the length

> of a single specimen.
> — *E. Turner, G. Narbonne,*
> *N. James,* Department of
> Geological Science, 1995

The comma is also more usual when two clauses with different subjects are connected. The length and complexity of the following example make such a comma almost essential:

10.22

> The United States is now
> facing serious problems for
> many medical facilities
> located in states which do
> not have access to low-
> level waste disposal facil-
> ities, *and* the reneging of

> the U.S. government on its
> high-level waste commit-
> ments has come close to
> forcing plant shutdowns
> this year.
> — *Nuclear Canada,*
> Jul/Aug 1994, P4

For statements any longer than this, you would be better off using two sentences connected by *In addition* or *Also.*

Exercise 10.5: Punctuating Connected Clauses

Explain why you would (or would not) use a comma for the following instances of introductory and connected clauses.

(a) *To get into college _ Lu had to pass college entrance examinations _ and also win the recommendation of his fellow workers.*

(b) *According to the legal documents filed _ Engineer S works for XYZ company _ and her husband runs a small company ABC Services.*

(c) *John Fisher is a justice of the peace with the Ontario court at Barrie _ but he is also a major in the Canadian Armed Forces Electrical and Mechanical Branch.*

(d) *With advice from Consumers Gas _ the university installed a 150 ton capacity chiller _ and a services package to facilitate maintenance.*

(e) *As explained in the leaflet _"Science is. . ." is the result of an eight year research project _ and involves educators, scientists, engineers and parents from across Canada.*

Commas before Final Effects

Writers always add a comma before a final clause that indicates the effect or enabling of the cause just given. The typical signal for such cause-effect relations is simply the -ing form of the verb reinforced by the comma. We see two examples of this use of the comma in:

10.23 The material ultimate strains are directly measured, thus enabl*ing* the verification of failure theory predictions. Preliminary failure results obtained with cruciform specimens (Figure 5) fall within the scatter of the strength data obtained with tubular specimens of the same material published by Swanson *et al.* (1989), thus confirm*ing* the adequacy of the specimen design . . .
— *Canadian Aeronautical and Space Journal*, Dec 1994, P161

The cause-effect relation is reinforced by *thus* in these sentences; *thereby* is also used in this context, though most writers use neither.

Commas with Lists

When there are three or more simple items in a list, most writers do not include a comma before the final *and* (although including one would not be wrong):

10.24 These included bleaching with laser light, ultraviolet light, blue light and others.
— *Pulp and Paper Canada*, May 1995, P14

This applies whether the list occurs at the end of the sentence, at the start, or elsewhere in the sentence. Note the absence of the comma after *TEM* in:

10.25 A number of exploration targets generated by the survey have been investigated on the ground using IP, TEM and magnetic techniques and anomalies located in the Hailal Safil region . . .
— *Canadian Mining Journal*, Feb 1995, PS5

As the items of the list become longer, however, there is more need for the final comma, and most writers will include one:

10.26 The company. . . has worldwide representatives including Geoterrex in Australia and Asia, CGG in Europe, Val d'Or Geophysics in Quebec, Geoexploracciones in Chile, and Geodass in southern Africa.
— *Canadian Mining Journal*, Feb 1995, PS4

Many writers include the comma before the final *and* when the items of the list are clauses, as in:

10.27 After a year of treatment, there was oxygen on the bottom, the biota had increased three-fold, enough sediment was digested that beaches re-appeared, and levels of toxic compounds had been drastically reduced, with heavy metals sequestered in plants.
— *Canadian Consulting Engineer*, Jan/Feb 1995, P29

When additional information comes after the last item of the list, the exact meaning may be unclear, and important legal decisions have depended on the interpretation. The problem can be seen in:

10.28 It will examine other nuclear waste management programs, alternatives to geologic disposal, and criteria for waste management from other energy and industrial sources.
— *Nuclear Canada*, July/Aug 1994, P2

Does the last phrase (*from other energy and industrial sources*) apply just to the last item of the list, or to *all* items of the list? The inclusion of the final comma might lead us to conclude the former, but it is not clear. Re-write this sentence in two ways to make each of these meanings clear enough to stand up to legal scrutiny. There is also the possibility that the second "item of the list" is really a verbless clause and not another item of a list. Rewrite the sentence (a) first to give this meaning, and (b) then to make an unambiguous list of three items.

Checklist 10.3: Major Uses of Commas

✓ *to separate non-restrictive clauses — usually mandatory*

✓ *to separate other "asides" including* however *and other connectors — usually optional*

✓ *to mark the end of clause-connecting introductory clauses — highly advisable*

✓ *to mark the end of other introductory clause — usually optional unless confusion or ambiguity arises*

✓ *between co-ordinated clauses (clausal ellipsis) — with* and *and* or, *not necessary unless the clauses are long or complex; with* but, *advisable*

✓ *between co-ordinated clauses with separate subjects — highly advisable unless the clauses are short and simple*

> ✓ *before final effects — highly advisable*
>
> ✓ *in lists — mandatory between most items; optional between the last two items but mandatory if confusion or ambiguity arises*

Colons, Semicolons, Dashes and Parentheses

Colons

As we saw in *Chapter 5*, the colon is *required* for introduced lists and *optional* for continuing lists. Here is an example containing first an introduced list and then a continuing list.

10.29
```
Task groups will study four      Visual Arts, Crafts,
areas: design demand,            Design, Ontario Arts
design capability, design        Council; consultants John
export and socially respon-      Lockyer, P.Eng . . . .
sible design. Members               — Engineering Dimensions,
include: Robert Jekyll,                    Nov/Dec 1994, P12
P.Eng., associate officer,
```

The first colon is required; the second is optional.

For introduced lists, the colon is where readers could ask "What are they?". A similar use of the colon is for an introduced "list" of one item:

10.30
```
But there was one problem:       knew what would happen.
a reverse DST had never             — Engineering Dimensions,
been attempted, and no one                 Sep/Oct 1992, P29)
```

For examples such as these, the colon is in the place where readers would ask the question: "What is it?" As this is an "introduced" item, the use of the colon is obligatory.

> ### Checklist 10.4: Major Uses of the Colon
>
> ✓ *obligatory at the start of an introduced list*
>
> ✓ *optional at the start of a continuing list*
>
> ✓ *obligatory at the formal introduction of a single item*

Semicolons

The semicolon is optional (instead of a comma or nothing) between two or more items of a list:

10.31

```
. . . use is made of two
other known solutions: two
collinear cracks in an
infinite sheet; and a crack
approaching a hole in an
```
```
infinite sheet.
        — Canadian Aeronautical and
                    Space Journal,
                Dec 1994, P155
```

When the list becomes long and the branches of the list contain commas or other punctuation marks (dashes or parentheses, perhaps), the semicolon is one way of indicating where the branches start and finish:

10.32

```
The five major areas
assessed are ozone layer
protection; environmental
impacts of energy use;
indoor environmental quali-
ty (acoustics, lighting and
indoor air quality);
resource conservation
```
```
including energy, water and
waste; and 'green' trans-
portation and site issues.
        — Canadian Consulting
                    Engineer,
            Jan/Feb 1995, P29
```

Note that, when semicolons are used in this way, the semicolon before the final item is *obligatory*, unlike the comma before the final item of a simple list. Another way is the use of lettering or numbering with or without the use of separate lines for each branch. If you decide to use separate lines, you could instead use bullets, dashes, or other symbols on your computer software.

Semicolons are also used between two clauses that are closely connected and either or both is quite short. We saw such an example connected by *however* earlier (*Example 10.13*). Here is an example of the semicolon with less overt connection:

10.33

```
The agreement among the
partners calls for the
Donhue mills at Amos and
Clermont, QC, and the
Maclaren mill at Masson to
receive about 50% of the
```
```
total produced; the rest is
sold.
        — Pulp and Paper Canada,
                May 1995, P12
```

As you can always use a period and a new sentence instead of the semicolon in such examples, you never *have to* use a semicolon in this way, although it is a useful ability to master. So, if you have difficulty with the semicolon at this stage in the development of your writing ability, only use the semicolon when you have to: in complex lists. See *Exercise 5.4* for correcting punctuation in complex lists.

Checklist 10.5: *Major Uses of the Semicolon*

✓ *to separate branches of a complex list (including the last two branches)*

✓ *to separate two closely connected clauses — usually when one or both are quite short*

Dashes

Dashes are a dramatic punctuation mark. Although ideal for separating notes and in personal or informal notes, they should not be over-used in formal writing. As noted earlier in this chapter, dashes are used in pairs as an emphatic indicator of non-restrictive clauses. We see this use in:

10.34

```
At the Halifax test, the        load — before punching
steel-free deck withstood a     through.
load of 94 tonnes —almost           — Engineering Dimensions,
10 times the                            Nov/Dec 1994, P11
maximum observed vehicle
```

Commas would be normal and neutral here, but the dashes make this non-restrictive verbless clause stand out in the text.

Note the difference between the *hyphen* and the *dash*, both illustrated in the previous example. The hyphen is a connecting mark that joins smaller parts into larger "words"; it is typed *without* spaces on each side of it. On the other hand, the dash is a separating mark that clearly indicates a change of direction for the coming material; it is typed *with* spaces on each side of it. Hyphens are discussed later in this chapter.

Dashes are used in pairs when there is no possibility of confusion with other punctuation marks. Unfortunately — like commas — the "start" and "finish" marks are the same, and also — as seen twice in this sentence —, dashes and commas do not mix well in English — though that is common practice in Spanish.

So, when you have complex combinations of non-restrictive clauses (especially in lists), you might need to use parentheses instead. Parentheses only work in pairs, and they work well in this role because they have separate "start" and "finish" marks, and because they can be combined with commas.

The dramatic quality of the dash — supported by the exclamation mark — is seen clearly when it is used at the end of the sentence:

10.35

```
On page six of this issue       step in your trip to the
of Canadian Consulting          podium at the awards gala!
Engineer you will find a            — Canadian Consulting
'Notice of Intention' form.                         Engineer,
Fill it out and send it to                  Jan/Feb 1995, P10
the magazine — the first
```

In more formal writing, we might need a separate sentence here: "This is the first step . . . " and a comma in the original would be rather odd and arguably a special sort of comma splice. But the original is quite acceptable — you can get away with a lot when using a dash!

Although the dash can be used where the comma cannot, it is often used instead of the comma to give a dramatic tone to the final element of a sentence:

10.36

```
During the entire northwest     Army — compiling an impres-
Europe campaign, 11,000         sive record.
RCEME engineers and techni-         — Engineering Dimensions,
cians provided repair ser-                  Nov/Dec 1994, P37
vices for the 1st Canadian
```

This cause-effect relation at the end of the sentence is typically signaled by the comma, as we saw earlier. In this case, though, the writer used a dash instead to give it added impact.

Even when there is no need for any punctuation before a final comment, you can still use a dash — to give added emphasis:

10.37
```
. . . its recommendations        cating effort.
will come to Council for              — Engineering Dimensions,
approval, giving it the                   Nov/Dec 1994, P41
opportunity to debate the
issue then — without dupli-
```

Dashes are also used at the end of the sentence in the same role as the colon — to answer such questions as "What is it?":

10.38
```
Terms and jargon are          — configuration management.
already complicating an              — Computing Canada,
already complex discipline              June 21, 1995, P46
```

Checklist 10.6: Major Uses of the Dash

✓ *for informal writing in many places*

✓ *instead of commas around non-restrictive clauses*

✓ *for dramatic effect instead of a comma for the final comment in the sentence*

✓ *for very dramatic effect instead of no punctuation for the final comment in the sentence*

✓ *in the role of the colon at the end of the sentence: to answer the question "What is it?"*

Exercise 10.5: Using Dashes

Use dashes to improve or correct the punctuation in the following:

(a) *There are no customers for nuclear power plants or indeed any other base line power plants in the US today.*

(b) *UPS lamps produce light which is yellow-orange not even hinting at white, with almost no blue-green component.*

(c) *The process control system efficiently responds to every request from all elements of the company achieving effective task co-ordiantion.*

(d) *This year's exhibition sponsored by engineers, scientists, architects and educators has a challenging title "Art in Steel".*

(e) To support these efforts, I as a professional engineer will offer this booklet on engineering education free to high schools throughout Canada.

Parentheses

As noted during the discussion about dashes, parentheses are often very useful in complex sentences in which we need either:

(a) to use marks with different "start" and "finish" indicators, or
(b) to use marks in combination with other marks, especially commas.

Parentheses are also used to add (usually quite brief) information to augment, explain or clarify part of the text, or to refer to something outside the text.

Checklist 10.7: Major Uses of Parentheses

✓ *to clarify the meaning of a pronoun: it (Lac)*

✓ *to provide or explain an acronym: its recently announced RETs (renewable energy technologies)*

✓ *to give references: (Aitken, 1998)*

✓ *to refer to figures: (Fig.3D)*

✓ *to explain a meaning: the geometrical (or ray path) and the dynamic (or displacement) parts of the problem*

✓ *to provide important identifying information: Airmag Surveys, Inc. (Philadelphia)*

✓ *to provide relatively unimportant information: General Condition 12.3.3. — Warranty (formerly General Condition 24.2)*

✓ *to clarify: short duration (usually less than 30 s)*

✓ *as mathematical product signs or identification: the flapping angles (a1, b1)*

✓ *identification on a diagram: NMP consists of a stainless-steel frame (1), high-resolution computer-controlled x, y, and z stages (2) . . .*

Note: It is considered impolite to place people's names in parentheses, but you can place parentheses around their positions.

Because references at the end of sentences to figures, tables, etc. are regarded as part of the sentence, the period comes *after* the closing parenthesis:

10.39	PEO Council has unanimously approved in principle the Fundamental Review Working Group's vision of the profession to the year 2000	(see Validation, pp 22-23). — *Engineering Dimensions*, Nov/Dec 1994, P43

When, however, the whole sentence is within parentheses, the period comes in front of the closing parentheses.

Exercise 10.7: Using Parentheses

Correct or improve the following:

(a) *Shi 1995 demonstrates that the outputs from these circuits are similar see Figures 6 and 7.)*

(b) *"Rent" includes the money or other consideration paid or given or required to be paid or given by or on behalf of the tenant to the landlord or the landlord's agent for the right to occupy and use the rented premises.*

(c) *Microscopic examination of high-fatigued specimens Test A revealed fibre-matrix interface cracking see the upper part of Feature 2 in Figure 3.*

(d) *Approval is needed from our Senior Engineer (Sarah Thompson) and our Personnel Director (Jean Matis).*

(e) *I am pleased to see Stewart Crampton's article on the Canadian Society for Professional Engineers CSPE Engineering Dimensions, March April 1995, p. 53.*

Other Punctuation

Punctuating With Quotations

The use of quotations — especially from speech — are indicators of a fairly informal style. In formal reports and proposals, you are more likely to paraphrase or summarize other people's written work than you are to quote their exact words. However, you still need to know how to punctuate quotations.

First, in formal writing at least, you should only quote someone when the words used are exactly what you want to present to your readers. That is, it must be important that you get the message right. We see this in:

10.40

```
. . . Mak said:              ies to practical problems,
''Engineering is a highly    making life better and
diverse profession, which    safer for people.''
promotes innovation and               — Engineering Dimensions,
good judgment. Engineers                   Nov/Dec 1994, P43
apply scientific discover-
```

Of course, *you* have to add correct punctuation marks to any speech you are quoting, as there were none in the spoken version. The colon is usual when the speaker or writer is introduced first (as in *Example 10.40*), but a comma is usually used when the quotation comes first (as in *Example 10.43*). Note that you may need to start a new sentence (with a capital letter) for the quotation, even though you are already within your larger sentence.

Example 10.40 consists of two independent sentences, and all you have to do is indicate their source. However, sometimes you may want to include something as *part* of a sentence you are creating. Here is an example:

10.41

```
The main difference between   what is, while engineers
science and engineering,      create that which never
she explained, is that        was.''
''scientists make known              — 10.40 continued
```

When you do this, make sure that the quotation fits in with the sense and the grammar of the sentence you have created.

When you wish to omit information from a quotation, use three periods:

10.42

```
''The failure to account     the essential value of
for the costs of using       energy in a sustainable
depletable resources is the  future.
biggest factor contributing         — Canadian Consulting
to the alarming environmen-                      Engineer,
tal news we receive daily .            Jan/Feb 1995, P23
. . The present accounting
of energy matters in the
growth-progress-wealth
equation does not represent
```

And when we want to add something to a quotation (often for clarification as it is now out of its original context), place your new material in square brackets:

10.43

```
''The whole idea behind      cient,'' she told
this research is to find     Engineering Dimensions.
new ways of catalyzing              — Engineering Dimensions,
[using a catalyst to alter               Jul/Aug 1992, P2
the rate of] chemical reac-
tions to make them more
energy- and yield-effi-
```

Logically the comma after the quotation should come after the quotation marks, as it is a mark *you* have added to a completed quotation. However, many style guides (especially in the USA) say that it should come before the quotation marks as shown in *Example 10.43*. It is only a small point, but be consistent.

If there is a small error (grammatical or other) in speech you have taken in note form, it is common practice to simply correct it. After all there is just as much chance *you* have made the error in taking notes. Strictly speaking, quotations from written work and taped comments should be verbatim — *exactly* what was written or spoken. However most writers will correct small errors (of spelling or number agreement, for example) in the quotation without noting the change. The original writer/speaker is not likely to object, and indeed will probably thank you.

If you notice a significant error in work you are quoting, you must *not* correct it in the quotation. Instead you should include *sic* (meaning *thus*) in square brackets as close to the error as possible.

10.44

```
Canadian law schools and        instruct law students on
Bar Admission courses           how to write better, plain-
should be urged [sic] to        er and clearer. [sic]
include a plain language            — Journal of Technical
drafting course in their        Writing and Communication,
curriculum in an effort to              24(3), 1994, P335
```

You cannot urge courses to do anything, and adverbs should have been used at the end ("better, more plainly and more clearly"). The writer calls attention to these errors by the use of *sic*. Use of *[sic]* in this way indicates that you are aware of the error and note its existence. Should you find material with many errors in it, it would be kinder to paraphrase or summarize it.

Both single and double quotation marks are also used to signal a newly-formed word, or one that has not yet been fully accepted, or one that is perhaps unusual in the context. Once the term has been introduced in this way, it is usually used later without the special punctuation:

10.45

```
The electronic vehicle          tags pay for themselves
"tags" will communicate         through reduced driver
vehicle identification num-     delays . . .
bers to inspection stations         — Engineering Dimensions,
as they approach . . . At a              Nov/Dec 1994, P26
cost of around $50, the
```

Quotation marks may also be used when titles of documents are included in a text.

Exercise 10.8: Punctuating Quotations

Correct the punctuation in the following.

(a) *We're definitely not going to accept their offer he stated.*

(b) *Beaver advised us, "to implement a few key performance indicators," to monitor our organization's pulse.*

(c) *The President replied we will consider your proposal and prepare a written response shortly.*

(d) *Lilly (1989) reported that: "The experiments conducted in flat-bottom columns produced similar results.*

(e) Roman said mine operators had developed 'lean and mean" operations, adding that we expect to operate Santo Tomas in an equally efficient manner.

Using Apostrophes

The major use of the apostrophe is to indicate possession. In formal and informal technical writing, possessives are used for organizations and things as well for people:

> **10.46**
> ```
> Also this year, two of
> three low-pressure turbines
> were replaced at the 900 MW
> Gosgen nuclear power sta-
> tion. Subsequent to
> installing the new
> ```
> ```
> turbines, Gosgen's power
> rating has increased to 928
> MW or 2.8 per cent.
>                 — Nuclear Canada,
>                   Jul/Aug 1994, P3
> ```

For singular nouns, add an apostrophe and an *s* (e.g. the ship's hull). When the noun is plural, the apostrophe comes *after* the plural *s* without another *s*:

> **10.47**
> ```
> MRO customers need profes-
> sional product- and ser-
> vice-oriented sales-people
> who know their objectives
> and effectively research
> ```
> ```
> and plan to meet their cus-
> tomers' needs.
>             — Machinery and
>               Equipment MRO,
>               Sep 1994, P17
> ```

Exceptions to the addition of the apostrophe after the *s* for plurals occur when the noun is plural without the *s*, as in women, men, mice, deer, etc. For these, the apostrophe comes before the final *s* (women's, men's, etc.). For names that end in the letter *s*, simply add the apostrophe at the end without an additional *s* (e.g. James').

Do *not* use the apostrophe when only the plural noun form is meant (e.g. customers, objectives). However some writers do use the apostrophe for indicating the plurals of acronyms (e.g. the seven ACT's), although simply adding the *s* is more usual (e.g. the seven ACTs).

Another function of the apostrophe is to indicate a "contraction" of two words into one:

> **10.48**
> ```
> It's a classic example of
> regional-to-site-specific
> exploration — the like of
> which cannot be seen any-
> ```
> ```
> where else in Canada at the
> present time.
>             — Canadian Mining
>               Journal, Feb 1995, P11
> ```

Note that *It's* is a contraction for *It is*; it is *not* a possessive form. The possessive form for *it* is *its* — without the apostrophe. There is no form *its'*.

Contractions are only used in informal writing — and speech of course. In fact if you do not use contractions in your normal speech, listeners will think you are very odd indeed. Typical contractions found in informal technical writing are *That's*, *don't*, *let's*, *you're*, *they're*, and *we've*.

Exercise 10.9: Correct Use of Apostrophes

Correct the following:

(a) *The mens and womens accommodation at the site are still in separate area's.*

(b) *Societies resource's for reducing risk are being poorly allocated when we judge such effort's against the criterion of life saving.*

(c) *Movement's of the measuring needle were barely perceptible over a days' recording.*

(d) *Its in its' infancy.*

(e) *Perhaps its our own personnels' smiling voices. Or maybe its our quality product's and services'.*

Hyphens

Hyphens are used to connect two or more words to create a single compound word.

Checklist 10.8: Major Uses of Hyphens

✓ *a number-unit adjective: the 1-second criterion*

✓ *equal noun combinations: plutonium-uranium fuel*

✓ *adjective-noun combinations: multi-impeller system*

✓ *noun-adjective combinations: cement-rich mixture*

✓ *noun-verb combinations: problem-solving criteria*

✓ *multi-word combinations: regional-to-site-specific*

✓ *a range: 30-40 per cent*

In informal writing — especially on e-mail (an adjective-noun combination) — you can create many new word combinations using hyphens. For formal writing, however, you should stay with accepted combinations. Note in *Example 10.47* how the first *oriented* is dropped, but the first hyphen is retained. This is standard practice.

Other Punctuation Marks

You may have occasional use for the following punctuation marks for special purposes.

Checklist 10.9: Other Punctuation Marks and Uses

✓ *the exclamation mark: to show surprise or other emotion in informal writing*

✓ *the question mark: (a) to indicate a question, (b) to indicate doubt in geology and other earth sciences*

✓ *the asterisk: (a) to refer elsewhere (e.g. a footnote), (b) three in a line to indicate a major break in the text*

✓ *the solidus (/): to indicate alternatives, ratios etc. (e.g. ac/dc, fuel/weight ratio)*

Exercise 10.10: General Basic Punctuation

Correct the following sentences. Note that there are often options and you should be able to defend your choices.

(a) *When the motor stopped I realized that it had not been oiled, since then I have oiled it, every day.*

(b) *We considered four groups of design criteria; engineering objectives, the profit criterion, laws ethics and standards and social and ecological factors.*

(c) *The next step to place the explosive in the hole cannot be done, until we have inserted plastic liners.*

(d) *The graph, that we drew from these data, (see Fig. 3), indicates, that the relationship is parabolic.*

(e) *As a result of this graph, (see Fig 6.) we produced a log-log graph (see Fig. 7.)*

(f) *Ours is a growing company, our sales have increased appreciably, for over 5 years; and I am convinced that this trend will continue.*

(g) *The companys new fire policy which was ratified by the Board at it's last meeting, will be announced next week.*

(h) *This discussion is largely a restatement of you're main theme, if you need to include it condense it, into one or two paragraphs.*

(i) *In my letter, dated November 30, (file AC/38) I informed them that our local representative, (Mr. T. Green) will visit them shortly.*

(j) *Before we proceed we need signatures from the following F. Galbraith our President, S. Lovell the Personnel Manager, and T. Bennington the President of the local union.*

(k) *They were dissatisfied with the results and therefore, decided to re-run the test.*

Exercise 10.11: General Advanced Punctuation

Correct the following using only punctuation. Note how good punctuation can create clarity out of gibberish — and vice versa!

(a) *With the construction of this plant located on the banks of the Roskilde Fjord in beautiful countryside about 65 km north west of Copenhagen see fig. 1 Det. Danske Staalralseeraesk A/S DDS, has doubled it's crude steel production, the facility is also proof that a steelworks can favourably blend with the environment, of a recreational area.* (Note: A/S means Ltd.)

(b) *Mr Caldwell outlined five signs, the supervisor should look for in the problem drinker absenteeism, three times the normal rate usually Mondays Fridays, or paydays lateness, three times the normal rate. Accidents, at twice the normal rate, morale the problem drinker has an adverse effect on fellow workers and drinking at, or prior to work.*

(c) *Firmly bonded to steel aluminum or galvanized steel these LAMINOL interpretations of maple walnut, teak, rosewood cherry or even weathered driftwood, offer a finish so realistic in texture and coloration, they virtually defy detection, yet LAMINOL can be worked, as easily as the base metal it'self, into cabinetry appliances, automotive, interiors decorative trim or even divider's or panelling.*

(d) *Soft low, friction non lamellar materials, provide lubricating actions solely, because they have an inherently low coefficient of friction, they are plastics such as fluorinated ethylene propylenes, FEP polytetrafluoro-ethylene, PTFE and chlorinated compounds and metals, (such as lead) silver; and gold.*

(e) *Preferred numbers, are based in theory on the pth root of 10 p being in practice, usually 5, 10 , or 20 — sometimes 40 — or very occasionally 80, the basic series are thus designated, R5, R10-R20 R40 — and R80, the last is referred to as an exceptional series, more rounded limited derived and shifted series, are derivations of the basic series.*

Review Questions

1. Why is it important that you understand where punctuation is optional as well as where it is wrong?

2. Where must you not place punctuation?

3. What is a comma splice? How can you correct it?

4. What is a run-on sentence? How can you correct it?

5. What punctuation can you use around non-restrictive clauses? What are the differences in emphasis?

6. What punctuation can you use around restrictive clauses?

7. What is the effect of commas around however in the middle of a sentence or clause?

8. What punctuation is acceptable before however at the start of a sentence or clause?

9. When should you use a comma after introductory clauses?

10. What is the difference between the punctuation for clauses connected with and and but?

11. What is the difference between the punctuation for clauses with the same (clausal ellipsis) and different subjects?

12. What are the major uses of the comma?

13. How should you use commas in simple lists?

14. What are introduced and continuing lists? How does this distinction affect punctuation?

15. What are the major functions of the colon?

16. How should you use semicolons in complex lists?

17. What other function does the semicolon serve?

18. What methods are there for separating the branches of a complex list?

19. What tone does the dash convey?

20. What are the major uses of the dash?

21. What are the limitations of the dash in complex punctuation?

22. What are the major uses of parentheses?

23. How do we indicate deleted information in quotations? How do we insert our own information?

24. How and when should we indicate the presence of an error in a quotation?

25. What are the major uses for quotation marks?

26. How should we introduce and then use a new term?

27. How are apostrophes used for singular and plural subjects?

28. What is the difference between possessives and contractions? When do we use these? What do its and it's mean?

29. What other punctuation marks are used in technical writing? What are they used for?

Chapter 11:
Grammar, Word Use and Editing

In this chapter you will review the most common grammatical errors, and learn the most important aspects of word use in technical writing. You will also learn about the approach and methods used in revising, editing and proof-correcting your own and other writers' work.

Common Grammatical Errors
Introduction
Parallel Structures
Dangling Clauses
Number Agreement
Sentence Fragments
Using Sentence Fragments
Pronoun Reference

Word Choice and Use
Simple and Complex Words
Concrete and General Words
Words Indicating Doubt
Using and Avoiding "Jargon"
Definition
Wrong Words
Using 'a' and 'an'

Revising and Editing
Computer Limitations
Revision
Editing Topics
Editing Approach
Making the Corrections on Computer
Making the Corrections by Hand (Informal Editing)
Correcting Proofs (Formal Editing)

11

Common Grammatical Errors

Introduction

It is assumed here that you have a reasonably sound understanding of how to create acceptable clauses and sentences in English. Thus there is no need to include instruction or practice in the grammatical rules of clause and sentence structure, or such things as how to use the articles, prepositions, or tenses. Those of you who need to learn about these topics for the first time (or perhaps need to review them), should refer to a more basic book and course of instruction in English grammar.

A few elements of grammar, however, often still cause difficulty for many technical students, and these are included in this section. These common grammatical errors will now be easier for you to understand and correct as you have learned some of the basic structural background in earlier chapters of this book.

Parallel Structures

The need to create "parallel" branches of text in ellipses and lists is explained in *Chapter 5*. All we need to do here is to extend that understanding into the use of parallel structures with prepositions and verbs.

Checklist 11.1: Criteria for Correct Parallel Structure

When a sentence has two or more branches:

✓ *each branch must make complete sense in the context of the sentence, and*

✓ *ideally the branches should be of the same grammatical structure.*

In the sentence

11.1 Special regulations apply to times of registration in and withdrawal from this course.

— Queen's University Applied Science Calendar, 1988

there are two branches co-ordinated by *and*. These can be illustrated as follows:

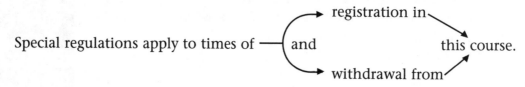

Figure 11.1: Correct Parallel Structure

As the two branches each make sense when read through with the main parts of the sentence, this is a correct parallel structure. Some writers like to emphasize the parallel structure by placing commas around the additional part which, if removed, would still leave an acceptable sentence:

> "Special regulations apply to times of registration in, and withdrawal from, this course."

Some writers omit the *in* after *registration*, thus creating faulty parallel structure. You can determine whether a parallel structure is faulty by drawing the diagram and checking whether or not the branches are complete and parallel.

Exercise 11.1: Correcting Faulty Parallel Structure

Correct the following faulty parallel structures.

> (a) *Cleavage is parallel or symmetrical about the axial surface of the fold.*
>
> (b) *Specialization was and continues a more effective approach.*
>
> (c) *The bus can turn corners as well or better than a regular transit bus.*
>
> (d) *Test results are not only scattered, but the amount is severely curtailed.*
>
> (e) *Their tools are shorter and just as expensive as the older ones.*

Dangling Clauses

When you place a clause before the subject of the sentence, that clause must refer to (i.e. provide information about) the subject that follows it. If that does not happen, the clause is said to "dangle", and you should correct it.

An example of a dangling clause is:

> "Weighing 12 kg, we have designed the hand-held or stationary Sword-Feeder for special applications . . . "

The clause *Weighing 12 kg* "dangles" because it should apply to the new design, not to *we*, the designers. Clearly the designers do not weigh 12 kg! Yet that is what the sentence appears to be saying.

To correct such errors, make sure that the clause applies to the appropriate subject:

| 11.2 | Weighing 12 kg, the hand-held or stationary Sword-Feeder is designed for special applications . . . | *— Machinery and Equipment MRO, Apr 1995, P28* |

Now the -ing clause provides information about the following subject, and the error has been corrected.

Although -ing clauses are frequent offenders of this grammatical error, the principle applies equally as well for *any* clause in first position: -ed clauses and verbless clauses as well as -ing clauses. Although you should correct all "dangling" errors, many readers will not notice such errors before passives, formulas, anticipatory *it* and existential *there*.

Exercise 11.2: Correcting Dangling Clauses

Correct the following errors involving dangling clauses:

(a) *Built by dendriform elements, we found that parts of the core have a great amount of core space.*

(b) *While injecting a sample into the chromatograph, my syringe needle broke.*

(c) *Available in three sizes, Ladbrooke now offers the new SFP-9 sausage foil-wrap packagers.*

(d) *Built in 1910 by Union Bag and Paper, many companies have since owned the mill.*

(e) *Using information based on ground geophysics, four exploratory holes were drilled by Diamond Mines.*

Number Agreement

If the subject is singular, the verb must be in the singular form; if the subject is plural, the verb form must also be plural. There is rarely any difficulty in applying this simple rule, but note that the addition of two singular subjects creates a plural subject:

11.3
```
The federal government's
recent budget and soon-to-
be-released science and
technology strategy are
examples of how it is
focusing on what it
```
```
does best.
    — Engineering Dimensions,
            May/June 1995, P15
```

Agreement is with the head noun of the subject, even if it is separated from the main verb by a restrictive or non-restrictive clause. A singular head noun requires a singular subject, even when there is an intervening plural topic:

11.4
```
The mathematical model_
based on the kinetic mecha-
nisms is a collection of
mass balances.
```
```
    — B Shaw, Department of
        Chemical Engineering,
                    1995, P10
```

Similarly, a plural head noun requires a plural verb, even when there is an intervening singular topic:

> **11.5** However, integrated circuit topograph*ies* created under contract *are* owned by the principal, unless the con- | tract states otherwise.
> — *Engineering Dimensions*, Jan/Feb 8, 1995, P14

Where something is added to a singular subject using *as well as, together with, in addition to, plus,* etc. (called "quasi conjunction"), the subject is still deemed to be singular.

Because, in speech, we often say *There's* even when the coming topic is plural, we might make this mistake in writing, where it is much more noticeable and serious. Whenever plural topics follow existential *there*, make sure that the verb form is plural too. Plural and singular forms are shown in:

> **11.6** In Canada, *there are* signs of renewed interest in gold exploration, in spite of 1994 stock market fluctuations, and in late 1994 *there was* even a staking | rush at the Voisey Bay nickel discovery in Labrador.
> — *Canadian Mining Journal*, Feb 1995, P2

Some words derived from Latin can cause a little difficulty with plurality. For example *criterion* is singular, whereas *criteria* is plural; and *fora* is the plural for *forum*. The word *data* is a plural noun, but in English it is not really the plural form of *datum* (meaning a fixed reference point); thus writers consider *data* as singular or plural — as long as they are consistent. The plural forms *antennas, premiums* and *stadiums* (instead of *antennae, premia* and *stadia*) are common in the USA and acceptable — though sometimes frowned upon — in Canada.

Exercise 11.3: Correcting Faulty Agreement

(a) *Miles of cabling has been installed to handle both existing and future requirements.*

(b) *One of the most common concerns of organizations who are considering implementing project management software are whether or not it is worth the effort.*

(c) *One of our clients was able to reduce their plant maintenance costs by 20%.*

(d) *Data production are where they are first captured and they occur in a variety of production systems.*

(e) *Multidimensional databases store the output results in a spreadsheet-like format, which make it easier for users to retrieve.*

Sentence Fragments

In formal writing, it is unacceptable to give the status of a sentence (capital letter and period) to a group of words that can only be a part (or "fragment") of a sentence.

Checklist 11.2: Criteria for Proper Sentences

✓ *Proper sentences must contain at least one main verb.*

✓ *Proper sentences must not be dominated by a word that converts sentences into dependent clauses (e.g. which, although, because).*

The second "sentence" of the following example is a sentence fragment:

11.7
```
Sometimes, negative public-     play where no one has
ity can be a good thing.        worked before.
Especially in the earliest            — Canadian Mining
stages of an exploration          Journal, Feb 1995, P10
```

The sentence fragment is being used here for dramatic effect, but if you were to do this, your readers might think you do not know how to construct sentences correctly. It is thus advisable to avoid sentence fragments in formal writing. At least until you are an established writer!

Sentence fragments can usually be corrected by using a comma (or more dramatically a dash) before the fragment. Occasionally you may have to reconstruct your sentence(s).

Exercise 11.4: Correcting Sentence Fragments

Correct the following to remove the sentence fragments.

(a) *The metacarpophalangeal (MCP) joint, or "knuckle," forms the articulation at the base of each finger. Providing the dexterity and stability required to perform intricate tasks with the human hand.*

(b) *The system includes an onboard computer containing a digitalized map of the city. And a GPS for vehicle location. Also a color video display on the car's dash.*

(c) *AutoCAD LT uses the same DWG file format as AutoCAD. Because it is descended from AutoCAD.*

(d) *The software can add special effects. Such as voice changing, echo and delay to phone calls.*

(e) *We are part of the industry identified with the leading edge of technology. Which makes it imperative for us to project this image.*

Using Sentence Fragments

Although sentence fragments are unacceptable in formal writing, they are used to give a punchy, dramatic effect in some advertising and other informal prose forms. Sentence fragments are quite acceptable — and very effective — when you are answering questions in informal conversation and when you are completing forms or answering questions in writing.

> **11.8** What is your impression of | reading text provided . . .
> the composing exercise? | — *Manuscript Review*,
> *Useless and misleading*. The | 1995
> principle of topic sentence
> is *not* demonstrated in the

The short summary answer provides an immediate, clear response, with supporting details to follow. The longer form ("My impression of the composing exercise is that it is useless and misleading.") is unnecessarily verbose.

When responding to several questions on e-mail, we often include the questions in our reply and respond using very brief sentence fragments:

> **11.9** <Sorry, I don't have JTWC and so haven't seen the
> <special Canadian issue. What issue is it? I'll try
> <to find it in my library.
> This year (1994!), I think — probably 24(3).
>
> — personal e-mail, 1995

Exercise 11.5: Using Sentence Fragments

Use sentence fragments to make the writing or speech more appropriate for conversation, completing forms and e-mail responses.

(a) *"What is your name and where do you live?"*
"My name is Michael Jordan, and I live in Kingston, Ontario, which is in Canada."
"What is your occupation?"
"I am a professor at a university."
(conversation on entering a country)

(b) *Date of arrival:*   *I will arrive on July 21, 1995*
Date of departure: *I will depart on July 31, 1995*
Type of room: *I would like to have a room that is suitable for two people and that contains its own separate bathroom facilities.*
(hotel reservation form)

(c) *< What was your figure for the output voltage between test points 24 < and 36?*
Thank you for your enquiry. The value of the output voltage which I measured between test points 24 and 36 was 30 mV. I hope this meets your requirements.
(e-mail messages)

(d) *While you were at your lunch meeting, Dr Bawley from the Research Department called you on the telephone. He will be in his office from 2.30 until 4.00 this afternoon, and he would like you to return his call. His telephone number is 545-0847. (message)*

(e) *"Welcome to Harvey's. May I take your order?"*
"Yes, I would like a quarter pounder and some fries. However please do not add chili peppers or pickles on it."
"What would you like to drink?"
"I would like to have a large Pepsi Cola to drink."
(conversation at a fast food restaurant)

Pronoun Reference

Through studying and practising the principles of continuity in *Chapter 5*, you should have developed a sound understanding of how topics are connected. Perhaps the most common error in pronoun reference is in the name itself, as most "pronouns" do not refer back to, or "re-enter," nouns at all — especially the word *this*.

When used on its own (without a noun following it), *this* can refer either to the immediately preceding noun group or to the entire preceding clause, sentence or even paragraph — depending on what comes next in the sentence. There is rarely any difficulty in deciding what *this* refers to, and it is no more "vague" or "unclear" than any of the connectors, which also have referents in the text. This can be demonstrated by paraphrasing the connectors to include *this*:

Checklist 11.3: Relationship Between 'This' and the Connectors

✓ *however — in spite of this, in contrast with this*

✓ *moreover — in addition to this*

✓ *therefore — it can be concluded from this that*

Thus *this* (also *that* for less formal writing) is used extensively without a following noun:

11.10   They're not waiting for 'the solution' but acting creatively without guarantees of success. *That* is what all of us must do.
   — *Canadian Consulting Engineer,* Jan/Feb 1995, P29

That re-enters the previous clause, and any attempt to use a following noun (e.g. *That action, That activity*) would only cause confusion.

There are, however, legitimate reasons for using a following noun after *this* or *that* (and *these* and *those* for plurals), as we see in:

| 11.11 | The comparison of predicted and experimentally observed locations of transition for several airfoils under different conditions shows that the results obtained with SCOLIC provide an estimate that is sufficiently | accurate for design purposes. *These predictions* are consistently conservative, which is desirable from a design perspective.
— *Canadian Aeronautical and Space Journal*, Mar 1991, P33 |

As there are several plural nouns in the preceding sentence, the writer needed a following noun to make it clear exactly what is being re-entered as subject of the next sentence. Note that the referent for *which* in this example is the whole of the preceding clause — a rare (for formal writing) but often useful technique. This technique parallels the use of *this* to re-enter clauses and sentences.

Exercise 11.6: Correcting General Errors

Each of the following examples contains many types of error: parallel structure, subject verb agreement, sentence fragments, consistency, wrong words/spelling, other (e.g. possessives, punctuation, capitalization). Correct them.

(a) *The record of achievement includes 60 hydro developments, 100 thermal projects, 8 000 km of transmission line. Contains hundreds of sub-stations around the world.*

(b) *The missive proportions of the 312m tall BP Magnis Platform — Three times the height of londons big Ben, are vividly captured in this picture showing an artists impression of the platform superimposed in an aerial view of London, with the house of Parliament in the foreground.*

(c) *The place and need for a SFIS in the hierarchy of manufacturing control systems is scene by examining two systems; the manufacturing shoppe and the control systems which regulate shoppe activities. A computerized costs control system is expected too: (a) monitor project costs accurately. This infers the existence of proceedings for automated and systematic collection of data on employee time charges, employee expenses, and on expenses which is generated by external supplier's (i.e. payments to sub-contractors): and (2) to trap unauthorized charges before it is posted against a project.*

(d) *Wastewater from food-processing plants represent a greatly untapped sauce of recoverable proteins. Given the worlds enormous*

> *protein shortage these effluents are becoming increasingly important for humane food and animal feed. Reclamation of proteins yields not only economically valuable produce , but also reduce the pollution loads of discharges released into municipal treatment works.*

(e) *Its estimated that the present hot rocks geothermal experiments in Cornwall, when projected to a reservoir deep of 6 km could provide about 7.5 MW from a twin hole system for some twenty-five years.*

(f) *The health center's are run by a Board of directors drawn from the Labour movement. (One centre is in Toronto and the other in Hamilton. Some employees may feel ambitious about labors control over the operation of a health service.*

Word Choice and Use

Simple and Complex Words

In general it is better, in all forms of writing, to use a simple word rather than a complex one if it communicates your message adequately to your readers. Simple words are more likely to be understood by more people, and they are often more concise.

It is especially important to choose the words you use very carefully when you are writing for members of the general public and to other professionals who are not specialists in your particular discipline. For these, you may need to introduce and define terms your readers do not know.

Some complex words are often over-used, and can usually be replaced with simpler ones:

Checklist 11.4: Some Complex and Simple Words

✓ More Complex Words	✓ Simpler Words
demonstrate	show
endeavor	try
initiate	start
most advantageous	best
technique	way
utilize	use

We can compare the clarity, conciseness and style of a text using complex words (*a*) with a similar one using simpler words (*b*):

(a) "The authors endeavored to demonstrate to them the most advantageous techniques of utilizing the instrument."

(b) "We tried to show them the best ways of using the instrument."

Concrete and General Words

Generally you should be as specific as you can be when writing to fellow professionals, although there is no need to inundate them with useless or barely relevant detail. Figures and scientific or engineering units are, of course, the most definite type of wording you can use, as they are measurable quantities. In reports, you will typically need to use very specific wording, as in:

11.12
```
To perform this test a por-      and the leachant were then
tion of the cylinder was         enclosed in a vessel which
ground down in size and          was tumbled end-over-end
separate samples of parti-       for 24 hours.
cles less than 0.075 mm                    — Canadian Civil
were leached with distilled           Engineer, May 1995, P5
water and with 0.1 N acetic
acid solution. The sample
```

The information you provide for such writing should be enough to allow others to conduct the same experiment to verify your results. Note that the text is still not absolutely precise where there is no need for such precision in the wording. How big is the portion? How finely was it ground down? How long was the leaching? What were the conditions in the vessel? Absolute precision in such matters is very hard to attain, and rarely worth the time and effort. An acceptable compromise is necessary.

Vague ("generic") words are extremely useful for re-entry purposes (e.g. *material*, *substance*) as long as their meanings are clear in the text. The sentence "This situation puts me in a difficulty position" is of course extremely "vague" out of context, but in context *This situation* refers to information just presented, and *difficult position* is about to be explained in detail. Such a sentence, then, could be a valuable pivotal statement linking two passages of text.

On rare occasions, you may not know the specifics of your subject. In a proposal, for example, you may only be able to guess at the expected outcomes:

11.13
```
The system will also            trucks onto
improve highway safety          the highway at inspection
through reduced truck merg-     stations.
ing manoeuvres and elimina-            — Engineering Dimensions,
tion of possible backups of                  Nov/Dec 1994, P26
```

How much improvement and reduction? How possible are the backups without this proposed system? Frankly, the writers do not know, and they can be no more specific than they have been.

Words Indicating Doubt

If you have no reason to doubt something, you should not indicate that you are unsure. That would give an impression that you are not sure of yourself and would give an inappropriate tone to your writing. On the other hand if you really are uncertain (and cannot determine the details), you must indicate that doubt to your readers rather than leave them with the impression that you *are* sure. Signals of doubt range from being almost certain to there being little chance, and it is often important for you to indicate the degree of certainty of your information or conclusions.

In statistical surveys, we give not just the range of certainty (e.g. ± 4%) but also the probability of the true value being within that range (e.g. 19 times out of 20, or 95%). The claim and the certainty of its correctness are mathematically linked. More typically, we often express a tolerance (e.g. *0.1% fsd*) without a probability, assuming that the figure will always be within this range. We provide a statement together with a general indication of its validity.

In the more mathematical subjects, doubt is often definitively determinable. If you do not know something, you can measure it or calculate it. However in other subjects (the age of ancient rock formations, for example), considerable doubt remains even after the most diligent efforts, and you must express that level of doubt.

There are many ways of signaling the level of doubt:

Checklist 11.5: Ways of Signaling Doubt

✓ *mathematically, by percentage and probability*

✓ *tolerance with presumed 100% occurrence within that*

✓ *anticipatory 'it': It appears that, It is our view that*

✓ *existential 'there': There is some doubt about*

✓ *adverbials: perhaps, possibly*

✓ *modal verbs: might, could, may*

✓ *main verbs: We believe that*

✓ *complementary assessments: We are fairly sure that*

✓ *reporting clauses: reported as, said to be, thought to be*

✓ *punctuation: the question mark in parentheses*

Using and Avoiding 'Jargon'

The term 'jargon' is defined in two ways: as the special vocabulary of a particular group or activity, and as confused unintelligible language that is often obscure and pretentious. Whether the use of specialist terminology is a necessary part of effective communication, or is instead the cause of incomprehension and the appearance of a pretentious tone, is all a matter of your audience.

When you are communicating technical details to fellow professionals, you *must* use the correct terminology. If you were to ask "How much electricity is there in those lines," an electrical engineer quite literally would not know what is meant. Are you asking about phase-phase or phase-ground voltage, current, power or KVA? You will have to be more precise if you expect an intelligent answer.

By asking such a question, you create another problem. You immediately brand yourself as someone who does not know the subject at all, and who has little or no understanding of the basic concepts or units of measurement. If, on the other hand, you *do* know what you are talking about, and you chose not to use the correct terms, your question would be condescending. The person you are communicating with would think that you thought he or she did not understand basic concepts or units.

Checklist 11.6: Reasons for Using Correct Terms for Professionals

✓ *to ensure clear, concise, precise communication*

✓ *to avoid giving the impression that you do not know the subject at all*

✓ *to avoid giving the impression that you feel that your readers do not know the subject at all*

Exercise 11.7: Using Appropriate Technical Terms

Make changes to the following to make them suitable for specialists in the subjects being discussed.

(a) *The amount of force pushing the electrons through the wire was measured at the output of the amplifier.*

(b) *We connected the device that interfaces between the computer and the mainframe computer via the telephone lines.*

(c) *The instrument used to measure current was set at 0-1 A.*

(d) *A chemical that would help the reaction to happen was added at this stage.*

(e) *The size of the component was measured using the special measuring device that closes on the component by twisting of the knob on the bottom and reading off the reading on the vernier scale.*

When you are communicating with those who are not specialists in the subject being discussed, you will need to use simpler words — or define the ones you use.

Definition

Readers rarely bother to check the meaning of words in a dictionary. Non-specialists who are reading about a technical subject are even less likely to do this — especially if they find many technical words, which may not even be in their dictionary. If they were to check technical terms in a technical dictionary, they still might not understand their meanings as they may not have enough background knowledge to understand the definition. So, if you need to use technical terms in writing (or speech) to the general public or to non-technical specialists in marketing, accounting, etc., you will have to define your terms.

You may also need to define terms if you need to use a term in a special way that is not quite the same as its usual, accepted meaning. Also if you discover a new concept, or invent a new product, you will have to give it a name and clearly define what you mean by it.

Checklist 11.7: Needs for Defining a Term

✓ *to explain a meaning for readers who do not know the term*

✓ *to stipulate a special meaning for an established term*

✓ *to identify something new you have discovered or invented*

Note: Never define a term to fellow professionals who already know it.

There are many way of defining a term. Frequently it is advisable to define your term quite subtly in case your readers (or some of them at least) do know the term. Thus we might write:

> "The home computer was connected via the phone lines to the mainframe computer. The connection was achieved by a Sportster 1440 modem from US Robotics."

In this way, readers learn what a modem is without you having to formally define it for them.

Checklist 11.8: Ways of Defining Terms

✓ *Place the term in a class of similar things and then distinguish between this term and others in the class (e.g. a screwdriver is a tool which . . .)*

✓ *Use a general class to indicate a special type of thing (e.g. Quality is that which . . .)*

✓ *Description, often including an illustration*

✓ *Synonym*

✓ *Saying what something "means"*

✓ *Special meaning (e.g. "Here quality means the best possible product at an acceptable cost.")*

✓ *Mathematical formula*

✓ *Chemical formula*

✓ *Using levels or limits*

✓ *Using a test*

In some cases, you may have to almost give up and define, for example, site cleanliness as being what is acceptable to the supervising site engineer, or what is "reasonable" under the circumstances. Such definitions *are* acceptable in the courts if there is no other way of defining your requirements.

Definitions are found as part of the main text in one or more sentences. However, they are also included in parentheses (or commas or dashes) immediately after the term:

11.14 Geoterrex now provides the ``analytical signal'' (a function of computed vertical and horizontal derivatives) to assist in the interpretation of magnetic data.

— *Canadian Mining Journal*, Feb 1995, PS7

or as a footnote with an asterisk or superscript number . When you have many definitions, it is often advisable to include a List of Definitions at the front of your document. Legal documents almost always do this, as definition is vital for unambiguous meaning.

Checklist 11.9: Definition Locations

✓ *in one or more sentences in the text*

✓ *in commas, parentheses or dashes immediately after the term*

✓ *as a footnote*

✓ *as a List of Definitions at the front of the document*

Writing definitions may not be as easy as you think, especially when your technical writing has legal implications. You have to be extremely clear about what you mean, and also what is excluded from the definition. If we need to define certain types of accommodation for rent, for example, do they include trailers, basements (and how do we define "basement"?), rooms with or without a bathroom (and again when is a bathroom a "bathroom"?), areas with separate entrances or not, and so on.

First you have to decide *what* you want to include and exclude — and then you have to write it so clearly that lawyers cannot possibly find a way of reading another meaning into it.

When you are defining, try to avoid common pitfalls of definition:

Checklist 11.10: Pitfalls of Defining

✓ *Do not include the term as part of the definition (e.g. "An attenuator attenuates . . . ")*

✓ *Do not include a term in your definition that also needs definition (e.g. "Entropy is a measure of the order in a system . . . ") unless you define that too.*

✓ *Avoid as many complex and technical words as you can.*

Writing Task: Writing Definitions

Write definitions for the following terms for the given readers and purposes:

(a) *a technical term of your choice for students in another technical speciality*
(b) *a technical term of your choice for the general public*
(c) *any of the following for a law or by-law: basement, bedroom, bathroom, garage, rent, parking, weed-free front lawns, tree, clear sidewalks, extension of a house, lawn watering*

Wrong Words

Many words (called "homonyms") sound like other words but have different spellings. Some cause real confusion — especially as your spell checker and style guide are unlikely to notice you have used the wrong words; even when they do, you have to decide which word to use.

Here is a list of the most commonly misused homonyms in technical writing:

Checklist 11.11: Commonly Misused Homonyms

✓ **advice/advise:** *You give* advice *(a noun), and* advise *(a verb) someone.*

✓ **affect/effect:** *You can* affect *or change something, and* effect *(or create) a change;* effect *is also the result of a cause.*

✓ **alternately/alternatively:** alternately *means doing something one after another;* alternatively *is a choice (writers in the USA do not always follow this distinction).*

✓ **auxiliary/ancillary:** ancillary *means on a lower level (subordinate to), whereas* auxiliary *means helping.*

✓ **censor/censure:** *Films are* censored *by removing unsuitable material, whereas people are* censured *(disciplined) for doing something wrong.*

✓ **cite/sight/site:** *You* cite *examples or quotations from another source;* sight *is the ability to see, and* site *is where you locate your building.*

✓ **complement/compliment:** *These mean to complete and to praise respectively;* complimentary *means free, whereas* complementary *means completing. Note that* supplementary *means adding to without completion.*

✓ **consequently/subsequently:** consequently *means as a result, whereas* subsequently *means after that.*

✓ **continuous/continual:** continuous *means without stopping (flow of water or electrons), whereas* continual *means going all the time but not continuously (continual interruptions). Note that* intermittent *means irregular occurrences (intermittent radio interference).*

✓ **discreet/discrete:** *You behave* discreetly *(with discretion) when you behave properly with consideration for others.* Discrete *means something that is a distinct individual item (discrete points of contact).*

✓ **farther/further:** *Use* farther *for distances, and* further *for other uses (further complications, furthermore).*

✓ **formally/formerly:** formally *means in a formal way;* formerly *means earlier.*

✓ **fewer/less:** fewer *is used for things you can count (fewer acci-dents), whereas* less *is used for things you cannot count (less top-soil).*

✓ **imply/infer:** *To* imply *is to hint at or suggest something without actually stating a conclusion. To* infer *means to reach a conclusion.*

✓ **its/it's:** its *is the possessive form;* it's *is the contraction meaning* it is.

✓ **personal/personnel:** personal *means something related to or private to a person (personal problems), whereas* personnel *means related to people generally (Personnel Department).*

✓ **principal/principle:** principal *means main or chief, including a Principal of a school or a business;* principle *is an accepted truth or idea.*

✓ **their/there:** their *is the possessive form for plural things and people, whereas* there *indicates location or existence. Note that* they're *is a contraction for* they are.

For further advice on word usage, refer to a handbook or reference book.

Using 'a' and 'an'

The rule concerning the use of *a* and *an* is quite simple, although there is some complication in practice. When the word following the indefinite article *sounds like* a vowel, use *an*; otherwise use *a*.

The difficulty arises when the following word is an acronym. When you sound out the acronym (as in *MTB, RSVP,* etc.), use *an* if the first letter *sounds like* a vowel. However, if you read the acronym as a word (e.g. *NATO*), then only use *an* if the word sounds like a vowel.

Checklist 11.12 Using 'a' and 'an'

✓ *use* an *if the following word (noun or adjective) sounds like a vowel*

✓ *use* a *otherwise (usually including 'hotel' and 'herbal' in Canada)*

✓ *for acronyms where each letter is pronounced, use* an *if the first letter sounds like a vowel: A, E, F, H, I, L, M, N, O, R, S, and X. Use* a *for the others.*

✓ *for acronyms read as words (e.g. NATO), follow the first two rules*

Exercise 11.8: Using 'a' and 'an'

Choose the appropriate indefinite article for the following: SFIS, MTB, NATO force, porous material, invisible light, NO2 solution, useful characteristic, low-frequency output, application, energetic employee, AE signal, low-amplitude output, adequate response, ZFT missile, EFT, Allard model, LCM approach.

Revising and Editing

Computer Limitations

Several humorous poems have been written on this subject filled with all sorts of mistakes which have been accepted by spell checkers and other computer aids. By all means use spell checkers to check your work (it is a rare writer who makes no mistakes in a document), but do not feel that this check is a substitute for your own detailed proof-reading of your writing.

Many students have become so dependent on their spell checkers they have yet to learn how to read their writing carefully to find mistakes their computers will miss. This is a difficult skill to learn, but it is a vital one if you are to become able to take full responsibility for the technical accuracy and clarity of your professional work.

Spell checkers are particularly weak with small words. If, for example, you mis-typed the word *new*, your spell checker will quite happily accept *nev, nee, nay, neg, net, news, newt, newf,* and even *mew* — the sound a cat makes! It will also allow all sorts of punctuation, wrong word, capitalization and consistency errors. Writing can be very badly flawed if you were just to rely on your computer to check your typing and spelling.

Style guides, too, can be unhelpful, and most professional writers ignore most or almost all of the advice they give. They will catch some errors, but they will also give you quite misleading advice about sentence length and complex sentence structures, for example. If you were to follow all the advice given by these guides, your writing might be suitable for Grade 8 — 10 readers, but it would appear childish and quite insulting to professional readers. You must develop your own understanding of effective technical style for fellow professionals, and be guided by that instead.

Revision

The term "revision" means to improve and correct the overall features of a document, whereas editing is the final correction of smaller elements of the text. If, for example, someone gave you a document to revise, you should initially be more concerned with the overall features of purpose, audience, style, structure and presentation than with the actual sentences and clauses. Revision is an opportunity to re-assess whether the document is doing the job it is intended to do, and doing it well. Only when such basic aspects of a documents are sound is it worth looking in detail at the actual language use (editing).

Checklist 11.13: Topics for Revision

✓ *the overall aims/objectives of the writer(s)*

✓ *the needs of the readers*

✓ *the structure of the document — organized sections*
   — sub-sections
   — headings
   — transitions

✓ *paragraphs*

✓ *style and tone*

✓ *clarity, logic, credibility*

✓ *overall conciseness*

✓ *illustrations and tables*

✓ *prefatory and appended material*

✓ *references*

✓ *layout and presentation*

It may not be possible for you to check all these at one reading, so you may have to read the document — or parts of it — more than once.

You should "revise" your own work too. If you have time, put it aside for a few days (longer if possible) and return to the task with a more detached, objective view. Also ask a colleague or perhaps your supervisor to go over the main elements of your work to ensure that it is, in general terms at least, what is needed.

Editing Topics

Editing is making sure the "nitty-gritty" parts of your work meet professional standards. In editing, you should be able to assume that the overall document is sound, and that you now have to fine tune the writing to achieve the desired effect.

> ### *Checklist 11.14: Editing Topics*
>
> ✓ *grammatical errors*
>
> ✓ *spelling/mistyping/wrong words/words omitted*
>
> ✓ *punctuation*
>
> ✓ *conciseness*
>
> ✓ *correctness and clarity at clause and sentence level*
>
> ✓ *style and tone*
>
> ✓ *numbers/symbols*
>
> ✓ *numbering of pages, illustrations, tables and appendices*
>
> ✓ *references*
>
> ✓ *a final check that everything is there and is in the correct order*

Editing Approach

When you become a technical manager or executive, you will spend less time actually writing, and more time assessing and editing the written work of others. Many students are poor editors of other people's work, not because of a lack of ability or effort, but because of a poor approach. When you are editing someone else's writing, you should not impose *your* way or style of writing (known as "idiolect") on the writer:

> If the writer consistently uses *which* and you use *that* for restrictive clauses
> — *leave it.*
> If the writer uses a comma after an initial *However* and you do the opposite
> — *leave it.*
> If a writer prefers to spell using USA usage and you prefer UK usage
> — *leave it.*

In effect, you should only change what needs to be changed, and not make changes just because it is not written the way you would have written it. You are the editor, not the writer. Your job is to help the writer produce an effective document written in the writer's own style — not yours. This is why it is important that you learn not just what is "right" or "wrong," but what is acceptable too. Only by being aware of other acceptable ways of expressing facts and ideas can you hope to become an effective editor of other people's work.

You must, of course, correct errors, and change style and tone if they are inappropriate for the purpose and readers. You should also make the work more concise if necessary — but not to the extent that you make the wording sound rigid or stilted. You might also need to combine sentences to improve the general maturity of the writing. Knowing when and when not to make changes is a very difficult task which requires considerable language skill and judgment. You should not expect to become a first-rate editor overnight — it could take many years.

Making the Corrections on Computer

If you are editing your own work, you make your changes directly on your computer, of course. If, however, you are editing work written by someone else, it is better to make the *suggested* changes so that the writer can see what you are suggesting and can decide what advice to accept and what to reject — as you do with style guides. To do this on your computer, simply use your *Tools-Track Changes* facility, elect to track your changes, and then edit the text in the normal way. The computer will highlight the changes you are suggesting in a selected color, e.g.,:

The first HSST trauck will be laid between a railrail-way station near Yokohama and a nearby theme park. The HSST will make the 5.3 km journey in 12 minutes. HSST Corporation, the Japan Airlines affiliate that will ruan the system, believes that it's train will be cheaper to run than conventional trains because theirer are no moving parts and therefore little where-wearand tear. The HSST track will be cheaper to layie than MAGLEV track because the expeansive electromagnets are all on the HSST, note on the track.

The writer can then review your corrections and accept or reject them. You can add notes and queries to the author on the computer by using the "Insert-Comment" facility; the writer can read them and make appropriate changes.

Making the Corrections By Hand (Informal Editing)

Many writers may prefer to make changes on a hard copy, especially if several people are editing the same document. It is particularly difficult to edit large documents on the screen as changes can affect text several pages away. For these reasons, editing on hard copy will probably never be totally phased out.

If you are given a hard copy to edit and it is 1.5 spaced or wider, you should be able to make the corrections *very neatly* between the lines, with deletions being made with a straight edge. A red pen is advisable, as this stands out best. If you make small changes — adding a comma, or deleting a letter or two, for instance — circle or underline the changes, and/or place an x in the margin so the writer knows you have made a suggested change there. If there are significant additions, type these separately and indicate where they should be inserted by large lettering: A, B, C, etc.

Here is an example of editing by hand:

Although Canada is the second largest country in the world and has very long coast line bordering ~~two~~ three oceans, as well as the worlds largest area of fresh water, its dredging markets are not significant. In 1695, dredging work for the Great Lakes connecting Channels became a Canadian responsibility; however, due to high water levels in recent years, little work has been done so far. Canada, therefore, is not a dredger ~~than~~'s paradise.

You should learn to use some of the symbols used for correcting proofs (see next section), but there is less need to follow all the "rules" or "language" of proof correcting. Here are a few rules you should observe:

Checklist 11.15: Rules for Editing by Hand

✓ *Make your corrections neatly and clearly.*

✓ *To move material, encircle it completely and indicate where you want it moved to. Correct the place it came from and also where it is to be placed.*

✓ *Do not write your changes in capitals unless you want them included as capitals.*

✓ *Do not include parentheses anywhere unless you want them inserted in the text.*

Correcting Proofs (Formal Editing)

Publishers and professional editors still use a special "language" to indicate changes in text that is nearly ready for publication. The special symbols they use are especially useful when you are editing "galley" proofs the same size as the final document. For these, there is no room to add words or letters between the lines. You have to keep the text (or "copy" as it is called) as clean as possible and place your instructions and additions in the margins.

There is some variety in the symbols used, and there are over forty of them for professional editing purposes. It is useful for you to know the most commonly used ones so that you can correct proofs adequately, and can "read" the editing when a professional editor edits your work.

Checklist 11.16: Commonly Used Editing Symbols and Meanings

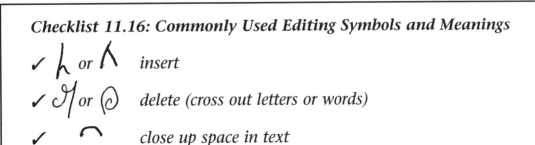

✓ ⅄ or ∧   *insert*

✓ ⅁ or ℮   *delete (cross out letters or words)*

✓   ⌒   *close up space in text*

✓ tr or trs	transpose letters or words (use in text)
✓ #	add a space (use insert symbol in text)
✓ np or para or P	new paragraph (use a solidus in the text)
✓ stet	leave as set before you changed it (place dots under the text)
✓ cap	capital letter (underline letters)
✓ lc	lower case: small letters (circle letters)
✓ ⌐	move right
✓ ⌐	move left
✓ ⸜	apostrophe or raised character

See, for example, Webster's New World Dictionary for a detailed list and explanation of these and many other symbols.

You need to know the language of editing as well — not just learn the "words." Here is a list of rules and advice:

Checklist 11.17: Proof-Correcting Practices

✓ *In general every symbol in the text must have a corresponding notation in the margin — so we do not miss anything.*

✓ *Use both margins and try to spread your changes out if there is more than one change in a line.*

✓ *When there are two or more changes in a line, ensure that the instructions follow left to right with the changes in the text.*

✓ *When you delete a single letter, cross it out with a clear oblique stroke (/) and place a delete sign in the margin.*

✓ *When you cross out two or more letters or words, use a single horizontal line and include a single delete sign in the margin.*

✓ *If you are replacing something you are deleting with something else, there is no need to place the delete sign in the margin, or to*

> place an insert sign in the text. Cross out in the text and write the new material with an insert sign in the margin.
>
> ✓ When you are moving text to another position, encircle it completely, and place a line to where it is to be moved; no mark is needed in the margin. Make changes to the punctuation and capitalization when you are moving parts of sentences.
>
> ✓ If you are not sure, place an encircled note to the author suggesting a possible change, or asking for guidance.
>
> ✓ Do not write your changes in capitals unless you want them included as capitals.
>
> ✓ Do not include parentheses anywhere unless you want them inserted in the text.

All this may sound quite complicated, but a little practice is all you need to be able to master this new "language." Here is a sample of proof-corrected text.

Although Canada is the second largest country in the worlds and has very long coast line bordering two oceans, as well as the worlds largest area of fresh water, it's dredging markets are not significant. In 1695, dredging work for the Great Lakes connecting Channels became a Canadian responsibility however, do to high water levels in recent years, little work has been done so far. Canada, therefore, is not a dredge man's paradise.

Exercise 11.9: Editing Sentences

Correct the following sentences, which have all been "approved" by a spell checker. Use informal editing unless your instructor tells you otherwise.

(a) Pattern recognition technique were use, to identify the damaged areas.

(b) The first test cell the Leachate Extraction procedure, LEP is new in use through out the country.

(c) Its not surprising to realise that some area of your companies performance is no optimum.

(d) There principle gaol was to determine the reason far the continual drain of power from the battery.

(e) The senior researcher (Tom Green), was censored for noted sighting his colleagues work in his paper.

Exercise 11.10: Editing Paragraphs and Small Texts

Edit the following texts, which have already been checked by a computer spell checker:

(a) Too engineering students one in Ontario and one in Quebec, are among 11 Canadian undergraduates who have, won 1992 roads scholarships. Emily Moore, a Queen's University engineering chemistry student and Catherine Beaudry, and electrical engineering student at Ecole Polytechnique will attend Oxford University in England this autumn, deceiving about $25,000 a year to cover academic and living expanses. The scholarship are for a maximum period of three year's. Canadian roads scholars are chosen buy six selection committees through out the country.

(b) In the old economy of the 1960's and 1970s, engineers new there roles and understood the opportunities that awaited them in such industries as steel, pulp and paper mining oil and gas utilities, an construction. But the job security of yesteryear has been replaced with an unspoken fear; "Am I employable in this new economy. Do I have the skills to compete in this new high tech word? Engineers are now alone in there concern for themselves and their children. Millions of Canadian's professionals and hourly paid workers a like feel lost and disoriented in a world that is changing rapidly and visibly before their i's. These changes have all ready created new and exciting opportunities for engineers armed with an understanding what the New Economy is all about.

(c) Mast environmental industry employers are small and medium-sized forms, with under 200 employers. Over 50% are concentrated in Ontario, the largest are companies that manage or dispose of waste. Or who operate waste treatments facilities. The second largest are manufacturer's of pollution control and other environmentally related systems, followed by consultants. As consulting forms grow they will be expected to require such technical professionals as hydrogeologists; environmental scientists; air quality specialists and project managers. Goodfellow Consultants and it's division Healthy Buildings International, are clean air technology specialists which have recently increased there engineering staff by over 30%.

(d) The British firm de Havilland established a Canadian subsidiary in toronto in 1928, to support the growing Canadian aircraft market and assemble its Moth aircraft. The companies came to realize that it's existing English designed aircraft were no entirely suitable fort *he country's bush operations. Fabric covered wooden construction was to fragile for rough conditions; and the buy plane configuration made loading and taxiing on floats awkward. To meat these special Canadian needs, de Havillands design team begun developing a modern, all metal bush airplane which would be come the Beaver.*

(e) *The airplane which defined canadian aircraft manufacture in the middle of this sentry, the de Havilland DFHC-2 Beaver — first flue on August 16, 1947, with the Beaver Canadian engineers developed a unique solution to the challenges, facing pilots in this countries unforgiving northland. At the same time, the aircrafts popularity over seas proved that Canadian expertise had international application, during it's 21 year success storey 1,692 were built.*

Review Questions

1. *What is "faulty parallel structure"? Give examples.*

2. *What are "dangling clauses"? Give examples.*

3. *What are the main problems with number-verb agreement?*

4. *What is a "sentence fragment" and what are the criteria for an acceptable sentence?*

5. *Under what circumstances should we use sentence fragments?*

6. *What is meant by the "referent" for such connecting words as* how-ever *and* therefore*?*

7. *What is meant by simple and complex words, and concrete and vague words?*

8. *What are the major methods of indicating doubt or uncertainty?*

9. *What is "jargon"? When should it be avoided, and when should it be used?*

10. *When should we define a term?*

11. *What are the major methods of defining?*

12. *Where do definitions often occur?*

13. *What are pitfalls in defining?*

14. *What are "homonyms" and why do they cause problems in writing?*

15. *What are the rules for using a and an?*

16. *What is the major weakness in computer spell checkers?*

17. *What topics should you be concerned with during revision?*

18. *What topics should you be concerned with during editing?*

19. *What is "idiolect"?*

20. *What is the editorial philosophy regarding what you change and what you leave alone?*

21. *How can you edit on the computer to indicate your suggested changes?*

22. *What is informal editing and when would you use it? What are the main rules to observe when editing informally?*

23. *What are the main proofreading marks and what do they mean?*

Chapter 12:
Graphical Communication

This chapter explains the importance of the many forms of illustrations, tables and other graphical aids that supplement written technical texts. Different types of graphs, schematic diagrams and pictorial representations suitable for published documents are discussed. The use of maps, photographs and tables is also explained here, and you will learn how to include your graphical communications as part of your technical documents. Visual aids displayed during oral presentations are discussed in *Chapter 13*.

The Importance of Graphical Communication
Drawings that Aid the Technical Work
Illustrations in Publications
Illustrations as Aids to Visualization
Other Functions of Illustrations
Choosing the Types of Illustration

Graphs and Tables
Basic Graphs
Graphs as Working Tools
Tables

Schematic Diagrams
Diagrammatic Representation
Circuit and Block Diagrams
Flow Charts and Algorithms
Organizational Diagrams

Graphic Presentation of Data
Bar and Column Charts
Pie Charts and Pictorials

Maps and Photographs
Maps
Photographs

Combining Text and Illustrations
Blended and Separate Illustrations
Titles and Numbering

12

The Importance of Graphical Communication

Drawings that Aid the Technical Work

In engineering, we are primarily interested in creating practical solutions to defined needs in society, and this means we actually make things. These things are physical realities that we can touch and see — and therefore draw, so that others can "see" them too. An ability to read and understand three-dimensional orthographic drawings and to produce them yourself is an essential skill of all technical professionals. Without it, you could not fully comprehend things that are being designed by others. More importantly, you would be unable to express your own embryonic three-dimensional design concepts, either to yourself (to allow you to refine your ideas) or to co-workers. A related ability is the use of isometric drawings of objects that do not yet exist.

Computer graphics programs have considerably enhanced our ability to "draw" such diagrams. They allow us to alter and rotate diagrams as we enhance our designs, progressing from general and quite vague notions to specific design drawings from which an actual products can be made. The uses of these illustrations are an inherent part of the thought/action process of inspiration, conceptualization, refinement and analysis — in fact of all aspects of the design process.

Similarly for analytical work, we often need to construct graphs, sketches, charts or maps as essential aids to our comprehension and analysis of the technical concepts we are seeking to understand. These enable us to determine mathematical relationships, to relate features spatially, and to construct models as the basis for our further study of the subject. They are a part of the thought patterns that produce our final conclusions based on the evidence we find.

Illustrations in Publications

Once we have completed our design or analysis, there is still often a need to use illustrations to help our readers to visualize what we have created or discovered. Engineering drawings become "working drawings," which are instructions for the manufacture and quality inspection of the finished products. We may also need to present our experimental results in graphs, tables or charts for publication or as the basis for further detailed study. This graphical information may also need to be made suitable as visual aids for presentations explaining our work.

Only occasionally can we take a drawing used for design or experimental purposes and include it in a publication. We often need to simplify it to meet the needs of our readers, or to have it fit conveniently into the pages of the document! Fortunately, we rarely need to communicate all the details of a project in the document. Just as we often need to summarize communications in written form, we should also consider the advantage of communicating only the essential elements of a design in our illustrations. Those interested in the finer points can be invited to see your sketches, detailed drawings, analyses and primary data.

Thus illustrations in documents are essentially quite simple, providing only enough information as is needed. As any illustration will often supplement or clarify the written parts of the document, or help readers to visualize spatial relationships or sets of data, it should be only as complex as is needed to achieve its purpose. This is especially true for visual aids used during oral presentations.

Illustrations as Aids to Visualization

Words are woefully inadequate as a means of communicating irregular sizes and shapes, or of showing spatial relations between parts of a design or other object. If you do not believe this, try describing in words the appearance of your computer keyboard, including the sizes and shapes of the keys and their spatial relationships. Although this can be done because keyboards have a relatively simple appearance with many identical features, a single illustration or photograph provides far better — and faster — communication.

When you compare your detailed description in words with a single illustration (check inside your keyboard manual), you will recognize that the drawing or photograph is much easier to "read" and remember than the words you have used — however well you have done your task. Now try the same exercise with more complex layouts such as the dashboard of a car, or the controls on a modern sewing machine, microwave oven or compact disc player.

Thus a prime function of illustrations is to help readers to visualize and recall sizes, shapes, colors and spatial relationships. Illustrations often convey information in a more "readable" way, as they allow readers to "see" what is being described and to comprehend how things or data relate to each other. Note how this is achieved below.

12.1

This U. of Calgary system was installed with a 36 m heading/pitch baseline, as shown in **Figure 2.**
— *Canadian Aeronautics and Space Journal*, Mar 1995, P14

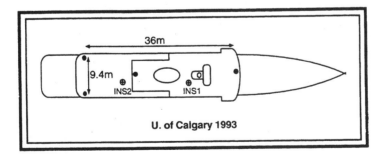

Figure 2.
GPS antenna array (view from above).

As we see here, an illustration may on some occasions almost completely supplant the text. Alternatively it may enhance and clarify the meaning of the text, as we see in:

12.2 A mine can be viewed as a system consisting of three structural components: firstly the mining process, e.g. exploration, fragmentation and materials handling, which relate to the mining methods and machine design. These are established and controlled by the second component, the support systems, e.g. systems for mine design, and production planning and control, see Figure 1. In recent years, these have been radically improved by advances in modelling, visualization, simulation, and database software. The efficiency and effectiveness of the overall mine system is dependent on the third component, the communications infrastructure, which links the mining process to the integrated support systems.

— *CIM Bulletin*, May 1995, P31

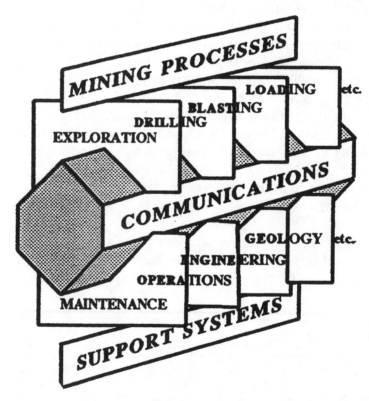

The key role of communications is made very clear in this diagram. Note how annotations or special dimensions or features may be essential parts of a clear illustration.

An added advantage of illustrations is that they can easily be found as readers scan the document, allowing a quick and easy review for readers of complex documents. The reference in *Example 12.1* is in bold type to help readers to find the part of the text where the illustration is introduced and discussed. When you are presenting your work orally, you will also find that your visual aids are extremely useful for reviewing designs or plans your have discussed in your talk — especially in response to a question for clarification or expansion. Note how the illustration in the previous example provides little more than is conveyed in the text, but provides it in a manner that is easy to recognize, recall and remember.

Exercise 12.1: Using Illustrations

Draw an illustration to help non-technical readers to visualize and remember the following description.

(a) *The High Speed Surface Transport (HSST) is a rail system supported and propelled by magnets. The rails, which are attached to sleepers secured to concrete girders, are cantilevered out toward the center of the track. Electromagnets are positioned under the rail by an L-shaped bracket attached to the undercarriage of the train. When energized, these electromagnets are attracted up toward the rails, thus lifting the train. Sensors between the underside of the rail and the electromagnets sense the distance between them. If the carriage starts to lower, the gap is increased, and the sensor boosts current through the electromagnet to raise the carriage. In this way the train is kept at a set height above the rail irrespective of the load it is carrying. A reaction plate on top of each rail interacts with a linear motor on the undercarriage and immediately above, but separated from, the reaction plate. The reaction plate and motor windings operate like a conventional ac motor opened up and laid flat.*

Draw an illustration (or several or a series of illustrations) to help technical readers to understand and remember the details given below. As this is for technical readers, two orthographic views (aligned and related in the proper manner of course) might be best for most of this information, but you may also need one or more other drawings (and/or notes to supplement the drawings) to indicate the sequence of movements.

(b) *The Skydome in Toronto is covered by four segments, three of which can be opened. Segment #1 is like a quarter of an orange, and is located at the north end of the dome. It does not move and is at the top of the segments when the dome is open. When the dome is being opened, Segment #4, of similar shape to Segment #1, is at the south end. It is the first moved as the dome is opened, and it moves on curved tracks to be situated under Segment #1. Segment #2 is the one nearer Segment #1 when the dome is closed. It is rectangular in shape in the top view and half a circle in the side view. It moves on straight rails to fit immediately under Segment #1 when the dome is open. Finally, Segment #3, of similar shape to Segment #2, is moved on separate straight rails (inside those for Segment #2) to lie between Segments #2 and #4 when the dome is open. The procedure is followed in reverse to close the dome.*

Draw two diagrams to help non-technical readers to understand the following text. The first diagram should be a plan view showing how the inflatable dams are situated and how they work as a system when a dyke is breached. The second drawing should show how a typical inflatable dam is located in the canal or river, how it is housed in normal circumstances, and how it works when inflated.

> (c) *In the Netherlands, many rivers and canals are* above *the level of the land, much of which is below sea level. The waterways are kept intact by dykes on each side. If a breach occurs in a dyke, water will flood the land both from the normal flow of the rivers and canals to the sea, and also as a backflow from the sea itself. As a solution to this problem, the Water Authority has installed inflatable dams in the floors of rivers and canals every 1.5 km. Now, if a dyke bursts, the dams on either side of the breach are inflated to isolate the faulty section to allow repairs. Water from upstream is pumped to an operating waterway. When out of use the dam is in a long, shallow box situated on the floor of the canal or river and traversing it. The top surface of the box has two steel plates hinged at the long edges (traversing the waterway). The inner edges of the plates meet and are attached to opposite ends of a sheet of rubber-nylon fabric, which normally lies folded inside the box. When a dyke breaks, water is pumped into the fabric envelope, causing it to rise out of the box and form a gigantic steel and fabric sausage across the waterway, blocking off the flow of water.*

For *Exercise 9.1*, try to tell the whole story completely as a cartoon series without any words. Then see how you could enhance the writing by using more than the one illustration stated for that exercise.

Other Functions of Illustrations

If you compare an illustration with the equivalent amount of text that gives the same information, you will realize that a good illustration can indeed often be worth more than many hundreds of words. *Example 12.1* and the drawing exercises above illustrate this principle. That is not always the aim, of course, as illustrations usually supplement the text. The combination of effective drawings and text often provides the best communication.

Although illustrations are often much more concise than the written alternative, some charts and graphs can take up several pages compared with perhaps a paragraph or two of text. On the other hand, well-designed pictorials or photographs with detailed captions can form a sort of illustrative summary of long articles. There are also whole books of "photographic essays," which convey the message graphically with the addition of a few brief notes and annotations. This useful combination of illustrations and explanatory captions is shown in:

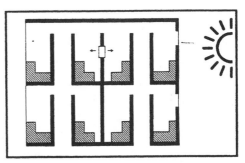

Restroom SupraSensors • reduce lighting costs by preventing unoccupied, overnight, week-end lighting powerful to detect occupants behind modesty walls, around corners, in stalls.

OmniSensors with Daylight Control Feature •automatically turns lighting on and off when ambient light reaches adjustable, preset level, even if area is occupied.

— *Canadian Consulting Engineer*, Jan/Feb 1995, P34

Another function of illustrations is to provide memorable — and even dramatic — communication. Illustrations and tables stand out from the remainder of the text, and thus draw the reader's attention to them. Charts and pictorials — especially with the use of color — have an immediate impact on readers, who will thus be more likely to remember the information being presented. Even though some illustrations can take up much more space than the corresponding information in written form, that is often justified by the impact they have on readers. Dramatic impact is shown in the following schematic diagram showing an automated control system.

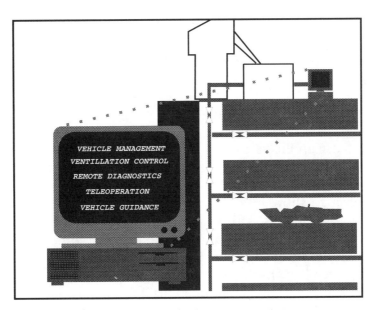

— *Canadian Mining Journal*, Dec 1994, P6 of supplement

Illustrations can also provide a note of reality. Photographs, in particular, show that something really exists (although they can be fudged), and are often strong "evidence" that support statements and conclusions. Much the same applies to automatic graph recordings of changes to temperature readings, pH values, humidity levels, etc. as a function of time. Photographs of current and voltage oscilloscope traces provide a clear statement of complex repetitive or transient wave forms. Similarly photographs of people are used extensively for profiles and bibliographic sketches. Much of the information presented in this way could not possibly be communicated at all effectively using words alone.

Graphics are also a means of presenting information in ways suitable for your readers. While a detailed description may be suitable for technical professionals, a clear illustration may be a better form of communication for non-technical management and sales personnel. The general public is more likely to be impressed with charts showing differences and comparisons than with the specific data — even if the illustrations take up much more space.

Checklist 12.1: Functions of Illustrations

✓ *to help readers to visualize and recall sizes, shapes, colors and spatial relationships, especially where that cannot meaningfully be communicated using words alone*

✓ *to provide immediate clear communication that can be reviewed easily*

✓ *to provide concise communication*

✓ *to indicate reality as strong evidence supporting conclusions*

✓ *to provide dramatic impact and memorable impression.*

Choosing the Types of Illustration

Your decision to use an illustration — and if so what sort — depends on all the factors listed in *Checklist 12.1*. If you have a lot of information dealing with sizes, shapes and spatial relationships, you should think of presenting it graphically. If you wish to show inter-connected elements of a complex system or organization, you should also think of providing the information in a graphic form. Or if you need to create a dramatic impact or to indicate reality, again a illustration might be the answer.

You will also need to think of your audience and determine the forms of graphical expression they will be familiar with and understand. Thus, for example, it would be totally unsuitable to include orthographic drawings in a document intended for non-technical professionals — or as a presentation for the public. They would not understand them, and you would be wasting your time. On the other hand, engineers could be insulted if you were to present experimental data in pictorial form instead of as a graph or in a table.

Your choice of the type of drawing to use also depends on the dramatic impact you might need for your audience, on the need to be concise in your writing and in the document as a whole, on the need to provide vital information for easy review, and on the need to give the impression of "real" products or evidence as the basis for conclusions.

Research Task

1. Look through all sorts of general and technical publications and note the types of illustration used. Determine what sorts of illustrations (schematic diagrams, graphs, photographs, charts) are used for different types of information being conveyed and the audience for the publication.

2. For some of these illustrations, determine whether some or all of the information they contain is, or could be, communicated by written text. If so, estimate how effective written text would be compared with the graphic form used. Also note whether the use of text would be more concise than the illustration.

3. Note the types of illustrations commonly used in your discipline.

Graphs and Tables

Basic Graphs

Graphs are indispensable as a means of plotting data on a mathematical screen so that we can "see" the relationship between two or more parameters, e.g. we can see what happens to the value of the current flowing through a resistor as we change the voltage applied cross it. By taking measurements and plotting the results on the graph, we can see that the relationship between the two variables is linear, and we can work out what that linear relationship is. Another example is the typical stress/strain graph for testing metals. From this we can learn much about the strength and ductility of the sample.

Such graphs are necessary parts of experimental reports, as they provide a graphic record of behaviour under specified conditions. If you are presenting a single copy of a report to your instructor (or perhaps one or two copies), you could submit the actual graphs drawn. However, if your work is to be published and many copies printed and distributed, you should consider re-drawing your graphs to make them more suitable. This usually means creating, on your computer, your own "graph paper" that does not contain all the lines on the sheets used for experimental purposes. We see this in the following example.

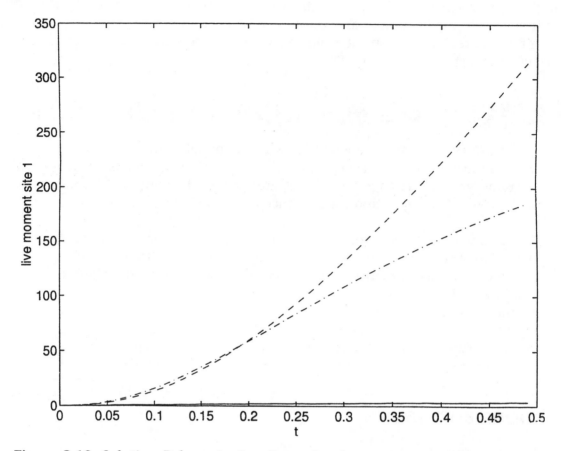

Figure 3.12: Solution Polymerization Example, the response variables plotted versus t, Y(0, 1)=solid line, Y(1, 1)= dashed line, Y(2, 1)= dashdot line

Graphs show how quantities change as a function of "variable" factors, which are placed on the horizontal axis of the graph. An exception is the well-known stress-strain graph for material strength test graphs. For these, the variable factor (the stress) is placed on the vertical axis, and the factor it creates (the strain) is on the horizontal axis.

Note how you can place several quantities, each changing as a function of the same variable, on your graph to indicate comparisons. For oral presentations, each of these can be placed on a separate sheet so that you can deal with the quantities first individually and then collectively.

If your graphs are being drawn for you automatically by a recorder, you might want to consider using the actual graphs produced. They may not look quite as neat as ones you produce yourself, but they have the advantage of being the real thing, as actually measured and recorded. They may therefore have greater credibility. Note how this is done in the following example.

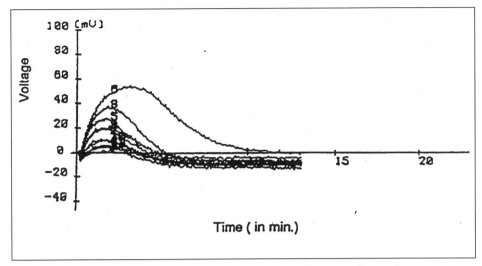

Fig. 2   Voltage-time curves for various electrodes for an industrial site

— *Canadian Civil Engineer*, May 95, P4

In this example, the figures of the different quantities are not very clear, and some of the values of time are overprinted by the recording of the data. In addition, every small change of voltage value is recorded, even if that is of little real consequence. However, these disadvantages are outweighed by the presentation of the actual values measured and recorded by the recording voltmeter. The credibility of that actual data would be reduced if we were to "tidy up" the graph to make it more presentable.

Graphs as Working Tools

Many graphs are used simply to display how quantities change as a variable changes. Others, however, are used as the basis for determining the mathematical relationship between two or more quantities. A simple example is shown in *Example 12.7*, in which the assumed linear relationship between voltage and force is determined by the "line of best fit" for the results obtained and identified on the graph. For this line, we can calculate the ratio (10.3) from the slope and any value of force (zero in this case) when the voltage is zero. These two values yield the formula F = 0 + 10.3 V, which is the mathematical relationship between the voltage and force. *Example 12.7* was designed for use as a visual aid to support an oral report of experimental work.

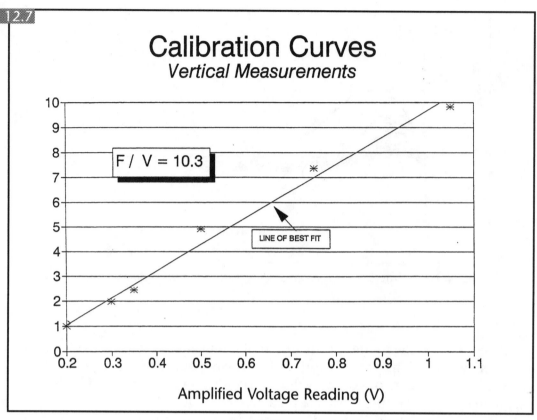

12.7

Calibration Curves
Vertical Measurements

F / V = 10.3

LINE OF BEST FIT

Amplified Voltage Reading (V)

— K. Haralampides, Department of Mechanical Engineering, 1995

Exercise 12.2: Working Graphs

Plot the three following sets of data with t as the abscissa (the horizontal or 'x' axis) on separate linear graph paper. Then find the lines of best fit and calculate the formulas.

D	t	Wb	t	pH	t
0.1	0	0.051	0	7.0	0
4.9	1	0.069	10	6.76	100
10.2	2	0.092	20	6.48	200
14.8	3	0.108	30	6.27	300
20.1	4	0.131	40	5.97	400
25.0	5	0.149	50	5.75	500
29.8	6	0.178	60	5.51	600

For more complex relationships involving exponentials and indices, you will have to use log-linear or log-log graphs. A linear "line of best fit" on such paper demonstrates that such a relationship exists between the two quantities being measured. From this line, you can calculate the formula that best describes the mathematical relationship between the two quantities. Again you may have to include the graphs and the calculations in your written or oral report of your work.

Tables

The actual measured data is often communicated in addition to, or instead of, the graphical form. For experimental work, the inclusion of the figures you measured is often a useful or even essential component of your report. For proposals and other reports, you may have more choice as to whether you use the data themselves, a graphical picture of the figures, or both. For many documents, the graphs and tables including the data are included as appendices. The table for *Example 12.7* is:

Voltage and Force Data

Voltage (V)	Force (N)
0.20	1.0
0.30	2.0
0.35	2.5
0.50	4.9
0.75	7.3
1.05	9.8

Tables are ideal for communicating lists of figures, as they give readers the exact data recorded and they are usually easy to read. It is far better to use a table than to try to explain the figures using normal sentences, as you will see when you complete *Exercise 12.3*.

Checklist 12.2: Advantages of Graphs/Charts and Tables

✓ *Graphs and charts:* - *provide clear communication of comparisons*
- *allow easy visual comparisons*
- *permit formula calculations*
- *give dramatic impact*
- *are ideal for oral reports and discussions*

✓ *Tables:* - *provide the actual data obtained*
- *allow specific comparisons*
- *provide information more efficiently*

There is, of course, often a disadvantage of using illustrations or tables, as only language can express the thoughts, views and opinions of the communicator. See what is *missing* after you have completed the following exercises.

Exercise 12.3: Converting Sentences to Tables

Prepare tables to convey the information in the following. Use an appropriate title for each table, and clearly label each series of figures in your tables. Make sure the order of the items of your tables is appropriate. When you have finished this exercise, compare the clarity of your tables with the original texts and draw your own conclusions.

(a) *If you want to find a job fast, look at the industries where jobs were created in 1993. We find that 8,132 were created in printing and publishing, 5,835 in communications and 499 in quarries and sandpits. In addition 5,174 jobs were created in the plastics products industry, while only 1,866 were created in industrial construction, 1,029 in machine shops but 1,556 in engineering surveying. Plastics and synthetic resins created only 676 jobs, and non-ferrous smelting and refining created a further 438.*

(b) *We counted 3,850 engineers working largely in engineering. They received an annual average salary of $61,148, an increase of 5.0% over the previous year. Those whose work is associated with engineering were also surveyed. The 3,233 we asked had an average salary of $68,592, which is a 4.6% increase compared with last year. The last category we studied was for engineers whose work is not associated with engineering at all. Their average salary was a surprisingly high $78,466, although their increment compared with the previous year was 1.3%.*

(c) *When we compare the number of engineers by industry and their average salaries, we find that most (39.5%) are in manufacturing with an average salary of $64,522, followed by 15.8% in consulting and 13.4% in government with salaries of $61,458 and $65,923 respectively. Significant numbers of engineers (12.3%) are employed in the non-manufacturing sector and in utilities (11.1%) earning respective salaries of $68,186 and $69,769. Smaller numbers work in construction (4.4% with an average salary of $65,931) and education (3.7% with an average salary of $69,444).*

(d) *There are two types of 1994 tax rates: the statutory tax rates and the actual effective rates. The statutory tax rates have three components: the federal income tax is 28.8%, the Ontario income tax is 13.5%, and the Ontario Mining tax is 20.0%. Thus the total statutory tax rate is 62.3%. In comparison, the actual effective tax rate has figures of 13.6%, 6.4% and 13.7% for the same three components of the statutory tax rates, yielding a total of 33.7%.*

We can also express this sort of information in a more graphic way by means of charts or pictorials, which your computer can easily create from the tables. These are discussed later.

Schematic Diagrams

Diagrammatic Representation

Schematic diagrams represent reality as diagrammatic metaphors. That is, they are not intended to illustrate exactly what something looks like, but merely to give a general "picture" of something. They use artistic licence to communicate the main elements of a topic clearly, while downplaying (or even ignoring) parts that are of little importance. Here is a clear schematic diagram of a new design for weaving material. Note how the illustration clearly labels components of the system, how the expanded sketch provides detail of a small but important element in the design, and how the diagram as a whole depicts everything in a non-literal manner.

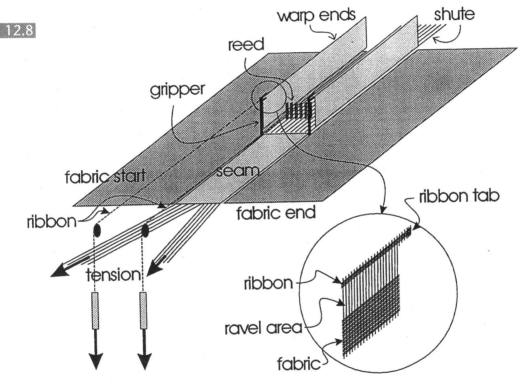

— E.Bacon, H.Iordanou, G.Logan, Stat 865, 1995

The diagrams you have drawn for *Exercise 12.1* are schematic diagrams, as they depict reality in a general way — not necessarily how the objects actually exist.

Circuit and Block Diagrams

When we need to communicate things that are connected together in various ways, we often need to use diagrams that indicate the circuit connections. For simple electrical circuits, for example, we would represent amplifiers and resistors as simple standard symbols, and thus produce a schematic diagram to represent reality:

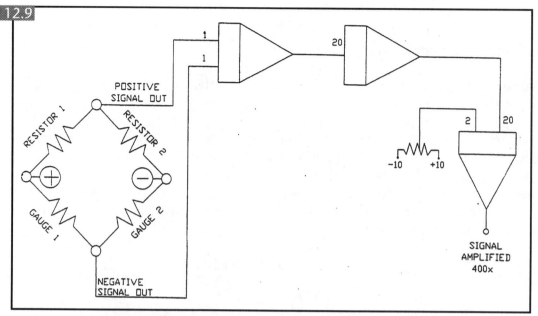

— K. Haralampides, Department of Mechanical Engineering, 1995

Standard symbols such as those in this example are used in diagrams for electrical circuits and hydraulic diagrams. In this diagram, there is also a standard pattern of connections of a balanced Wheatstone Bridge of the four resistors on the left.

Even more simply, we can depict things as rectangular "boxes" interconnected with each other to create block diagrams:

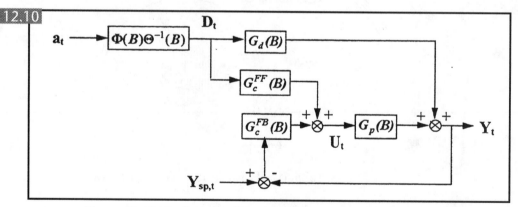

Figure 2. Block diagram for a multi-input, multi-output process

— C. Seppala, Department of Chemical Engineering, 1995

The formulas inside the boxes indicate their functions, and the lines and arrows indicate the connections and direction of flow for the process. Many of these illustrations can be drawn directly on your computer, using the "Draw" facility.

Flow Charts and Algorithms

Block diagrams usually show the flow of electric current or hydraulic fluid within a system. We can, however, depict the flow of anything in very complex arrangements through the use of flow charts. By this means, the flow of ore from the mine to finished products, the flow of activities from start to end of a design process, the flow system of a car assembly plant, etc. can all be shown in clear schematic diagrams. Here is an example of the flow of products and control mechanisms for a complex mine operation:

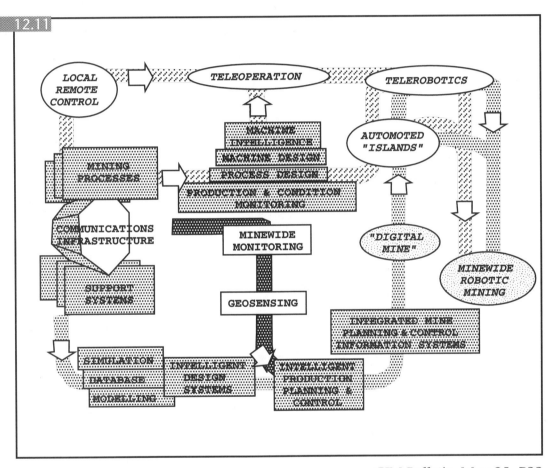

— *CIM Bulletin*, May 95, P33

The boxes of this illustration indicate activities, and the connecting lines and arrows show us how these activities are interconnected within the whole operation. Obviously such a diagram could not stand on its own; discussion in written text or by oral presentation would be needed to explain and elaborate on the flow system depicted here.

A special kind of flow chart is the algorithm, which shows the procedure whereby a complex task is performed. These charts ask such questions as "What is done next?" and "What is done if the answer is Yes/No?." Here is an example of an algorithm, which would be equally suitable for a written report or as a visual aid to support an oral presentation.

12.12

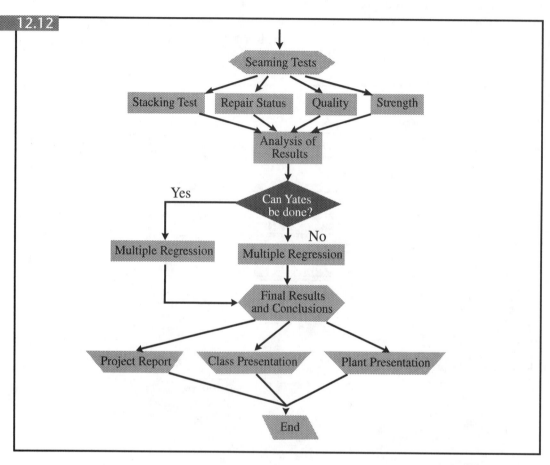

— E.Bacon, H.Iordanou, G.Logan, Stat 865, 1995

Organizational Diagrams

In contrast with circuit and block diagrams, which depict some sort of flow or movement, organizational diagrams are essentially static. They represent the way things are in an organizational way, with the positioning of the blocks indicating levels of hierarchy and lines between them showing connections. The way a college or university is governed is best shown in this way, with the Board of Trustees and Senate at the top, faculties and schools underneath, and then departments below them. Company organizations are typically shown in this way.

Exercise 12.4: Organizational Block Diagrams

Draw block diagrams to show the levels of hierarchy and within your educational institution or your faculty. Do the same for your student organization. For these, start with the positions, and then add the names of those currently occupying them.

Example 12.2 is a block diagram for a more technical topic. In that diagram, the mining processes of exploration, drilling, blasting, loading, etc. are at the top with the support systems of maintenance, operations, engineering and geology at the bottom. Communication is shown as the link between these activities. A more elaborate illustration of this static picture is shown as *Example 12.13*. It shows what the mine processess and support systems are and how they interact with each other, with the Communications Infrastructure coupling together these two main branches of activity.

Such complex organizational diagrams often need quite considerable amounts of explanation in the text or as oral discussion. However, the combination of such a diagram with supporting description is often a powerful method of communication.

12.13

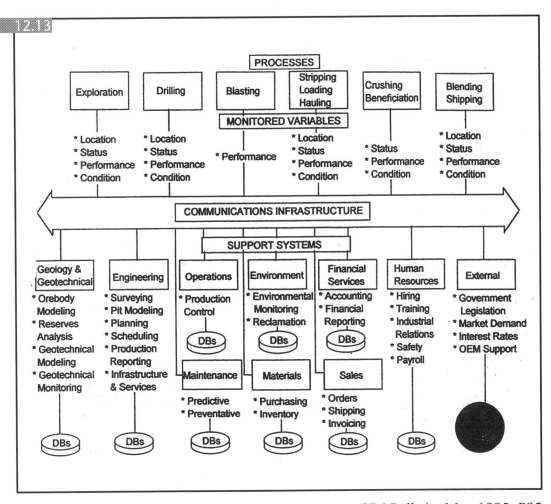

— *CIM Bulletin*, May 1995, P32

Graphic Presentation of Data

Bar and Column Charts

Although data presented in tabular form is very concise and clear, it takes readers time to assimilate the information, to compare the figures and to note trends. We can help readers to do that by presenting the information graphically in the form of bar or column charts. Bar charts are horizontal and are usually used for comparing quantities, whereas column charts are vertical and are usually used to show changes as a function of time, e.g. growth for the last few years.

Many writers prefer the appearance of the column chart and tend to use them for any sort of information. On the other hand, you might prefer to use a bar chart if you have many quantities to compare, as you have more room on the page vertically than you have horizontally. Bar charts are often called "horizontal bar charts," and column charts are often called "vertical bar charts."

As computer programs now allow us to construct high quality bar and column charts in a matter of minutes, you should consider using them when you need to emphasize your data. They are especially suitable for oral presentations or for technical proposals that include estimates of growth and financing. Here is a typical bar chart:

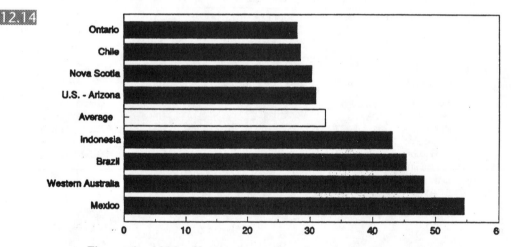

Figure 1. 1993 effective tax rates, low profitability mine

— *CIM Bulletin*, May 1995, P51

Although this information could be communicated in a table in much less space, the message the writer wishes to present would not have been as obvious. Even stating the comparisons would not give the desired impact, which only a chart such as this can achieve.

Example 12.14 shows one attribute for each location. Often, though, we have several attributes, as we see in the following table:

12.15

Table 8. Annual Salaries by Job Category

Proportion of Job Related to Engineering	Count	Average	Low Decile	High Quartile	Median	High Quartile	Decile	%Incr. 90/91 Median
Not associated with engineering	536	78,466	48,800	59,520	69,900	86,000	117,000	1.3
Associated with engineering	3,233	68,592	45,000	53,630	65,000	78,630	95,000	4.6
Largely engineering	3,850	61.148	41,000	48,900	59,850	70,420,	82,000	5.0

— *Engineering Dimensions*, Salary Details, 1992, P9

There are only three groups being compared here, but no fewer than eight features for each three. Thus a table is probably the best way to communicate this information. However, to emphasize the differences, we could present the five features from low decile to high decile for each of the three groups. This can be done (a) by showing all five features together for each of the three groups separately (i.e. three clusters of five features), or (b) the three groups compared for each of the five features (i.e. five clusters of three groups). In this case the former methods would show the comparisons more clearly.

Of course, color and/or shading can also be used to clarify the information and to make differences stand out. Note how shading is used to help readers follow the numbers; this is especially useful when you have many rows and columns. Also, for complex bar and column charts used in oral presentations, you can start with one feature and then use successive overlays to "build up" the complete illustration. This technique gives your listeners time to assimilate quite complex sets of information.

Pie Charts and Pictorials

Pie charts are ideal for demonstrating percentages — especially in business documents — and we see their frequent use by governments and businesses to show where their income comes from and what it is spent on. The slices of pie represent the percentages of the whole pie, and the percentage and actual figures are usually included too. Here is an example showing the employment status of engineers in Ontario. First we are given the table of data, and then the pie chart as of December 1, 1991.

12.16

Table 1. Respondents' Employment Status Over Six Years (%)

	1991	1990	1989	1988	1987	1986
Full-time employee	80.8	83.3	81.8	85.5	84.3	84.1
Retired	10.3	9.3	11.3	9.1	9.5	8.6
Self-employed	5.0	4.4	5.0	4.5	4.7	5.5
Unemployed	1.8	0.9	0.7	0.5	0.9	1.1
Part-time employee	0.7	0.8	0.7	0.4	0.6	0.7
Other	1.2	0.8	0.5	—	—	—

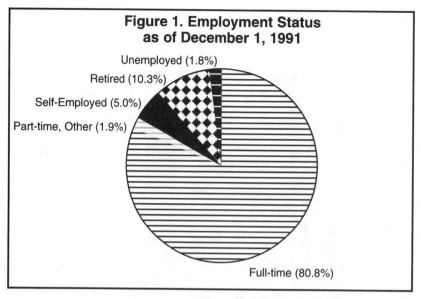

Figure 1. Employment Status as of December 1, 1991

Unemployed (1.8%)
Retired (10.3%)
Self-Employed (5.0%)
Part-time, Other (1.9%)
Full-time (80.8%)

— *Engineering Dimensions*, Salary Details, 1992, P4

Note the use of different types of shading on this chart to help readers distinguish the slices of the pie.

Although pie charts clearly communicate percentages at a given time, changes over time cannot be seen easily from a series of pie charts. We would therefore be better off using column charts if we wanted to show any trends over time.

Another way of making information more noticeable and dramatic is to use pictorials: pictures representing or highlighting the data. As an example, readers may overlook the rather surprising data in *Example 12.15* concerning salaries earned by engineers in different job categories. Those employed largely in engineering earn less than those in work associated with engineering, who earn even less than those working in areas not associated with engineering at all! To bring this information to the attention of readers, the writer noted it in the text and also provided a pictorial:

12.17 APEO members whose jobs have a large engineering component earn a median salary of $10,050 less than those who have no engineering content or responsibilities.

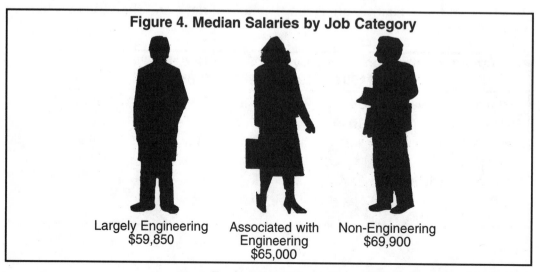

Figure 4. Median Salaries by Job Category

Largely Engineering
$59,850

Associated with Engineering
$65,000

Non-Engineering
$69,900

— *Engineering Dimensions*, Salary Details, 1992, P10

This pictorial provides no additional information — in fact it uses only three of the 24 figures presented in *Example 12.15*. However, it provides them in a very clear and dramatic way, making sure that readers note this rather surprising information.

This pictorial does not use the size of the people in the diagram as an indicator of salary, as that could have been misconstrued as saying something about how big the people are. For other topics, though, we could use size in that way; this is essentially what we are doing with bar, column and pie charts. To indicate different quantities in pictorials we can use different numbers of items in the diagram.

Checklist 12.3: Advantages of Graphic Presentation of Data

Graphic presentation of data:

✓ *emphasizes something you regard as important.*

✓ *provides an effective attention-getting device.*

✓ *enables readers to grasp the levels of the data presented.*

✓ *often provides clear comparison of data.*

✓ *provides clear review of important information.*

Exercise 12.5: Graphic Presentation of Data

(a) *Present the information in Exercise 12.3 (a) first as a bar chart, and then as a pie chart. State which you feel is more effective and what you might prefer to use them for.*

(b) *Illustrate the information in Exercise 12.3 (b) as a bar chart.*

(c) *Draw a pie chart with clear labeling to illustrate the data provided in Exercise 12.3 (c).*

(d) *Use any appropriate method to illustrate the information in Exercise 12.3 (d).*

(e) *Draw two different types of column chart for the five categories from low decile to high decile for Example 12.15 — see the discussion following that example. Compare the effectiveness of the two methods for this example.*

(f) *Present the information given in the table for Example 12.16 as six separate column charts for each employment status. Prepare them so they can be used as overlays to build up to an overhead containing all the information together.*

Maps and Photographs

Maps

The use of illustrations in technical communication is a vast subject, and this chapter can do no more than introduce you to the principles of using illustrations and the most important types. One such important method of illustration is the use of maps, especially in the earth sciences. They are ideal as representations of geographical locations, areas, relative distances and topographical details. Location maps show where the area of study is, and regional maps show the special detail you wish to impart. Often a location and a regional map are placed together to provide locational and detailed information. Only rarely can you expect to use an existing regional map for your report — you will usually have to draw or trace your own without the extraneous detail on standard maps.

In mining and geological engineering, you may need "maps" that show readers important details beneath the surface. These are often schematic rather than depicting the actual features in true scale. Such maps allow readers to view a special part of the earth horizontally rather than the usual vertical downward view of conventional maps. Detailed maps of mines, oil or gas deposits, rock formations, earthquake or volcano activity, and many other underground features are shown by such vertical maps.

Specialized maps drawn by other workers can often be used in your document — as long as you give full references and credit of course. Many writers of technical reports and papers also adapt existing maps already published elsewhere. When they do this, they indicate what they have done by using, for example, (*after Wells, 1995*) to give credit and origin and to indicate that the original has been changed.

Photographs

Aerial photographs can be used instead of maps if they are available and they show your readers features that are not shown on maps. Special aerial photographs using infra-red or other systems are used for surveying purposes, and often find their way into technical reports. Aerial photographs of volcanoes, glaciers, woodlands, floods, etc. provide information which clearly cannot be presented in a conventional map with the same clarity or sense of reality. Nor could that sort of information be communicated at all adequately using words alone.

Photographs are also used whenever you need to "show" readers what actually happened or what exists. We use photographs to verify a person's identity for various purposes (e.g. licences, examinations, passports), and they are thus useful supplements to descriptions of people. Manufacturers also use them in advertising to show potential purchasers what a product looks like. Photographs are also useful in showing relative sizes and shapes, although to indicate size you may have to include something of known size (a ruler or a person) to allow comparison. (Advertisers used to include scantily-dressed women next to large engineering products such as transformers or motors, using the excuse that it indicated the size of their products! This practice, however, is now considered inappropriate.)

The great advantage of photographs is that they show real information as opposed to schematic information, although you should be aware that even photographs can be altered! However, photographs are often useful as "evidence" — see *Chapter 7*. For example, a photograph of charred wood or electrical wire may be vital evidence in a report on the cause of a fire. Photographs are also useful in showing the existing state of, say, housing inadequacies, corrosion of material, mussel build up in pipes, oscilloscope traces, and many other features that need to be recorded and communicated.

Photographs can be included as part of the main text, although larger photographs are often included as appendices. A large photograph, or other illustration, at the front of a document is called a "frontispiece."

Combining Text and Illustrations

Blended and Separate Illustrations

In informal writing, it is usual to blend simple diagrams or sketches with the text without formally referring to the illustration. That is, the illustration supports the text in a clear or general way, and there is often no need to discuss it or explain it in the text. You should try to place such illustrations as close to the most relevant discussion as you can, as this helps readers to see their relevance. They do not need to have a figure number or title.

For more formal documents, illustrations are given figure numbers and titles to help readers to identify them. The figure numbers also enable writers to refer specifically to the illustration at the most appropriate point in the text:

12.18 The pull-out tests were performed with a hollow cylinder hydraulic ram with a 150 mm stroke, a load cell, and a rotary potentiometer displacement transducer (Fig. 3).

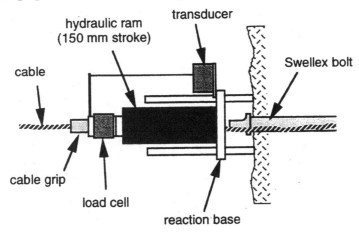

Figure 3: Pull test Setup

— *CIM Bulletin*, March 1995, P100

Such introduced illustrations do not have to be placed next to the text that refers to them, leaving you more free to arrange your material conveniently on the page. Large diagrams could even be placed as an appendix, although it is always easier for the reader to have the text and related illustration on the same or the facing page. Important large documents could be presented as "pull-outs," which can be seen wherever you are in the document. If your illustration has several parts or sub-sketches, or is a sequence of illustrations, you could indicate these separate components (e.g. by letters) and use these in the text to help readers follow your text and your illustration.

Titles and Numbering

Illustrations that are given figure numbers should also be given titles. Try to make your titles as meaningful as possible, ideally allowing readers to understand the illustration without having to read the supporting text. Readers should be able to recognize what the diagram is about simply by reading its title in the Table of Illustrations at the front of the document. Titles for illustrations are usually placed underneath the illustration. In some documents you might, in addition, find it useful to provide some further textual detail under the title (see *Example 12.3*). This provides a summary of the whole article, allowing readers to understand the gist of the communication by looking at the illustrations and reading the captions underneath them.

Illustrations with figure numbers should be placed in the order of their numbering, so that readers can find them easily. In addition, for many reports and proposals, the list of figures (their numbers and titles) should be included as prefatory material, together with the page numbers on which they appear to help readers to find them. If there are only a few illustrations, they could appear on the Table of Contents; if, however, you have many illustrations a separate Table of Illustrations would be more suitable (see *Chapter 13*).

Much the same applies to tables. They can be blended in with the text or, more usually, given a table number and title, which is more typically placed at the top of the table:

12.19 Five pull-out tests were conducted in norite rock, four at the Big Nickel mine and one at the Levack mine in the Sudbury basin. The support properties and dimensions for each test are listed in Table 1.

TABLE 1. Swellex bolt, cable, and borehole dimensions for pull-out tests					
Cable	No. 1	No. 2	No. 3	No. 4	No. 5
Swellex type	yielding	yielding	yielding	standard	standard
Swellex length in hole (m)	2.12	2.17	2.15	0.86	1.75
Cable length in hole (m)	2.36	2.36	2.36	1.17	2.08
Cable free length[1] (m)	0.20	0.15	0.15	0.27	0.30
Wire rope dressing class[2]	D	D	D	D	A

[1]Distance between the end of the Swellex bolt and the cable end-bushing.
[2]All cables were coated with a regular wire rope dressing (lubricant). Cables No. 1 to No. 4 contained a class D coating. This coating is much thicker than the class A coating on cable No. 5.

— *CIM Bulletin*, March 1995, P101

As with illustrations, tables should have a clear title (usually above the data) and sometimes also explanatory notes as in this example.

While some organizations prefer to regard tables as illustrations, it is more usual to treat them separately and to provide a List of Tables in the prefatory material. Again, include this in the Table of Contents if there is room; otherwise use a separate prefatory page or use a single page for your Table of illustrations and List of Tables. Although a few quite small tables are probably better included with the main text, masses of tubular data are often included as appendices.

Exercise 12.6: Incorporating Illustrations and Tables

a) *Provide titles for Examples 12.2, 12.9, 12.12, and 12.13.*

b) *For Exercise 12.2 a), provide a number and title, and then use letters (A, B, C) in the text to refer to parts of your diagram*

c) *For Exercise 12.1b), use a series of sketches to illustrate the sequences of movements to open or close the roof system. Letter these and refer to the letters in the text. Also provide a number and title for your overall illustration.*

d) *For Exercise 12.1c), provide figure numbers and titles for the two illustrations and refer to them at appropriate parts of the text. For the second diagram, use numbering as well as labels to identify the major parts, and again indicate that in the text,*

e) *For Example 12.4, provide a figure number and title, and also include some brief discussion to help readers understand what the illustration is depicting.*

f) *Provide table numbers and suitable titles for the three sets of data presented in Exercise 12.2 and also for all parts of Exercise 12.3.*

Writing Task

1. In a report to first-year college or engineering students, explain in general terms how the latest computer software can be used to create, change, and blend different types of illustrations into documents.

2. Choose a certain type of illustration and computer software, and explain in detail how we can create and adapt them on the computer.

Review Questions

1. *What are orthographic drawings used for, and how have computers revolutionized their production?*

2. *Why are drawings in documents usually different from working documents for manufacture and quality control?*

3. What sorts of information are illustrations particularly good at communicating?

4. Can an illustration really be worth a thousand words? Discuss the use of illustrations to replace or complement text.

5. What are the main functions of illustrations?

6. How does audience background affect the choice of illustrations?

7. How can graphs be used a) to determine how one or more quantity varies as a function of another, and b) to determine the mathematical relationship between two quantities?

8. What are the advantage and disadvantage of using graphs that are drawn automatically by monitoring/recording equipment?

9. What are the relative advantages and disadvantages in communicating data as graphs or tabular material?

10. What information does text often contain that you will not find in tables?

11. What are schematic details, and how can they be seen as a form of metaphor?

12. What are circuit diagrams, and what are their main characteristics?

13. What are block diagrams, and what are they used for?

14. What are organizational block diagrams, and what do they communicate?

15. What are flow charts and what sort of information do they convey?

16. What is an algorithm and what does it do?

17. What are bar charts and column charts? How else are they named? What sort of information do they best communicate?

18. How can bar and column charts be used to indicate several parameters for different features?

Chapter 13:
Oral Presentation

This chapter explains the most important principles of oral presentation of technical information. Advice is given regarding how you can benefit most from group work and discussions, how you should plan, prepare and deliver formal oral presentations, and how to answer questions. The planning, preparation and use of visual aids to support your presentations are also discussed here.

General Principles
Importance of Oral Presentations
Writing and Speaking — The
    Differences

Informal Presentations
Discussions and Meetings
Telephone Conversations
Job Interviews

Formal Presentations
Do Your Homework
Plan Your Presentation
The Start
The Body of the Speech
Nervousness
Attitude
Stance
Voice
Audience Contact

Answering Questions
Importance and Circumstances
Procedure
Techniques

Visual Aids
Visibility, Clarity, Simplicity
Preparation and Use
Types of Visual Aid and their
    Uses

13

General Principles

Importance of Oral Presentations

Although your written documents provide a lasting record of your technical work and ability to communicate it, the way you present your work and yourself orally can have a much more immediate effect on others. Through knowledgeable explanation of your work and your ideas, you could be perceived as a competent individual worthy of further advancement. On the other hand an *in*ability to explain your work to others orally could have the very opposite effect.

Technical professionals engage in oral communication every day of their professional lives. They may talk to fellow technical specialists, managers and executives, personnel officers, accountants, marketing executives, and tradespeople in many technical branches. They may also talk to those in other companies as suppliers, customers or clients; and they may have to present their work and proposals to a board of directors or to outside organizations such as municipal councils. Some are called as expert witnesses in court cases.

Much of this discussion will be face-to-face conversation or group interaction. You will also be talking to others by telephone, in interviews and through video links. You may also be required to explain your ideas, designs and proposals in formal presentations. You will need to master all these forms of oral discussion to be an effective professional.

Writing and Speaking — The Differences

The biggest difference between writing and speaking is that all forms of oral discussion and presentation involve *personal* communication. When you are speaking to someone (formally or informally), you can see (or hear on the telephone) immediately what effects your message is having on your listeners. Are they bored or nearly falling asleep? Or are they obviously interested in your point of view? Or are they openly skeptical, or showing signs of bewilderment. These and other reactions are apparent to experienced oral communicators by subtle (sometimes not so subtle) signs of body language. These signs are essential parts of effective two-way communications, and you will need to note them and take them into account if you wish to become an effective oral communicator.

With writing, you have to think of the needs of your readers and then write in accordance with those defined needs. If you are badly mistaken in your assessment of reader needs, your writing will fail, and there is no opportunity to alter your approach to meet those needs during your communication. With speaking, however, you should obtain immediate and continuing feedback from your listeners, and this gives you the opportunity to accommodate your listeners' needs during your discussion or presentation.

The key to being able to make necessary changes as the discussion or presentation proceeds is flexibility. If you have over-planned your talk in great detail and then present it exactly as planned, then you are losing the great advantage that oral reporting presents to you. Actual reading of a presentation not only sounds wooden and often too formal, but also fails to acknowledge the essence of the humanness of oral presentations.

Another difference between writing and speech is that listeners cannot stop for a break, or go back and check something earlier in the presentation — as readers can. You, as the speaker, are in complete control of the order and pace of the material you are presenting. So if part of your material is quite difficult, you should slow down a little, or go over it again, or summarize it to help your audience understand the information. Often a written form of your work is presented as well, and then you have the best of both forms of communication.

Another difference is that it is often more difficult to explain complex concepts when speaking and referring to complex drawings than it is in writing. There is a practical limitation on the amount of information people can comprehend in a given period of time; and also how much a speaker can reasonably explain in a short time. So you may have to keep your presentation relatively simple, leaving more complex issues for a written argument you have more time to think about. The need for simplicity in your visual aids is extremely important — more on this later.

Informal Presentations

Discussions and Meetings

Informal discussion with two or more people may have a fairly clear subject, but there is rarely an approved "agenda" — a list of the contents and order of the topics to be discussed. Many discussions are totally unplanned — you meet one or more colleagues in an informal setting, and discuss items of mutual importance almost at random.

Do not underestimate the importance of such discussions, as they can produce many important ideas and suggestions — especially by those who might be reluctant to voice their opinions during more formal discussions or meetings. To help yourself to remember important topics raised, you should consider making brief notes of any interesting points raised during informal discussions immediately afterwards.

Meetings are nothing more than formalized discussion periods. They can be quite informal, as when a group leader gets everyone together to discuss progress, problems, suggestions, etc. For these there may be no formal agenda, but the meeting co-ordinator or chairperson should have a list of items for discussion. Notes should be taken at informal meetings, although the writing of formal "minutes" (an account of what was said and decided) may not be necessary.

Formal meetings have an agenda (contents and order) and they are usually organized and controlled, in Canada, by Robert's Rules of Order, or less commonly by Bourinot's Rules of Order. The speaking, voting and other elements of the running of the meeting are defined in the rules of order and any other rules used by the organization. Formal minutes of the meeting are taken and approved at the next meeting.

Oddly, perhaps, speaking may not be the most important aspect of your participating in discussions, although you *are* expected to participate and not just sit there and say nothing. But listening can be important too. If everyone talks and nobody listens, you will all be wasting your time. You need to learn from the views and experience of others. When you are speaking, make your points firmly and clearly (but not too dogmatically). When you are listening, do not interrupt unless it is really necessary (make a note and comment later), and try to think of the positive things you are hearing and not just how you can have *your* ideas accepted by the group.

If you are "chairing" an informal meeting, try to involve all members of group in the discussion. You may have to encourage some members to comment, especially if they are being polite and not taking the chance to express their views. Try to guide the group in a full and meaningful discussion of all relevant points, and try to arrive at decisions that are acceptable to all — or at least most — members of the group.

As chair of a formal meeting, you will have to become familiar with all the rules of order. You should seek and take the advice of a knowledgeable professional secretary in planning and controlling the meeting and related documents.

Telephone Conversations

Although you have obviously had a great deal of practice with the telephone for personal use, professional conversations on the telephone require some thought. This is especially true for discussions regarding a summer or permanent position you are seeking.

First plan what you want to say — not the exact words as that would sound rehearsed and wooden, but the questions you wish to ask and the points you want to make. Write out your "agenda" and cross off items you have discussed, usually after making a note or two to remind yourself of what you (or your respondent) have agreed to. Bear in mind, however, that you may not be able to stick rigidly to your plan if you find the conversation moving in another direction. You may have to allow that to happen, but return to points you have not covered later in the conversation.

Your next task is actually making voice contact with the person you wish to speak to. Voice answering systems and secretaries who screen calls for their bosses often make this first task quite difficult. If you have too much difficulty, you could leave a voice message perhaps asking the person to return your call or suggesting a time you might be able to contact each other. Alternatively, you might try sending an e-mail message and perhaps make arrangements to discuss some matters personally — or of course try to do everything via e-mail.

When you do get through to your respondent, make sure that you are speaking to the right person, and then introduce yourself clearly and explain why you are calling. In some cultures in the world (especially Pacific Rim countries), it would be rude to launch straight into the main reason for your call. Instead you first need to establish some rapport with your respondent, or discuss something personal first if you know the person. That is less necessary in North America, although some basic pleasantries at the start are usually appropriate.

Unlike face-to-face discussions, telephone conversations cannot rely on facial expressions or body language as part of the dialogue. So you must be clearer than usual with your responses, and you need to make "continuity" noises (*mmm, yes, I see*, etc.) during long speeches by your respondent. These indicate that you are still there and that you are paying attention. Always appear friendly and helpful on the phone. A gruff officious tone does not impress anyone — they will only think you are being rude.

Similarly at the end, try not to appear too abrupt by clicking off your respondent the instant you say "Bye." Let the conversation wind down naturally, and make sure you have achieved the main objectives of your call before you stop the discussion.

When you are receiving telephone calls, you may not have had the opportunity to plan what you want to say or ask. Always have a pad and pen available on your desk, and make notes as you go. Make sure you have the person's name and phone number clearly recorded. Also note anything you have promised to do, or anything your caller has agreed to do or send you.

Checklist 13.1: Telephone Techniques

✓ *Plan what you want to say and ask.*

✓ *Check who you are addressing and introduce yourself.*

✓ *Do not be in a rush to get your points across at the start; some pleasantries may be appropriate.*

✓ *Be flexible in your agenda, and check you have discussed all important issues before hanging up.*

✓ *Speak clearly and appear friendly.*

✓ *Make notes of what you and your respondent have agreed to or promised to send.*

✓ *Ensure a smooth unhurried ending.*

Job Interviews

One of the most important face-to-face discussions you will have over the next few year will be interviews for summer and later permanent employment. Your purpose is to convince the interviewer that you are the best person for the job available. You can go a long way toward achieving this object by adopting the following guidelines.

Preparation

Go to your Career Planning and Placement Office or library, and find out about the organizations you are applying to. Find out what sorts of things they do or make, who their customers or clients are, where they are located, what sorts of technical professionals they employ and why, and what they are best known for. The more you can find out, you more prepared you will be to understand what their positions involve, what your prospects for advancement might be, and what you might want to ask to have clarified at the interview.

Make a list of questions to ask the interviewer about the position and about their organization. These might involve what your duties would be, whether you would be expected to travel, or whether the organization would encourage you to continue studies in certain areas — or perhaps for an MBA. You will almost certainly be asked at the end if you have any questions to ask, and a lame "No, not really." response is hardly likely to impress anyone. If your interviewer is a technical professional, you might be able to ask one or two technical questions about their products or work — if you know what you are talking about, that could be very impressive.

Just before the interview, go over your notes about the company and the questions you would like to ask. You should also quickly review the information you have sent them by letter, resume or application form. This will prepare you to answer the inevitable questions about your education, experience, interests, etc.

Appearance and Manner

Dress formally, conservatively and comfortably. While purple hair, nose rings and long dangling earrings might appeal to some students at some time in their personal lives, these and other "marks of individualism" are inappropriate for job interviews — see *Chapter 8* on propriety. For the same reason, elaborate jewelry, strong perfume or aftershave, flowers, unusual clothes, colors or combinations should all be avoided.

Try to appear as a professional person — someone interviewers would feel comfortable accepting as a representative of their organizations. This applies to manner as well as appearance. In the way you hold yourself, the way you present yourself and your views, and the way you appear alert, interested and intelligent, you must give the impression of someone they should be employing.

Contents and Structure

Interviews usually follow a clear structure. First there are the introductions in which you will learn the names and positions of the interviewer(s) (try to remember them) and you introduce yourself. As they will have your resume and/or an application form, there is no need to go into any detail yet. Then you will be asked about your education, experience, and perhaps your personal interests. Answer clearly and elaborate on any significant feature you wish to emphasize. Be concise with your responses, but do not simply answer with one or two words or simple sentences. You need to demonstrate that you can speak fluently and clearly.

The interviewer is then likely to describe the position(s) available, the skills they are seeking, and the company and its aims. It is appropriate to interject with one or two brief questions during this period, but do not try to take over the interview — let the interviewer control the direction of the discussion. You will probably then be asked if you have any questions, and of course you should have two or three that you thought of before the interview or that you think of as a result of the discussion to that point. Ask other "supplementary" questions if you feel you need clarification, but do not be too pushy as your interviewer may not know the answers to some of your questions.

At the "closing" of the interview, you will learn about the next step in the procedure. For permanent positions, it is unlikely that the interviewer will have the authority to offer you a position on the spot, although that is possible for summer employment. It is more likely that you will be told that they will be in touch with you — and perhaps invite you to attend other interviews with those you might be working with.

The interviewer might try to find out from you just how interested you are in the position offered, and you should be as honest as you can at that time. Just as you are aware that they are interviewing many other candidates, they are also aware that you are attending several interviews — this is a reciprocal selection process *(see Chapter 2)*. You might try to find out when you will be hearing from them, and perhaps point out that although you are extremely interested in the position, you will need to make a decision in a reasonable time. Interviewers understand that, and will appreciate a delicate tone in these all-important final last few minutes.

Follow-up

If you are really interested in a particular position, write a letter to the interviews expressing your gratitude for the interview and your strong interest in the position. You could state that you hope to hear from them shortly. If necessary, you could follow up by e-mail or phone. If you have been offered another position but would prefer to accept theirs, tell them so and request an early response. This is where personal discussion on the telephone is the best way to communicate.

Checklist 13.2: The Job Interview

✓ *Find out as much as you can about the company.*

✓ *Prepare questions to ask the interviewers and review the information you have sent them.*

✓ *Dress formally, conservatively and comfortably; do not try to appear "different."*

✓ *Introduce yourself and try to remember the names and positions of your interviewers.*

✓ *Listen attentively while the interviewers explain their company and the position(s) available; ask the occasional question for clarification if you like.*

✓ *When you are asked questions, answer clearly and emphasize your relevant skills and interests; be concise but answer in a fluent, confident manner.*

✓ *Find out about the procedure and time schedules.*

> ✔ *Follow up the interview.*
>
> ✔ *If necessary and appropriate, follow up interviews with letters or by e-mail or telephone.*

Formal Presentations

Do Your Homework

If you are to give a formal presentation — on your own or as part of a group — you will need to know the subject of your presentation and the time allotted for it. Find out if the time allowed includes time for questions or whether there will be additional time for them. You also need to know roughly how many will be in your audience, who they are and why they will be attending (general interest, expert interest, those opposing your proposal, etc.), as this information will enable you to plan your talk to meet the needs of yourself and your audience.

You should also find out where you will be giving your talk, and especially the size and shape of the room. This will allow you to plan your visual aids, and you might also wish to re-arrange tables to create a less or more formal atmosphere. You should check (or ask if you are traveling to give the talk) what facilities are available (e.g. computer display, overhead projector, chalkboard) for your talk. Check that they work beforehand, rather than find out during your speech that there is no power to the projector, or the light bulb has blown, or there is no chalk for the board. You should also find out how to dim lights, operate screens and do anything else in the room that you may need to do during your presentation.

You also need to know the procedures for your presentation. Will you be formally introduced, for example? If so, prepare brief notes on a card about your background and professional interests so that the chairperson can introduce you adequately. Find out about the use of microphones, and be prepared to clip or hang one on yourself before you start — when you will be most nervous.

Also ask about the procedure for selecting questions at the end — will you do it, or the chairperson? If a member of your audience asks you if they may tape record your talk, ask them for a copy! If your talk is to be simultaneously translated, prepare a list of new or specialist words, and discuss them with the translator before you give your presentation.

Plan Your Presentation

First collect your material and group it into "themes" or topics to be discussed during your talk — like this section on formal presentations, for example. If you are presenting work as part of a group, decide among you who will be presenting each part, and who will introduce the team and perhaps provide a brief final summary. Transitions from one topic to another should be much more "marked" or emphatic than in writing, especially if this also coincides with a change of speaker in a group presentation.

You should either memorize your introduction, or write it out very legibly. This way you will be able to present the all-important introduction well even if you are extremely nervous at the time (which is quite likely). You should also have your conclusion well prepared. The reason for this is that if you run out of time (as often happens), you will at least be able to provide a clear conclusion even if you have had to leave out some material.

Try to know your subject rather than learn it verbatim. You should present your work, not read from a prepared text. You will, of course, need notes to help yourself to recall the main points of your speech. Several numbered cards with clearly legible points are ideal for your notes. Do not feel you have to hide these during your presentation; most of us need some reminder, even for quite short speeches. Your visual aids might also double as notes for yourself.

Once you have planned your talk, go over it several times and check for timing. The actual talk usually takes longer than your practice sessions, so make some allowance for that. During your talk you may be informed as you approach the end of your allotted time — and you may be stopped if you take longer. It is better to stop a little early than to go over time. Also resist the temptation to cram in too much information in the time you have been given.

The Start

Before your presentation, it is often better to sit quietly on your own and go over the main elements of your talk. You can also make final checks to your clothes or hair, so that you can forget them once you walk to the front and start. Make sure your prompter notes are in order.

If your presentation is a formal one, the chairperson will introduce you, using the information you should have provided on a card. You should walk at a normal speed (do not leap up to the front), and place any microphone on your clothing. Take your time (but not too much) in arranging your prompter cards, thank the chair for introducing you, and start.

Nowadays presentations are a lot less formal than they used to be, so "Ladies and Gentlemen" could seem rather quaint. For most technical presentations, simply start by saying what you will be talking about. This is where a prepared introduction might be useful, as you are likely to be most nervous at this time.

The Body of the Speech

Go through your planned themes methodically, making clear transitions between the major parts of your presentation. Use your visual aids as you proceed (mark their use on your prompter cards), pointing to parts of the visuals where appropriate.

Do not be afraid to go back to something if you realise you have missed out important information. Listeners do not expect you to give an absolutely "perfect" presentation. In fact if you did, it would probably sound very over-rehearsed and dull.

Watch your progress through the presentation against time estimates — again these should be on your prompter cards.

If you are running out of time and the chairperson is trying to stop you, you might try something like "Finally . . ." or "In conclusion then . . . ," as these may win you another minute or two. But do not bank on it, as most chairpersons probably do the same when they give talks. Finish with a clear conclusion, summary or other ending. This avoids having to stand like a dummy waiting for applause that does not come for a while because listeners are not sure you have finished.

Nervousness

You *should* be nervous. If you are not, you obviously do not care about your talk and that will be apparent to your audience. You should not go to extreme measures to hide nervousness from your audience — they all know you are nervous anyway — but you do need to be aware of what nervousness is, and how to make it less obvious. This will make you feel more confident in your presentation.

Nervousness is caused by a chemical signal from your pituitary gland to your adrenal gland, causing adrenaline to be pumped throughout your body. Adrenaline creates the "fight-or-flight" response, which was very useful when, as prehistoric creatures, we were perhaps suddenly faced with a ferocious animal. Blood is pumped to the brain, allowing us to think more quickly, and this is a great advantage the speaker has over sleepy listeners. Blood is also pumped to the large muscles of our arms and legs (fight or flight); this may help us when faced with ferocious animals, but is not helpful when we are giving a presentation.

The trouble is all this blood has to come from somewhere. It comes from the smaller muscles in the arms and hands, for example, and this means we may have less control over our hands and fingers — we may shake or our palms may go cold and damp. The blood also comes from the feet and, quite literally, we may get "cold feet" about giving this talk at all. Blood is also taken from the face (we go gray or white) and from the bladder (we need to visit the bathroom). None of these are helpful physiological changes.

Knowing how our bodies are likely to react in such circumstances helps us to reduce the effects. First try to get *behind* something (a table or a podium), as you will feel far more secure that way. However do not clutch a microphone stand or stroke a microphone cord, as this could cause crackling, and do not lean on tables or hold on to a podium as if your life depended on it. Ironically, it is far more difficult to give an informal presentation immediately in front of your audience than it is to give a formal presentation behind a table or podium. So make your first few presentations as formal as you reasonably can.

Also do not try to hold a sheet of paper in front of you (it might shake), or try to casually take a drink of water (you might spill it over yourself, or break a tooth!), or use a long pointer with an overhead projector. By limiting the apparent effects of your nervousness, you will not appear as nervous, and this in turn will make you less nervous.

Only time and a great deal of practice will reduce your nervousness. Remember, though, that if you ever reach the stage when you are not keyed up and a little nervous about your talk, it is time to retire because that would indicate you no longer care.

Attitude

First of all show that you care about your subject and your talk. If you do not care, you can hardly expect your audience to care either. Be firm and positive with your explanations and proposals, and try to give an air of authority in your voice and in what you present.

There is no need for you to appear perfect. Your listeners expect you to be human and to speak normally, and "normal" speech includes the occasional pause, voiced hesitation and changes in pitch and volume. Do not try to speak like a machine. Instead try to be your normal (relaxed) self, and try to let your personality come alive through your work and how you present it.

Stance

Similarly, do not stand rigidly or woodenly, rooted to the spot, throughout your talk. Try to bring in natural movement of your arms, facial expression and body — but without creating "forced" movement as if you were acting.

Move a little and as naturally as you can, without pacing the deck, or rocking from side to side, or making back-and-forth movements with your body or head. Also avoid poking glasses or your nose or scratching or pulling your ears, or making other distracting movements. The odd poke or scratch will probably go unnoticed, but any nervous repetitive mannerism will distract your audience and detract from your message.

Voice

You *must* be heard well by all members of your audience — if some of them cannot hear you, they are likely to say so very clearly. If you are using a microphone, check out the volume you need (do not speak *too* loudly) and perhaps ask the audience at the back if they can hear you.

Speak clearly and distinctly, but without making it sound as if you are rehearsing for a Shakespeare drama part. Most of us speak more quickly when we are nervous, so try to slow down a little and give a more measured pace to your speech. Do not garble or slur your words in an effort to cram too much information into the time available.

Some speakers — especially in Canada, eh — have developed the unfortunate habit of using *eh, um, ok* or *like* after every few words. This is unacceptable. The occasional voiced hesitation of *eeeeer* or *uhhhhhm* is not distracting, and indeed is an acceptable way of informing your listeners you are thinking about something (very useful in meetings). But any repetitive use of a nervous voiced syllable that has no meaning will be most annoying to your audience and must be avoided.

Audience Contact

As oral presentations are a personal medium, you need to make eye, as well as voice, contact with your listeners. This is strangely very difficult for many speakers, who would rather do almost anything than make direct eye contact with members of their audience. However, you should endeavor to do this.

There is also the temptation to talk only to one or two people in the audience — especially if some of your friends are there. Again this should be avoided. Try instead to engage *all* members of the audience in all parts of the room, not just those at the front or at one side of the room. Make a conscious effort to look at all your listeners to prevent them feeling left out. Above all, do not give your presentation to your shoes, or to a clock above the audience at the back of the room. Talk to your audience, and try to make each of them feel you are talking to them.

Checklist 13.3: Giving Formal Presentations

✓ *Do your homework*
- *topic of speech*
- *audience*
- *room size and shape*
- *equipment and lighting controls*
- *procedures*
- *recording and translations*

✓ *Plan your talk*
- *select subthemes*
- *prepare introduction and conclusion*
- *know your subject*
- *prepare visuals and prompter cards*
- *check your timing*
- *notes for chairperson*

✓ *The start*
- *check clothing and get ready*
- *walk to the front*
- *take your time — relax*
- *read or present your introduction*

✓ *The body*
- *introduce and follow your themes*
- *make clear transitions*
- *go back if you miss something*

✓ *The end*
- *watch your timing*
- *include a conclusion or summary*
- *make your finish clear*

✓ *Nervousness*
- *you should be nervous*
- *reduce effects by planning*

✓ Attitude	- care about your talk - be your normal self - do not try to appear perfect
✓ Stance	- try to stand naturally - avoid distracting body movements - avoiding distracting mannerisms
✓ Voice	- speak loudly enough - speak clearly and not too quickly
✓ Audience contact	- look at your audience - make them feel you are speaking to each of them

Answering Questions

Importance and Circumstances

Ironically, the actual speech may be the easy part, for it is in the question period that your real understanding of your technical work will be assessed. During your formal presentation, you are not likely to be interrupted and no one is likely to challenge your work or your conclusions. In the question period, however, you may face some very tough questions that may be difficult to answer adequately.

In your professional career, after you have delivered a presentation, members of the audience may well challenge your views or proposals. Some might even be rather hostile if, for example, you are recommending that a new hydro line be erected near their homes or village. In a professional setting, fellow professionals are also likely to be quite searching and persistent in seeking answers to matters they feel you may have omitted or dealt with inadequately.

In college and university, undergraduate students are rarely asked to face such circumstances. Professors and fellow students are likely to be very reasonable in their questioning and their expectations of you. At the graduate level, though, you must expect to face very rigorous questioning as you "defend" your thesis.

Procedure

There is sometimes a stony silence at the end of a presentation — no one apparently wants to ask you a question! A good chairperson will always have a question or two ready in case this happens, and this is often enough to stimulate questions from the audience. If not, you should have one or two "questions" ready yourself. You can present these by using something like "As there are no questions, there is an interesting point I would like to add concerning . . ." Some students have been known to ask colleagues to ask them certain questions they are prepared for.

In many formal presentations, the chairperson will select those who will ask questions. At very formal functions, questioners will line up at microphones at different parts of the room and be allowed to present questions in turn, alternating from one microphone to another. If you have the task of selecting questioners, make your selections from different parts of the room. Do not allow someone to present more than one question before others have had the opportunity to ask a question; in particular do not pick only those in the front row.

Some "questioners" try to use *your* question period by discussing *their* views and what *they* have done. Should that happen, you should, as politely as you can, ask the person to present a question for you to answer. Others may try to present interminable "supplementary" questions once you have answered their first one. If you are chairing the proceedings, you have the right not to accept these questions (though it is often difficult) on the grounds that others wish to present theirs. If there is a chairperson, you must accept the chair's way of doing things.

If you are asked a question which you think all members of the audience may not have heard, you should repeat it for the audience. Your response may mean very little if you fail to do this. Repeating the question has two other advantages: it gives you a little time to think of a response, and it gives you the chance of perhaps rephrasing the question in a way more suitable to you.

Techniques

Here is some advice about how to respond to questions.

Checklist 13.4: Techniques for Answering Questions

✓ *Keep your responses fairly brief, although if there are few questions and you have time, you can spread them out a little.*

✓ *Try to answer the question presented and not wander off onto a related question. At the end of your response, you could look at the questioners and ask if your response was adequate, although that is almost inviting a "supplementary" question.*

✓ *For specific questions relating to one of your visual aids, you should find and show that visual aid again and answer the question with reference to that aid.*

✓ *If you are asked a question you cannot answer, say so rather than waffle along for a minute or so demonstrating that you cannot answer it. You might well be able to point out that that was beyond the scope of your work, or thank the questioner and say that that is an interesting point you will consider in later analyses.*

✓ *If you receive a question with very wide-ranging implications, you should give a brief answer, and point out that there is obviously much more to consider. You could suggest that interested people might like to get together afterward to discuss it further.*

✓ *Throughout the question period, maintain an appearance of being calm and in control — even if you are under heavy pressure and are sweating profusely! Try to smile!!*

✓ *Always be polite.*

Visual Aids

Visibility, Clarity, Simplicity

The golden rule for all forms of visual aid is that they must be clearly seen by all members of the audience. An otherwise splendid presentation can be marred by unclear or cluttered visual aids. Audiences have been known to call out from the back of the room that they cannot see the visuals. This is upsetting, and rarely can anything be done about it at that stage. So plan ahead.

Although there are formulas regarding the size of lettering that can be read at certain distances, it is easier to create one or two visuals and try them out in a room of the size you will use for your presentation — or the actual room if you can. Remember that some of your audience may not see as well as you do, so make some allowance for that.

Keep your visuals as clear and simple as you can. It may not be advisable to use a complex wiring or systems diagram on an overhead as the basis for a detailed description. If you really need such a diagram, provide it as a handout, and perhaps use a simplified version for your overhead. Keep lettering clear and bold, and use it quite sparingly on a technical drawing.

Preparation and Use

Use your PowerPoint program or acetate sheets to create suitable overheads, and include schematic drawings when appropriate.

When you have completed your visual aids, number them in the order you will use them, and make sure they are all the right way up and not upside down. Speakers often get very flustered when they place visuals upside down or the wrong way round; you need to be very organized to avoid such embarrassments. Similarly slides must be placed in order and the right orientation — an upside down slide in the middle of an otherwise polished presentation destroys the effect.

You should practice using your visuals. You may need to find pages in your computer file, or control complex computer outputs on a screen, or point to features on a screen, or turn over large sheets of flip chart paper, or write legibly on a chalkboard. None of these is easy under the pressure of a formal presentation, so do not take anything for granted. You might consider having someone else place overheads on the projector for you, as this is one thing less you have to worry about. If you do this, of course, numbering and orientation must be checked before you start. Make sure you know how to adjust the focus and image size for overhead projectuals.

When visual aids are not in use, they should be switched off so the audience is not staring at the visual aid when they should be looking at you and listening to your every word. You may have to co-ordinate the dimming of lights with the switching on and off of your visual aids.

Visual aids may become especially important during question time. Listeners may ask you about something on a visual aid, or you may need to go back to one to answer a question adequately. Because of this you must be able to find any particular visual aid at a moment's notice, and you might consider making a list of your visuals so that you can do this.

Types of Visual Aids and their Uses

Each type of visual aid has its advantages and limitations, and you should select whichever is most suited to your needs as a communicator. Sometimes a combination of techniques is ideal.

Checklist 13.5: Types of Visual Aid

✓ *Computer Projection:*
You can project your computer screen image directly onto on overhead screen, and perform all the normal computer functions in front of your audience. This facility is ideal for showing variations of designs as drawings, and you are able to change parameters and see resultant effects on the final design in response to queries from listeners.

✓ *Overhead Projectuals :*
These are still commonly used visual aids for formal presentations; overhead projectuals range from hastily prepared sketches or notes to professionally computer-drawn works of arts. Color can be used effectively and you can overlay several sheets to show a progression. Text and diagrams are equally suitable, and photographs can be screened onto the projectual. You can point to features on the projectual (use a pencil) or on the screen (use a pointer), and you can write on the projectual as you talk.

✓ *Handouts:*
If you want your audience to see detailed drawings, involved discussion or mathematical derivations, handouts are ideal. Listeners like to have something tangible to take away with them,

and they can add their own notes to a skeleton lecture or other form of handout if they wish. Handouts are an excellent way to prepare for your talk, but do not give out a full version of your talk and simply read from it. The audience can read too, and they will probably walk out in disgust. Handouts can be distracting — the audience may look too much at the handout and not enough at you.

✓ **Flip Charts:**
These large sheets of paper on a stand are ideal when you are leading a discussion and making notes of ideas. They can also be prepared ahead of time and presented instead of overheads or slides. They give a more informal impression than projectuals and slides, but their visibility is quite limited. Prepared sets of charts cannot easily be modified, as can other visual aids.

✓ **Chalkboard:**
Use of the chalkboard is the standard technique in schools, colleges and universities. It is extremely versatile, a fact which can annoy your audience if you erase parts and add other notes — something they cannot easily do with the notes they are taking. The writing and drawings must *be legible, and this may require considerable practice. You must also learn to write with chalk without creating horrible squeaking noises. You can use black chalk (green chalk on green boards) to prepare complex illustrations or mathematical derivations that your audience cannot see. This gives the impression that you carry it all in your head!*

✓ **Slides:**
Used with a carousel and remote control, slides are still used. You can go back and forth in your series, but it may take time if you need to find one to refer to again during the question period.

✓ **Physical Objects**
You can pass round samples (of rock or bearings, for example) to members of the audience. This has the advantage of showing them the physical reality of something, but is rarely effective as the object(s) may not be seen by all members of the audience. It may be better to have a display for the audience to look at after your presentation. Simply holding up objects has little effect as they cannot usually be seen well enough.

Review Questions

1. Why is speaking important to technical professionals? Make a list of situations in which they present facts and ideas orally.

2. What are the main differences between oral presentations and written work?

3. What are the differences between informal discussion, informal meetings and formal meetings? What is an " agenda"? What are "minutes" in this context?

4. How can you prepare for a telephone conversation you are about to make?

5. What are the main principles of an effective telephone call?

6. What do you need to know before having a job interview?

7. What sorts of dress are, and are not, appropriate for job interviews?

8. What is a typical structure for job interviews?

9. What preparatory work is advisable in preparing for a formal presentation?

10. What should you put on prompter notes? Why are the introduction and conclusion so important?

11. What is the importance of "themes" for oral presentations? Why are they even more important for group presentations?

12. What are the physiological effects of nervousness? What can you do to counter these?

13.. What elements of attitude and stance can annoy an audience?

14. What are the important elements of your vocal presentation?

15. What is meant by "audience contact" and why is it important? How can you achieve it?

16. Why is the question period so important?

17. What are the ways that questioners are selected?

18. *What difficulties might you have with some "questioners" and how should you handle specific difficult situations?*

19. *What are the main elements of a good response to a question?*

20. *What are the overriding requirements for visual aids?*

21. *What are the main types of visual aid? Explain their uses, advantages and limitations.*

Chapter 14:
Technical Documents and Their Parts

In this chapter you will learn about the many components that make up a complete technical document, including the title page, contents, summary, abstract, appendices and references. You will also be introduced to the wide variety of technical documents used in industry and government — not just reports, but proposals, instructions, specifications, contracts and others.

Parts of Documents
Large and Small Documents
Cover and Title Page
Table of Contents and Illustrations
Other Prefatory Material
Appendices
References
Other Appended Material

Summaries and Abstracts
The Problem with Terminology
Summaries
Abstracts
Summary/Abstracts

Types of Technical Documents
Reports, Papers, Articles
Types of Reports
Other Technical Documents

Parts of Documents

Large and Small Documents

If you are writing a one or two-page document, it would be silly to present it formally in a cover with a title page, abstract, summary, list of contents, etc. If you did, all this "prefatory" material would swamp the real message of your writing. So you are more likely to present short documents in letter or memo format, or simply with a title followed by your name.

On the other hand, if you have produced a significant document (or even a few pages if they are important), you should consider "dressing up" your document to help your readers to follow and understand it. For large documents, it becomes essential for you to present it with full prefatory and appended material. You will not need *all* the additions discussed in this chapter for any one document, of course. You will have to decide what is needed for the purpose and audience of your communication.

Cover and Title Page

Many sorts of covers are available, including clear acetate sheets, plastic clamp spines, multi-slotted spines (if you have the equipment), and simple covers with and without title windows. For larger documents, you should consider a three-ring binder, or formal binding for theses or other important documents. Much depends on the size of the document, its importance, and how it is to be used. Some organizations (and university and college departments) have their own report covers to ensure a consistent appearance for their documents. Use them if they are available.

If you use a cover with a title window you must, of course, ensure that your title fits into that window. The title itself should be as explanatory as possible — not just "Accident Report" but something like "Report of a Fatal Accident Caused by Cadmium Poisoning." You may need to add a subtitle if you cannot put all the information you want to include in the title itself; for this, place a colon or dash after the title and provide further information as a subtitle.

In addition to the title itself, the title page should include the name(s) of the author(s), the date, and the name and address of the organization for which the report has been written. At college or university, you may wish to add the course and course instructor. Some title pages also include a short abstract of perhaps two or three sentences (more on abstracts shortly), a report number, and a copyright claim. See *Example 14.1* for a typical example of a technical title page written in an educational setting.

Tables of Contents and Illustrations

Tables of Contents, or simply Contents, are usually presented on a separate page. Their role is to identify *everything* that is in the document, including the summary and any lists of illustrations, tables, symbols or acronyms or any appendices you include. List all appendices by letter and title.

Include all the headings you have used throughout the document in the same size, form (e.g. bold), and font used in the document itself, and make sure that any numbers for these headings are included. Also use indentation and/or capitalization consistent with the use throughout the document and add page references. If a numbering or lettering system is used in the document, include it in the Table of Contents (see *Example 14.2*). Your computer can do all this for you.

Example 14.1: Sample Title Page

Design Related Advantages
of the
HP54603B Digital Oscilloscope

Written By

James Fry and Danny Yung

in association with

**Department of Electrical and Computer Engineering
Faculty of Applied Science
Queen's University
Kingston, Ontario**

Produced May 1995

— J. Fry and D. Yung, Department of Electrical and Computing Engineering, May 1995

Example 14.2: Sample Contents Page

Table of Contents

Page

1. Introduction
1.1 Anatomy   1
1.2 Pathology   7
1.3 Background   9
1.4 Overall Measurement System   9
1.5 Objectives   10

2. Biomechanics of the Metacarpophalangeal Joint
2.1 Models of Joint to Predict Muscle Force 11
2.2 Choice of Model   12

3. Design Considerations
3.1 Strength Analyzer   13
3.2 D/A System   15
3.3 Software   16
3.4 Model   18

4. System Testing
4.1 Set-up and Preparation   21
4.2 Running the Program   21
4.3 Storing and Printing the Data   24
4.4 Comparative Studies and Databases   24

5. Recommendations for Future Work   25

6. Conclusions   26

7. References   27

Appendices
Appendix A: Voltage-to-Force Calibration Curve
Appendix B: Circuit Diagram for Half-Bridge Configuration
Measurement
Appendix C: Sample Calculations for Electrical Connections
Appendix D: Computer Code in Visual Basic

— K. Karalampides, Department of Mechanical Engineering, 1995

Although the title page is regarded as Page i, it is rarely indicated as such. But the Table of Contents, as Page ii, *is* usually indicated as such, and so are subsequent prefatory pages until you get to the start of the document proper which is Page 1. Appendices are often separately numbered (A1, A2, A3, ... B1, B2, B3, etc.). Page numbers are usually bottom center or right or top right, but the other possibilities on your computer software are occasionally used.

If you have a short table of contents and just a few illustrations, you could include your Table of Illustrations (or simply Illustrations) on the same page as your Table of Contents. If either is long, however, start your Table of Illustrations on a separate page (iii). You may also need to include a separate List of Tables, although some organizations regard tables as illustrations. The summary should be on a separate page (iii or iv). Other prefatory pages (e.g. lists of acronyms or symbols) usually have their own pages.

Other Prefatory Material

Other prefatory material is included in some technical documents, and you may occasionally need to include some of them.

Checklist 14.1: Types of Prefatory Material

✓ *cover*

✓ *table of contents*

✓ *table of illustrations (and/or other tables)*

✓ *abstract*

✓ *summary*

✓ *list of symbols, usually in alphabetical order (English then Greek) of the symbols*

✓ *list of acronyms and/or definitions, usually in alphabetical order of the acronyms or definitions*

✓ *scope or purpose of your document*

✓ *preface, written by the author to explain the background and/or motivation for the document*

✓ *foreword (note the spelling), written by an authority or senior administrator explaining the relevance or importance of the document*

✓ *frontispiece, a photograph or drawing to provide a dramatic image of the document contents or emphasis*

Appendices

Appendices are really little documents in their own right, with separate titles and page numbering. For a detailed report or proposal, you may decide to place complex mathematical derivations, or a complete separate supporting article, or some detailed information as appendices rather then cluttering up the main body of your document.

Checklist 14.2: When to Use Appendices

Use appendices when:

✓ *the information you wish to include is known to some of your readers,*

✓ *the information is too technical or is otherwise of little relevance or interest to some readers, or*

✓ *the information is too big or does not fit conveniently into the structure of your main document.*

References

There are essentially two types of referencing systems, each with its own minor variations. Most published technical work follows the "numbering" system, in which the writer refers to references by consecutive numbers in the text. The numbers are added either in superscript form or in parentheses or square brackets:

14.3 Acoustic emission (AE) received increasing attention in recent years in order to assess damage initiation and cumulation in composites. However, the conventional interpretation of AE events through their measured overall parameters in the time domain, such as peak amplitude, duration, and counts, could cause difficulty in correlating the AE signals with the different failure modes.[2]

— *Canadian Aeronautics and Space Journal*, Mar 1995, P21

To create your reference numbering and actual references, use your "Footnote" and/or "Endnote" facility on your computer. For just one or two references, you could use footnotes; but if you have several references, they should be placed at the end and listed in numerical order:

Example 14.4: Sample Endnotes

1. Garg, A.C. (1988) "Delamination — A Damage Mode in Composite Structures,"*Engineering Fractures Mechanics*, Vol. 29, No. 5, pp. 557-584.

2. Wang, A.S.D. (1989) "An Overview of the Delamination Problem in Structural Composites," *Key Engineering Materials*, Vol. 37, pp. 1-29.

3. Gustafson, C-G. and R.B. Selden. (1985) "Monitoring Fatigue Damage in CFRP Using Acoustic Emission and Radiographic Techniques," *Delamination and Debonding of Materials," ASTM-STP 876*, W.S. Johnson (ed.), American Society for Testing and Materials, pp. 448-464.

4. Awerbuch, J and W.F. Eckles. (1986) "Detection of Failure Progression in Cross-Ply Graphite/Epoxy Through Acoustic Emission," *Testing and Evaluation*, pp. 888-898.

— *Canadian Aeronautics and Space Journal*, Mar 1995, P27

The typical order for information in numbered references is: author, title, publication, volume, year of publication, pages but some variation is often acceptable, as we see above where the year follows the author(s). Often the title of the publication comes first, followed by the author(s), publication, year and pages. Be consistent in any one document and follow the system used by the instructor, editor, magazine or journal you are writing for.

The numbering system has the advantage that you can usually find the place any document is referred to in the text because of the consecutive numbering. This cannot be done for the "author-year" referencing system, as reference to Aitken (1988), for example, could be anywhere in the text. However, the author-year system provides a "bibliography" of works referred to in alphabetical order of the authors. Its immediate reference to established work in the text itself is also useful for readers who are familiar with the literature.

This second system, using author and year, is occasionally used in technical documents. The reference is made in the text to the author (last name only) and year of publication; a page or other reference may also be added:

14.5

```
Such  crusts  are  identical
to  those  shown  by  Aitken
(1988,  Fig.  13)  and  inter-
preted  by  him  as  reproduc-
tive  structures
```

```
— E. Turner, G.
Narbonne, N. James,
Department of Geological
Sciences, 1995
```

The bibliography at the end of your document lists the publications cited in alphabetical order of the authors:

Example 14.6: Sample Bibliography

Gelperin, N.I., V.G. Ainshtein, E.N. Gelperin and S.D. L'vova., "Hydrodynamic Properties of Fluidized Granular Materials on Conical-Cylindrical Sets," in "Proceedings of 1st International Conference on Fluidized Technology", Prague (1961), p. 14-24.

Kalwar, M.I., G.S.V. Raghavan, A.S. Mujumdar and M.A. Fanous, "Aerodynamics of Grains in a Large Scale Two-Dimensional Spouted Bed with Draft Plates", in "Drying '89", A.S. Mujumdar, Ed., Hemisphere Publishers, New York (1989), pp. 433-439.

Kmiec, A., "Simultaneous Heat and Mass Transfer in Spouted Beds", Can. J. Chem. Eng. **53**, 18-24 (1975).

— *Canadian Journal of Chemical Engineering*, June1995, P312

The order of the bibliography is usually author, year, title, publication, volume, pages, but again considerable variation is possible and quite acceptable, as we see above. Be consistent within each document you write, and make sure you use the system of referencing used or preferred by the instructor, editor or publication accepting your work.

In engineering and science, most published papers are written by several authors (even five or six is not unusual). When referring to such publications using the author-year system, use the first author's name followed by *et al.* (meaning "and others"). However, you must include *all* authors of multi-authored works in the bibliography, as shown above. In any field of study, a detailed bibliography (in alphabetical order of first authors) of work in a defined speciality (especially if "annotated" with comments) can be very valuable indeed. The "references" in the author-year system is such a bibliography, and is often named as such. A thorough literature review and compilation of a bibliography is often a high-priority activity for students starting graduate work.

Other Appended Material

Other material is often appended to technical documents, and you may occasionally need to include some of it.

Checklist 14.3: Types of Appended Material

✓ *appendices*

✓ *references or bibliography*

✓ *acknowledgements, usually for the help of your supervisor and for any substantive financial or scholarly assistance provided by others*

✓ *indexes for very large complex documents*

Summaries and Abstracts

The Problem with Terminology

Unfortunately, the terms "summary" and "abstract" are not used consistently. It is therefore sometimes difficult to know what is needed when you are asked to write one or the other. For the purposes of understanding the subject, we need to define the two terms, and definitions are given below. However, you should not expect that others will always follow these definitions, or even understand the distinction between the two types of synopsis. As long as *you* understand the differences in purpose and style, it does not really matter what others call them.

Checklist 14.4: Definitions of Summary and Abstract

✓ *A "summary" (also called an "informative abstract") is a brief synopsis of the document, highlighting major features of the details, results and any recommendations. For busy readers it is often regarded as an alternative to the whole document; for others, it includes key elements of the main document as useful preparation for a detailed reading of the full document. Most summaries are at the front of the document; however, review summaries at the end are sometimes provided to remind readers of the main points of the document.*

✓ *An "abstract" (also called a "descriptive abstract") overtly states what is in the document, i.e. it is a sort of Table of Contents in prose form. It is often published separately from the document it describes, and it provides enough information to allow readers to decide whether or not they need to obtain and read the document. A brief (two or three sentence) abstract is sometimes included on the title page.*

Summaries

A summary is typically a single prefatory page of a document. Summaries provide a brief overview of the document, largely as an alternative to reading the whole document. In some documents, they are called "Executive Summaries," implying that they are intended for very busy executives. These executives may read only the summary and not the whole document, or they may only read parts they consider most important (conclusions and recommendations, for example). In any event, the summary must provide a clear, very concise account of the main features of the whole document.

Summaries follow the same structure and style as the main document. Thus a summary of a large description is a short description (see *Chapter 5*), a summary of a problem-solution document will still follow the problem-solution framework (see *Chapter 6*), and the summary of a thesis-backing document is also a thesis-backing structure (see *Chapter 7*). The form of language used is also the same as the main document — unlike abstracts, as we will see shortly.

The summary stresses the main points of your document. Your decision as to what the main points are depends on what you consider your readers need to know most. Depending on the type of technical document you are writing, the summary will have typical types of information.

Checklist 14.5: Typical Types of Information for Summaries

✓ **Descriptions** (e.g. measuring instrument): what it does, how it does it, ranges and scales, accuracy, how it works, applications, how it is used, size, appearance

✓ **Proposals:** established need, previous solutions and their limitations, importance of the need, proposed solutions, rejected new solutions, reasons for selection, assessment of proposed solution, implementation

✓ **Reports** (e.g. of an accident): those involved, seriousness of the accident, causes and reasons, related safety codes and standards, whether codes and standards have or have not been followed, recommendations to prevent a recurrence

✓ **Technical Research Papers:** earlier background research, details of the current work done, method and conditions, level of success of the work, the results of the investigation, any overall conclusions

---

Here is an example of a summary of a technical research paper:

14.7

The methane oxidation coupling performance of a fixed-bed reactor was successfully translated to a bubbling fluidised-bed reactor and this reaction mode was superior to spouted-bed, inclined and mechanically-agitated fluidised-bed units. Also, a two-stage bubbling fluidised-bed reactor with inter-stage addition of oxygen had the same performance as the single-stage unit, for the same total oxygen input over a wide range of operating conditions. Overall the bubbling fluidised-bed is preferred, catalytic reactions dominate over non-catalytic gas phase reactions in determining the reactor performance, the gas phase exhibited plug-flow behaviour and the performance was independent of the gas phase oxygen partial pressure for a given oxygen input. The best hydrocarbon yield achieved in this study was 19.4%.

— *Canadian Journal of Chemical Engineering*, June 1995, P327

This summary tells readers what was done to what, and how well the technique worked in comparison with other methods. It also compares other related techniques and their relative effects. Overall conclusions are provided with a final assessment of yield effectiveness. For other types of document, of course, other types of information will be needed.

Many published technical papers also include "key words," which are another way of informing readers of the subject and main topics of the document.

Here is a title and related key words:

Intensification of Vortex During Free Draining
Key Words: vortex, free-draining, air cave, discharge ports, rotational flow

— *Example 14.8: Canadian Journal of Chemical Engineering,* June 1995, P292

The key words elaborate on the title, and are thus useful to readers. More importantly, when entered into a computer retrieval system, they allow very fast retrieval of information. Note that key words do not all have to be single words.

Writing Task

For any technical document larger than a page or two, identify the main features of the document and then write a summary. Also include some key words.

Abstracts

Abstracts are often filed separately from the document (in volumes of abstracts or library filing systems) as well as with the document itself. Abstracts are invaluable in literature searches, as their function is to indicate what is in the document. Enough information should be provided so that, if only the abstract is read and the full document is not at hand, the reader will know whether or not it is worth the effort obtaining and reading the full document. A short (two-three sentence) abstract may be added to the title page of a report or proposal.

Abstracts overtly state what is in the document, and so have a distinctive style. In a "true" or "pure" (descriptive) abstract, every sentence and main clause clearly states what is in the document. There are only two main linguistic forms.

Checklist 14.6: Linguistic Forms for (Descriptive) Abstracts

✓ *the document (or part or association of it) or the author(s) as subject of the sentence, saying what the document does*

✓ *the passive voice in* present *tense (occasionally future), saying what is presented, demonstrated, calculated, etc. (in the document, by the author)*

Typically (though not necessarily) the first sentence uses method (a) and subsequent sentences use method (b). This is demonstrated in:

14.9 *The purpose of the present paper* is the experimental study of the deposition of particles conveyed by a gaseous turbulent jet onto a flat and horizontal surface. The size distribution of settled particles *is studied* as a function of the distance from the jet stagnation point by image analysis. The measurements *are made* with several particle samples and under very different experimental conditions. The values of the settling diameters *are gathered* in a dimensionless representation dependent on a Stokes number Sto. The results *are finally correlated* as a function of a dispersion parameter J.

— *Journal of Chemical Engineering*, June 1995, P300

The document-as-subject form has the disadvantage that many writers do not like to say that an inanimate document can evaluate, assess, calculate, or do other thinking activities. This is avoided in two ways:

Checklist 14.7: Avoiding Animacy of the Document

✓ *by using an expanded verb structure, creating, for example, "This paper includes an assessment of . . . " instead of "The paper assesses . . . "*

✓ *by using the passive form, which says that things are evaluated, assessed, calculated, etc. by the author, in the document (not by the paper)*

The passive form is often found at the end of the sentence if the sentence is short, and overt triggering (*in this document,* etc.) is occasionally added to clearly mark the abstract genre.

14.10 *In this paper,* a newly-developed DSI instrument called the NanoMechanical Probe (NMP) *is described.*

— *Canadian Aeronautical and Space Journal,* Dec 1994, P16

For longer sentences (which are typical of technical abstracts), several options are available.

Checklist 14.8: Avoiding End-of-Sentence Passives

✓ *placing the passive form in the middle of the structure (often "splitting" the noun group, as in the third sentence of Example 14.9)*

> ✓ *using anticipatory* it *(as in "It is shown here that...," "It is demonstrated in this paper that...," etc. Note that very few verbs fit this pattern and that overt mentioning of* in this paper *is necessary*
>
> ✓ *"fronting" the verb, as in "Shown here are...;" the present passive is the inverted* Shown ... are.

The overriding criterion for the true style of (descriptive) abstracts is that each sentence and main clause must overtly or implicitly say *what is in the document*. In a (descriptive) abstract, we do not state what was done or what the results are — we simply say what is in the document.

Exercise 14.1: Converting to Abstract Style

Change the style of the following to make them conform to the true style of (descriptive) abstracts. Use a variety of techniques.

(a) *Numerical examples were calculated for a cubic and an orthorhombic material.*

(b) *Waveforms for a point source in a uniform medium and for fast and slow shear waves in a gradient, with and without coupling have been determined.*

(c) *Thermal conductivities for the CWM from thirteen kinds of coal were determined by measurement, and a simple and accurate method to predict the thermal conductivity of coal was created.*

(d) *A simulation program was developed and was used to compare a purge system to a conventional non-purge permeator.*

(e) *The effects of impeller type and diameter, particle size and loading, and gas flow rate were studied.*

Summary/Abstracts

Many synopses are a combination of summary and abstract: they say what was done, give background, results and assessments, but also say specifically what is in the document. These may be labeled "summary" or "abstract" — or sometimes nothing at all. Here is a clear summary-abstract combination, in which the writer first explains what was done and finally indicates the main information presented in the paper.

14.11   The heat transfer coefficient for the laminar flow of the coal-water mixture (CWM) in a round tube *was measured* in a preheater which included three inner pipes of radii 5 mm and an outer pipe of radius 40 mm and a length of 1.8 m. It *was found* that the heat transfer coefficient for the CWM could be estimated

from a Newtonian correla-
tion within the experimental error. Furthermore,
thermal conductivities of
CWMs from thirteen kinds of
coals *have been measured*.
A simple and accurate

method to predict the thermal conductivity of coal *is
proposed* in this study.
— *Canadian Journal of
Chemical Engineering*, June
1995, P400

The experimental work culminates in a useful prediction model. The first three sentences tell readers what was done (note the use of the *past* passives). The final sentence indicates what is in the document, using the *present* passive.

As many people do not understand the difference between "abstract" and "summary" as defined here, and others use the terms in different (and sometimes the opposite!) way to the definition here, you often cannot be sure what is required. So if you are asked to write a summary or an abstract, you will need to find out what is required. You can do this by following examples of the sort of document you are writing or the magazines or journals appropriate for your discipline. You could also ask your supervisor, perhaps by first writing a draft and then asking if that is the sort of thing required.

Technical Documents

There are many different types of technical document. In college and university, you will probably be asked to write laboratory reports, analytical reports, proposals, and project reports. You will also be writing letters to prospective employers and to manufacturers seeking information about their products.

In government and industry, you may also become involved with letters and memos, instructions, installation procedures, test procedures, research papers and notes, proceedings, contracts, specifications, standards, solicited and unsolicited proposals, and many different types of technical report. This section provides you with an introduction to all these documents as well as others you may meet in academic circles.

Reports, Papers and Articles

Perhaps the most confusing set of terms are reports, papers and articles, and so these are best dealt with separately. Reports are written for use within an organization (or for a specific purpose for a client) on a defined technical subject. They say what you, the investigator, researcher or designer, have done, what your results and conclusions are, and perhaps also what you suggest or recommend. They are published by yourself or your department or organization, usually for limited circulation within the organization. There are many types of report — see *Checklist 14.9*. Readership of reports depends on their purposes, ranging from perhaps a small group of engineers and technicians to wider readership including other professionals (accountants, marketing executives), public bodies (governments, municipal councils), and clients.

Papers are scholarly accounts of technical work done in a specialist area of research and/or design. They are often first presented at regional, national or international conferences, and may first be published in brief form as "Notes" or as part of the conference "Proceedings." Published papers are "refereed" by other experts in the discipline, and may have to be modified to overcome objections raised or suggestions made by the referees. Papers are published by professional societies in their journals, and are intended for those specializing in the particular area of expertise. They usually include a summary/abstract and detailed references to related published work.

Articles range from short discussions of a general or humorous nature to serious highly technical analyses. They are published by commercial magazines and journals, and are suitable for a wider range of readers than are papers. Articles are usually not refereed and rarely have references (or perhaps one or two). Some are presented dramatically and graphically with photographs to enhance eye appeal. Unlike reports and papers, they do not have a captive audience, and so more attention is paid to making the contents and the writing interesting to readers.

Types of Report

The term "report" is often used almost as a synonym for "document." You may be asked to write a "report" on something, only to find that what is really needed is a proposal or some other document. So make sure you know what it is you are expected to produce. Reports are by far the most frequently written technical document written by technical specialists. Here is a partial list of different types.

Checklist 14.9: Important Types of Report

✓ *Laboratory Report: an account of the aims, apparatus, method, results and conclusions of a laboratory experiment*

✓ *Accident Report: an explanation of the details and causes of an accident, together with conclusions regarding the causes and reasons for the accident and recommendations to prevent a recurrence*

✓ *Feasibility Report: an analysis of a possible project to determine whether it can, and perhaps also should, be undertaken*

✓ *Design/Project Report: a discussion of a specified need (problem) and a design or developed idea (solution) together with an assessment of the merits and limitations of the solution*

✓ *Progress Report: an account of details of continuing work to a specified time*

✓ *Interim Report: a report providing preliminary information before the main report is completed*

Other Technical Documents

Here is a partial list of other technical documents and their functions. Note that the "essay" is not included here, as technical professionals rarely if ever write them.

Checklist 14.10: Important Technical Documents

✓ **Codes**: *Minimum requirements for the quality of materials and workmanship in specified specialities, e.g. electrical, plumbing, welding.*

✓ **Contracts**: *Legal agreements to buy or do something. They are often in the "legal" style, in which companies "shall" do something in a certain way to meet the requirements of the contract.*

✓ **Instructions**: *Step-by-step sets of instructions, frequently supplemented with illustrations. The imperative mood (e.g. "Turn the adjusting screw slowly clockwise.") is the main stylistic feature of this form of technical writing.*

✓ **Notes**: *Short papers, often refereed, published in journals.*

✓ **Proceedings**: *Published papers presented at a technical conference. These range from brief unrefereed discussions to refereed scholarly accounts of research work.*

✓ **Proposals**: *Problem-solution documents that suggestion that work be done to meet specified needs. For solicited proposals, the need is usually specified by the person or organization requesting the proposal. In unsolicited proposals, the writer defines the need and then provides a solution to it. Both types include an evaluation of the proposed solution.*

✓ **Reports**: *See the previous section.*

✓ **Specifications**: *Details of the technical requirements for a large project, written in one of three styles: "instruction" (imperative) style, "legal" style (using shall), or in note form. A list of technical details added at the end of some descriptions is also often entitled "Specifications."*

✓ **Standards**: *Documents that provide answers to recurring needs, ensuring a consistent solution. Companies, countries and other organizations (e.g. NATO) often have their own published standards.*

✓ **Theses**: *Extremely detailed accounts of research work written by graduate students as their final submission for an MSc or PhD degree — also known as "dissertations."*

Review Questions

1. *What is prefatory material? Why is it not needed for short documents?*

2. *What information is typically found on a title page?*

3. *How is prefatory material page numbered? How are appendices page numbered?*

4. *What information should be included in a Table of Contents? How can you make your computer software create Tables of Contents?*

5. *What is the difference between a preface and a foreword? What other sorts of prefatory material are there?*

6. *What is appended material? What may be included as appended material?*

7. *What are the two main methods of referencing, how are they used and what are their advantages and limitations.*

8. *What are the differences between summaries and abstracts as defined here (a) in relation to their purposes, and (b) in relation to their writing styles?*

9. *What are similarities between summaries and the documents they summarize?*

10. *What forms of writing distinguish abstracts as defined here?*

11. *What is a summary/abstract?*

12. *What are the differences between reports, papers, and articles in relation to (a) their publishers, (b) their readers, and (c) their technical levels?*

13. *What sorts of reports are there? Explain their functions.*

14. *What other sorts of technical documents are there? Explain their functions and styles.*

Chapter 15:
Correspondence

This chapter explains the contents, structure, formats and styles of electronic mail (e-mail), letters and memos. Emphasis is placed on correspondence for job applications inside and outside your institution; the resume and how to complete application forms are also discussed. Advice about job interviews is given in *Chapter 14*.

Electronic Mail (e-mail)
Modern Use
Format, Response and Copies
Style and Tone
e-Words

Letters
Uses of Letters
Styles
Letter Formats
Component Parts
Optional Extras
Addressing the Envelope
Letter Style and Tone
Letter of Application for Employment

Resumes and Forms
Resume Contents and Structure
Resume Components
Resume Design and Layout
Completing Employment Application Forms

Memoranda (Memos)
The Roles of Letters, Memos and e-Mail
Memo Format
Optional Extras
Memo Style and Tone

Electronic Mail

Modern Use

Although electronic mail (e-mail) has only been in general use for a few years, it has already become an indispensable method of correspondence. Its use for person-to-person and broader internet connections now allows us to communicate effectively, rapidly and cheaply to others throughout the world. All forms of electronic communication will probably become the medium of choice for brief, personal messages in the decades ahead.

The advantage of e-mail over the telephone, apart from the lower cost, is that you can always get your message through whether someone is there or not. With e-mail you are not left in a complex answering machine algorithm — only to end up having to give up or leave a message.

Earlier systems do not provide the same editing facilities as even basic computer programs. If you are using such a system, you may need to re-type several lines if you want to correct quite a simple error. Also line overlaps may not be included, meaning you will have great difficulty in normal editing of your messages. More modern systems, however, do provide line overlap and insertion of new text without obligatory "typeover" of your message with the additions. For long messages you need to edit, you should prepare the document first, then edit it, and finally download it electronically.

Electronic mail is still limited in not providing underlining, font, appearance (bold, italic, etc.) and size changes, which we have become used to with modern desk-top publishing software. Some writers use asterisks to depict underlining, while others use quotation marks. The latter, often used wrongly for this purpose in consumer stores, is not recommended as quotation marks indicate something strange or different rather than something to be emphasized. "Smileys," for example :-) and :-(, are intended to be viewed from the right to express various emotions (happy and sad, above). A large selection of smilies has been created.

A possible disadvantage of e-mail is that it may not be completely private — there is always the feeling that someone could tap into your messages and read what you are saying. So bear this in mind if you are thinking of sending something personal or sensitive. Another slight problem is that you may not be absolutely sure your message has been received (only a response can confirm that) although the same applies to letters of course. Also remember that as your e-mail messages can easily be printed in hard copy by recipients, any inappropriate messages could come back to haunt you

You can, of course, print any of your e-mail messages you wish to keep as hard copy, and you can always use e-mail for informing your recipient that you have just sent something — and they can confirm its receipt by e-mail. Transmission by FAX will however still remain useful for sending copies of documents, hand-amended corrections, and more-formal letters that need to be received immediately Recent acceptance of e-mail signatures for legal purposes will reduce the need for FAX messages.

Format, Response and Copies

The format for e-mail messages is like that for memos (see later), headed by details of the date and time of the message, the sender's name and e-mail address, the recipient's name and address, and a subject line. The recipient's name and the *Subject* line may be omitted. Here is a typical example of the prefatory material for an e-mail message:

15.1
```
Date: Fri, 10 Nov 1995, 23:40:47
From: Lamertz Kirsten F <3kfli@qlink.queensu.ca>
To: Michael Jordan <jordanm@qucdn.queens.ca>
Subject: Re: Chapter 6
```

The *To* line can include just one recipient or a large number with their e-mail addresses. You can also list other recipients under the *cc* line, meaning "complimentary copy." When there are many recipients, you do not have to include them all with this initial information, but can instead indicate that other recipients are not listed. Then any recipient can see who else has received a copy if they wish to retrieve that information.

Try to make your subject line as clear as possible. As many recipients receive dozens, often scores, of e-messages each day, they will want to know which ones really need to be read. A poorly considered title for your message could mean that it is assigned to the computer trash without being read!

You can respond directly to a message, in which case the Subject line will indicate that your message is in response to a message with a specified receiver and date. A useful feature on many e-mail systems is the ability to separate the incoming message, and to add your response to each part. When you do this, the original message is shown within "less than" signs (<), and your new message is shown without it:

15.2
```
Date: Fri, 8 Dec 95 11:26:25 EST
From: ''B.Brown'' <brownb@qucdn.queensu.ca>
To: ** All Faculty ** <me.faculty.qucdn.queensu.ca>
Re: Upcoming PhD Comprehensives

At 11:32 AM 12/7/95 EST, J.Selkirk wrote:

<Please keep in mind that students will discuss the
<contents of their exams with other students. For this
<reason you should not plan to use the same questions for
<different students.

Just as we operate take-home examinations on an honor
basis, I think we can fairly expect students not to dis-
cuss questions with other students. Bob
```

Another useful feature of e-mail is that you can relay a message you have received from one person to another person, or several others. The relayed message is prefaced with an indication of who sent the original message and the original recipient. You may wish to indicate why you are sending the message on when you do this. You can also forward a message already forwarded to you. Single and double "less than" markers indicate the original and forwarded parts.

Style and Tone

E-mail messages tend to be less formal than letters. This is partly because of the medium itself and its immediacy of communication — the message gets there almost as soon as you send it. This encourages brief, friendly notes rather than more formal discussion. Also when you are communicating to someone you know (as you often are on e-mail), there is a tendency to use language that is more like informal speech than formal writing.

We thus often find many of the signals of informality discussed in *Chapter 8*, including colloquial and slang words, dashes, contractions, exclamation marks, and liberties with grammar. Many writers sending quick notes to friends or colleagues may not bother to fully check or edit their text, and so we often see spelling and typographical errors (typos), which would be unacceptable in any other medium. Your work should not include such errors.

Another feature of the style of e-mail messages is that they are often very brief and to the point. They can sound rather like the style we use when answering questions orally, or answering questions on forms. For these the comment you are responding to may not be included in detail with the answer. Here is a typical short e-mail message:

```
15.3   <Good idea. An informal r-e-minder should be fine. Do you
       <have her address?

       Yep, I've got her address. I'll send her a quick note and
       ask for an update.
       Thanks for the advice.
                          — M.P.Jordan and S.Crawford, Nov 1995
```

This is a perfectly clear — and very efficient — exchange of communications between two people who know each other. The brevity, colloquial use, and contraction do not detract from the clarity of the message, and the tone is appropriate in this situation. However, when you are sending a message by e-mail to someone you do not know — especially if your recipient is above you in status (e.g. a prospective employer) — a more formal style would be appropriate. In that case you should adopt the style appropriate for letters, at least for the first message or two until you feel you can become less formal.

For longer e-mail messages, we often compose them as we go with little planning before we start. This often results in a rather rambling, often repetitive text — but one that is nevertheless usually acceptable as an e-message. You should not do this for important messages, of course. For those, take the time to plan the contents and order just as you would for any important communication.

e-Words

You may have noticed the use of the newly-created word *r-e-minder* in *Example 15.3*. Some writers use such words to indicate commonly-used terms in the messages. Here are some examples with their meanings:

Checklist 15.1: Some e-words

✓ *commun-e-cate*   *communicate via e-mail*

✓ *director-e*   *directory of e-mail addresses*

✓ *e (noun)*   *an e-mail message*

✓ *e (verb)*   *you can e someone, or be e-d; the -ing form is e-ing*

✓ *r-e-minder*   *reminder sent by e-mail*

✓ *r-e-ply*   *reply by e-mail (noun or verb)*

✓ *r-e-spond/r-e-sponse*   *respond/response by e-mail*

Writing Task

Think up more e-words and write an article for your student newspaper explaining their meanings and how they can be used. This should be a "fun" article — a bit tongue-in-cheek.

Checklist 15.2: Major Stylistic Features of E-Mail Messages

✓ *often include informal indicators such as contractions, sentence fragments, colloquial and slang terms, personal pronouns, dashes, and exclamation marks*

✓ *often contain typographical, spelling and grammatical errors*

✓ *brief messages, very much to the point*

✓ *direct responses with little reference to the original message*

✓ *may include e-words*

Note the signals of informality in the following extract of a rather long e-mail message.

15.4

```
<Dear Mike!
<Can't say how sorry I am about not having gotten chap<ter
6 back to you. I was ill for some time and have since <sim-
ply been buried in work.
<Anyway in the hope that it's not altogether too late now
<for you, I decided I would e you the suggestions I had
<for changes — god, I imagine the chapter has already <been
revised a few times. Anyway, for what it's worth, <here
are a few comments I thought might be useful to <you. I
also added some editorial comments on the paper, <but
since I only had a hard copy, I didn't do anything <too
drastic and I can't e them to you as well. They are <main-
ly changes in words, or sentences. If you want <those as
well, let me know, and I'll mail the copy back <to you —
at this time of term, there is just no way <I'll make it
down to McLaughlin Hall. So, here goes for <some struc-
tural suggestions . . . .
<That's it. I really liked the section on argument as <evi-
dence, and thought the categorization of evidence <worked
out really well. Please let me know if I can be <of more
help — preferably next term though.
<
<Sorry again, for this embarrassing delay, Kirsten.
```

Editing Task: Editing for E-Mail Style

Change the style of the following messages to make them more suitable for e-mailing to friends or colleagues.

1. I am greatly indebted to you for sending me the comments on the structure of *Chapter 6*, which I received yesterday. You mention that you also have additional comments regarding suggestions for some words or sentences. I would also appreciate receiving those if you could possibly send them to me. Unfortunately I have not been able to edit that chapter at this point in time as a result of my being rather heavily occupied over the last few weeks or so. However, I will be editing the entire book starting at the end of term. I plan to re-issue the book for use in January, and I would be pleased to send you a copy in the event that you might find it interesting. Perhaps you would let me know how you feel in regard to that.

2. Thank you very much for inviting me to give two presentations at your planned summer school in English linguistics in Cuenca next July. I will prepare a letter of formal acceptance of your offer and this will be sent to you using the FAX equipment by no later than tomorrow. (Transtate your answer into Spanish using www.babelfish.altavista.com.)

3. Please note that there will be a graduate seminar at 2.00 pm in Room 312, McLaughlin Hall, which is the usual time and place for these seminars. This

particular seminar will involve a discussion of wind tunnel experiments of cantilever bridge structures. The speaker for this presentation will be Marilyn Goldsmith. All recipients of this e-mail message are welcome to attend the seminar and to participate in the discussion which will be held after the presentation.

4. The purpose of this message is to confirm that there will be a meeting of the First Year Studies Committee shortly. In fact it will be held in Room 312 of Ellis Hall and it will start at 3 pm next Monday November 27, 1995. The first item of the agenda will be a discussion of the results of the recent post-admission English proficiency text. As representative of first-year students on this committee, it is to be hoped that you will attend this meeting and that you will present the views of students regarding the test and the results.

5. This is to inform you that we will no longer be creating a hard copy of the minutes of departmental meetings, and that instead the details will be made available to you and other interested parties by means of the electronic mailing system. It is expected that you will all read these minutes, and that you will make hard copies only if you think you really need them. One hard copy of the minutes will be filed in the departmental office as a permanent record of transactions at departmental meetings. You are welcome to consult this collection at any time if you wish.

Letters

Uses of Letters

Letters are usually sent to those who are geographically separated from the writer, and you should use a letter rather than an e-mail message or a memo when the situation calls for a more formal communication. However, letters can be very informal — those between close friends, for example. Another use of letters (rather than memos) is as a formal communication within an organization. For most communications within a department or company, we use memos or, more frequently nowadays, the e-mail. For formal communications, however, a letter may be preferred. Thus you should use a letter for accepting a promotion, filing a complaint, informing your company of your resignation, or any other formal situation.

Similarly you would expect to receive a letter if you are receiving a salary increase, or being fired or officially cautioned, or if you are being informed of an important new policy. Communication of new plans for development and growth — or of the impending takeover — of your organization should be sent to you and your co-workers by letter and not by memo or e-mail.

Checklist 15.3: Uses of Letters

✓ *generally for communications between people or organizations that are geographically apart. These are either formal communications (instead of informal e-mail messages), or very friendly informal messages between friends*

✓ *within an organization, letters are used for formal communications (e.g. promotion, firing), where memos and e-mail would be too informal*

Styles

You can create and use standard presentations for your address, phone and e-numbers as a "style" on your computer, which you can simply retrieve as a standard way to start your letter. Companies and departments usually create and use these, as they ensure standardization, and also reduce typing time. The computer "wizard" will help you with letter formats; just type the salutation (Dear . . .) and start a new paragraph, and the wizard will appear.

Letter Formats

"Format" means the way material is presented in a document, and there are several standard methods of doing this for letters. Perhaps the most common nowadays is the "Standard Block Format," in which all material (including the beginning of each paragraph) starts at the left-hand margin. This is obviously an extremely easy method to use, and a standard format is assured even if several people are typing letters to this format. This is why many companies prefer its use. An example of this format is shown as *Example 15.5.*

In the "Modified Block Format," the sender's address (with the date) is placed to the right of the page, and the complimentary close and signature are usually placed to the right of center. In this format, the starts of the paragraphs are indented — sometimes three spaces, or more usually five spaces so you can use the *Tab* key. An example of the modified block format is given as *Example 15.6.*

The modified block format is often regarded as a more pleasing arrangement of material on the page compared with the block format. However, the exact placement of the sender's address and signature block, and the spaces used to start paragraphs can lead to minor inconsistencies in format unless there are clear instructions to all those using the format. That is, you do have to think a little when using the modified block format, and you may not regard the possible esthetic advantage of the modified form worth the effort.

Checklist 15.4: Differences for the Modified Block Format

✓ *The sender's address and date are placed to the right of the page.*

✓ *Each paragraph start is indented a number of spaces (usually three or five).*

✓ *The complimentary close and signature are placed just to the right of center.*

Other combinations of arrangement of material are possible, and thus there are other letter formats. However one or other of the two discussed here will certainly be acceptable for most purposes. There is little to be gained by experimenting with other letter formats, unless you wish to make a special "statement" by your original graphic design.

Example 15.5: Standard Block Format

36 Elm Street
Kingston ON K7L 2G1
(613) 531-5374
<woodsb@qlink.queensu.ca>

May 23, 1995

Dr M.P. Jordan
Professor, Department of Mechanical Engineering
McLaughlin Hall
Queen's University
Kingston ON K7L 3N6

Dear Professor Jordan:

I am a third year Queen's student currently enrolled in Mining Engineering, Mechanical option. I understand you are looking for a summer student to carry out research in technical communication, and this is my application for that position.

In addition to my technical courses, I have completed your course in Effective Technical Communication MECH 380. I have also been a reporter (sports and reviews) for *The Gazette* student newspaper for the last two years.

My summer employment experience includes work as a customer service representative for a long-distance carrier, and as an assay supervisor for an open-pit mine operation. In both positions, I had to complete forms, keep accurate records, and write monthly reports.

I am extremely interested in the position you have to offer. I hope you will consider my application, and that I will hear from you shortly.

Sincerely,

. . . .
Barbara Woodstock

Example 15.6: Modified Block Format

127 Avenue Road
Kingston ON
K7M 5P8
<3fti@qlink.queens.ca>

January 10, 1996

Mr F. Williams
Personnel Manager
Bell-Northern Research
P.O.Box 3511, Station C
Ottawa ON K1Y 4H7

Dear Mr Williams:

I will shortly be graduating from Queen's University with a BSc in Electrical Engineering, Electronics Option, and I am a seeking permanent employment as a design engineer in your electronic design division.

For the last two summers, I have been employed in your organization, working first with your team creating new systems for home telephone/computer equipment, and more recently on voice recognition systems for computer telephone control networks. Mr. James Collingworth and Ms. Jessica Strange were my immediate supervisors, and they have both agreed to provide references.

My grades in courses in computer communications networks, solid state electronic devices and microprocessor systems have all been very high (see details in my attached resume and transcript), and I am looking forward to taking advanced courses in IC engineering and electronic circuits in communication this term.

My career objective is to develop my expertise in the design of electronic devices and systems in the telephone and home computer industries. I am fully conversant with all the major computer software and internet systems — see details in my resume.

Would it be possible for me to come for an interview on a Friday afternoon in the next few weeks? I look forward to hearing from you.

Sincerely yours,

....

encl: Resume and transcript   Rupert C. Black

Component Parts

The Format of letters is made up of standard parts, which are discussed below.

Addresses

Place your addresses as shown in *Examples 15.5* or *15.6*. When you are employed by an organization, use letterhead paper (for the first page only) to communicate your address. Do *not* include your name above your address — that will appear at the end of your letter. For all addresses, including that on the envelope, follow the following recommendations adapted from those issued by Canada Post:

Checklist 15.5: Recommendations for Addresses

✓ *Use no punctuation where it can be avoided (i.e. between the number and street, and between city and province). Do not add periods in addresses.*

✓ *Use a three-line address (typically street number and street, city and province, postal code).*

✓ *Use two-letter provincial codes in capital letters (NF, NS, NB, PE, PQ, ON, MB, SK, AB, BC, YT, NT).*

✓ *When the postal code occurs on the same line as the city and province, use two spaces to separate the province from the postal codes.*

It is good idea to include your telephone number with your letter — usually just under your address. If you will have two addresses in the next few weeks after writing the letter, include them both with the dates you will be there. Your e-mail address is worth including too. Add "Canada" if your letter is being sent abroad.

Date

The date is usually placed one space below the sender's address. The usual method is *December 21, 19XX* although *21 December 19XX* is acceptable. Note the use of commas, and type out the month in full — not as abbreviations. Use of *th*, *st*, *nd*, and *rd* after dates is usual in the UK and many other countries, but not in North America.

Although the use of figures in the day-month-year order is logical (e.g. 3/4/95), your readers will have to *think* to understand the date! Also there is possible confusion, because many people in North America think of addresses in the order month-day-year, while others use day-month-year. For these reasons, the figures-only method is not recommended, especially for 04/02/03 etc.

Courtesy Titles

If you know the person you are writing to, place that person's name immediately above the recipient's address. Use *Ms.* or *Mr.* as appropriate or use other titles (e.g. *Prof., Dr., Rev.*), although some married women prefer to be addressed as *Mrs.*. If you do not know the sex of the person you are writing to, you could use initials only (e.g. Dear F. Jones).

Place your reader's position immediately under the name. Be as specific as you can, e.g. *Senior Engineer, New Products Division.* If you do not know the name of the person you are writing to, you could find out (by Internet or phone, or through your Career Planning and Placement Office). Alternatively you could address your letter to an unnamed person in a specified position, e.g. *The Personnel Manager.* A further — often very useful — method is to use an "attention" line instead of (or as well as) the salutation. For this, address your letter to the company and add the attention line (e.g. *Attention: Mr. S. Mak, Chief Engineer*).

Salutation

The salutation is a quaint convention of letters, which few writers ignore. Type *Dear* followed by the person's courtesy title and name. If you know the person you are writing to very well, you could use the first name (e.g. *Dear Susan*) or abbreviation or nickname (e.g. *Dear Mike*). The usual punctuation after the salutation in North America is the colon, although the UK tradition of using the comma is quite common and acceptable in Canada.

If you do not know your reader's name, use *Dear Sir/Madam* or the department, e.g. *Dear Personnel Department.* You should not assume that your readers are all women or all men, so do not use *Dear Mesdames* or *Dear Sirs* unless you know you are only writing to women or to men.

If you are really stuck, you could omit the salutation and use an attention line for the position instead. Some companies use attention lines instead of salutations as standard practice.

Complimentary Close and Signature

Place your complimentary close and signature as shown in *Example 15.5* or *15.6.* Many writers simply use *Sincerely,* although *Sincerely yours,* and *Yours truly* are common and acceptable. You should only use *Respectfully yours* or *Yours respectfully* if you really mean that. *Yours sincerely* (informal) and *Yours faithfully* (formal) are more common in the UK, and acceptable in Canada. *Your humble and obedient servant* is archaic.

Capitalize only the first letter of the complimentary close, and place a comma after the complimentary close. Sign your letter the way you wish to be addressed by your reader. For formal letters you should sign your letters with your initials and family name. If you wish to be a little more familiar, you could use your first name, initial and family name. Even more familiar is the use of an abbreviation or nickname (e.g. *William (Ed) O'Neill*).

You should sign your letters legibly. If you insist on using an illegible scrawl for your signature, place a translation under it to make sure your reader knows your name. The sender's position in a company usually comes just under the sender's name.

Optional Extras

The above elements are essential components of letters. In addition, there are several other features that writers often include.

Subject or Title

You could include a title for your letter to inform your reader of the subject matter. It is usually underlined and centered, and occasionally prefaced with *Re:*, meaning *Regarding*. The usual position for the subject line is between the salutation and the start of the letter, but some writers place it above or in line with the salutation.

Reference Lines

When you are replying to a letter that has been given a reference line, it is courteous to include that reference in your reply. This can be done by including, for example, *Your ref.: RB/jr/pf2/00-3* after your own address. Such a reference usually refers first to the writer, then the typist and then the file number, which in this case would perhaps include a reference to the third such letter in the file in 2000.

If you find you have a lot of correspondence you need to keep track of, you should include such a reference in your letters — even if you do not have a typist! Your reference system could refer to letters on different topics — probably in different files — together with the directory and document referencing. Your own referencing should be placed below your signature on the left-hand side of the page.

Including Attachments and Enclosures

You will often have to include additional material with your letter. The inclusion of a resume with a letter for application for employment is a good example. To do this, add *attach.* (attachment) or *encl.* (enclosure) under your signature. If you have several appendices, number these A, B, C, etc. and list them either as part of your letter or under your signature.

Indicating Copies

You may wish to send copies of a letter to readers other than the person it is addressed to. There are many reasons for this, including the need to keep others informed, the desire to put pressure on your main recipient by sending a copy to a mutual supervisor, or the need to demonstrate that the letter has been sent (for legal purposes).

Whenever you send copies to others, you should indicate that by listing all other recipients. This list is prefaced by *cc:* (meaning "complimentary copy"), or simply *Copies sent to:* or *Copies:*. The list of other recipients is placed at the end of the letter.

Confidentiality

When you wish to send a letter (or memo) only to one person that others are not to read, you should mark your correspondence as CONFIDENTIAL near the top of the document. Also include that word on the envelope so that potential readers (e.g. a secretary or colleague) will not open such correspondence. If your correspondence contains something personal to the recipient, you should include PERSONAL at the start of your letter or memo, and again also on the envelope. For correspondence that is both personal *and* confidential use PERSONAL AND CONFIDENTIAL instead. Many companies use colored stickers to indicate this sort of correspondence.

Addressing the Envelope

Place the recipient's address a little to the right of center and a little below halfway down. The address should be exactly the same as that used for the recipient in the letter itself. Remember to follow the advice given by Canada Post for addressing envelopes (*Checklist 15.5*). For packages, use all capital letters.

If you are using pre-printed envelopes, as you probably will after you graduate, you may not need to add your own address, although you may still have to add a building or division to a generic address. If you are writing as an individual, type your own address — again exactly as you have typed in on the letter itself — at the top left-hand side of the envelope. Better still have your return address printed for you on sticky labels.

Letter Style and Tone

Most letters deal with a single topic and are generally quite simple in structure. The purpose of your early letters may be to ask for an interview (for employment), or for advice (for a research project), or for information (as the basis for a possible purchase). Later your letters as a technical professional may include proposals to sell equipment or services, requests for legal variances or approvals, and responses to fellow professionals regarding your area of specialization.

For all these, style and tone are extremely important. You are not just conveying information or requests for information; you are, by your style and tone, also expressing yourself as an individual. Your tone can be friendly or curt, businesslike or sloppy; you can appear to lack self-confidence, or to be belligerent or insensitive; you can instill confidence in your abilities and judgment, or you can leave your reader feeling somewhat uneasy about being associated with you.

Style and tone are dealt with in some detail in *Chapter 8*, and you should review that chapter now, and complete the exercises in preparation for writing letters and memos — and also for e-mail messages to some extent. Some stylistic features specific to correspondence are given below.

Checklist 15.6: Stylistic Features for Correspondence

✓ *State your purpose clearly at the start (perhaps also in the subject line) — a climactic build-up is inappropriate for correspondence.*

✓ *Make your requests or points clear in simple, and usually quite short, sentences.*

> ✓ *Use fairly short paragraphs — even if some have only one or two sentences.*
>
> ✓ *Try to avoid starting all your sentences with the pronoun I, as this can give a self-centered impression. You could use the possessive form* my *instead on some occasions.*
>
> ✓ *Pay particular attention to the style of your writing and the tone you are imparting.*

Letter of Application for Employment

Of special importance to you at present is the letter of application for employment — initially for summer work, and then for a permanent position. You may be given the opportunity to attend an interview at your college or university, and you may be asked to complete an application form before the interview. But good jobs that provide useful technical experience are difficult to obtain nowadays. To obtain such a job, you might consider writing to companies you are interested in working for.

Your letter should follow an acceptable format of course, and you should try to find the name of someone you can write to directly — rather than just the Personnel Department, or the Engineering Department. Find out as much as you can about the organization you are writing to, as this will enable you to appear knowledgeable and more potentially useful to the company. If you actually know someone who works there, or who has recommended that you write to a specific person, that may help you to gain an interview. It certainly makes your initial sentence easier to write.

Your letter should start off by saying who you are — not your name, but what you are doing and your technical interests. State that you are seeking summer (or permanent) employment, being as specific as you can and making sure that your plans could fit in with the needs of the company.

State your notable academic achievements if you have any — if not, just mention your program and interests. Also include details of special abilities, technical interests, computer knowledge, and communications skills you have. You should also mention any language (other than English) abilities you have, and any interesting or different elective courses you have taken. A brief mention of your earlier work experience should also be included — perhaps with reference to your resume for further details.

Make sure your claims are of substance, i.e. what you have done or achieved. You should include few, if any, unsubstantiated self-evaluations (e.g. that you feel you are a diligent worker, have an interesting personality, work well with others). Let your referees say such things for you, or let your interviewer form that opinion during the interview.

Your final paragraph should be a request for an interview. Providing some times you could be available is a useful way of being businesslike without appearing too pushy. You could ask your reader to phone or e you to set up an appointment.

Checklist 15.7: Features of Letters of Application for Employment

✓ State who you are and what you want clearly in the first paragraph.

✓ Include details of your academic achievements, your current program, and your technical interests and skills.

✓ Make sure your tone is friendly yet businesslike.

✓ Avoid unsubstantiated claims about yourself, and also avoid too many I's.

✓ Make your final paragraph a request for an interview.

✓ Enclose your resume (details shortly).

Research Tasks

1. Analyze advertisements for positions in your specialty, noting the qualifications, duties and personal qualities the companies are seeking.

2. Examine the positions available to you that are posted in your Career Planning and Placement Office. Note their requirements for the positions and how the companies want you to apply for them

3. Search the files of your Career Planning and Placement office for companies who employ those in your technical specialty. Make a list of them classified by location, types of employer (consulting, manufacturing, mining, research, municipal, educational, etc.), and types of positions they offer. Find out the name of the Chief Engineer or Senior Personnel Officer for companies you might be interested in.

4. For a few companies in your area of specialization and an acceptable location, find out precisely what they do, who their customers are, what their developing interests are, and any other relevant information.

5. Find the e-mail addresses of key personnel in one or two of these companies. Send a brief e-mail message to each of them, introducing yourself and asking if they are seeking technical students such as yourself for summer or permanent employment. Offer to send then your resume.

Writing Tasks

1. Write a letter seeking summer or permanent employment in a company of your choice. Assume that you have had no previous contact with the organization or employees.

2. Find an advertisement (or details in your Career Planning and Placement Office) for a position you are qualified for. Write a letter applying for the position, and submit your resume and the details of the position with your letter.

3. Write a letter to a professor in your college or university seeking employment as a summer research assistant for a position of your choice. Again assume your resume will be enclosed with your letter.

4. Write a letter to the manufacturers complaining about something that has annoyed you with their equipment. Some suggestions are:

   (a) unclear instructions for a computer,
   (b) missing pieces for a home-assembly desk or table,
   (c) some difficulty with a computer program,
   (d) receipt of wrong electrical components by post,
   (e) buzzing from a new fluorescent desk lamp.
   (f) write to the Department of Health and Safety, pointing out that snow clearing on steps to your building is slow and could result in injuries.

5. As year president for your specialty, write a letter to a local company of your choice asking them if your class (perhaps in groups of 20) could visit their facilities to see their operation.

6. Write a letter to your local member of the provincial parliament, pointing out the hardships being caused by increased tuition fees and asking that better student loan systems be created.

7. Write a Letter to the Editor of your student newspaper on a subject of your choice.

8. Assume that your department or faculty has decided to hire a new instructor in a position of your choice (e.g. technical writing). Decide what qualifications, experience and qualities are appropriate for the position. Write a detailed description of the duties of the position and the requirements of the successful candidate, making sure you avoid sexist pronouns. Append your descriptions to a letter addressed to your Dean with a copy to the Personnel Director of your organization. Find out their names.

9. Do the same for a new position as a tutor in the Writing Center. Write your letter to the Director of your Writing Center.

Resumes and Forms

Resume Contents and Structure

The word "resume" is a French word meaning summary, and in French it has acute accents on *both* e's. You are not obliged to include the accents when using the word in English, but if you do, you must include both of them. Another term for our use of *resume* (meaning an account of your career and qualifications) is the Latin *curriculum vitae* (or simply *c.v.*), but that is used more by academic specialists. Some writers prefer to use "Personal Data."

Your resume should include some personal detail and your qualifications to date, together with details of your current educational program. Your work experience should be presented in order, and you should either include references, names and addresses of referees, or state that these are available on request.

Resume Components

Resumes have standard components and a recognized order, both of which you should observe.

Introductory Material

Your resume can be headed *Resume* if you like, though the type of document is clear enough without that. Your name (full or with middle initial(s) if you like) comes at the top — usually bold type centered. Then include your full address (or addresses if applicable), your full telephone number and your e-mail address. A statement of your "Career Objectives" may be included; it can be useful, although it can also appear to limit your interest for a particular position if your objectives do not coincide with a company's plans.

You are not obliged to provide any information about your racial origin, religion, age, marital status, or whether you have any handicaps. Some students, however, include their place of birth or citizenship (or landed immigrant status) if it is Canadian and they are applying for employment within Canada, as some jobs in Canada are available first to citizens or landed immigrants. The applicant's date of birth is also often provided, and sometimes also height, weight and marital status. All such information could come under a heading of "Personal Details."

You might also want to include special interests and hobbies, especially if they are relevant to the position you are seeking. Work for a student newspaper as a member of a debating team, or on a student, departmental, faculty or senate committee are all worth noting. You could also list memberships in clubs or associations, or any special projects you have been involved in. For the best jobs, employers are seeking students with broad-based knowledge and abilities, not just technical specialists.

Try to achieve the appearance of a balance in your interests (and thus in your resume). A list including *"chess, ballet, cooking, and art appreciation"* may not help you to obtain summer work in an open pit mine. On the other hand, a list of *"beer, women/men, internetting, football, television sports watching"* could be less than helpful for the best engineering positions, for which some intellectual qualities are required.

As computer skills are nowadays often of vital importance, you might consider providing a separate list of the systems you know well and have worked with, and perhaps also those you have some familiarity with.

Education

List your education so far in reverse-chronological order (your current program first). Include the dates, the institutions you attended, the programs you completed, and any special awards or recognitions you achieved. For your current program, list not just your overall program, but also any specialization and special concentrations you are following.

Also include any notable achievements, such as Dean's scholar, top 10 percentile, scholarships and awards. Note any detailed report or proposal you have prepared and would be proud to take to an interview. If your academic work and achievements are not noteworthy, do not mention them!

Experience

List your work experience in reverse chronological order — the latest first. Include the dates of employment, the organizations you worked for (names and full addresses), your job titles and your duties. It is also useful to include your supervisors' names, addresses, phone numbers and e-mail addresses if you think prospective employers might want to contact them and they will give you a good reference.

Include details of any significant work you have done and any noteworthy documents you have prepared; take them with you to the interview. Provide more detail for experience related to the position you are seeking, and emphasize that experience in your letter. Your letter could include "see resume for further details" in parentheses to cross refer to important experience you wish to highlight.

References

You could state at the end of your resume that "References will be supplied on request.," but few prospective employers will bother to do that if they have several suitable candidates for a position who *have* listed referees. If you have (good!) letters of reference from suitable people, by all means include them with your resume. More usually, though, you will have to ask permission from those who know your academic work, your experience and your character to agree to provide references in confidence.

The references are the actual letters of reference, not the people (the referees) who write them. So you should include an introductory statement to the effect that "The following have agreed to provide references on request:." List the names, titles, positions, full addresses (snail and e), and telephone numbers. Ideally one referee should be able to discuss your academic abilities, another should be able to describe your work habits and abilities, and a third should be able to vouch for your organizational or personal qualities. Talk to possible referees first, and try to find out if they feel able to give you a good reference. If not, find someone else.

Checklist 15.8: Contents of Resumes

✓ **Introductory material:** *names, addresses, phone number(s), special interests, personal details, career objectives*

✓ **Education:** *dates, places, programs, achievements, awards*

✓ **Experience:** *dates, companies, addresses, positions held, duties, accomplishments, supervisors*

✓ **References:** *introductory statement, names, positions, addresses, phone numbers*

Resume Design and Layout

The presentation of the details in your resume can be very important, as it should give a clear impression of your professional attitude to your work and to the way you present yourself. While a rather tacky resume prepared on a pre-Windows computer and basic printer is acceptable, you will create a far better impression by designing and presenting your record and achievements using more modern methods and a laser printer. Use different type sizes, bold lettering and even different fonts to create a pleasing and professional appearance for your resume. If you need help, companies can do this for you at very little cost.

Space your details out well and in an orderly fashion, making your major section headings (usually Personal Details, Education, Experience, References) stand out clearly. You do not have to cram everything onto a single page, although a one-page resume may be suitable until you have compiled more experience and achievements. If you really have a lot to say, your resume can be two or even three pages. Academics and professionals with many achievements, presentations, publications and awards can have resumes in the 10-20 page range, but you may have to wait a few years before you could justify such a detailed resume. *Example 15.7* is a sample resume.

Example 15.7: Sample Resume

JULIE HOWES

469 Earl St.
Kingston, Ontario
K7L 2K2
(613) 549-8003
howes@conn.me.queensu.ca

EDUCATION

1994-Present   M.Sc. Mechanical Engineering, specialisation in Biomechanical Engineering,
In Progress, Queen's University, Kingston.
1994 B.Sc.(Hons.) 1st Class Mechanical Engineering, *Queen's University.*
1990   OSSHGD, *A.N. Myer Secondary School, Niagara Falls, Ontario.*

AWARDS AND SCHOLARSHIPS

1990 Stirling Scholarship	$ 1500	1994 K.L.Murray Award in Mechanical Engineering	
1995 Queen's Graduate Award:	$ 5920		
1994 Queen's Graduate Award:	$ 3000	1993 NSERC Summer Research Award	$ 3000
1994 R.S. McLaughlin Fellowship	$ 7000		

WORK EXPERIENCE AND QUALIFICATIONS

1994-1996   **Teaching Assistant,** *Mechanical Engineering, Queen's University*

Assisted in grading assignments and provided individual assistance to students in class and during office hours for Mechanical Engineering 122, 212, 215 and 399.

1993
(Summer)   **Research Assistant,** *Terray Corporation*

Responsible for design and implementation of static testing of biomedical implants. Assisted in the design and manufacturing of these devices and accompanying instrumentation. Designed and prepared Design Assurance Documents for the project.

1990-1992 **Head Lifeguard,** *City of Niagara Falls Parks and Recreation*
(Summer)

Responsible for planning and running all training sessions. Organised and ran one special event per week. Supervised staff and ensured smooth operation of facility. Vital communication link between lifeguards and supervisors. Performed general lifeguarding duties.

PROFESSIONAL AFFILIATIONS

1994-Present Registered as Engineer in Training with Professional Engineers of Ontario

1992-Present Canadian Society for Mechanical Engineering
American Society of Mechanical Engineers

COMPUTER SKILLS

Familiar with DOS, Windows 95 and Windows 3.1 platforms, and have experience with UNIX and Macintosh systems. Proficient with data-entry packages Excel and Quatro-Pro and drawing tools AutoCAD 12 and Corel Draw. Also familiar with programming languauges including FORTRAN and Pascal.

CERTIFICATIONS

Canadian Red Cross: Water Safety Instructor
Royal Life Saving Society Of Canada: National Lifeguard

Heart and Stroke Foundation of Canada: CPR Instructor
Canadian Red Cross: First Aid Certificate

ACTIVITIES AND INTERESTS

Campus Involvement: Internal Graduate Student Representative in Mechanical Engineering (1 year), Member of the Queen's Society for Mechanical Engineers (3 years), Mechanical Engineering Club Executive (2 years)

Athletics: Queen's Women's Varsity Rugby Team member (2 years), Queen's Curling Club (5 years), Intramural athletics member and manager (past 6 years)

Interests: Enjoy sailing and water sports, playing French Horn and listening to music.Enjoy reading, gardening and travelling

REFERENCES

Dr. Genevieve A. Dumas, *Associate Professor, Mechanical Engineering, McLaughlin Hall, Queen's University, Kingston ON., K7L -3N6. Tel: (613) 545-2648*

Mr. Paul Debenham, *Micro-Computer Cluster Supervisor, Faculty of Applied Science, 306 Jackson Hall, Queens' University, Kingston, ON., K7L 3N6. Tel: (613) 545-2780*

Mr. Colin Smith, *Development Engineer OSTEONICS, 59 Route 17 S., Allendale NJ., USA., 07401-1677. Tel: (201) 825-4900 ext. 210 Fax: (201) 934-4390*

Writing Tasks

1. Prepare your resume in draft form following the guidelines in this chapter.

2. After you have received advice regarding the contents, structure and order, re-arrange your information as necessary. Then design and produce your resume to a high level of presentation quality.

Completing Employment Application Forms

Many companies, especially those who visit campuses looking for technical students to hire, ask students applicants to complete an application form as part of their hiring procedure. This helps them to make quick comparisons among many applicants. Some forms are quite brief, on the assumption that you will attach your resume with your completed form. Others, however, can be quite detailed, and they are then an alternative to your resume. If you have prepared a resume you are proud of, there is no reason why you should not also include that — even if your completed form contains the same information.

If you have the choice, your own well-prepared resume will probably be better for you than a completed form. This is because, for your own resume, *you* decide what to include and what to emphasize. When completing forms, you may be less able to do that. Also your own resume should be a masterpiece of clarity and presentation skills, whereas a completed form — however neatly you complete it — never looks quite the same.

When completing forms pre-prepared typed responses are best, as your answers can be read easily. However, many companies prefer hand-written answers to their questions, in which case you should write your answers very neatly. If your spelling is dreadful, you should type and spell-check your responses first. Answer the questions as directly, clearly and concisely as you can.

Writing Task

Complete the following application form for a position of your choice. If you like, attach a letter and/or resume and refer to either or both to provide more complete responses.

SUMMER WORK PROGRAM
STUDENT EMPLOYMENT APPLICATION

A. Personal Information

Family Name: Given Names:
Term Address:
Permanent Address:
Telephone: Alternative:
e-mail Address:
Student Number:

Dates Available:
Position Applied For:

B. Education

Program: Year: Area of Concentration:
Faculty/School:

Other Post-Secondary Institution Attended:
Institution: Address:
Program: Qualification:
Period of Study:
Highest Grade or Level Completed:
Type of Certificate or Diploma Obtained:
Overall Grade of Final Year:

C. Employment History

Company Name: Address:
Type of Business: Job Title:
Supervisor: Telephone:
                                        e-mail:

Period of Employment:
Duties:

Company Name: Address:
Type of Business: Job Title:
Supervisor: Telephone:
                                        e-mail

Period of Employment:
Duties:

Company Name: Address:
Type of Business: Job Title:
Supervisor: Telephone:
                                        e-mail:

Period of Employment:
Duties:

D. Relevant Job Skills

E. Career Objectives

F. References (List three people we can contact for references.)

Name: Position:
Company: Division/Department:

Address: Telephone:
                                    e-mail:

Name: Position:
Company: Division/Department:
Address: Telephone:
                                    e-mail:

Name: Position:
Company: Division/Department:
Address: Telephone:
                                    e-mail:

Signature: _____ Date: _____

Memoranda (Memos)

The Roles of Letters, Memos and E-Mail

As mentioned earlier in this chapter, letters are primarily for correspondence between organizations that are geographically separated, i.e. letters are usually sent via the postal service. Important exceptions are for important, formal correspondence within an organization. Before the advent of e-mail, the "memorandum" ("memo" for short, also called "Internal Communication") was used for most normal correspondence within an organization — both within departments, and among members of different departments and divisions of a company. A compromise between the letter and the memo is the "memo-letter," which is a standard reply form sent through the mail. The sender adds the recipient's name and address, writes a line or two of information, and sends it in the mail.

However, the growing use of e-mail means that memos are becoming less common for everyday communications and reminders, and are now only used for more-important issues. Some informal memos used to be handwritten on standard memo paper, signed or initialed and given or sent to the recipient(s). Now such informal correspondence is more likely to be sent by e-mail, which is quicker, saves paper and reduces filing time and costs. If you need a hard copy for a file, you can simply print a copy, but for much correspondence that is not necessary.

The memo will probably continue to be used, though only for the more formal correspondence that needs to be clearly and permanently documented. Perhaps as memos become more formal, they will overlap with the use of letters for important matters within an organization. Thus letters will only be used for *very* important issues within an organization.

Many short technical reports will continue to be written in memo format; they are often called "memo-reports." That is, the report writer completes the information at the head of the memo paper and then types the report. Longer or more important reports are given a separate cover, title page, etc. and a

"Memo of Transmittal" may be sent with the report as a record of its transmission. When such reports are sent outside the organization, the Memo of Transmittal becomes a "Letter of Transmittal," of course — using the letter format and not the memo format.

Memo Format

Most organizations of any size have their own computer "memo style," which includes their name and logo and usually the title "MEMORANDUM" or simply "MEMO." Standard information lines are also included, typically To:, From:, Date: and sometimes Re: or Subject:. These are completed by the sender before typing the memo. Pre-printed memo paper may also be available.

Complete the "To" line by adding your recipient's title, rank and position (e.g. "Dr. R. Melton, Head, Department of Civil Engineering"). As memos can be quite friendly, you could use the person's first name (e.g. "Dr. Ruth Melton") if you feel that level of informality is appropriate. If your message is *really* informal, send the message by e-mail instead. Add other recipients if you like.

Add your own name on the "From" line, using the form appropriate for the level of formality you wish to convey. Use your name and position (e.g. Ignacio Perera, P Eng, Group Leader, Quality Control Department) for more formal occasions. For less formal messages, you could use a shorter form (e.g. I. Perera, Quality Control), or just use your name and include your position with your signature at the end.

Complete the date line the way you would include the date for letters (see the earlier discussion). Write the month out rather than using abbreviations or the often confusing system using only numbers (e.g. 2000:7:6 or 02/03/00).

The Re: or Subject: line should be completed with a clear statement of what your message is about. Such titles can be important as they can indicate not just the subject, but also the writer's perspective or emphasis. Thus "Dispute Resolution: Working Conditions in the Welding Shop" has a different tone and emphasis than "Various Grievances: Unsafe Conditions in the Welding Shop." Note how you can use both a title and a sub-title to provide readers with a clear statement of the substance of your memo.

Note that memos do not normally have a salutation; nor do they have a complimentary close. You should, however, always sign (or at least initial) all your memos at the end of your message, as this signifies that you have checked the document and take responsibility for it.

Optional Extras

Memos can have other features, which are similar to those used for letters. Occasionally writers do include a salutation, especially if the memo is quite formally addressed and the writer adds, for example, "Dear Angela:" before starting the message. However, this is not necessary and is considered by some to be poor practice.

Copies are often sent to other than the main recipient(s). This is done by adding their names and positions after your signature. As with letters, use *c.c.*

(complimentary copy) or *Copies sent to:* to indicate who besides the recipient in the To: line has been sent a copy of your memo.

You can also add attachments, enclosures, or appendices with your memo. These are indicated below the Copy line as *attach., encl.,* or as a list of appendices in the memo itself or at the end after your signature and any copy line. Personal and/or confidential notes may also be added to memos, as with letters.

Memo Style and Tone

The principles for style and tone in memos are similar to those in letters (see earlier discussion). However, memos tend to be more businesslike in tone, and many organizations insist that memos be written as isolated numbered points. This prevents writers from producing long rambling "essays" instead of clear, concise memos.

Checklist 15.9: Elements of Memo style

✓ *State your purpose clearly in the Subject line.*

✓ *Make your points clearly and concisely, usually with quite short sentences.*

✓ *Use fairly short paragraphs even if one or two have only one sentence.*

✓ *Many memo writers number their points (paragraphs).*

✓ *Observe the conventional format.*

Writing Task

1. Write a memo to Dr. J. Milligan, Director of Environmental Health and Safety, about an accident to your senior secretary, Mrs F. Gore, who slipped and fell outside her office at about 11.10 this morning. There was a pool of liquid soap outside her office and dribbles of soap from the women's washroom along the corridor (past Mrs. Gore's office — Room 214) to the elevator. She injured her left wrist and ankle and bruised her chest. At about 10.45 that morning Prof. G. Spragge of your department had seen two janitors dismantling the old soap container in the men's washroom and emptying it into a container in the corridor. When you heard of the accident, you had phoned the janitorial service to have the soap cleaned up; that was not done until 12.30. The soap trail goes along corridors C5 and D5 to the elevator at the end of D5. At about 11.10 Mrs. Gore left her office (making a left-hand turn) to go to the washroom. She is now in hospital being examined. Create your own memo paper and send a copy of your memo to Catherine Johnson, who chairs the Health and Safety Committee.

2. As New Products Leader, you have just invented and designed a new paper roll holder (see sketch below), which you would like your company to manufacture and market. Write a memo to Janice Prentice, your Chief Engineer, explaining the problems of too-loose holders (paper runs all over the place) and too-tight holders (paper tears off in little pieces) and explaining your design and how it works. Append your sketch of course. Create your own company and memo paper.

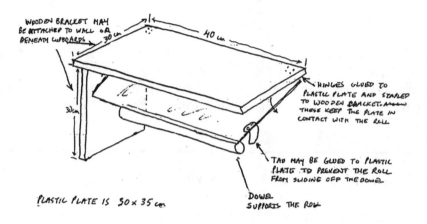

3. Invent, create and design other solutions to common household problems, and write separate memos explaining the problems and your solutions. Include sketches where appropriate. Some suggestions are:
   - a better can opener
   - a better mouse trap/killer
   - a modular desk for computer, printer, disc files, manuals, etc.
   - a support used for sawing large sheets of wood (see *Exercise 9.1*)
   - a squirrel-proof bird feeder

4. Edit the following using memo format and style.

Dear Boss:

This is an accident report and is further to your request for some more information regarding the accident that occurred in the electric shop this morning. After digging through all the personal records, I found that Mr Bankoski is not employed by our company Ontario Land Fill Ltd. I found out that they we have a contract out for him, but they operate on there own as independant truckers. They own there own truck and have been moving fill from a pit about 10 km away east of Highway 541, they leave the fill at the site dump point, which as you know we have established near the north-east corner of the site about 150 m from the electric shop. Further investigation on my part revealed that Mr. Bankoski emigrated to Canada from Italy only five months ago — perhaps he couldn't read the warning signs and that is why he took the acid to his uncle instead of water? His uncle, Mr. Lucini gave him jobs as his assistant in his independant trucking business. The to of them had started work at 6 am this morning and had stopped for a break by the damp point when the accident occurred. Mr Lucini drank the acid which his nephew had brought to him thinking it was water I imagine. I asked the electric shop foreman, whose name is Mr. Fred Gordon, why Mr. Bankoski had not used cups we put near the tap outside the shop and he said they keep getting "nicked" (stolen, I presume), so he doesn't provide them any more. You know the sign we have "No Entry to Unauthorized Personal" above the counter in the electric shop? Well I found it all muddy on the floor. Fred isn't sure whether it was up this morning or not. I hope this clarifies the situation for you. Please let me know if I can be of any further assistance in this matter.

Yours truly,

Review Questions

1. *What are advantages of e-mail? What are the limitations of editing on e-mail? What are "smilies"?*

2. *What does cc mean? How can you avoid a huge list of people at the start of an e-mail message when you want many people to receive your message?*

3. *Explain the use of the forwarding facility and responding to separate parts of a message you have received.*

4. *What are the main features of the style of e-mail messages?*

5. *What are e-words and how can they be used?*

6. *When are letters used rather than memos and e-mail?*

7. *What are the "standard block format" and the "modified block format" for letters? How do they differ?*

8. *What are the main and other elements of letter format?*

9. *What are the conventions (a) for addresses and (b) for dates?*

10. *What is the "salutation"? How do we avoid sexist reference in salutations?*

11. *What is the "complimentary close"? What is the conventional wording? How can informality be indicated in the signature?*

12. *What other items, apart from the message itself, might we include in a letter? How and where are these noted?*

13. *What are the Subject and Reference lines in a letter used for? Where should we include the sender's reference in our reply?*

14. *How, where and why are letters and memos marked as confidential and/or personal?*

15. *What are the conventions for addressing the envelope?*

16. *What are the major elements of style and tone for letters?*

17. *What are the main features for letters of application for employment?*

18. *What do "resume" and "cv" mean and what is an alternative?*

19. *What are major contents of a resume?*

20. *What information could you include as "personal information"?*

21. *What is the advantage and the disadvantage of stating your "career objectives"?*

22. *What information should you include about (a) your education and (b) your experience?*

23. *What do "references" and "referees" mean? What information should we include under the heading "References"?*

24. *What can you use to enhance the appearance of your resume?*

25. *Why is it often better for you to prepare your own resume rather than complete an application form?*

26. *What is a "memo" and why is it used less frequently nowadays?*

27. *What are the elements of the format for memos?*

28. *What are the main stylistic features of memos?*

Appendix A:
Information Retrieval

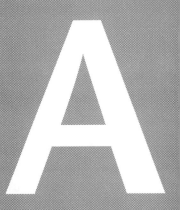

Information Retrieval
Background
Defining the Task

Primary and Secondary Sources
Locating Information
Documenting Your Sources

Types of Secondary Sources
Reference Works
CD-ROMS
The Internet
The Web
Search Engines

Information Retrieval

Background

During your university career and later as a professional, you will need to conduct research into many specific topics. You may need to explore the history of an invention or theory, determine the cause(s) of an occurrence or disaster, or accumulate relevant details about a subject as the basis for a report. Computers have revolutionized the process of information retrieval, so that technical research no longer entails hours of reading in the hope of coming across suitable information. However, the variety of data retrieval tools available can be just as daunting, although they are easy to use once you get started. The key to successful and time-efficient retrieval is not just knowing what you are looking for: you also need to know what sources are available, which ones are likely to be the most appropriate for the task at hand, and what the procedures are for using them.

Defining the Task

First define the initial task as clearly as you can. This means determining exactly what you have been asked to design or evaluate, the purpose of your work and document, and also the intended audience. Next, decide whether you need to broaden or limit your research objectives to provide a suitable response in the time you have available. The initial task may point to some underlying concerns or issues which could direct your research. If so, you may be able to narrow or reformulate the initial task. You may have to engage in some preliminary research at this point.

During your preliminary research, you may find that the initial task leads to other questions which need to be answered before you can deal with the basic issue. Also if your audience is non-technical, you may have to retrieve information beyond the initial task to provide a broader context for your readers. This may create more work, but it will help you produce a more effective document. As a bonus, such background information could be useful for a detailed introduction to your project.

No matter how clearly you define your task, your research objectives may change as you gather more and more information. Be flexible — if you discover information that indicates you need to re-assess you objectives, you would be doing yourself and your readers a disservice by ignoring it. On the other hand, if expected information is not available, adapt your plans and outline accordingly. If you change the plans for your work significantly, it would be wise to check with your supervisor before proceeding.

Checklist A.1: Procedure for Information Retrieval

✓ *Identify the initial task* - *initial question*
- *purpose of work and document*
- *audience*

✓ *Redefine the question* - *What do you need to study — and why?*
- *What are the underlying issues and concerns?*

✓ *Check with your supervisor*

✓ *Decide how and where to retrieve information.*

Primary and Secondary Sources

Locating Information

Now you need to decide where to look for relevant information. There are two types of information: primary and secondary sources. Primary sources are first-hand sources of information, including interviews, letters of inquiry, and personal experimentation and observations. Research using primary sources involves active investigation and discovery, as opposed to researching information resulting from investigations and discoveries by others.

Secondary sources include any information researched, written or documented by someone other than yourself (literally secondhand information); when using secondary sources, keep track of the sources of each piece of information, so that you can give appropriate credit later. Papers, articles, reports, interview transcripts, and documentary films are all examples of secondary sources, which you can find in your university or college library.

Your library will have a computerized catalogue system that allows you to access all available holdings very quickly. To look for books or documents on a specific topic, enter a word or phrase as a key word (k= . . .) or subject (s= . . .). Be as specific as you can, as a general key word (e.g. *science)* could give you over 20,000 entries! The computer will search the system and return a list of texts, including authors, publishers and call numbers; some systems also include a brief summary of the text. Most also allow you to enter a specific author (a= . . .) or titles (t= . . .) to check on a specific author or text.

Computerized catalog systems are easy to use, and you can access them from home via your modem. Once you know how to use them to locate books on your topic, you should learn how to access other reference works (papers, articles, reports) that will further assist your search for articles and information relevant to your project.

Documenting Your Sources

Once you have located all promising sources and begun the actual research, keep in mind that accurate documentation of your sources is *crucial*. If you use someone else's words, ideas or illustrations, you must say where they came from. Whether you quote directly or paraphrase, pay close attention to accuracy, and make sure you cite your sources in detail.

The best way of avoiding accidental plagiarism (and having to delve through your notes for a particular quote or source) is to make careful and complete notes on computer or index cards and cite the source at the bottom of each card. This takes longer, but could save you hours of frustrating repetition of your work. Of course, use of the photocopier or your printer is often a better alternative to your notes.

Types of Secondary Sources

Reference Works

Most students are familiar with the format and function of at least two basic reference works: encyclopedias, which provide general information on a broad range of subjects (e.g. McGraw-Hill's *Encyclopedia of Engineering*); and dictionaries, which provide a large variety of detailed definitions (e.g. Van Nostrand's *Scientific Encyclopedia*). Other reference documents such as handbooks, bibliographies, almanacs, directories, journals, indexes and abstracts allow you to conduct research far beyond the basic information provided by the above and they will also give you specific locations for the information you need. A list of common sources follows.

Handbooks

Engineering disciplines have handbooks that provide detailed information about basic theory and design parameters in specialist subjects. You will probably need to refer to these throughout your professional careers, so you should become familiar with their contents and uses. Some of the major handbooks are:

- *Chemical Engineers' Handbook* (Perry)
- *Materials Handbook* (Brady and Clauser)
- *Standard Handbook for Electrical Engineers* (Fowle)
- *Standard Handbook for Mechanical Engineers* (Mark)

Ask your technical librarian for other reference books applicable to your engineering or scientific discipline.

Bibliographies

Bibliographies are a stepping-stone to information sources pertaining to your topic, and are indispensable for more advanced work. They are lists of publications, by author, on topics in given disciplines, and include full details of authors, dates of publication, and titles.

An annotated bibliography is particularly helpful, as it provides an abstract or summary of the text, giving you a preliminary sense of whether the text will be helpful to you or not. Examples of bibliographies in technical subjects are:

- *Information Source in Physics*
- *Mechanical Engineering: The Sources of Information*
- *List of Publications available from the Department of Natural Resources and Energy, Minerals and Energy Division*, 1996.

Almanacs

While they often also suggest references on certain topics, almanacs are primarily factual information sources in their own right, offering collections of facts and statistics pertinent to given subjects. Almanacs vary in scope from general to quite specific. This means, for example, you might find helpful statistics on radioactive emissions in the Almanac of Applied Science and Technology, but you would also want to check the Nuclear Almanac for a more comprehensive set of facts and figures. For a listing of almanacs which might be helpful to your research, enter "almanac" as a key word or subject along with those you would normally use for your search; the computer will respond with a list of almanacs pertinent to your topic.

Examples of almanacs are:

- *The World Almanac Book of Inventions*
- *The Pacific Rim Almanac*
- *Facts Plus: An Almanac of Essential Information*

Directories

Directories provide information about organizations, companies, people, products, and services, often including addresses, phone and e-numbers and contact names. The wide scope of directories as a resource is indicated by titles which range from the Directory of Canadian Architects to the Alberta Biotechnology and Pharmaceutical Directory. Further examples of directories are:

- *The Canadian Environmental Directory*
- *Energuide Directory: Energy Consumption Rating of Major Household Appliances*
- *1989 Directory of the Association of Professionals Engineers of the Province of British Columbia.* (Available for all other provinces.)

Journals and Indexes

Scientific and engineering journals and periodicals are invaluable resources as they contain reports and updates on current technology and scientific development. To find articles relevant to your area of research, you will need to use the Journal Indexes in your library. These classify articles appearing in given journals according to topic, and tell you exactly where to find them. You may need to ask a librarian for help, as the indexing system can vary from library to library. Some publications, e.g. *The New York Times*, provide their own annual index (The New York Times Index), while many libraries carry a comprehensive index of their own journal holdings e.g. the Applied Science Technology Index at Queen's University.

Abstracts

A combination of indexes and annotated bibliographies, abstracts perform the same function as an index in terms of listing and classifying journal articles, while providing brief details about the articles themselves. Like indexes, abstracts may index specific publications, or focus on a few journals in a specific discipline. Abstracts allow you to decide in advance whether or not an article is worth finding on the shelf or obtaining through inter-library loan.

CD-ROMS

Increasingly, many of the reference works just described are becoming available on CD-ROM. The Compact-Disc Read Only Memory Systems operates in easy-access CD's which are copies of on-line data bases. The great advantages of the CD-ROM are that it permits the storage of volumes of information in a single disc and allows an extremely rapid search, with highly accurate results. Once you locate the appropriate CD, the computer will sift through thousands of articles in seconds, searching for the key words or phrases you type in, and listing all pertinent articles.

Ask your librarian which CD's are appropriate to your research; many libraries carry discs specifically geared toward technical disciplines. For example, Compendex provides a comprehensive index and texts of current engineering journals and conferences. The CD-ROM is a powerful and time efficient search tool, although the gradual transference of the information available in data bases, and on CD, to the readily-accessible Internet may eventually render it obsolete.

The Internet

The Internet ("the Net") is a global network of computer networks linked via specific hardware and software. Anyone with the right equipment and software can log on to the Net and link up to computers used by universities, government departments, companies, organizations and individuals. The wealth of information available over the Net has resulted in its label "The Information Super-Highway." Some of the resources include e-mail, news groups, on-line library catalogs, computer file archives, and electronic journals.

The Web

The rapid growth of the Net has resulted in the development of superstructures such as the Gopher (gopher-space) and the World-Wide-Web, which index and organize the resources into an easily-accessible order. Increasingly, the World-Wide-Web is the search tool of choice for Net-users, indexing millions of home pages and computer sites around the world. These are maintained by individuals (fan clubs, hobbies, interests) or the institutions and organizations already mentioned. The Usenet is a global network of newsgroups also accessible through the Web. These are a particularly valuable resource as they allow you to post a request or express interest in certain information or experiences. Individuals around the world may help you with your work, although you will need to check for accuracy and legitimacy.

Search Engines

Navigating this ocean of information is surprisingly simple as you use Search Engines. These are Web Indexes that allow you to scan vast sections of the Web and retrieve information, using key words to begin your search. Some of the major Search Engines on the Net include: Microsoft Network, Lycos, Altavista, Web Crawler, Excite and Yahoo.

Your college or university will have computer sites which allow immediate access to these engines through software such as "Netscape." Companies such as Compuserv also provide access to them for a fee, after you enter a password to log on to the net from local computer sites, or from your personal computer.

To use a Search Engine, simply type in a key word or phrase, and click on the "search" or "go" icon. Once the engine has completed the search, it will provide you with information about websites that fit your query in descending order from the best match. The number of articles retrieved ("hits" in Net terminology) may be in excess of several thousand even when you give very specific keywords and describe their context. Be wary of over generalizing when entering a category, as the engine could take a long time to produce a list so long it could be useless. Different search engines react in different ways to input. If you asked Altavista to search for *Michael Jordon*, it would search for all occurrences of *Michael* or *Jordan* or both anywhere on a page! For a more efficient search put the two in quotation marks: *"Michael Jordan"*. However, if you did this for Yahoo, it would not find anything as it describes names with first name last: *"Jordan, Michael*. Thus if one search engine fails to give you what you want, try another.

The Net is arguably the easiest way for users to locate and retrieve information. Taking the time to familiarize yourself with the Net will ensure that you have a wealth of information at your disposal whenever you need it. Refer to an Internet handbook (e.g. Harley Horn's) to learn about techniques and procedures. You should learn about security and privacy, search procedures, downloading software, usenets and mailing lists, creating your own website, talking on the Net, and video net communications.

Checklist A.2: Types of Information Sources

✓ *Primary:*

- *interviews*

- *surveys*

- *letters of inquiry*

- *experiments*

- *observations*

✓ *Secondary:*

- *On-line catalogue system:*

    - *Encyclopedias*
    - *Bibliographies*
    - *Handbooks*
    - *Directories*
    - *Almanacs*

- *CD-ROMS*

- *Internet*

Appendix B:
Describing People
(Including 60 ways of Avoiding Sexist Pronouns)

Describing People
People as Descriptive Topics
Profiles
Biographical Sketches
Avoiding Sexist Pronouns
The Need to Use and Avoid Sexist Pronouns
Methods of Avoiding Sexist Pronouns
Some Advice on Correcting Sexist Pronouns
Avoiding Other Sexist Forms of Language

Describing People

People as Descriptive Topics

Chapter 5 explains the methods used by skilled writers and editors to describe technical instruments, machines and other objects. As the principles of describing people differ only slightly from those described there, this appendix uses and extends those principles. The use of repetition and other basic re-entry devices apply also to people, although of course there is considerable choice in the partial repetition of people's names, from the full formal name to nicknames.

Checklist B.1: Partial Repetitions for People's Names

✓ *Ms. Kristiina Valter McConville*

✓ *Kristiina Valter McConville*

✓ *Kristiina V. McConville*

✓ *Kristiina McConville*

✓ *Ms. McConville*

✓ *McConville*

✓ *Kristiina*

✓ *Krissy*

✓ *Kris*

The full name would only be used for legal purposes, others for very formal or formal uses, and still others by colleagues, friends and relatives.

Another difference when describing people is that the relative pronoun is *who* for both restrictive and non-restrictive clauses, unlike the option of *that* and *which* for things. Thus we must be more careful with commas around incidental material when describing people. Also, associated re-entries are used extensively when describing people, especially the pre-triggered forms (e.g. *my* interests, *her* abilities). In fact, unlike with the description of things, we find that possessive connections are the more usual form of associative connection for people.

Substitution is used extensively when writers are describing people. When the topic is a specific person, this causes no difficulty. When, however, we are describing an unspecified person belonging to a group (e.g. students, engineers, employees, executives, managers, scientists), we often run into difficulties because there is no gender-neutral pronoun system for singular people. All we have are *she* and *he*. Because the use of such "sexist pronouns" is a breach of propriety (see *Chapter 8*), we must avoid them, and this chapter provides 60 ways of doing that. Related to the avoidance of sexist pronouns are other inappropriate terms (e.g. *fireman*, *manhole cover*, and *woman principal*), for which we must find suitable alternatives.

Thus this appendix first explains the general case of describing specific named people (whose sex we know) in profiles and then biographies; then gives advice about and lists 60 ways of avoiding sexist pronouns followed by related exercises; and finally provides advice concerning alternatives to generic "man" forms and other unacceptable sexist terms.

Profiles

We often find "profiles" of interesting and talented people in technical magazines. Obviously the topic is the person being profiled, and that topic is re-entered many times into the text using a variety of techniques — just as when we describe things. Here are some details extracted from one such profile:

B.1

One such ''frontier engineer'' is *Kristiina Valter McConville*, P.Eng, *who*'s anxiously awaiting the results of Dr Roberta Bondar's experiments, to be announced at the Canadian Aeronautics and Space Institute meeting in November. *McConville, who* worked as an engineering assistant at the Canadian Space Agency, helped to set up the experiments Bondar performed aboard the U.S. space shuttle Discovery . .

. .*She* thinks astronauts must master more than one field of knowledge. . . . *Her present studies* link two fields — physiology and biomedical engineering . . . As a teaching assistant in engineering, *she* was troubled by the static enrollment of women in engineering school, _ and is relieved that this seems to be changing.
— *Engineering Dimensions*, Sep/Oct 1992, P39

O n c e the topic is introduced here, the writer uses a variety of re-entry techniques. *P.Eng.* is a verbless clause, and there are two instances of relative clauses, dominated by *who*. The subject is re-entered into the text by the partial repetition *McConville* and also the pre-triggered associate *Her present studies*. Substitution (*She*) is also used twice, and ellipsis is used to connect the final clause. Note how a minor topic of this profile (*Bondar*) is also re-entered in the text by partial repetition.

If the subject is a man, of course, we use *He* as the substitute word. Here is a very brief profile as part of a wide-ranging narrative structure:

B.2
A significant appointment was Dr A.L.Clark in 1906 to head the physics department. *Clark* had a BSc in electrical engineering from Worcester Polytechnic Institute in Massachusetts _ and a PhD in physics from Clark University in the same state. *He* was the first U.S.-trained engineer to join the Queen's faculty and only the second with an earned PhD.

— *Engineering Dimensions*,
Sep/Oct 1992, P48

Partial repetition, substitution and ellipsis are used in this brief profile.

Writing Tasks

1. Write the profile of Dr Sastri (a man) using the following notes. All information refers to Dr Sastri.

   Winner of Morris Cohen Award for corrosion in 1995 — a CIM Member — graduated with Bachelor and Masters degrees in chemistry from Sri Venkateswara University, India — subsequently received PhD in chemistry from the University of New York at Buffalo — brief period of post-doctoral work at the University of Southern California — taught chemistry at the Haileybury School of Mines — also taught chemistry at Carleton University and the American University in Beirut — during this period guided students to BSc, MSc and PhD degrees — joined CANMET in 1972 as a research scientist — published three books and 115 refereed papers — published 50 technical reports — has chaired and presented many invited papers at national and international conferences — received the Howard Taylor Best Paper Award of American Foundrymen's Society in May 1994 — will be presented the Morris Cohen Award at the CIM annual conference in Vancouver in August 1995.

2. Write your own third-person profile to give to the chairperson of a meeting, who will use it to introduce you.

3. Interview colleagues to obtain information about their lives, achievements and interests; choose both men and women. Then assume each colleague has been elected to serve as student representative on the Board of Trustees, and write brief profiles for each of them for the Board of Trustees' profile publication. Note and identify the re-entry techniques you use. Ask each colleague to check your profile and give advice as to how it might be improved.

4. Present some of these profiles orally as if you were introducing each colleague to a wider audience.

Biographical Sketches

Profiles are usually quite brief accounts of the major achievements of a person. More detailed accounts including the life history of a person are called "biographies," which can be full-length books or hour-long TV documentaries. Biographies written by the person being described are called "autobiographies." Be careful not to confuse biographies with bibliographies, which are lists of related published documents.

Short biographies (often called "biographical sketches") often accompany articles, theses or other publications, and are used as introductions for speakers at conferences. They are sometimes little more than a brief note of the author's position and relevant background:

B.3

Professor George Richardson, of Queen's' Faculty of Applied Science, has been researching, teaching and writing about Canadian engineering history since 1967. *He* has just completed the book *Queen's Engineers, a Century of Applied Science, 1893-1993*, from which this article was excerpted.
— *Engineering Dimensions*,
Sep/Oct 1992, P49

More typically biographical sketches are highly condensed summaries of the qualifications and main experiences and achievements of the author:

B.4

Alan G. Galley was born in 1954 in Hull, Quebec. *He* received *his BSc degree* in geology from Carleton University in 1978, _ *his MSc degree* in geology from the University of Western Ontario in 19812, and _ PhD in geology from Carleton University in 1994. After doing a little consulting work, *Alan Galley* joined the Mineral Resources Division of the Geological Survey of Canada in 1983. *He* has since worked on the gold metallogeny of Early Proterozoic Trans-Hudson Orogen _ and mineral deposit research on massive sulphide deposits from Archean and Early Proterozoic island arc terranes and Cretaceous ophiolite terranes. *His present interest* is in researching the role of subvolcanic intrusions in developing regional scale hydrothermal systems and associated massive sulphide deposits.
— *CIM Bulletin*,
May 1995, P15

As well as using partial repetition and substitution, the writer of this biographical sketch uses three pre-triggered associations, a list in the first sentence, and ellipsis in the fourth.

Writing Tasks

Write biographical sketches based on the following information.

(a) *Malcolm J. Scoble — Webster Professor of Mining at McGill University — Graduate of Camborne School of Mines, Leicester University and Nottingham University — previously professor in the Department of Mining Engineering in the University of Nottingham for twelve years — has current research, teaching and consulting activities — these are in the fields of rock mechanics and fragmentation — also mine design and automation — has worked in several mines in Canada, Sweden, Portugal, and England — has a PhD — has been a member of CIM since 1967 — is a member of the Order of Engineers in Quebec.*

(b) *Michael P. Jordan — early life as an electrical apprentice — became an electrical engineer — later worked as a technical writer and publications manager — now Research Associate at the Strathy Language Unit in the Department of English at Queen's University — also full professor of linguistics and technical communication in the Queen's Faculty of Applied Science — has PhD in linguistics/English language — teaches technical writing to engineering and science students and linguistics to arts students — published four books and many refereed papers and articles on technical communication and linguistics — past President of the Canadian Association of Teachers of Technical Writing — former director of the Linguistics Association of Canada and the United States.*

Avoiding Sexist Pronouns

The Need to Use and Avoid Sexist Pronouns

As we saw in the examples discussed so far in this appendix, we can, and should, use the female and male pronouns (*she, he* and their variants) when referring to a person whose sex we know. We can also use them when referring to a class of people (male or female) when the members of that class can only be one sex — mothers and fathers, brothers and sisters, for example. This also applies when we are referring to classes of people who can only be of one or other sex by virtue of the definition of a word or physical reality (e.g. lesbians, victims of prostate cancer). An oddity of English to note here is the use of the female pronoun for nature (mother nature), ships and space craft, although the earlier inclusion of hurricanes in this class is no longer acceptable. Some people (probably only men) might lovingly also refer to their new car using *she*.

Checklist B.2: When to Use Sexist Pronouns

✓ *when referring to a person of known sex*

✓ *when referring to a class of people who inherently must be of one sex or the other (e.g. young girls, sons)*

✓ *when referring to a class of people who can only be of one sex by definition or physical reality (e.g. victims of breast cancer, beard wearers)*

✓ *use of female pronouns for nature, ships and space craft*

When, however, we need to refer generically to a class in which there is or could be members of either sex (which of course means most classes of people), we cannot use either *she* or *he* as that would give the impression that *only* that sex is or should be members of that class. Also when we refer to someone we cannot yet identify (e.g. the successful candidate for an award, the student with the highest mark in the course next term, the next dean or principal), we cannot use sexist pronouns as such people could be of either sex. This does not apply if the person can be only of one sex, however (e.g. next year's captain of the women's or men's hockey team). Finally, when we are writing about the rights and obligations of an unspecified person of either sex (e.g. the plaintiff, the complainant, the accused, the murderer), we cannot use male or female pronouns, as that would imply exclusion of the other sex. Once that person is known in any given case, of course, we can then use the appropriate sexist pronoun.

Checklist B.3: When Not to Use Sexist Pronouns

✓ *when the class does or could include either or both sexes (e.g. nurses, engineers, supermarket customers, astronauts, caregivers, truck drivers)*

✓ *when we are referring to a specific individual we cannot yet identify who could be of either sex*

✓ *when writing about the rights and obligations of as yet unknown individuals of a class (e.g. the grievor, the accused)*

Avoiding Sexist Pronouns

Pronouns form the "substitution" system in English, and the language has evolved with substitution as a key element in the re-entry system. You should have realized this in your earlier work on profiles and biographies. As we cannot use substitution in certain instances (see *Checklist B.3*), we have to find alternatives. As substitution is just one of many ways of re-entering topics, we can use the many other methods available.

The next section of this appendix provides examples of how you can avoid sexist substitution mainly using the methods of topic connection you learned in *Chapter 5*. The methods of avoiding sexist substitution are listed here with examples in the order of the material in the book. This takes us through repetition, generic nouns and synonymy, acronyms, substitution, ellipsis and lists, relative clauses, non-finite and verbless clauses, and finally associations and perspectives. Other methods are also included, with reference to discussion in other parts of the book noted where applicable.

Each of the examples consists of two elements: first an unacceptable sexist version, and then a version avoiding the sexist substitution using the method identified in the heading. Key words or other language features are italicized in both versions to help you to recognize how the technique is being used.

It is important to realize that when we change a sentence to avoid sexist substitution, we may be changing the emphasis or tone of the writing. These changes are usually acceptable as long as we do not significantly change the meaning of the writing or make the writing stylistically inappropriate.

When you have finished studying the paired examples provided, read the advice given in the next section and then try using the methods by editing some of the exercises provided. The first set of exercises is of single sentences, which are relatively easy to correct. The second set consists of examples each several sentences long, and these are much more challenging.

Methods of Avoiding Sexist Pronouns

Repetition (*Chapter 5*)
  1. Full Repetition

      How can *the teacher* help language learners. *She* can . . .
      How can *the teacher* help language learners? *The teacher* can . . .

  2. Partial Repetition

      The director of nursing quality and scheduling should be a member of the personnel committee. *He* should also . . .
      The director of nursing quality and scheduling should be a member of the personnel committee. *The nursing director* should also . . .

General Nouns and Acronyms (Chapter 5)

3. Generic Noun

    When *a student* makes a statement that requires explanation, *she* can be encouraged to provide this.
    When *a student* makes a statement that requires explanation, *the speaker* can be encouraged to provide this.

4. Synonym

    The student needs to acquire the ability to infer meanings in words. *He* must also discover . . .
    The student needs to acquire the ability to infer meanings in words. *The pupil* must also discover . . .

5. Acronym

    The psychologically deprived child can become a serious problem in society. *She* often resorts to violence and crime.
    The psychologically deprived child (PDC) can become a serious problem in society. *The PDC* often resorts to violence and crime.

Substitution (Chapter 5)

6. First-person Singular

    The course instructor would like to receive your opinions of *his* instruction on the course.
    As *course instructor*, *I* would like to receive your opinions of *my* instruction on the course.

7. First-person Plural

    The teacher seldom gets ready-to-use directions from grammarians. *She* can however make *her* own.
    We seldom get ready-to-use directions from grammarians. *We* can however make *our* own.

8. Second-person Explicit

    The student is required to purchase a set of notes for the course. *He* must also buy the required text of course.
    The student is required to purchase a set of notes for the course. *You* must also buy the required text of course.

9. Second-person Implicit (Imperative)

The student should answer the easiest question first. *She* should then re-read the remainder and answer the next easiest one.
Answer the easiest question first. Then *re-read* the remainder and *answer* the next easiest one.

10. Third-person Singular (Impersonal)

The student should always leave time to re-read *his* examination answers.
One should always leave time to re-read *one's* examination answers.

[The use of *one* — and especially *one . . . one* — is thought to be rather affected in Canada and it is not recommended; however it must now be preferred to the usage of *One . . . he* found in the USA.]

11. Third-person Plural (Consistent)

The successful language student can be encouraged to explain how *she* has analyzed *her* exercise.
Successful language students can be encouraged to explain how *they* analyzed *their* exercises.

12. Third-person Plural (Inconsistent)

No one failing this course can complete *his* program.
No one failing this course can complete *their* program.

[This technique is not advisable, as it is inconsistent with number.]

Ellipsis and Passives (*Chapters 5 and 8*)
13. Subject Ellipsis (Active)

The teacher can collect sentences of various structures. *She* can then group them . . .
The teacher can collect sentences of various structures and can then group them . . .

14. Subject Ellipsis (Active-Passive)

The student pays fees to the Home university; *he* is classed as a "visiting graduate student" at the Host University, where no fees are paid.
The student pays fees to the Home University and is classed as "visiting graduate student" at the Host University where no fees are paid.

15. Subject-Modal Ellipsis

The student must attend regularly and *she* must submit all assignments on time.
The student must attend regularly and submit all assignments on time.

16. Subject-Verb Ellipsis

The student needs a great deal of encouragement. *He* also needs praise for continued hard work.
The student needs a great deal of encouragement and also praise for continued hard work.

17. Subject-Modal-Verb Ellipsis

The student may feel that certain things are inadequately expressed in English. *She* may also feel that other things are unclearly expressed in Spanish.
The student may feel that certain things are inadequately expressed in English and also that other things are inadequately expressed in Spanish.

18. Subject-Verb-to Ellipsis

The student will want to use only simple well-known words. *He* will also want to use only repetition and co-ordination for sentence connection.
The student will want to use only simple well-known words and use only repetition and co-ordination for sentence connection.

19. Clause Ellipsis

The student will work hard to achieve well-established goals. *She* will also work hard to please respected teachers.
The student will work hard to achieve well-established goals and also to please respected teachers.

20. Passive (Agentless)

The teacher asks a question, and throws a ball to a student, who answers the question and returns the ball. *He* can vary this procedure in a number of ways.
The teacher asks a question, and throws a ball to a student, who answers the question and returns the ball. This procedure *can be varied* in a number of ways.

21. Passive (Agentive)

The student sometimes submits essays written by others. To receive credit, all work *she* submits must be *her* own.
The student sometimes submits essays written by others. To receive credit, all work *submitted by a student* must *be written by that student*.

22. Intransitive Verb

The graduate student needs a supervisor who can assist and stimulate *him* effectively throughout the program.
The graduate student needs a supervisor who can *lead* effectively through out the program.

23. Direct Verb

The student may make *her* selection of electives from those listed for the department.
The student may *select* electives from those listed for the department.

Lists *(Chapter 5)*
24. Continuing List

The teacher can bring humor into the classroom. *He* can change the pace and type of instruction. *He* can seek to make learning a joy.
The teacher can bring humor into the classroom, change the pace and type of instruction, and seek to make learning a joy.

25. Introduced List

The teacher can encourage interest by asking students to bring in their own examples from newspapers. *She* can also do this by playing taped television interviews. Finally *she* can encourage interest by taking students to museums where they will have to read descriptions in English.
The teacher can encourage interest in several ways: by asking students to bring in their own examples from newspapers, by playing taped television interviews, and by taking students to museums where they will have to read the descriptions in English.

Relative Clauses *(Chapter 5)*
26. Relative Clause (Non-Restrictive)

The teacher should always consider the use of visual aids. *He* may find them unsuitable for some purposes, however.
The teacher, who should always consider the use of visual aids, may nevertheless find them unsuitable for some purposes.

27. Relative Clause (Restrictive)

A teacher may try to bully weak students into trying harder. If *she* does this, *she* may cause the student to give up altogether.
A teacher who tries to bully weak students into trying harder may cause the student to give up altogether.

Non-finite and Verbless Clauses (*Chapter 5*)

28. -ed Clause (Non-Restrictive)

The language learner is often faced with living in the target country. *He* will then undergo culture shock.
The language learner, when fac*ed* with living in the target country, will undergo culture shock.

29. -ed Clause (Restrictive)

Imagine *a language learner* faced with living in the target country. *She* will then undergo culture shock.
A language learner fac*ed* with living in the target country will undergo culture shock.

30. -ed Clause (Single Word Post-Modifier)

The student only attempted three questions and did poorly on the questions *he* did attempt.
The student only attempted three questions and did poorly on the questions attempt*ed*.

31. -ing Clause (Non-Restrictive)

The teacher writes the vocabulary on the board. *She* then separates the different parts of speech.
The teacher writes the vocabulary on the board, separat*ing* the different parts of speech.

32. -ing Clause (Restrictive)

We will select *a student* with high academic standing. *He* must also excel at sports.
A student hav*ing* high academic standing and hav*ing* excelled in sports will be selected.

33. Verbless Clause (Informational — Non-Restrictive)

The student is usually eager to learn real-life language. But *she* may be less keen to learn grammar.
The student, usually eager to learn real-life language, may be less keen to learn grammar.

34. Verbless Clause (Informational — Restrictive)

If *a student* is aware of damage being done in residence, *he* has a duty to report it.
Any student aware of damage being done in residences has a duty to report it.

35. Verbless Clause (Appositional)

The whale is the biggest mammal on earth. *She* constantly migrates along continental shores.
The whale, the biggest mammal on earth, constantly migrates along continental shores.

36. Verbless Clause (Prepositional)

One student will achieve top standing in class. *He* should receive special recognition.
The student at the top of the class standing should receive special recognition.

37. Verbless Clause (With)

We are considering *the highly motivated student. She* generally has a broad linguistic background.
We are considering *the highly motivated student*, generally *with* a broad linguistic background.

38. to-infinitive Clause (Passive)

The winner will be announced next class. *He* will be presented with the award on Founders' Day.
The winner, to be announced next class, will be presented with the award on Founders' Day.

39. to-infinitive Clause (Active)

The writer's aim is to create a plausible sales message. *She* can only achieve this by providing convincing information.
The writer's aim, *to create* a plausible message, can only be achieved by providing convincing information.

Associative, Perspective and Implicit Connection (Chapter 5)
40. Post-triggered Association

If a student fails to complete all required courses and with an overall average of at least 55 per cent, *he* will be required to withdraw from the program.
If a student fails to complete all required courses and with an overall average of at least 55 per cent, *withdrawal from the program* will be required.

41. Pre-triggered Association

The student may, within two days, rewrite the essay rejected by *the teacher* and ask *her* to re-mark it.
The student may, within two days, rewrite the essay rejected by *the teacher* and request *its remarking*.

42. Untriggered Association

Should *a student* prove disruptive during a session, *he* may be required to withdraw.

Should *a student* prove disruptive during a session, *withdrawal* [from the session] may be required.

43. Untriggered Perspective

The diligent student can expect to receive high grades for *her* work.
The diligent student can expect to receive high grades.

44. Implicit Indirect Object

It is easier for *a student* to remember the correct use of words and expressions if they are presented *to him* in meaningful sentences.
It is easier for *a student* to remember the correct use of words and expressions if they are presented in meaningful sentences.

45. Implicit Direct Object

If *the student* is asked for the passive counterpart, it does not help *her* much to know the transformational "rules."
If *the student* is asked for the passive counterpart, it does not help much to know the transformational "rules."

46. Implicit Reflexive

If *a student* misbehaves *himself* on the trip, appropriate action will be taken.
If *a student* misbehaves on the trip, appropriate action will be taken.

47. Anticipatory 'It' (*Chapter 9*)

The teacher can simply state that something is wrong. Or *she* can ask the student to explain the answer.
The teacher can simply state that something is wrong. Or *it* might be a good idea to ask the student to explain the answer.

48. Definite Article

If *the teacher* is aware that *his* lesson will be assessed . . .
If *the teacher* is aware that *the* lesson will be assessed . . .

49. Indefiniteness

. . . for *the teacher* to walk into *her* classroom . . .
. . . for *the teacher* to walk into class . . .

50. Indefinite Article

Perhaps *the student*'s problem is more basic still: *his* inability to . . .
Perhaps *the student*'s problem is more basic still: *an* inability to . . .

51. Unarticled Plural

The teacher should use visual aids in presenting *her* lessons.
The teacher should use visual aids in presenting lessons.

52. Unarticled Singular

The successful applicant must send *his* acceptance within one month.
The successful applicant must send acceptance within one month.

53. Consistent Plural

The successful language student can be encouraged to explain how *she* has analyzed *her* articles.
Successful language students can be encouraged to explain how *they* analyzed *their* articles.

54. Substitute Clause (Inverted)

The writer may wish to delay stating the agent as long as possible. *He can do this* by using the by-phrase at the end of the sentence.
The writer may wish to delay stating the agent as long as possible. A by-phrase at the end of the sentence can achieve this aim.

55. Substitute Clause (Combined)

The teacher can guide learners into habits of intelligent guessing from context. *She* does this by a kind of catechism of leading questions.
The teacher can guide learners into habits of intelligent guessing from context by a kind of catechism of leading questions.

56. Temporal -ing Clause

It is inadvisable for *a trainee* to use a new aid if *he* is giving a practical test.
It is inadvisable for *a trainee* to use a new aid *while giving* a practical test.

57. Time Adjunct

The gifted student may lose interest in academic work in *her* youth.
The gifted student may lose interest in academic work *during youth*.

58. Modal Infinitive

The student needs to be seated so *he* can see all information presented.
The student needs to be seated *so as to be able to see* all information presented.

59. Existential 'There' (*Chapter 9*)

> *The teacher* often has difficulty teaching articles and prepositions to ESL students from China. *She* can, however, simplify the task.
> *The teacher* often has difficulty teaching articles and prepositions to students from China. *There* are ways, however, of simplifying the task.

60. Purpose Clause

> *The successful local candidate* will be sent an application form and *he* will be asked to complete and return it for the regional competition.
> *The successful local candidate* will be sent an application form *to* complete and return for the regional competition.

Some Advice on Correcting Sexist Pronouns

In some legal documents the male substitutes are still used, but with a covering note indicating that these are intended to mean both sexes. This is not acceptable in normal use, and some writers use combinations such as *s/he him/her* and *herself/himself* instead. This method is very obvious, and is usually extremely confusing (see *No. 4* in the multiple-sentence editing exercise later), especially as we really should alternate first positions to be fair to both sexes. Some writers choose to alternate female-male-female etc. substitutes without the combinations. However even this can be very confusing (see *No. 5* in the multiple-sentence exercise later) and is not recommended. Ideally you should avoid sexist pronouns without your readers being aware that that is what you are doing.

   You should now recognize that the sex-specific substitutes are part of a wider substitute sub-system and that that sub-system is just one method in the wider system of continuity. Thus you could seek alternative re-entry methods within the substitution sub-system itself (using *you, we, one, they,* for example). You can widen your search for a suitable method by trying the basic re-entry techniques of repetition, generic nouns, and acronyms — and also associations and implicit connections. Methods within the clause are also often useful techniques to consider; these include all the relative, non-finite and verbless clauses as well as the associative and perspective connections within the sentence.

Checklist B.4: Tips for Avoiding Sexist Pronouns

✓ *If you can change the style to an informal one, use you, we or I. For more formal prose try the passive form and implicit connections.*

✓ *For possessive pronouns, try the various methods of the article system (including no article at all).*

✓ *You can only use plurals if the text makes sense in the plural. You cannot, for example, write about students submitting reports if you mean each student must submit one report.*

> ✓ *If you do use plurals, be consistent: "Customers place their products in carts," for example.*
>
> ✓ *Use a variety of techniques rather than unthinkingly using a single method. No one method will work all the time.*

Editing Exercise: Short Examples

Edit the following sentences to remove the sexist pronouns. Use a variety of re-entry techniques.

1. To be safe, the committed professional over-prepares for all his classes. As a result he tends to arrive for his classes a bit early, and he finishes a bit late.

2. In discussion, the teacher should withhold her opinion almost all of the time. Her general aim should be to encourage a variety of opinions from her students.

3. The well-prepared teacher arrives on time as he wants to make every minute count. He has little time to accomplish all his objectives, so he often insists on punctuality.

4. Each applicant must name two people whom she has asked to submit confidential letters of reference about her.

5. If the response of the accused is unsatisfactory, he may be required to appear before a committee at a hearing to determine his guilt and his possible penalty.

6. A candidate for this award must be a citizen of Canada or she must have held landed immigrant status for one year prior to her submitting the application.

7. If a student can demonstrate that his transcript is in error, he may appeal to the Board of Studies to have his transcript corrected.

8. Unsatisfactory performance by the student may lead to a decision requiring that she withdraw from her program.

9. The instructor should explain that she will require the student to read from his journal.

10. If the instructor wants the student to react to class lectures and respond to readings, he should give her a model entry for her journal so that she can prepare answers to possible questions he might give in class.

Editing Exercise: Multiple-Sentence Examples

1. The customers makes her selection from about 2,000 items displayed behind transparent panels so that she can see the products but she cannot remove them. After she has decided to purchase an item, she inserts a plastic card into a slot, and she presses a button to select her item. She then receives the item she has selected, places it into her shopping cart, and continues her shopping.

2. If a student wants to study at another approved university, he must pay his fees at the other university. During his period away from his university, he must retain his registration here; however, he will be exempted from paying his fees here for that period. For the period to count towards his residence, the work he performs must be equivalent to the work he would have been required to do in his program at this university.

3. If any member allows her subscription to fall six months in arrears, the membership secretary will inform her of this, and he will request her to make immediate payment to make her membership current. If she does not pay her subscription within a further six months from the date of mailing of her notification, the Council may declare her as an inactive member. The secretary will then delete her name from the active roll, and he will cease all membership services to her.

4. A student withdrawing voluntarily before January 31 is not considered to have failed his/her year, but she/he should apply immediately for admission into the following year to continue his/her program. However, if she/he withdraws after January 31, he/she is considered to have failed her/his year, and he/she must then apply for re-admission if she/he wishes to continue his/her program. The Dean may at any time require her/him to withdraw from his/her program if he/she deems that her/his attendance or work is unsatisfactory. In addition she/he may recommend to Senate that he/she be required to withdraw from her/his program if he/she deems that her/his conduct is unsatisfactory.

5. The teacher must take one further precaution: she must skim his lesson plan shortly before entering her classroom to refresh his memory of the major topics she feels he must include in that class. She must think carefully about what he has to do to get her major points across to his students. She can then enter his classroom with greater confidence, and she can pace his class according to her plan. He will be sure that she will not accidentally omit something he feels is important, and she will make sure he covers all her essential points.

Avoiding Other Sexist Forms of Language

Although sexist pronouns are an importance part of achieving balanced writing that will not offend either sex, there are other forms of sexist language you should avoid. An obvious one is the use of the word *man* to refer to all human beings. *Mankind* is better (or simply *people*), although some writers prefer *humankind* as this is less likely to be interpreted as meaning men only and not also women. The recent change of the name of the Canadian Museum of Man to the Museum of Civilization is a good solution. Use of the Latin *homo sapiens* is probably going too far.

Another source of impropriety is the use of the suffix *man* or *men* in occupations such as *fireman, policemen, draftsmen* as these give the impression that only men do those things. For these, we should use *fire fighter, police officers*, and *drafting specialists* instead. *Workmen* is easily changed to *workers*, and *Chairman* is better avoided in favor of *chairperson* or simply *the chair*. However, *personhole* instead of *manhole* would not be a good alternative; *inspection hole* is preferable. Occupations that traditionally have had male and female forms (e.g. *actor/ actress, conductor/conductress*) are now usually referred to by the *-or* form for both sexes. It is impolite to refer to a "female" actor or a "male" doctor or a "woman" driver, unless there is a really good reason (e.g. someone suffering pre-menstrual stress might legitimately prefer to consult a *woman* doctor).

When, however, the *man* component of a word is truly embedded in the meaning and cannot possibly refer to men as opposed to women, you should not change it. This occurs, for example, in words such as *maneuver, manipulate, manual* and *manage*. Even where the *man* is perhaps sexist, you may find it hard to find an acceptable alternative; we find this in *horsemanship*, for example, which would be a little odd as *horsepersonship*. Only rather sick humorists would seek to criticize *person* for including the "sexist" *son* and rewrite *Manual of Horsemanship* as *Peroffspringual of Horseperoffspringship*.

Much the same applies to the word elements *her* and *his*. We might think that both *hernia* and *hysterectomy* are a little peculiar, but you are not likely to be understood if you change them. The use of *history* is more debatable, as it derives from *his story*; some writers use *herstory* — especially for profiles of women — but this and the more logical *theirstories* are not commonly accepted.

The term *master* as in "Master's Degree" could perhaps be changed using a Latin term, but its use in mastering a subject cannot easily be altered. A person claiming to have *mistressed* a subject could cause bewilderment. Similarly a *masterly* job has no reasonable alternative.

Appendix C:
Using Numbers, Symbols and Units (SI)

Using Numbers, Symbols and Units (SI)
Use of Numbers
SI Symbols
Prefixes with Numbers
Writing Symbols

Using Numbers, Symbols and Units (SI)

Use of Numbers

Practice varies as to when to spell out numbers or use figures. Organizations and most editors and magazines have their own ways of doing it, and you should follow any system you are given. If you are not given a system to follow, you will find the following to be generally acceptable.

Checklist C.1: The Use of Numbers

✓ *Use numbers at all times with measurable quantities (e.g. 0.4 Cd, 110 V, $5) and also for percentages and ratios (e.g. 3% , 6:1). In general the values for time (hours, days, months, years) under ten are often spelled out, but specific measured units (e.g. 3.56 s) are usually numbered.*

✓ *For quantities of things that are not measurable quantities, use numbers above ten, and spell out the numbers for 10 and below (e.g. seven amplifiers, 26 resistors). The need for consistency may override this.*

✓ *Try to avoid starting a sentence with a number.*

✓ *Make sure you use the appropriate keys for 0 and 1, rather than using O and l.*

There are also conventional ways of writing numbers:

Checklist C.2: Writing Numbers

✓ *Try to use decimals rather than fractions.*

✓ *Include a zero before all values less than 1. Use a period in English (0.35) and a comma in French (0,35).*

✓ *Use a comma or a space between blocks of three for large numbers (3,574,863 or 3 574 863). Be consistent.*

SI Symbols

Use approved Systeme International (SI) units if you possibly can, although the imperial system is still in use in some disciplines and in the USA. Use the approved symbols.

Checklist C.3: Approved SI Units and Symbols

✓ Unit	✓ Name	✓ Symbol
angle (plane)	degree	o
	minute	‘
	second	“
angle (solid)	radian	rad
area	hectare	ha
electrical capacitance	farad	F
electrical current	ampere	A
electrical potential	volt	V
electrical resistance	ohm	Ω
electricity (quantity)	coulomb	C
force	newton	N
frequency	hertz	Hz
illuminance	lux	lx
inductance	henry	H
luminous flux	lumen	lm
magnetic flux	weber	Wb
magnetic flux density	tesla	T
length	metre	m
mass	gram	g
power	watt	W
pressure	pascal	Pa
substance (amount of)	mole	mol
temperature	kelvin	K

time	*second*	*s*
	minute	*m*
	hour	*h*
	day	*d*
	year	*a*
volume	*litre*	*L*
work	*joule*	*J*

Prefixes With Numbers

Prefixes are added directly to the basic unit (e.g. *cm* or *centimetre*). Here are the accepted prefixes for SI units.

Checklist C.4: Accepted Prefixes

✓ Prefix	✓ Symbol	✓ Multiplication factor
micro	μ	10^{-6}
milli	*m*	10^{-3}
centi	*c*	10^{-2}
deci	*d*	10^{-1}
deca	*da*	10^{1}
hecto	*h*	10^{2}
kilo	*k*	10^{3}
mega	M	10^{6}

Writing Symbols

In addition to the rules for the units and prefixes, there are several other rules which will help you to make your work consistent with published documents.

Checklist C.5: Rules For Writing Symbols

✓ *Never pluralize symbols (36 V, not 36 Vs). Except when they end a sentence, they are not followed by a period (5 L, not 5 L.).*

✓ *Except for angles (56˚ 24'36"), and Centigrade temperature (18˚C), leave a space between the number and the symbol (5.6 kg, not 5.6kg).*

✓ *When two or more units are used together, separate them with a period for multiplication and a solidus for division (e.g. kg.m/s). Do not mix names and units.*

✓ *Use the symbols when accompanied by numbers but the name when there are no numbers (e.g. 20 kg, but several kilograms).*

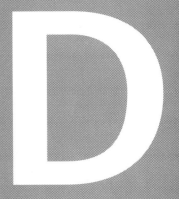

Appendix D:
Conventions

Conventions
  General
  Including Equations
  Commonly Used Foreign Abbreviations
  Consistency

Conventions: Equations, Abbreviations, and Consistency

General

In addition to the use of numbers, symbols and units, there are other important "conventions" in technical writing. You need to master these to ensure that your communication is clear and that you follow an accepted system of use for your writing. Discussed in this appendix are the use of equations, commonly used foreign abbreviations, and consistency.

Including Equations

When your equations are short, are on one line, and you will not need to refer to them later, you should include them as part of the text:

D.1

However, the *n* factor curves predict transition to occur at x/c = 0.57 (f=144 Hz and 162 Hz) versus the experimental observations placing transition in the range between x/c = 0.61 and 0.65.
— *Canadian Aeronautics and Space Journal*, Mar 1995, P33

If you wish to include a larger equation within the text, you may have to use extra lines to give enough space for the equation:

D.2

L is the distance from the wall to the location where

$\dfrac{U}{2e}$ =-U and N is the number of grid points used to

discretise the linear stability equations.
— ibid, P30

For larger equations, use separate lines and give each equation a number so that you and your readers can easily refer to them:

D.3

The sound transmission loss plate/porous/plate system is defined by

$$TL=10_{\log} \dfrac{Wi}{Wt} \qquad\qquad (10)$$

— ibid, P8

You will not go very far in any technical discipline without having to make quite extensive use of mathematical and other symbols to express yourself clearly. Thus equations can become an important aspect of your communications work.

As you advance in your technical discipline, you will need to become familiar with many different symbols, and how to use your computer to create them. If you have not done so already, you should now practice using your computer facilities to work with numbers and equations. (You may wish to take advantage of your computer's *Help* file to do this). When you have a large number of symbols, you should include a List of Symbols (sometimes called "Nomenclature") at the front of your document. This allows readers to find a meaning for a symbol quickly without having to find its definition when it is first mentioned in the text.

Writing Tasks

1. Write the following single-line equations on your computer:

    i) $\epsilon_g = 3.34 \, (D/T)^{1.55} \, Fr^{0.52} \, Fl^{0.48}$

    ii) $N_{js} = 330.6 \, v_{soc}^{0.5} \, v_g D^{-0.75}$; SD 12%

    iii) $n_{cj}(r_k) = \pi \, r_k \, (r_{k+1} - r_{k-1}) \, nj(r_k)/S_{ref}$

    iv) $(Sh - Sh')/Sh' = 0.237(N_U/Mv^4)^{0.144} e_G^{0.602}$

    v) $\ln (\Phi_i Z) = \ln (\Phi_i^{ph} Z^{ph}) + \ln (\Phi_i^{ch} Z^{ch})$

2. Write the following multi-line equations on your computer.

    i) $\mu_{fi} (X) = \exp \left[- \left(\dfrac{f_i (X) - f_i (X_R)}{r_i} \right)^2 \right]$

    ii) $D = \tan^{-1} \dfrac{2 \, \zeta^{0.5} v + A x_a}{x_a \, c^{0.5}} - 2 \tan^{-1} 1$

    iii) $N_{js} = \dfrac{3.5 \, \gamma^{0.1} \, (g \, \Delta\rho/\rho_l)^{0.42} \, x^{0.15} \, d_p^{0.18} \, T^{0.58}}{D^{1.5}}$

Commonly Used Foreign Abbreviations

A few foreign abbreviations (especially *e.g.* and *i.e.*) have become so much part of our writing that it would be hard to imagine them not being available. The fuller versions (*for example* and *that is*) are often used rather than the abbreviated forms, but the abbreviations are particularly useful for brief additions within examples.

Other foreign abbreviations are used in referencing documents. Note that while *et al.* is commonly used in the text to refer to more than two authors, the full list of authors is always included in the bibliography itself.

Checklist D.1: Common Foreign Abbreviations

✓ *etc.*   (short for *et cetera*) *means* and so on *or* and other things.

✓ *e.g.*   (short for *exempli gratia*) *means* for example *and is used when you wish to give an example of something.*

✓ *i.e.*   (short for *id est*) *means* that is *and is used when you wish to explain or elaborate on something.*

✓ *viz.*   (short for *videlicet*) *means* namely *and is used instead of a colon in front of an introduced list.*

✓ *et al.* (short for *et alii*) *means* and others *and is used with the first author to refer to multiple authors in the text.*

✓ *ibid.*   (short for *ibidem*) *means* in the same place *and is used to refer to the title in the preceding reference.*

✓ *loc.cit.* (short for *loco citato*) *means* in the place cited *and is used to refer to the precise passage or page mentioned in the preceding reference.*

Consistency

You should be consistent within any one document you are writing, although of course you may need to change spelling and other details when writing for different purposes and in different countries.

Consistency means doing the same thing for the little things of your writing where there is a choice. This includes some uses of hyphenation, capitalization, heading weights, underlining, paragraph indentations, and a host of other elements. Many organizations and magazines have their own "house style" for such matters, and "style guides" are available if you wish to follow an authoritative set of uses.

In Canada one difficulty is in the spelling you use, and again you should use one or other system (that used in the USA and that used in the UK and elsewhere) in any given document. Both systems are used in Canada, and some organizations insist on the use of one or the other. Spell checkers come in "UK" and "USA" versions. As some may accept both *organise* and *organize*, but not *analyse*, it is often difficult to be totally consistent. This book uses USA spelling in the general discussion, but any UK spelling in the examples has been left of course. Here are some important spelling differences in UK and USA use.

Checklist D.2: Some UK/USA Spelling Differences

✓ UK	✓ USA
analyse	analyze
behaviour	behavior
fibre	fiber
centre	center
colour	color
manoeuvre	maneuver
organise	organize
programme (except computer)	program
travelling	traveling

Note that, in Canada, the UK use of tyre (tire) is not acceptable, and the UK use of aluminium (aluminum) is sometimes regarded as questionable.

Appendix E:
Multiple-Choice Test Questions

E

Multiple-Choice Test Questions

This appendix provides an easily marked set of test questions for review of the book. It can also be used as the basis for a test, or as a means of stimulating class discussion. For each question, indicate the answer that *most correctly* completes the sentence.

1.   A summary is

  A.   *a sales document used to advertise books.*
  B.   *prefatory material that tells readers what is in the document.*
  C.   *prefatory material in which the writer explains the motivation for writing the document.*
  D.   *information that briefly highlights the main points of a document.*

2.   An -ed clause is

  A.   *a clause dominated by an adjective ending in -ed.*
  B.   *any clause in the past tense.*
  C.   *a clause dominated by an -ed form of a verb.*
  D.   *a special type of verbless clause.*

3.   Acceptable punctuation after the salutation in a letter is

  A.   *a dash.*
  B.   *nothing.*
  C.   *a semicolon.*
  D.   *a colon.*

4.   A "comma splice" is

  A.   *the use of a comma when stronger punctuation is needed.*
  B.   *the separation of a main clause from a subordinate clause with a comma.*
  C.   *omission of a comma before a final effect clause.*
  D.   *any improper use of a comma.*

5.   A major element of verbosity corrected during revision is

  A.   *overuse of existential* there.
  B.   *including unnecessary or known information.*

C. *tautologies and pairing.*

D. *overuse of anticipatory* it.

6. Acronyms

A. *are the opposite of generic nouns.*

B. *are useful for re-entering topics with long names.*

C. *must always be surrounded by commas.*

D. *mean the same as homonyms.*

7. Lists

A. *must always be preceded by a colon.*

B. *are always at the end of the sentence.*

C. *always answer the question "What are they?"*

D. *may include semicolons between the branches.*

8. One advantage of the author-year referencing system is

A. *it avoids repetition in the text when there is more than one reference to the same publication.*

B. *it is easier to locate where the reference is made in the text.*

C. *it enables you to list all authors in the bibliography.*

D. *it gives immediate reference to readers who know the author and year of major publications in the subject area.*

9. An outline has a disadvantage for some writers in that

A. *they have to decide what information to include and what to exclude.*

B. *it can restrict them in later re-organizing their work.*

C. *it allows their supervisors to give them advice on the progress of their work.*

D. *it requires them to organize their thoughts and their topics into groups and subgroups.*

10. Full repetition

A. *is always poor practice.*

B. *can be more emphatic than partial repetition.*

C. *is another term for* generic noun.

D. *can only be used when the topic is a single word.*

11.   Untriggered associations

A.   *are the most concise form of associations.*
B.   *are used when there are two or more possible topics.*
C.   *provide the means for adding adjectives.*
D.   *provide perspective for the statement.*

12.   Commas

A.   *provide more emphasis than dashes around non-restrictive clauses.*
B.   *are necessary around all restrictive clauses.*
C.   *provide a useful pause between a long subject and the main verb.*
D.   *can be used in front of a short introduced list.*

13.   Verbless clauses

A.   *are dominated by non-finite verb forms.*
B.   *are not dominated by any verb form at all.*
C.   *mean the same as appositions.*
D.   *are always indicated by the preposition* with.

14.   Continuing lists

A.   *must be introduced by a comma, a dash, or a colon.*
B.   *have introductory punctuation only when they are very complicated and/or long.*
C.   *cannot be presented with bullets.*
D.   *answer the question "What are they?" about the root of the list.*

15.   Clausal ellipsis

A.   *only occurs when two clauses are connected with* and, but, or or.
B.   *provide more emphasis than substitution.*
C.   *must always have a comma between the branches.*
D.   *is another name for faulty parallel structure.*

16.   For reports to members of the public

    A.   *jargon is useful because it tells them you know your subject.*
    B.   *jargon helps you to be precise.*
    C.   *jargon is confusing and should be avoided.*
    D.   *jargon aids in effective communication.*

17.   Sexist substitution

    A.   *occurs whenever* she *or* he *is used.*
    B.   *is apparent in such words as "Mr. Manson," "hernia" and "history."*
    C.   *only applies to women and not to men.*
    D.   *can be avoided by using almost any of the re-entry techniques.*

18.   Dashes

    A.   *are the same as hyphens.*
    B.   *can always be used instead of commas.*
    C.   *can be used at the start of an introduced list.*
    D.   *can be used at the start of a continuing list.*

19.   Problem-solution texts

    A.   *reflect the thoughts and actions of technical workers.*
    B.   *can only be used for engineering writing and not scientific writing.*
    C.   *apply only to large texts.*
    D.   *all have four parts to them.*

20.   You should *not* define something when

    A.   *only some of your readers know the term.*
    B.   *you need to use a word in a special sense.*
    C.   *you have invented something and it needs a name.*
    D.   *you need to provide an example to illustrate a point.*

21.   -ing clauses

    A.   *are dominated by an adjective ending in* -ing.
    B.   *can only be used in Positions 2 and 3.*
    C.   *always have commas within them.*
    D.   *can be restrictive or non-restrictive.*

22.   Signals of doubt

    A.   *are always poor style as they indicate that the writer lacks self confidence.*

B. *provide misleading information about the certainty of conclusions.*
C. *are useful in indicating the writer's level of uncertainty.*
D. *are "weasel words" that hide the real message.*

23. A "dissertation" is

A. *another word for "thesis" but more commonly used for graduate work.*
B. *a formal brief presented to a commission of enquiry.*
C. *an oral report of research work.*
D. *a written version of a paper presented at a conference of a professional society.*

24. Relative clauses

A. *are always dominated by* which *or* that.
B. *can often be converted to -ed, -ing or verbless clauses.*
C. *are clauses that indicate family relationships between topics.*
D. *can occur before the subject, between subject and verb, and at the end of the sentence.*

25. Square brackets are used for

A. *enclosing references to figure numbers.*
B. *enclosing references to tables.*
C. *including your own comments in a quotation.*
D. *including a full sentence in brackets.*

26. The trigger

A. *indicates what is being re-entered into a new clause.*
B. *is the punctuation used for introduced lists.*
C. *is an indication that you are re-entering the main topic into the text.*
D. *is another name for the topic when used for associations.*

27. When revising a major document you should pay attention to

A. *reader needs.*
B. *punctuation.*
C. *spelling.*
D. *consistency of terminology.*

28. Definition can occur as

    A.   *one or more sentences.*

    B.   *footnotes.*

    C.   *parenthetical interruptions in a sentence.*

    D.   *any of the above.*

29.   Appositions

    A.   *indicate the position of something.*

    B.   *are a special type of -ed clause.*

    C.   *provide more emphasis than their relative clause counterparts.*

    D.   *are useful for indicating a person's name, or position.*

30.   You should *not* indicate the structure of a document in

    A.   *headings.*

    B.   *the introduction.*

    C.   *the conclusion.*

    D.   *the contents page.*

31.   In problem-solution texts, description is usually found in the

    A.   *situation.*

    B.   *problem.*

    C.   *solution.*

    D.   *evaluation.*

32.   A tautology is

    A.   *any verbose structure.*

    B.   *two adjoining words where one is redundant.*

    C.   *an expanded verb structure.*

    D.   *a brief presented in some legal cases.*

33.   Evaluations

    A.   *contain whatever elements of basis, assessment and skilled opinion are necessary.*

    B.   *always contain basis and assessment.*

    C.   *depend largely on skilled opinion and experience.*

    D.   *never contain skilled opinions without detailed basis.*

34.   The relative pronoun *that*

    A.   *must always be used when re-entering things into restrictive relative clauses.*

    B.   *can only be used in restrictive relative clauses.*

    C.   *often has commas, dashes or parentheses around the clause it dominates.*

    D.   *can be used to re-enter places and times as well as things.*

35.   It is correct to say that

    A.   continual *and* continuous *mean the same.*

    B.   intermittent *and* continual *involve interruption whereas* continuous *does not.*

    C.   continual *and* intermittent *mean the same.*

    D.   continuous *and* continual *involve people whereas* intermittent *does not.*

36.   Semicolons

    A.   *can be used to separate parts of a list when any one part contains at least one comma.*

    B.   *are used to indicate that a list is coming.*

    C.   *are used after the salutation in a letter.*

    D.   *are used before final effect clauses.*

37.   A correct sentence is

    A.   *Its in its initial stage.*

    B.   *Its in it's initial stage.*

    C.   *It's in its initial stage.*

    D.   *It's in it's initial stage.*

38.   Sentence fragments

    A.   *are unacceptable.*

    B.   *are useful in expressing formal conclusions.*

    C.   *are normally acceptable only in very informal communications.*

    D.   *are accepted by style checkers.*

39.   A correct parallel structure is

    A.   *He not only tried to help practically, but also to provide financial backing.*

    B.   *This is as good or better than the earlier version.*

    C.   *Excellence always has, and will always continue to be, the prime concern.*

    D.   *The plane is neither parallel to, nor symmetrical about, the axial surface.*

40. A correct statement is that

    A.   i.e. *and* e.g. *mean the same.*
    B.   viz., namely, *and a colon all mean the same.*
    C.   etc. *is used in author-year references when there is more than one author for a publication.*
    D.   i.e. or ex *is used to indicate an example.*

41. It is correct to say that

    A.   *a paper is a formal article.*
    B.   *reports are published in magazines for wide readership.*
    C.   *articles can be very informal or quite formal.*
    D.   *papers are brief informal notes handed out at conferences.*

42. *Stet* means

    A.   *leave it the way it was before I was silly enough to change it.*
    B.   *that an error exists in a quotation.*
    C.   *a brief form of situation in problem-solution texts.*
    D.   *we are in a hurry to complete the work.*

43. When used to join two independent clauses *but* and *however*

    A.   *have no difference in punctuation.*
    B.   *differ in that* but *needs a semicolon preceding it whereas* however *must have a period preceding it.*
    C.   *differ in that* but *can have no punctuation or a comma, whereas* however *must have a semicolon or a period preceding it.*
    D.   *differ in that in that* but *must not have any punctuation preceding it, whereas* however *must.*

44. In editing you should pay attention to

    A.   *punctuation.*
    B.   *reader needs.*
    C.   *overall objectives of the document.*
    D.   *how the document relates to other documents.*

45. All technical documents

    A.   *follow the problem-solution pattern.*
    B.   *contain patterns of description.*
    C.   *contain basis-assessment patterns.*
    D.   *have an introduction, body and conclusion.*

46.   An apostrophe

    A.   *cannot be used to indicate a plural acronym.*
    B.   *is used with an s after all plural nouns to indicate possession.*
    C.   *indicates contractions in informal writing.*
    D.   *in it's indicates the possessive form.*

47.   *sic*

    A.   *is an editing signal indicating very poor writing.*
    B.   *is an editing signal reversing an earlier instruction.*
    C.   *is used in references to refer to the previous reference.*
    D.   *is used in square brackets in quotations to identify an error.*

48.   Subordinators (e.g. *because*) at the beginning of the sentence

    A.   *indicate that the information in the subordinate clause is known by readers.*
    B.   *is very poor practice.*
    C.   *is a verbose method of expression.*
    D.   *often leads to confusion.*

49.   Formality is indicated by

    A.   *euphemisms.*
    B.   *tautologies.*
    C.   *particle verbs.*
    D.   *contractions.*

50.   Wordy phrases (e.g. the city of Quebec) are

    A.   *useful for providing emphasis.*
    B.   *never useful.*
    C.   *useful when you need to distinguish between one type of thing and another.*
    D.   *useful for impressing your readers of your command of English.*

Appendix F:
Glossary of Terms

F

Glossary of Terms

The following brief definitions are intended as quick reminders. See the text pages listed for more extensive definitions and uses.

Abstract nouns: vague or generic nouns (e.g. device).   63

Abstract: (descriptive abstract) a table of contents in prose style; tells readers what is in the document.   294

Acknowledgements: details of who has helped with the work and/or document and how they have helped.   294

Acronyms: initial letters of a name (e.g. *IBM* for International Business Machines).   64

Active voice: voice used to say what was done and who did it (e.g. "The explosion caused 59 deaths.").   148

Agenda: list of contents and order for discussion at a formal meeting.   269

Algorithms: charts showing actions resulting from different decisions.   255

Anticipatory 'it': sentence starter that anticipates the rest of the sentence (e.g. *It* is clear that . . .).   167

Appended material: all information added to the end of the main part of the document.   292

Appendices: small documents added to the end of larger documents; can also be data, illustrations, photographs, etc.   292

Appositives: verbless clauses that identify or explain something.   79

Articles: (a) definite (the) and indefinite (a/an);
  (b) documents ranging from short general interest accounts to quite detailed discussions of scientific discoveries.   300

Asides: any non-restrictive information.   189

Assessment: the decision, conclusion or judgment made based on evidence or other basis.   115

Associations: topics associated with previously introduced topic; can have the previous topic (the trigger) after the new noun (post-triggered), before the new noun (pre-triggered), or left out (untriggered).   86

Audience (readership): the people who will read your document or hear your speech.   18

Bar charts: horizontal bars showing comparative quantities.   257

Basis: the evidence, grounds, support, data, or observations on which conclusions and judgments (assessments) are made.   115

Branches (of a list): the elements following the introduction.   73

Block diagram: use of connected rectangular blocks to depict a system.   253

Chair(person): person controlling a meeting.

Circuit diagrams: those depicting electrical circuits.   253

Clause: a group of words that present an idea but not as a complete sentence; types are *main, subordinate, relative, -ed, -ing,* and *verbless*; the last four can be *restrictive* or *non-restrictive.*   78

Clausal ellipsis: two main clauses connected by *and, but,* or *or* with the same subject, but the subject is missed out (or "elided") in the second (e.g. *"The current* flows through R1 and ___exits via terminal B-39.").   70

Colloquialism: non-standard usage (e.g. "She *shoved* the *plug* in the *electric hole.").*   150

Column charts: vertical bars showing comparative quantities.   257

Conjunctions/conjoiners: weak connecting devices (e.g. *and, but, or*)   175

Comma splice: two sentences placed together with a comma.   185

Complimentary close: the "Sincerely yours," part of a letter.   316

Condensed structure: two or more parts of the four-part problem-solution structure placed in one or two sentences, or as the title.   105

Connectors: words used to show meaning between two sentences (e.g. *However, Moreover, Therefore*).   175

Contents table: prefatory material giving details of all the contents of a document.   288

Continuing list: where the elements of the list are essential for the completion of the sentence.   72

Contractions: two words made into one (e.g. *can't, isn't*).   205

Credibility by insistence: insisting that something is true or valid.   122

Dangling clause: an initial dependent clause in a sentence that does *not* modify the first noun in the following main clause.   213

Definition: explanation of something, or the meaning of a word.   224

Description: text detailing what something is, what it does, how it works, etc.   62

Document: a complete communication (letter, report, proposal, etc.).   300

-ed clause: a clause dominated by the -ed form of the verb (e.g. "The component, *manufactured by DuPont*, is now available.").   78

e.g.: (*exempli gratia*) for example.   372

e-mail: electronic mail.   306

Editing: making final changes to a document before publishing it.   230

Ellipsis: generally when something is deliberately "missed out" in a sentence (see Clausal Ellipsis).   70

_et al._: (and others) used to refer to other authors of a cited publication in the main body of the text.   372

Euphemism: saying something unpleasant in a more delicate way (e.g. "He is not perhaps the most suitable candidate." for "He is totally unsuitable for the job.").   152

Evaluation: (a) any thoughtful assessment, judgment or conclusion;   115
(b) the final part of the four-part problem-solution structure; often has basis and assessment.   94

e-words: new words relating to transmission by e-mail (e.g. r-e-ply, director-e, commun-e-cate).   309

Existential 'there': the 'there' that provides formal introduction (e.g. "*There* are different ways of looking at this.").   165

Expanded verb structure: use of a noun plus verb instead of just the verb (e.g. *make an examination* instead of *examine*).   172

Expanded modifiers: phrases used instead of single-word adjectives or adverbs (e.g. *in a short time* instead of *soon*).   173

Flow charts: illustrations depicting the flow of material, information, etc.   255

Foreword: prefatory material written by an authority or company executive   291

Format: the appearance of, or way of presenting, a document.   312

Frontispiece: prefatory photograph or illustration depicting the theme or significant feature of the document   291

Generic noun: nouns with a general meaning (e.g. *material, tool*).   63

Graphs: graphic presentation of data; can have linear or logarithmic scales.   247

Headings: topic indicators heading part of a document; can be conventional, general or creative.   54

Hierarchies: levels of generality and specificity.   24

Homonyms: different words that sound alike, (e.g. *their-there*).   226

ibid.: (*ibidem*) in the same place; refers to the title previously mentioned.   372

i.e.: (*id est*) that is (followed by reformulation or elaboration).   372

Index: alphabetical list of topics covered in a document with page locations.   294

-ing clause: clause dominated by the -ing form of the verb (e.g. "The connecting rod, *weighing 3.7 km*, was secured in place.").   76

Idiolect: the way individuals write and speak.   231

Imperative: the mood used when giving instructions (e.g. "*Turn* Switch S3 to ON.").

Interactive problems: where a solution or attempted solution by one person or group is a problem to another person or group.   105

Intransitives: verbs that cannot take an object (e.g. *be, become, happen*).   148

Introduced list: where the root of the list could be a complete sentence.   72

Jargon: inappropriate use of technical terms.   222

loc.cit.: (*loco citato*) in the same place; refers to the precise passage previously referred to.   372

Macrostructure: the overall structure of a document.   33

Marking: emphatic forms of expression.   63

Memo (memorandum): internal communication on standard paper or computer style.   329

Metaphors: statements that implicitly compare one thing with another (e.g. "He *flew* down the left wing.").   150

Microstructure: structures that control smaller parts of a document.   34

Minutes: accounts of what happened at a meeting.   269

Natural orders: orders of material based on a natural division of information (e.g. chronological, hierarchical).   43

Narrative: structure based on an orderly time sequence.   33

Non-restrictive clauses: information that is incidental to the meaning of the preceding noun; they do not define or restrict the meaning of the noun.   80

Number agreement: how a singular subject takes a singular verb form, and a plural subject takes a plural verb form.   214

Orthographic: (a) three-dimensional engineering drawings;   240
                           (b) using appearance (e.g. size, font, underlining) for emphasis.   154

Outline: a plan for a document made up of headings and subheadings in order; a table of contents for the planned document.   48

Overlaps: items of information that overlap adjoining subject areas; can be inappropriate or desirable.   40

Pairing: two words connected by *and* which means much the same thing (e.g. *produce* and *manufacture*).   168

Papers: scholarly documents explaining research published by professional organizations.   300

Parallel structures: two or more branches of text connected by prepositions, or as clausal ellipsis or in lists.   75

Particle verbs: two- or three-word verbs containing one or more particles (e.g. *throw up, get on with*).   150

Passive: the voice used to say what was done (e.g. "The motor was switched on." is an agentless passive and "The motor was switched on by our TA." is an agentive passive.); can be in different tenses (e.g. *will be assessed* (future passive), *is examined* (present passive), *was determined* (past passive)).   148

Perspective connection: explicit or implicit cohesion of a main clause or sentence with a previous topic (e.g. *in this paper, in this region*).   84

Pictorials: pictures depicting relative quantities, movement, or other features.   259

Pie charts: circular charts sliced into portions depicting percentages of the whole.   260

Politeness strategies: saying things in a less direct or face-saving manner to meet acceptable standards of politeness (e.g. "Do you think you could print this chapter for me?" instead of "PRINT!").   177

Political correctness: using terms more acceptable and less hurtful than more direct language (e.g. "mentally challenged" instead of "mentally retarded").   153

Preface: prefatory material written by the author explaining the motivation for, or background of, the document.   291

Prefatory material: all information placed before the start of the main part of the document.   288

Problem-solution structures: organization of information according to situation-problem-solution-evaluation or related combination.   94

Pronoun reference: the material in a text that a pronoun re-enters into the text.   66

Proof reading (and correcting): (formal editing) correcting page proofs ready for publication.   233

Proposals: documents that propose the design or implementation of a solution to a problem; can be solicited (asked for) or unsolicited.   302

Propriety: being "proper", i.e. behaving in a manner appropriate to the circumstances.   138

Purpose-means structures: like problem-solution structures but stressing purpose and means rather than problem and solution.   104

Re-entry: the process of referring again to a topic already introduced into the text.   62

References: (a) lists of works cited in a document;   292
(b) letters commenting on the abilities and character of a candidate for a position.   326

Relative clause: clauses dominated by relative pronouns (*which, that, who, when, where*).   68

Repetition: re-entry by means of repeating the topic; can be full or partial.   63

Reports: documents published by the author or the author's company; describe work done often with conclusions and recommendations.   301

Restrictive clause: those that define or restrict the meaning of the preceding noun.   80

Resume: (*curriculum vitae* or *c.v.*) a document detailing a person's professional achievements.   322

Revision: improvement of the higher level elements of a document (e.g. aims, structure, general style and approach).   229

Rhetorical question: asking a question and then answering it. 146

Root (of a list): the part leading up to the start of the separate elements. 72

Run-on sentences: long rambling sentences containing many clauses. 186

Salutation: the *Dear Dr Smith* part of a letter. 316

Sentence fragments: parts of sentences given the appearance of a sentence (i.e. capital letter and period). 215

Sexist pronouns: *he* or *she* referring to a person who could be female or male. 348

sic: (*thus*) indicates an error observed and left in a quoted passage. 203

Simile: overtly signaled comparison of two things (e.g. *like* a bull). 150

Smileys: graphic symbols typed on e-mail messages and read from the right to depict emotion or other standard messages (e.g. :-) means "happy"). 306

stet: editing symbol meaning leave as set (i.e. the way it was before the editing change). 234

Style: (a) personal ways of expression (idiolect);
(b) standard ways of punctuation, use of numbers etc.;
(c) different forms of writing (e.g. advertising, legal, technical);
(d) formal or informal;
(e) pre-programmed format on computer. 142

Subordinators: words that dominate dependent clauses (e.g. *although, because, since*). 175

Substitution: use of substitute words (including pronouns) to re-enter a topic. 66

Summary (informative abstract): concise account of the principal information in a document. 295

Synonyms: words with the same or very similar meaning. 64

Task identification: understanding and definition of the task to be performed; often a document. 26

Tautologies: two adjoining words where the meaning of one is part of the meaning of the other (e.g. *past history*). 168

Tone: manner of expression in writing or speech (e.g. pleasant, businesslike, aggressive). 155

Trigger: the referent for associations. 82

Verbless clauses: clauses not dominated by any verb form; include appositives; can be restrictive or non-restrictive.   79

Visual aids: any device to support oral presentations.   281

viz: (namely) used instead of a colon in front of an introduced list.   372

'You' tone: use of *you, your,* etc. in a style appealing directly to the reader.   154

Appendix G:
List Of Checklists

LIST OF CHECKLISTS

Page

2.1	Aims of Educational Writing	19
2.2	Audience Requirements - Some Useful Questions	20
2.3	Requirements for Writing Tasks	21
2.4	Techniques for Finding a Suitable Topic	23
2.5	Questions for Task Selection and Specification	26
2.6	Task Identification	27
2.7	Writing Preliminaries	28
3.1	Relating Structure to Contents (Examples)	33
3.2	Typical Contents for Describing People (Examples)	35
3.3	Initial Selection of Contents for Description	36
3.4	Methods of Dividing Descriptive Work	38
3.5	Features of Division of Information (Examples)	39
3.6	Natural Orders as the Basis for Sequence	43
3.7	Arranging Your Material	44
4.1	Factors Affecting the Need for an Outline	48
4.2	Major Outlining Structures	50
4.3	Advantages of an Outline	52
4.4	Some Systems of Standard Headings	54
4.5	Conventional, General and Creative Headings	55
4.6	Structure Signaling Devices	57
5.1	Criteria for Obligatory Colon Before a List	73
5.2	Types of Restrictive and Non-Restrictive Clauses	80
5.3	Ways of Expressing Associated Information	82
5.4	Methods of Re-entering the Topic	85
6.1	The Four-Part Problem-Solution Structure	94
6.2	Typical Information for Problem-Solution Texts	99
6.3	Reasons for Curtailing the Four-Part Structure	102
6.4	Typical Purpose-Means Signaling within Sentences	104
6.5	Some Complexities of Problem-Solution Texts	109
7.1	Two Elements of Evaluation	115
7.2	Possible Evidence for Armed Robbery of a Store	116
7.3	Types of Evidence	127
7.4	Types of Evaluative Writing	133
8.1	Special Styles for Technical Documents	140
8.2	Elements of Propriety	140
8.3	Some Meanings of Style in Writing	142
8.4	Signals of Formal Technical Writing	144
8.5	Signals of Informal Technical Writing	146
8.6	Summary of Transitivity Statements	149
8.7	Reasons for Excluding the Agent	149
8.8	Connections Between Voice and Formality	150
8.9	Types of Words Creating Informality	152
8.10	Range of Emphasis for "cannot"	154
9.1	Material to Avoid to Achieve Conciseness	162
9.2	Basic Re-Entry Techniques and Conciseness	164

9.3	Condensing Relative Clauses	164
9.4	Examples of Verbosity with Existential 'There'	166
9.5	Some Uses of Existential 'There'	166
9.6	Some Uses of Anticipatory 'It'	167
9.7	Examples of Tautologies	169
9.8	Examples of Wordy Phrases	170
9.9	Examples of Verbose General Words	171
9.10	Examples of Expanded Verb Structures	172
9.11	Examples of Expanded Modifiers	173
9.12	Comparing Three Types of Connection	175
9.13	Methods of Achieving Conciseness	178
10.1	General Rules for *Not* Punctuating	185
10.2	Ways of Correcting the Comma Splice	185
10.3	Major Uses of Commas	195
10.4	Major Uses of the Colon	196
10.5	Major Uses of the Semicolon	197
10.6	Major Uses of the Dash	199
10.7	Major Uses of Parentheses	200
10.8	Major Uses of Hyphens	205
10.9	Other Punctuation Marks and Uses	206
11.1	Criteria for Correct Parallel Structure	212
11.2	Criteria for Proper Sentences	216
11.3	Relations Between 'This' and the Connectors	218
11.4	Some Complex and Simple Words	220
11.5	Ways of Signaling Doubt	222
11.6	Reasons for Using Correct Terms for Professionals	223
11.7	Needs for Defining a Term	224
11.8	Ways of Defining a Term	224
11.9	Definition Locations	225
11.10	Pitfalls of Defining	226
11.11	Commonly Misused Homonyms	227
11.12	Using 'a' and 'an'	228
11.13	Topics for Revision	230
11.14	Editing Topics	231
11.15	Rules for Editing by Hand	233
11.16	Commonly Used Editing Symbols and their Meanings	233
11.17	Proof-Correcting Practices	234
12.1	Functions of Illustrations	246
12.2	Advantages of Graphs/Charts and Tables	251
12.3	Advantages of Graphic Presentation of Data	261
13.1	Telephone Techniques	271
13.2	The Job Interview	273
13.3	Giving Formal Presentations	278
13.4	Techniques for Answering Questions	280
13.5	Types of Visual Aid	282
14.1	Types of Prefatory Material	291
14.2	When to Use Appendices	292
14.3	Types of Appended Material	294
14.4	Definitions of Summary and Abstract	295

14.5	Typical Types of Information for Summaries	296
14.6	Linguistic Forms for (Descriptive) Abstracts	297
14.7	Avoiding Animacy of the Document	298
14.8	Avoiding End-of-Sentence Passives	298
14.9	Important Types of Reports	301
14.10	Important Technical Documents	302
15.1	Some e-words	309
15.2	Major Stylistic Features of e-Mail Messages	309
15.3	Uses of Letters	312
15.4	Differences for the Modified Block Format	312
15.5	Recommendations for Addresses	315
15.6	Stylistic Features for Correspondence	318
15.7	Features of Letters of Application for Employment	320
15.8	Contents of Resumes	323
15.9	Elements of Memo Style	331
A.1	Procedure for Information Retrieval	337
A.2	Types of Information Sources	342
B.1	Partial Repetitions for People's Names	344
B.2	When to Use Sexist Pronouns	349
B.3	When Not to Use Sexist Pronouns	349
B.4	Tips for Avoiding Sexist Pronouns	359
C.1	The Use of Numbers	364
C.2	Writing Numbers	364
C.3	Approved SI Units and Symbols	365
C.4	Accepted Prefixes	366
C.5	Rules for Writing Symbols	366
D.1	Common Foreign Abbreviations	372
D.2	Some UK/USA Spelling Differences	373

Subject Index

Subjects are in normal type with key words in italics. Page number references are given; locations of main discussions or definitions are in bold type. See the Glossary of Terms (Appendix F) for brief definitions of terms marked with an asterisk.

Abbreviations 147, 371
Abstract nouns* **63-64**, 69, 85, 164, 178, 221, 350-351
Abstracts* 56-57, 140, 288, 291, **294-295**, 297-300, 340
Acknowledgements* 22, **294**
Acronyms* 6, **64-65**, 85, 144, 164, 178, 200, 204, 228-229, 350-351
    list of 65, 288, 291
Active voice* 107-108, **148-150**, 156, 352
Address 315
Addressing mail 318
Advertisements 62-63, 216, 321
Advice/approval (obtaining) 52
Agenda* 269-271
Agent (with passive) (see Passive)
Agreement
    pronoun reference 66, **218-219**
    subject-verb (number) **214-215**, 219
Aims (of writing) 10, **18-19**, 230
Algorithms* 255-256
Almanacs **339**, 342
although 132, 175, 185, 191, 216
Analogy, 125-126
Animacy 298
Apostrophes **204-205**, 234 (also see Contractions and Possessives)
Appearance (at interviews) 272
Appended material 230, 288, **292-294**
Appendices* 10, 22, 101, 231, 263, 289, 290, **292**, 292-294
Appositives 79, 355
Argument 114, 121, **123-128**
Articles
    definite* 167, 212, 357
    indefinite* 212, **228-229**, 357
    documents* 111, 120, 145-146, **300-301**
"Asides"* 189, 191, 195
Assessment* 6, **115**, 116, 118, 120, 124, 126, 146, 189, 191
Associations **82-84**, 86, 165, 179, 344-345, 348, 356-357
    post-triggered **82-84**, 165, 356-357
    pre-triggered **82-84**, 165, 344-345, 348, 356-357
    untriggered **82-84**, 165, 356-357
Asterisks 57, 206, 225, 399
Attitudes (about writing) 2
Audience (readers) 3, 9-10, **18-20**, 21, 28, 32, 64, 144, 147, 155, 162, 175-177, 220, 223-224, 229-230, 243, 246-247, 268, 274, 278-279, 295, 308
Authority 119-120, 127

Balance 53
Bar charts* (see Charts)
Basis* 6, **115**, 116-118, 124, 126, 130-132, 145, **168**
because 105, 132, 175, 191, **216**
Binders 21, 57, **286**
Bibliographies **292-294**, 338-339, 342, 347
Biographical sketches 347-348
Biographies 36, 347
Block diagrams* 253-257
Body language 268
"Body" of text 62, 275, 278
"Boilerplate" sections 15
both 67
both...and 75
Brackets (square) 202-203
Branches (of list)* **73-74**, 212-213
Brainstorming 36
Bullets 73-74, 197
but 71, 75, 97, 132, 147, 151, 175, 186, 190, 193
by/through...ing **104**, 191

Canada 2-4, 19, 86-89, 120, 168, 277, 315, 372-373
Capitalization 219, 233-235, 289, 372
Cartoon 244
Cause-effect 99-100, 109, 144-145, 191, **194**, 196
CD-ROMs **340**, 342
Chair(person) 270, 274, 276, 278-280, 346
Chalkboard 274, **283**
Charts 244-245, 251-252, **255-257**
    bar* 257-258
    column* **257-258**, 259
    pie* 258-260
Circuit diagram* 253-254
Certainty (see Definiteness)
Clausal ellipsis* (see Ellipsis)
Clauses
    relative **68-70**, 76-80, 85, 164-165, **188**, 345, 350, 354
    -ed* **78**, 80, 86, 164-165, 179, 188, 214, 354-355
    -ing* **76-77**, 86, 164-165, 179, 188, 194, 213-214, 355, 358
    verbless* 79, 80-81, 86, 164-165, 179, **188**, 214, 345, 350, 355-356
    to-infinitive **80-81**, 356
Closure 271, 273
Codes (documents) 120, 302
Cohesion 145
Cold feet 276
Collaborative writing/speaking (see Team writing/speaking)
Colloquialisms* 143, 146-147, **150-152**, 308-309
Colons 72-73, **196**, 202
Color (use of) 245, 259, 282
Column charts* (see Charts)

Commas 184-186, **187-196**, 197, 200, 213, 216, 225
    after introductory clauses **191-192**, 195
    before final effects **194**, 196, 198
    in lists 73-74, **194-195**, 196-197
    with clausal connections **192-193**, 195
    with quoted speech 202
    with non-restrictive clauses 70, 76, 80, **187-189**, 195, 198-199
Comma splice* **185-186**, 190
Comparison 33, 62, 126-128, 133-134, 191, 218, 251, 258, 260, 295-296
Complimentary close* 312, 316
Complimentary copy (cc) 307
Composition techniques 17
Computer graphics 240, 252, 254, 274, 281
Computers 4, 32, 142, **229**, 232, 282, 289, 291, 306-312, 336, 340-341
    master document control 53
    outlining 48-53
    spell checkers (see Spell checkers)
    style 312
    style checkers (see Style checkers)
Concession (in argument) 132
Conciseness 4, 10, 71, 78, 138, **162-182**, 220, 230-232, 246, 272, 280, 295, 308-309
Conclusions 23, 62, 114-116, 118-119, 121, 123-124, 128, 168, 278, 296
Condensed structures* 105-108
Connectors* (*however*, etc.) 175, 186, **190-191**, 218
Conjunctions/conjoiners* (*but*, etc.) 147, 151, **175**
Consistency 219, 293-294, 352, **372-373**
Contents (table of)* 21-22, 50, 52, 55, 288, **290**, 291, 295
    of document 32-39
Continuity 62-91
Contractions* 143, 146-147, 153-154, **205**, 308-309
Contracts 5, 11, 15, 140, **302**
Contrast (see Comparison)
Conventions (of writing) 139, 364, **370-373**
"Copy"/copywriter 62, 98, 233
Core instruction 3-4
Correction (in argument) 130
Correspondence 138, 156-157, **306-334** (also see e-mail, Letters and Memos)
Counter-argument 114, 132
Courtesy titles 316
Covers (see Binders)
Creative headings (see Headings)
Credibility **113-136**, 230
    by insistence* 122
Crudities 152
Curtailed texts 102-105

Dangling clauses* 213-214
Dashes 73, 143, 146-147, 153, 188, 196-197, **198-200**, 225, 308-309
Dates 315
Decisions 115, 117, 123, 128
Definiteness 115-116, 119

Definitions* 6, 99, 109, **224-226**
   list of 225
Denial 130
Describing people 6, 35, 69-70, **88-89**, **343-362**
Description* 5, 21, 50-51, 95-96, 224, 295-296
      contents and order 32-45
      language 62-91
Design methodology 94
Diagrams (see Illustrations)
Directories **339**, 342
Dividers 53, 57
Division of contents 38-45
Documents* 300-302 (also see Reports, Articles, etc.)
Document parts 288-300
Doubt (signals of) (see Hypotheticality)
Dramatic effect 154, 184, 198-199, 216, 245-247, 251, 257, 260, 262-263, 301
Drawings (see Illustrations)
Dress 138-139, 272-273

-ed clauses (see Clauses)
Editing* 17, 32, 138, 177, 184, 229, **230-237**, 306, 332-333
Effects (final) (see Commas)
*e.g.** 371-372
either...or 75
Elements (of lists) (see Branches)
Ellipsis/eliding* 62, **70-72**, 76, 85, 164, 179, 192, 346, 350, 352-353
Ellipsis points 202
e-mail* 11, 17, 139, 147, 177-178, 205, 217, 270, 274, **306-311**, 320, 329
Emphasis 21, 153-155, 166, 184, 188-189, 192, 213, 258, 260-274, 291,
Encyclopedias 120, **338**, 342
Endnotes 292
Engineering 94-95, 202
Equations 6, **370-371**
Essays 3, 302
*et al.** 371-372
Ethics 118, 149
Euphemisms* 145, **152-153**
Evaluation* 22, 94-99, 101-104, 107, 109-110, **115**
Evaluative texts 33, 115, **133-134**, 138
Evidence 33, **115-133**, 246, 262
Examples (as evidence) **124-125**, 128,
Exclamation marks 147, 153-154, 198, **206**, 309
Expanded verb structures* **172-173**, 179, 298
Expanded modifiers* **173-174**, 179
Experimentation 2, 114, 118, 127
Expert testimony 119-120, 127
Exploratory texts 133-134
e-words* 147, **309**

Facts and figures 114, 119, 123, 127
Figures (see Illustrations)
Figure numbers and titles 263-264
Flip charts 283
Flow charts* 255-256
Footnotes 206, 225, 292
Foreword* 291
Formality (see Style, formal and informal)
Format* 22, 28, 142, 288, 307, **312-314**, 319, 330-332
Forms 15, 217, 327-328 359
Formulas 214, 249, 370-371
Four-part structures (see Problem-solution structures)
Fronting 299
Frontispiece* 263, **291**

Generic nouns* (see Abstract nouns)
Genre 22, 28
Grammar 9, 72-73, 138, 147, 185-186, 203, **212-220**, 231, 308-309
Graphic communication 240-266 (also see Illustrations)
Graphs* 118, 240, 244, **247-250**, 251

Handbooks **338**, 340
Handouts 282-283
Headings* 289
    general 54, **56**
    standard 32, **55**
    creative 55
Hierarchies* 24-26
Homonyms* **226-228**, 231
how 104-105
however 97, 132, 151, 186, 189-190, 197, 218
Hyphens 198, **205-206**, 372
Hypothetical argument **125**, 126
Hypotheticality (doubt) 115-116, 168, 170, 206, **221-222**

*ibid.** 372
Idiolect* 142, 231
*i.e.** 371-372
Illustrations 5, 22, 100, 125, 138, 140, 162-163, 224, 230-231, **240-266**, 291, 301
    list of 264, 288-289, 291
Image (professional) 9, 155
Imperative mood* 140, **156**, 351
Importance of writing 2, **8-9**, 14
Important information 44, 70-71, 189, 260, 295
Indexes* 6, 21-22, **294**
Information retrieval 6, **336-342**
-ing clauses* (see Clauses)
(in order) to 104, 105, 191
Instructions 11, 100, 140, 142, 302
Insulting readers 64, 223, 246
Interactive problems* 105-106

Internet **340**, 342
Interviews (see Job application)
Intransitive verbs* **148**, 156, 353
Introductions 50, 55-56, 58, 62, 166, 275, 278
-ion words 150
Irregular verbs* 78
it
    anticipatory* 6, **167-168**, 176, 179, 214, **222**, 299, 357
    pronoun 66-67, 200

Jargon* 222-223
Job application
    forms 322-328
    interviews 270-274
    letters 15, 142, **319-322**
    resumes 35, 272, 320, **322-329**
Judgement 115, 120, 123

Key words 296-297
Known information 121, 128, 147, 162, 175, 292

Latin-derived words 215
Legal matters 15-16, 116-117, 140, 142-143, 169, 171, 195, 226, 344
Length of document 22, 28, 48
Letters
    correspondence 11,15, 139, 142, 147, 177-178, 273, **311-322**, 329
    in lists 73-74, 197
    in outlines 50
    in illustrations 264
Levels
    of hierarchy (see Hierarchies)
    in outlines 50-53
Line of best fit 249-250
Listening 270
Lists **72-76**, 86, 140, 142, 164, 179, 194-197, 350
    continuing* **72-74**, 196, 354
    introduced* **72-74**, 124, 196, 354
Literary approach to writing 2-3
Linguistic approach to writing 2-3
*loc. cit.** 372

Maps 262
"Macro-structures"* 33-34
"Marked" 63, 71, 73, 274
Mathematical calculations/symbols 2, 127, 200, **222**, 225, 240, 364-367
Means (ways and) **103-105**, 191
Meetings 269-270
Memoranda (memos)* 11, 17, 139, 142, 147, 156-157, 177-178, 311, **329-333**
Metaphors* 143, 147, **150-52**, 253

"Micro-structures"* 34
Minutes (of meetings)* 269
moreover 175, 186, 218

Naming **64**, 85, 344
Narrative* **33-34**, 133-134, 345
Natural orders* (see Order/structure)
Negation 118, 130
Nervousness **276-277**, 278
nevertheless 97
Non-restrictive clauses* 68-70, 76-77, **80-81**, 187-189, 195, 354-355
Notes
    as documents 302
    informal 147, 271
    on drawings 243
Numbers
    in lists 73-74, 197
    use of **364**, 370-371
Number agreement* (see Agreement)

Observations 118, 127
one (person) 352
Opinion 120, 122, 128, 130
Oral presentations 5, 23, 76, 139-141, 178, 241-242, 251, **268-285**, 347
Order/structure 32, **42-45**, 52, 56, 100-101, 229-230, 272, 295
Organizational diagrams 256
Orthographic drawings* 240, 246
Orthography (appearance)* 57, **154-155**, 306, 372
Outlines* 6, 26, **48-55**, 128, 138
Overhead displays 274, 282
Overlaps* 40-42

Page numbering 231, **291**
Pairing* **168-169**, 179
Papers (documents)* 120, 296, **300-301**
Paragraphs 143-144, 146, 163, 189, 230, 331
Parallel structure* 75-76, 146, **212-213**, 219
Parentheses 146, 188, 197-198, **200**, 225, 233, 235
Paraphrases 201, 203, 218
Particle verbs* 147, **150-151**
Parts (of documents) 288-300
Passive voice* 22, 107-108, 140, 143-144, **148-150**, 156, 214, 297-298, 300, 352-353, 355
"Past participles" (see Clauses, -ed forms)
Patents 11, 140
Period (punctuation) 175, 1990, 201, 215
Personal credibility 120-121, 128
Personal interest 26
Personal preference 26, 48, 139
Personal pronouns 146, 157, 319-320

Perspectives* **84**, 85-86, 165, 179, 350
   triggered **84**, 298-299
   untriggered **84**, 357
Photographic essays 244-245
Photographs 22, 118, 241, 246-247, **262-263**, 291, 301
Physical objects 283
Pictorials* 245, **259-261**
Pie charts (see Charts)
Plain language 175, 178
Planning 4, 26, 32, 48-53, 268-269, 274, 278, 281, 308
Plagiarism 15
Plurality 214-215, 219, 359-360, 366
Politeness strategies* **177-178**, 200, 270-271, 281
Political correctness* 145, **153**
Positions (of clauses) 77, 79, **80**
Possessives 146, **204**, 219, 228, 319-320, 344, 359
Preface* 291
Prefatory material* 230, 264-265, **288-291**, 294-300
Prefixes 97, 366
Prepositional groups 80-81
Prepositions 151, 212-213
Presentations 5, 178, 230, 268-285, 324
Problem 6, 24, 94-112
Problem-solution texts* 4, 16-17, 33-34, **94-112**, 138, 145, 295
Problem with competing views 127-131
Proceedings 302
Processes
   creative 14-16
   reciprocal **14**, 273
   reiterative 32-34
   selection 14-16
   writing 33-34
Professional etiquette 141
Professional standards 9, 230
Profiles 345-347
Prominence (see Emphasis)
Pronoun reference* (see Substitution)
Proof (evidence) 114-121, 125
Proof correcting* 233-237
Proposals* 4-5, 15, 21, 33, 98, 108-109, 143, 178, 268, 296, **302**
Propriety* 5, **138-142**, 272
Pros and cons 129-130
Punctuation 6, 9, 138, 152-154, **184-209**, 219, 222, 231, 315 (also see the individual punctuation
   marks)
Purpose
   of writing **18-20**, 32
   of document 98, 160, 229, 291
   -means structures **104-105**, 145, 191, 359

Quasi-conjunction 215
QED 114
Question marks 206, 222
Questions
    answering 279-281
    supplementary 272, 280
    use of 33, 73, 124-125, 199, 256
Quotations 143, 146-147, **200-204**

Readers/readership (see Audience)
Reason(ing) (see Argument and Basis)
Rebuttal 130-133
Recommendations 99, 101, 115, 130-131, 295
"Re-entering"* 62, 63-91, 218, 344-345, 359
References
    for job applications* 324, **326**, 328
    to figures and tables 200-201, 243, **263-264**
    to other work* 22, 27, 120-121, 127-128, 145, 230-231, **292-294**
    pronoun (see Agreement)
    within the document **57-58**, 263-264
Reference works 338-340
Relative clauses (see Clauses)
Relevance 36-37
Repetition* 69, 85, 350
    full **63-64**, 85, 164, 350
    partial **63**, 85, 164, 344, 346, 348, 350
Reported speech 143
Reports* 3, 5, 9-10, 102, 106, 110, 114, 120, 139, 143, 178, 296, 300, **301**, 302, 332
Restrictive clauses* 70, 77, **80-81**, 184, 188, 354-355
Resume* (see Job application)
Revision* 17, 32, 138, **229-230**
Rhetorical questions* 146, 147, **154**
Root (of lists)* **72**, 124
Rules of order 269
Run-on sentences* 186-187

Salutation* 154, **316**
Schematic diagrams 253-257
Science (texts in) 94-95
Search engines 341
Sequence (see Order)
Semicolons 72-74, 175, 185, 190, **196-197**
Sentence 202, 216
    combining **174-176**, 179
    complexity 143, 146
    fragments* 147, **215-218**, 219
    length 144, 146
Sexist language 361-362
Sexist pronouns (avoiding)* 6, 345, **348-361**
Shading 259

shall 140, 142

SI units and symbols 364-367

sic* 203

Similes* 147, **150**

Singularity 214-215

Situation 24, 94-99, 102, 107, 109-110, 221

Sketches 240, 332

Slides 283

Smileys* 306

Solidus (/) 206, 234

Solution 6, 33, 94-112

so 175, 190

some 67

Source identification 146, 202

Sources of information 337-342

Speech 139, 155, 177, 201-203, 205, 224, 272-273, 276-279

Specifications 5, 15, 120, 140, **302**

Spell checkers 4, 8, 226, 229, 235-236

Spelling (wrong words) (see Homonyms)

Square brackets 202-203

Stance **277**, 279

Standard headings (see Headings)

Standards 100, 120, 140, **302**

Statistics 119, 222

stet 234

Strikeout 154

Structure (see Order)

Style 22, 28, 138-140, **142-154**, 170, 176, 178, 220, 229-231, 295, 308, 312, 318-319, 331-333
   abstract 56, **297-300**
   formal **143-145**, 147, 150, 178, 311-312
   informal 138-139, 142-143, **145-147**, 150-155, 201-204, 216-218, 308-310, 312, 359
   semi-formal 145
   personal 4, 11, 142, 231
   technical 4, 11

Style checkers 4, 8, 144, 176, 202, 226, 229

Subject (of sentence) 140, 144, 146, 185, 297

Subjective words 150-152

Subordinators (*because* etc.)* 175, 185, 191

Substitution* **66-68**, 71, 85, 164, 178, 218, 344, 346-351, 358
   embracing 67
   partitive 67
   (also see Personal pronouns, *it, they,* etc.)

Summaries* 10, 21-22, 56, 106-107, 120-121, 201, 203, 217, 240, 264, 278, 291, 294, **295-297**, 299-300, 346

Summary/abstracts 299-300

Surprise 191, 206

Swear words 152

Symbols
   editing 233-234

units **364-367**, 370
    list of 291
Synonyms* **63**, 64, 85, 225, 351

Table of Contents (see Contents)
Tabs 53, 57
Tables 22, 118, 230, 240, 245, 247, **250**, 251-252, 259, 264-265
    list of 264-265, 291
Talk (see Presentations)
Task identification* **26-27**, 32, 336
Tautologies* 6, **168-170**, 179
Team writing/speaking 24, 27, 52, 274-275
Technical documents 300-302
Technical level 143-145
Technical vocabulary 144-145
Telephone (use of) 268, **270-271**, 274, 306, 318
Tenses 212
    future 78, 297
    past 78, 148, 300
    present 78, 140, 148, 297, 300
    tenseless forms 78
that (pronoun) 62, 70, 218-219, 231, 344
there (existential)* 6, 125, **165-167**, 176, 178, 214-215, 222, 359
thereby 194
therefore 151, 167, 175, 218
these 66-67, 142, 144, 219
Theses 302
"Thesis-Backing" structure 33, 133-134
they 66-67
this 6, 66-68, 97, 144, 218-219
those 218
thus 167, 175, 194
Timing (of speeches) 269, 276, 278
Time 189, 192
Title page 21, 56, **288-289**, 295
Titles 107-108, 171, **288**, 297, 307, 330
to-infinitive clauses (see Clauses)
Tone* 9, 138, 140-141, **155-158**, 230-231, 271, 308, 318-320, 331
too 103
Topic selection **22-24**, 32, 278
Transitions 40, 57, 275, 278
Transmittals (letters and memos) 330
Trigger* (see Associations)

Units (scientific and engineering) 221, **365-367**
UK usage 231, 372-373
USA usage 200, 231, 372-373
Verbless clauses (see Clauses)
Verbosity (see Conciseness)
Very short texts 105-106

Visual aids* 241, 269, 274, 2768, 280, **281-283**
Visualization 241-242, 246
*viz.** 372

"Weight" 51, 54
when 69-70
where 69-70
which 6-7, 62, **68-70**, 76-77, 79, 216, 219, 231, 344
White space 57
who 69-70, 344-345
Word choice 138, 147, 150-152, **220-228**

Special Indexes

These indexes will enable you to study various aspects of language use in technical writing by examining how skilled writers use them in actual texts. All entries refer to example numbers and also paragraph numbers within the examples when relevant. Thus "6.5/4 It's" means that the contraction It's occurs in paragraph 4 of example 6.5.

When two or more occurrences appear in the same example or paragraph, this is indicated in brackets; thus "9.3 TCF, TEF (2)" means that there is one instance of the acronym TCF in Example 9.3 and two instances of the acronym TEF. For many of the occurrences of continuity and punctuation, key words are cited to help you to find and identify the items referred to.

Special Index: *Structure-Signaling Words*

SUBORDINATORS

after: 10.27, B.4 *although*: 6.11, 7.21, 8.3/3, 8.10, 10.15 *as:* 6.11 (2), 7.8, 8.13, 8.25 *because*: 6.9/3, 6.9/5, 7.10, 7.13/2, 7.16, 7.20/2, 7.21, 8.2, 10.16 *despite*: 9.7 *during*: 10.08, 10.36, 7.3 *if:* 7.5/2, 7.14/1, 7.14/2, 7.20/2 (2), 8.17, 8.27 (2), 8.29/1, 8.30, 15.4 *once*: 7.11/2, 8.30, 7.18/4 *should*: 8.9 *unless*: 7.13 *when*: 8.5, 8.28 (2), 10.1 *whereas*: 7.16 *while*: 7.13, 7.19, 10.41

CONNECTORS

first, etc.: **5.19** First, Second, Third and Fourth **7.12** First, Second, Third **12.2** *firstly finally*: **4.3** *furthermore*: **14.11** *however*: **6.11**, 7.10, 7.14/1, **8.15**, 10.9/2, 10.11, 10.12, 10.13, 14.3, D.1 *in addition*: 7.4, 7.8, 7.18/3, 14.7 *nevertheless*: 6.4/1 *numbers*: 5.18 1), 2), 3), 4), *on the other hand*: 3.1 *therefore*:

9.4 *then*: 6.7/2 *thus*: 6.2, 6.9/3, 6.9/5, 10.23

CONJUNCTIONS

and (at start of sentence): 5.19, 6/2, 6.6/2 *but*: 3.1, 5.15, 6.6/1, 7.18/4, 8.11, 8.14, 8.21, 8.24, 10.5, 10.21, 10.30, 11.10 *so* 5.7, 5.18, 6.4/2, 7.7, 8.14, 8.27 (2), 11.9/1 *either . . . or*: 5.11, 8.6

Special Index: *Indicators of Meaning and Style*

SIGNALS OF DOUBT

chance: 7.14/2, *conceivably*: 7.21 *could*: 7.21, 8.2, 14.3 *doubt*: 7.20/2, 8.8 *dubious*: 7.20/2 *indicate*: 7.21, 10.3, 10.9/2 *may* 5.15, 7.1, 7.14/2, 8.8 (2), 8.21, 8.22, 8.23, 8.30, 10.11 *possibility* 7.12 *probably* 11.9/2 *seemed* 10.17 *sometimes*: 7.18/4 *state*: 7.19 *suggestion/suggests*: 7.1, 7.8

SIGNALS OF INFORMALITY

abbreviation: 12.1 U. *collo-*

quialisms: 8.3/2 up to 8.5 thanks, dig up, get back to you, a day or so, surface for air 8.10 the beauty 8.11 a catch-22 situation 8.12 gearing up 8.15 grab 8.16 hung in there 8.17 started from scratch 8.18 Start-up, went off, without a hitch 8.19 cleaning up its act 8.21 gains an edge *contractions*: 3.1 isn't 5.29 what's 6.5/1 you'll 6.5/3 that's, you'll 6.5/4 It's 6.5/5 there's, won't 8.4/3 It's 8.4/4 There's 8.11 It's 8.21 It's 8.23 don't 8.24 that's, It's 8.27 don't 8.30 (2) can't, you've 10.48 It's 11.9/1 don't, haven't, I'll 11.10 They're B.1 who's *e-word*: 8.5 e *imperative mood* :6.7/2 Use, Press, Remove, Use 8.30 think 10.35 fill it out, send it *metaphor*: 8.10 as a sideline 8.13 in the spotlight 8.16 turnaround 8.21 the push, on the power map, quixotic 8.29/1 caught between a rock and a hard place 8.29/2 the competitive edge *orthography*: 8.26, 8.27 (2), 10.35 *particle verbs*: 8.5 dig up 8.12 gearing up 8.16 hung in 8.18

start up, went off **8.19** cleaning up **8.25** looking for **8.27** spell out *personal pronouns:* **4.5** I **6.5/1** you (2) **6.5/2** you, **6.5/3** you **6.5/4** you **6.7/2** you, your **7.4** our (2) **7.6/1** I, you **7.6/2** I (2) **7.14/1** our, us **7.19** You, our **8.3/2** we **8.3/3** I, we (2) all of us **8.5** your, I (2), you **8.11** we (3), our **8.23** We **8.24** your, we **8.27** you (3), your **8.28** I **8.29/1** you, **8.29/2** we, you (3) **8.30** you (3), yourself **10.35** you, your **10.42** we **11.1/1** your **11.9/1** I (2), my **11.9/2** I **11.10** all of us *quotations:* **7.13/3, 7.15, 8.4/2, 8.15, 8.23, 8.24, 10.40, 10.41, 10.42, 10.43** *rhetorical quotations:* **3.1, 8.3/2** (2), **8.25, 8.28, 8.30, 11.8/1** *sentence fragments:* **6.8/1** To . . . States **11.7** Especially . . . before **11.8/2** Useless and misleading. **11.9/1** Sorry. **11.9/2** This year (1994!) I think *similes:* **8.21** like . . . pin *summarized speech:* **5.19** Boulle points out that **7.5/2** His opinion . . . was that **7.9** MacMillan . . . said **7.21** The . . . official . . . gave evidence **8.4** Barrett . . . describes **8.24** Wright added that **9.3** The authors point out that **10.12** Beaulieu explained that

OTHER INDICATORS

it (anticipatory): **5.19** it appears **7.10, 7.12** it possible (2) **7.14/1** It is **8.3/3, 8.14, 8.15, 8.17, 8.21, 9.4,** **9.5, 9.6, 10.17, 14.11** *there (existential)* **3.1** (2) **4.4, 6.5/5, 7.12, 7.20/3, 7.21, 8.4/4, 8.30, 9.1, 9.2, 9.3, 10.12, 10.18, 10.27, 10.38**

Special Index: *Methods of Continuity*

BASIC METHODS

acronyms **5.1** AEM **5.2** NBSK **5.6** OLTP (4) **5.8** AVI, GIS, GPS **5.10** DIN **5.11** RMS, HDS **5.23** GPR **5.28** C. M. D. **5.29** PEO **6.4/2** SKF **6.9/6** TV **7.1** GRB **7.2** AFT (2) **7.6/2** CIDA **7.9** CEO (2) PPG **7.10** OD **7.12** GPS **7.13/2** VHS **7.17** INS, GPS (2) **7.20/1** ACES (2) **7.20/2** ACES **8.2** ASR **8.3/1** APEO **8.20** ECF, TCF **9.3** TCF, TEF (2) **10.4** IVHS **10.5** HPS **10.9/1** AECB **10.9/2** AECB **10.13** NASTRANTM FE **10.17** EPA **10.25** IP, TEM **10.26** CGG (2), U. S. **10.32** DST **10.38** PEO **10.47** MRO **11.11** SCOLIC **14.3** AE **14.10** DSI, NNMP **14.11** CWM (3) **B.2** U.S. *repetition (full):* **5.1** (3) GEOTEMRIII **5.5** HUMMINGBIRD **7.4** Canadians (2) **7.11/1** the 407 **7.13/2** Beta (2) **10.45** the tags *repetition (partial)* **5.1** the system **5.2** The . . . program **5.6** These systems **5.19** Boulle **5.25** the computer system **6.1** Model MS-2 **7.5/1** M78 **7.5/2** M78 **10.1** The soil (2), the value **B.1** McConville, Bondar **B.2** Clark **B.4** Allan Galley *naming* **5.5** the HUMMINGBIRD **5.6** OLTP sys-

tems **5.7** The **1250** Series *generic nouns and synonyms* **5.4** lights **5.11** system **5.13** system **5.19** deposit, discovery **5.21** instruments **5.22** report **5.24** instrument **5.26** instrument *Also see substitutions followed by a noun*

SUBSTITUTION (also see personal pronouns under INFORMALITY)

he **7.5/1, 7.13/2, 7.13/3, B.2, B.3, B.4** (2) *she* **B.1** (2) *his/him* **7.5/2, 14.5** *his or her* **8.30** *it:* **5.7, 5.18, 5.19** it will be **6.5/4** It's **7.11/1, 7.11/2, 7.13/2** (2) It (Beta), It **7.20/2, 8.4/2** it **8.4/3, 8.9, 8.10, 8.11, 8.15, 8.24** (2), **10.9/2, 10.15, 10.28, 10.35** (2) **10.37, 10.48, 11.3** (2) **1.9/1** (2) *they:* **5.8, 7.16, 7.19, 7.21** (2) **10.9/1, 10.45, 11.10** *them:* **8.1, 10.43** *this* **5.9, 5.30, 6.4, 7.1, 7.8, 7.14/1** (2) **7.20/2, 8.2, 8.25, 8.27, B.1** *this (followed by a noun):* **4.5** This . . . system **5.26** This . . . instrument **6.10** This . . . system **7.4** This . . . industry **7.5/2** This code **7.8** This explanation **7.10** This factor **7.11/1** this project **7.14/2** This control scheme **7.19** This statement **8.3/1** This issue **10.35** this issue **10.43** this research **11.1** this course **11.12** this test **12.1** This . . . system **14.7** This . . . mode **B.3** this article *these:* **7.12** All of theses **10.24, 12.2** (2) these (followed by a noun) **5.21** these . . . instruments **7.5/2** these rules **7.21** these results **8.2** (2) These concerns, These factors **8.6** These . . . instruments **10.14** these negotiations **10.18** these new materials **11.11** these predictions *those:* **8.21, 14.5** *those (followed by a noun):* **8.3/3** those theories *that* **6.6/2, 7.13/4, 7.20/2, 8.24, 11.10**

ELLIPSES AND LISTS

clausal ellipsis (subject) **4.2** Section 2 . . . and also **5.6** Data production . . . and occurs **5.13** and advises, and is **5.19** the deposit . . . and will be **5.30** Preliminary . . . testwork has been done . . . and is **6.1** Model MS-2 incorporates . . . and **6.2** The brochure covers . . . and includes **7.3** our mining industry . . . and is **7.6/2** I . . . and **7.8** This explanation . . . and is **10.19** The company has . . . and is **10.20** The next . . . program analyses . . . and allows **10.20** The diameter rod . . . can be . . . but is **10.47** who know . . . and . . . research **11.9/1** I . . . and so **14.5** those shown by . . . and interpreted by **B.1** she was . . . and is *clausal ellipsis (other):* **4.2** The third section **5.13** contains . . . and a **5.13** The . . . computer . . . advises the pilot of . . . and **5.14** Tubules have **5.26** This . . . instrument combines . . . and a **6.9/3** Signals can . . . and

instantly **9.3** There is . . . and a **14.11** which included . . . and **B.2** Clark had a . . . and a, He was . . . and **B.4** He has since worked on . . . and *lists (introduced):* **3.1** devices **4.2** follows **4.3** systems **4.4** splice **5.1** components **5.18** reported **9.7** assets **10.29** areas **B.1** fields *lists (single item)* **4.2** the . . . process **7.14/1** scenario **7.14/2** scenario **10.30, 10.31, 10.38** discipline **12.2** components *lists (continuing:)* **5.2(2)** include **5.5** comprising **5.6** are **5.7** records **5.8** use **5.9** for **5.11, 5.16** have been **5.17** including **5.20** include **5.27** include **5.29** to **6.4** designed to **6.5/2** to be a **6.5/4** software programs **7.11/2** it will **8.3** process is **8.4/4** There's **10.29** including **10.32** are **B.4** He received

DESCRIPTIVE CLAUSES

relative clauses (non-restrictive): **5.10** which . . . algorithms **5.11** which . . . interface **5.20** which . . . leaks, which . . . occur **7.6/2** in which **7.14/2** which **8.1** which were submitted **8.3/1** which **8.8** which **8.28** where **10.8** where **10.40** which **11.11** which **12.2** which (2) **B.1** who (2) **B.3** from which *relative clauses (restrictive):* **3.1** that (3) **4.2** which **5.15** that **5.19** where **5.28** that **5.29** that **6.5** who **6.5/4** that **6.5/5** that **7.1** that **7.5/1** which **7.8** which **8.1** which confirmed **8.4** that **8.9** that **8.12** we all face

8.15, 8.25 that **8.28** that **8.29/2** that, you need **8.30** who **10.3** who **10.22** which **10.42** we receive daily **10.47** who **11.7** where **11.11** that **11.12** which **14.11** which **D.2** where *-ed clauses (non-restrictive):* **4.3** Followed by **5.20** released . . . May 27 **5.26** Founded . . . engineers **5.25** Managed . . . section, called . . . Census, entitled . . . Score **7.1** dated . . . 1991 **7.3** reduced . . . deviations **7.5/1** hereinafter referred to . . . **9.1** descriptively called . . . elements **10.4** held . . . 1994 **10.19** spaced . . . apart **10.26** now owned . . . Canada **12.1** as shown in figure 2 *-ed clauses (restrictive):* **4.3** carried out . . . systems **5.1** intended . . . exploration **5.6** gathered and stored . . . systems **5.16** hosted . . . sandstones **5.25/1** ever produced . . . Resources **6.4/2** designed . . . downtime **6.7/2** made . . . Duxseal **6.10** developed . . . Montreal **6.10/2** based on . . . parameters **7.1** observed . . . GRB **7.5/2** specified in M78 105 consumed **10.8** aimed . . . industry **10.13** calculated . . . code **10.17** presented . . . Brazil **10.22** located . . . facilities **10.25** generated . . . survey **10.25** located . . . region **10.33** produced **11.4** based . . . mechanisms **11.8/2** provided **11.11** obtained . . . SCOLIC **14.9** conveyed . . . surface **D.2** used . . . equations *-ing clauses (non-restrictive):* **5.5**

compromising **5.7** so isolating **5.19** making **5.20**
offering **5.2** Weighing . . .
lb **6.5/4** including **7.2**
enhancing . . . and con-
tributing **7.14/1** meaning
. . . increases **7.20/2** casting **8.6** weighing **10.23**
enabling **10.40** making
11.2 Weighing *-ing clauses
(restrictive):* **5.7** causing . . .
distortion **5.16** overlying
7.8 having **7.18/1** requiring **8.1** framing **8.2** regarding **8.3/3** researching . . .
theories, applying . . . solutions **8.25** surrounding
10.2 ranging **10.42** contributing **12.2** consisting . . .
components **D.1** placing
*verbless clauses (non-restric-
tive):* **5.1** a . . . system **5.13**
in real time **5.18** similar . . .
derivative **5.24** An . . .
instrument **7.9** president
. . . Inc. **7.13/3** most . . .
conferencing **7.17** including . . . altitude **7.21** an . . .
loss **8.2** such as lead **8.4/1**
a . . . ago **8.4/2** the bank's
. . . officer **8.13** As . . .
envelope **10.5** the amount
. . . consumed **10.29** associate . . . council, Visual
Arts . . . Council, P. Eng (2)
11.14 a function . . . derivatives **12.2** the systems,
the infrastructure **B.1** P.Eng
B.3 of . . . Science, a
Century . . . Science *verbless clauses (restrictive):* **4.2**
relevant . . . contributions
4.3 relevant . . . systems
7.8 similar . . . **7.20/3** open
to government **8.11** necessary . . . face **8.30** both . . .
respect *to-infinitive clauses
(non-restrictive):* **B.1** to be
. . . November

**ASSOCIATIONS AND
PERSPECTIVES**

associations (post-triggered):
4.2 the document, the
body of the proposal **4.5**
the new towed bird . . .
system **5.2** Benefits of the
program **5.6** Examples of
OLTP systems, the data . . .
OLTP systems **5.30** the
excellent . . . paper **7.2** the
application of AFT **7.20/1**
The recommendations of
the ACES report **10.10** the
flowmeter **10.20** The next
. . . program **10.21** the
diameter . . . rod **12.2** The
efficiency . . . system **14.9**
The purpose . . . paper,
The size . . . particles, The
values . . . diameters **14.11**
the heat . . . CWM, ther-
mal . . . coals *associations
(pre-triggered):* **5.11** its . . .
recording **5.29** The
Association's Code of
Ethics **6.9/1** their signals
7.5/2 His recommenda-
tions **8.4/2** The bank's
officer **8.9** meeting's opinion **10.37** its recommendations **10.39** PEO Council
B.1 Her . . . study *associations (untriggered):* **4.2**
Section 2, the third sec-
tion, section 4, section 5
5.27 Features **5.28** the 35
production employees
7.5/1 the drawings **8.9** the
President, members,
Executive Committee,
Council **14.9** the measurements, the results *perspectives (triggered):* **4.3** in this
section, in section 2.1, in
section 2.5, in section 2.6
8.4/4 on the premises **8.27**
in your contract, in the

contract **14.10** In this
paper **14.11** in this study
perspectives (untriggered):
5.31 Tests . . . underway
(at Lakefield)

**Special Index:
*Punctuation***

COMMAS

before introduced lists: **3.1**
devices **5.1** components
9.1 *after introductory word
or phrase:* **3.1** hand **5.6**
Unfortunately, **5.19** First,
Second, Third, And fourth,
6.4/1 Of these failures, In
other words **6.5/1** run,
6.5/2 notice, **6.5/5** In fact,
6.6/2 Over . . . birds **6.6/2**
bonus **6.9/5** Thus **6.11**
However, As professionals,
7.7 in . . . system, **7.8** In
addition, **7.10** However,
7.11/2 At . . . billion **7.12**
First, Second, Third **7.13/2**
Not that long ago **7.14/1**
However **7.15** For . . . corridor, unlike . . . travel
7.17 However **7.18/1** also,
7.18/2 On the downside
7.18/3 Also, **7.18/4** more
importantly **7.19** On average **8.2** In the meantime,
8.3/1 Similarly, **8.3/1**
Technically, in . . . issues,
8.7 Before analysis, **8.13**
As . . . envelope **8.27** More
important **9.4** Therefore,
10.9/2 However **10.11**
however, **10.12** however,
10.13 however, **10.34** at
. . . test **10.36** During . . .
campaign, **10.45** At . . .
$50, **10.46** Also this year
11.5 However **11.6** In
Canada, **11.7** Sometimes,
12.2 In . . . years, **14.3**

However, **14.7** Also, **14.11** Furthermore, **B.1** As . . . engineering **B.4** After . . . work **D.1** however *after introductory clauses:* **6.4/2** To overcome . . . opera-tion, **6.9/3** Because . . . earth, **6.9/5** Because . . . country, **6.10/2** By provid-ing . . . rocks, **6.11** Although . . . situations, As . . . and as . . . entwined, **7.5/2** If . . . met, **7.8** as . . . increased **7.11/2** Once . . . **1988 7.13/4** To . . . high-way **7.14/1** If . . . load, as . . . equation, **7.14/2** if . . . used, **7.17** advantages, **7.18/4** once installed, **7.21** Although . . . addition **8.8** When . . . way **8.9** Before . . . meeting, **8.9** Should . . . meeting **8.10** Although . . . difficult , **8.17** If . . . scratch **8.22** To mediation, **8.25** As . . . expected, **8.27** if . . . appeal, if . . . law **8.28** When . . . yearbooks **8.29/1** If . . . place, **8.30** If . . . yourself, **8.30** Once . . . directly, **9.7** Despite . . . properties, **10.14** To expe-dite these negotiations, **10.15** Although . . . it, **10.18** During . . . materi-als, **10.27** After . . . treat-ment, **10.46** Subsequent . . . turbines before clauses **7.16** because, **7.18/1** assuming, **7.20/2** first because, before final -ing clauses of effect **5.7** so, **5.19** making, **6.2** thus reducing, **6.10/2** resulting in, **7.4** contributing, **7.14/1** meaning **10.23** thus enabling, **10.37** giv-ing, **10.40** making *in lists:* **4.3** (2), **4.4** (2), **5.2** (4), **5.5** (2), **5.6, 5.7, 5.8, 5.9, 5.16**

sandstones, **5.17** (4), **5.18** (3), **5.20** (2) hydraulic chemical, and, **5.27, 6.1** (2), **6.2** (3), **6.4** (2), **6.5/2** (4), **6.5/4** (4), **6.5/5** (3), **6.9/2** (2), **6.9/6, 7.7** flood-ing, **7.11/1** scale, **7.11/2** highways, jobs, **7.12** sur-veys, rapidly **7.17** inexpen-sive, time, **7.20/3** that, and that, **8.3** fair, consis-tent **8.4/4** (4), **8.16, 10.24** (2), **10.25, 10.26** (5), **10.27** (3), **10.28** (2), **10.29** (4), **12.2** (5), **14.3** (3), **B.1** researching, **B.4** (2) *with ellipsis:* **5.6** and occurs, **5.13** and advises, and is, **6.2** and includes, **9.3. B.1** and is *with non-restrictive clauses and phrases:* **5.10, 5.13**(2), **5.18** similar, **5.19** and very importantly, **5.20** which identifies, which offers **5.20** offering **5.21** 2-1/2 lb **5.22** (2) released . . . May 27, **5.23, 5.28, 6.5/4** (2) including . . . designs, **6.11** including engineers, **7.1** and GRB, **7.3** reduced . . . deviations **7.5/1** here-inafter **7.6** with concern, **7.9** president . . . Inc., **7.11/1** (2) in fact, **7.12** i.e. . . . aircraft **7.13/3** dead **7.17** including . . . alti-tude, such as, **7.20/1** in, **7.20/2** casting . . . extrapo-lation **7.21** in . . . perfor-mance, **8.1** which were, **8.2** (2) such as lead, (2) along . . . recycling, **8.3/1** which, **8.4/1** Learning, **8.4/2** (3) the bank's . . . officer (2), an . . . employ-ees, **8.8** (2) which, **8.11** (2) as . . . individuals **8.12** including, **8.28** where, **10.3** (2) primarily female, **10.4** (2) held . . . 1994,

10.8 where, **10.19** spaced **10.33** (2) QC, **10.40** which, **11.2** Weighing 12 kg, **11.11** which, **12.1** as shown in Figure 2., **12.2** e.g. . . . handling (2), which (2), the support sys-tems (2), **14.3** (20 such as . . . counts, **B.3** of . . . sci-ence, a Century . . . Science, from which *between pre-modifiers:* **5.16** oxidizing **5.26, 6.6/2** healthier **6.7/1** confined, **7.7** agitated, **7.11/2** 69-kilometer, **7.17** small, **10.23** (2) acoustics, energy, **14.7** spouted-bed *between clauses:* **7.5/2, 7.3/2, 7.18** but **7.20/2** first because, and that, **7.20/3** and, **8.3/3** although, **10.21** but, **10.22** and, **10.30, 14.7**(2) *with source:* **5.19** Boulle remarked, **7.13/1** says, **7.13/2** he says, **7.13/3** he said, **7.13/4** Klinkhammer said, **7.15** Evans said, **10.41** she explained, **11.9/2** I think

OTHER PUNCTUATION

apostrophes (possessives): **5.11** user's **6.4/1** Today's **6.5** moment's **6.6** Mr. Kallagi's **6.8/1** (2) Canada's, **7.11/2** Canada's, worlds, **7.12** platform's, **7.20/2, 8.4/2** bank's **8.9** meeting's **8.19** Canada's **8.28** Beckers', society's **9.7** Mexico's **10.2** Fundamental Review Working Group's **10.46** Gosgen's **10.47** customers' **11.3** government's **B.1** Bondar's **B.3** Queen's' Queen's *bracket pairs:* **4.3** (3), **5.1** (3), **5.2, 5.6, 5.8,**

5.30, 6.9/1, 7.1 (3), 7.5/1, 7.6/2, 7.7 (2), 7.8 (2), 7.10, 7.13 (2), 7.19, 7.21, 8.2 (2), 8.3/2, 8.7, 9.6, 10.32, 10.39, 11.14, 14.5, D.1 *colons before introduced lists and single items*: **4.2, 4.3, 4.4, 7.14/1, 7.14/2, 9.7, 10.29, 10.30, 10.31, 12.2,** *before continuing lists*: **5.17, 5.18, 5.29, 10.29** *in lists*: **5.29** *preceding quoted speech*: **10.40** *dashes* **4.2, 5.29, 7.12, 8.3/3, 8.22 (2), 8.23, 10.5 (2), 10.34 (2), 10.35, 10.36, 10.37, 10.38, 10.48, B.1** *exclamation marks*: **10.35, 11.9/2** *hyphens*: **3.1 (5), 4.3 (2), 4.4(4), 5.1(7), 5.5, 5.13(2), 5.15(2), 5.16, 5.17, 5.19, 5.21, 5.24, 5.25, 5.26, 5.27, 6.1 (7), 6.4, 6.5/4 (2), 6.7/1, 6.9/4, 6.10/1, 6.10/2, 7.1, 7.11/1, 7.12, 7.11/2 (3), 7.14/2, 7.15, 7.16, 7.18/1, 7.21 (2), 8.4/4, 8.6 (3), 8.7, 8.8, 8.17, 8.21, 9.7 (2), 10.3(3), 10.6, 10.7 (4), 10.12, 10.22, 10.27 (2), 10.34, 10.42 (2), 10.43 (2), 10.46, 10.47 (3), 10.48 (3), 11.2 (2), 11.3 (3), 11.12 (2), 14.7 (10), 14.10, 14.11, B.2, B.4** *quotation mark pairs (double) (also see quotations under* INFORMAL INDICATORS*)*: **6.9/4, 6.10/1, 7.5/2, 7.6/2, 7.12, 7.13/3, 8.4/2, 8.28 (2), 9.6 (3), 10.45, 11.14** *quotation mark pairs (single*: **10.32, 10.35, 11.10** *semicolons in lists*: **5.20 (2), 10.29 (2), 10.31, 10.32 (3),** *semicolons between clauses*: **7.11/1, 7.19, 10.2, 10.13, 10.31, 10.33** *soliduses*: **D.1,**

D.3 (3) *square brackets (pairs)*: **10.43, 10.44 (2)**

Special Index: *Logical Connections*

basis: **6.10/2** based on **7.14/1** one reason **7.20/2** rests on, evidence, basis **7.20/3** evidence **8.1** evidence, revealed **9.6** from examining **10.3** A systems, practices, Further investigation **10.13** experimental results **10.16** because **10.17** data assessment **7.6/2** so **7.20/2** conclusion **8.28** offensive **10.32** assessed **11.9/1** and so **11.11** desirable **B.1** relieved *purpose*: **5.2** to update **5.4** to reduce **5.7** to provide **5.8** to help and avoid **5.9** for **5.18** to estimate **5.20** to reduce **5.24** for the use of **5.25** to design and develop , to analyze **5.28** to ensure **6.1** to verify, to test **6.4** to overcome this **6.4** to ease, **6.7/2** to measure **6.9/1** Purpose, To prevent **7.14/1** to control **7.14/2** to control **8.1** to study **8.12** to deliver **8.22** to establish **8.30** to bring **10.8** to apply **10.9/1** to amend, to fulfill **10.10/2** fiction, to measure **10.12** is used for **10.14** to expedite **10.43** to make **10.44** to instruct **10.47** plan to meet **11.2** designed . . . applications **11.12** to perform **11.14** to assist *means*: **5.20** by standardizing **6.2** how **6.7/1** how **6.9/3** how **6.10/2** by providing **6.11** how to avoid them **7.2** how **7.11/1** way **7.11/2**

through **8.7** through **8.8** by, through, in this way **8.30** ways **9.5** how **10.1** by **10.25** using **10.43** new ways **10.44** how to **10.46** through delays **11.3** how **11.13** through **12.2** by **14.9** by *cause*: **6.9/3** because **6.9/5** because **7.9** partially to blame for **7.12** as a direct result of *effect*: **5.7** so isolating, causing **5.18** so **5.19** making **5.25** resulted in **6.2** thus reducing **6.3** Result **6.4/2** and so **6.6/2** the result **6.9/3** thus **6.9/4** Results **6.10/2** resulting in **6.10/2** the result **7.2** enhancing, contributing **7.4** contributing, balance **7.12** have led to **7.14/1** meaning, This will cause, in order to, This will result in **7.14/2** causes **8.2** resulted in **8.2** have created, have made **8.16** meant **8.25** cause **10.22** come close to forcing **10.23** thus enabling **10.27** plants **10.40** making **14.3** cause *problem*: **5.28, 6.2** expensive **6.3, 6.4** fail, incorrect, inadequate, problem, error, unfit, failure **6.5/1** have to do **6.6/1** The Problem, need, stress, panic, death **6.7/1** PROBLEM **6.10/2** problem **6.11** serious problems, more litigious, more entwined, conflict of interest **7.13** failure **7.18/4** limitation, inconvenience **7.20/2** fault **7.20/3** problem, fails **8.1** concerns, overstressing **8.2** concerns, difficulties, major problems, unsatisfactory **8.10** difficult **8.11** problems **8.30** can't resolve the dispute **10.3** problems, exclude, cannot see **10.13** failed prematurely **10.18** a need **10.22** serious problems, plant shutdown **10.30** problem, no-one knew **10.42** failure **10.47** need **11.8/2** not demonstrated **14.3** difficulty **B.1** troubled *solution:* **5.20** free training, advice **5.28**, **6.3**, **6.6/2** Light Solution **6.7/2**, **6.10** improve productivity and cut costs **6.10/2** reduced the need for, improved, less . . . wasted **7.18/4** overcome, offset **8.30** solution **12.2** radically improved **B.1** seems to be changing

Special Indexes: *Tense, Voice, Modality and Mood*

Note: the distinction between transitive and intransitive is not always clear.

INTRANSITIVE VERBS

future tense: **5.19** will be **6.5/4** won't **6.6/2** will save **7.11/3** will become, will be **7.13** will be **7.14/1** will increase **7.20/2** will continue **8.3/2** Will be **8.3/3** will take **8.5** I'll **10.9/1** will . . . allow **10.37** will come **11.9/1** I'll **15.3/2** I'll . . . ask **15.4/2** I'll make it *present tense*: **3.1** are, is, function **4.2** is, contains, occurs, are **5.1** is **5.2** include **5.5** consists of **5.6** is, occurs, are **5.9** is **5.10** comes **5.13** is **5.14** have **5.15** is **5.18** contains, are,

is **5.19** points, lies, is, hovers **5.20** include **5.21** have **5.23** has **5.27** include **5.29** have, goes beyond, 's, requires **5.30** were, make **5.31** is, were **6.4/1** are, fail, is **6.5/1** know **6.5/3** 's **6.5/4** 's **6.6/1** are, get **6.6/2** dim, is, means, **6.9/3** are **6.9/5** reach **6.11** becomes, become, constitutes **7.1** is **7.4** is **7.5/2** states, is **7.6/2** feel **7.8** suggests, is **7.9** is **7.10** is **7.11/1** is **7.11/3** is **7.12** are, is **7.13/1** says **7.14/1** is, increases **7.14/2** increases **7.15** advocates **7.16** differs, are **7.17** has **7.18/1** offers, entails, exceed, exists, is **7.21** are, imply **8.3/1** is, meets, have **8.9** are **8.10** is **8.11** 's, are **8.14** is **8.15** 's **8.20** is, are, stand **8.21** believe, is, gains an edge **8.24** is, that's happening, 's, need **8.25** is **8.27** want **8.28** find, are, see **8.29** think, need **8.30** Is, is **9.1** are **9.3** is **9.4** seems is **9.5** is **9.6** is, are **10.1** is **10.2** are **10.3** has, have, see **10.5** are **10.8** is **10.10** is **10.11** suggest **10.12** are **10.15** have **10.16** hopes, are **10.18** is **10.20** allows **10.22** have, has come close **10.23** fall within **10.26** has **10.33** are **10.34** class for, is **10.40** is **10.41** is **10.42** is, represent **10.43** is **10.45** approach, pay **10.46** need, know **10.48** is **11.1** apply **11.3** are, does **11.4** is **11.5** states **11.6** are **11.8** is **11.9/1** have **11.10** is **11.11** shows **12.2** relate to **12.2** is **14.5** are **14.7** is **14.9** is **15.2/2** think **15.3/1** do you have

15.3/2 I've **15.4/1** am **15.4/2** it's, imagine, are, want, is, goes **15.4/3** That's **B.1** thinks, seems **B.4** is **B.5** predict, is *present continuous tense:* **6.11** is increasing **7.12** are beginning **8.12** are also gearing up **8.17** is starting **8.25** What is . . . looking for **10.22** is facing **11.3** is focusing **11.10** They're waiting . . . but acting **B.1** 's . . . aiding *Past tense (generally in the past):* **6.11** have been **7.6/2** have lived **7.13/3** have come and gone, have existed **7.18** has gained **7.20/2** has accumulated **8.2** have arisen **8.3/1** has begun **8.13** have been **10.6** has been **10.9/2** has indicated **11.7** has worked *past tense (specific time in the past):* **5.28** arose **7.3** showed **7.5/1** was **7.5/2** was, were **7.6/1** read **7.6/2** retired **7.7** were **7.8** was, showed behaved **7.9** said **7.11/1** decided **7.11/2** was **7.13/2** battled it out, was, lost, said **7.15** said **7.20/2** was **7.21** was, indicated **8.1** confirmed, had, considered **8.3/2** was, indicated **8.4/1** opened **8.16** hung, in, had, meant **8.18** went off **8.24** added **9.2** was **10.12** explained **10.13** confirmed, failed **10.17** seemed, was, showed, were **10.27** was, reappeared **10.30** was, knew **10.34** withstood **10.40** said **10.41** explained **10.41** was **10.43** told **11.6** was **14.7** was, had **15.4/1** was **15.4/2** decided, thought, added, had, did **15.4/3** thought, worked out B.1 worked, helped B.2 was, had *continuous past tense*: 15.4/1 have been buried *past in past tense (pluperfect)*: 10.27 had increased *infinitives* 6.4/2 to ensure 7.12 beginning to change 7.14/1 cause to increase 7.14/2 cause to increase 7.20 ought to ensure 8.3/2 continue to adapt 8.3/3 to continue 8.1 best way to ensure 8.14 not enough to achieve 8.24 to make use of 10.17 seemed to consider

MODALITY

can: 6.2 can be 6.5/2 can keep up with 6.9/3 can be 7.18/4 can offset 7.19 can start 8.3/2 Can we adapt 8.3/3 we can 8.26 can communicate 10.21 can be 11.7 can be 15.2/2 can expect 15.3/1 Can't say 15.4/3 can be could 8.2 could leach out *have/need to:* 6.5/2 will have to do, need to be 7.4 need to know *may:* 6.5/2 may need to be 7.1 may be 7.5/2 may not be 7.14/2 may have 8.8 may begin 8.22 may be 8.23 may be 8.30 may need 10.11 may represent *might:* 7.14 might be 15.4/2 might be *must:* 6.11 must be 7.20/3 must be 8.3/3 we must 8.24 must be 8.26 must communicate 11.10 must do *ought:* 7.20/3 ought to ensure *shall:* 7.5/2 shall not be *should:* 7.4 should be, should know 8.26 should communicate

15.3/1 should be *want:* 6.5/2 want to *would:* 5.19 would have, would bring 7.20/2 would be 8.17 would be 8.25 would be 10.3 would indicate, would reveal

TRANSITIVE VERBS-ACTIVE VOICE

future tense: 4.5 I shall examine 5.2 will invest, will include 14.1 will cause 7.14/1 will result in 8.5 I'll dig up 8.29 will give 10.9/2 will prescribe 10.28 will examine 10.29 will study 10.35 will find 10.45 will communicate 11.13 will improve 14.2/1 will discuss 15.3/2 I'll send 15.4/2 I'll mail *past in present (future perfect)*: 7.11/3 will have created *present tense:* 3.1 requires 4.2 presents, completes 5.1 provides 5.4 monitors and controls 5.7 records 5.8 use, avoid 5.10 uses 5.11 offers, uses, provides 5.13 reads, advises 5.20 identifies, offers 5.26 combines 6.1/1 describes 6.1/2 incorporates 6.2 describes, covers, includes 6.4/2 results in 6.5/3 lets, enable 6.6 contributes to 6.6/9 use 7.2 improves 7.4 employs, provides, accounts for 7.6/1 condemns 7.14/2 causes 8.4/2 describes 8.23 don't make 8.25 includes, cause 8.28 look at 8.30 respect 10.2 hold 10.7 feature 10.15 codifies 10.20 analyses 10.40 promotes, apply 10.42 receive 11.13 pro-

vides 12.2 links 14.7 dominate 15.2/2 operate B.1 link *present continuous tense:* 5.9 is stocking 6.10/1 is helping 8.19 is cleaning up 10.19 is developing 10.38 are complicating *past tense (generally in the past)*: 4.5 Having explained 5.7 has introduced 5.9 has announced 5.25/1 has resulted in, has led to 7.18/4 has overcome 8.2 has resulted in, have created, have made 8.29 has caught 8.30 have exhausted 9.7 has narrowed 10.14 has withdrawn 10.19 has drifted through 10.39 has approved 11.9/1 haven't seen B.3 has completed B.4 has worked *past tense (specific time in the past)*: 5.5 reported 5.15 permitted 5.17 supplied 5.22 recommended 5.28 spent, wanted, received 6.3 made 6.6/2 converted 7.1 intruded 7.3 recorded, revealed, submitted 8.4/1 invested 8.9 advised 10.24 included 10.36 provided 14.3 received 15.4/3 liked B.4 received, joined *continuous past tense:* B.3 has been researching *past in past tense (pluperfect)*: 7.5/1 had reviewed *infinitives:* 3.1 used to describe 4.5 can be used to meet 4.6 pleased to announce 5.1 designed to collect 5.2 to update 5.4 coordinated to reduce 5.7 to provide 5.8 to help, how to reach 5.18 can be used to estimate 5.20 how to avoid, offering advice to reduce 5.25

to design, to analyze **5.28** to ensure **5.29** an ethical duty to preserve an ethical duty to preserve **5.30** to study this **6.1/1** used to verify **6.1/2** to test **6.2** expensive to dispose of **6.4/2** To overcome this and ensure, designed to ease . . . minimize . . . and so to reduce **6.5/2** need to be, want to look **6.5/3** enable you to create . . . solve . . . solve . . . access . . . keep . . . and run **6.7/1** How to measure **6.7/2** want to measure **6.9/1** To provide, use to broadcast **6.9/2** used to provide **6.10/2** monitored to identify **6.11** how to avoid **7.4** intended to focus **7.10** used to relate **7.11/1** decided to apply **7.12** made it possible to determine, made it possible to determine, made to possible to install **7.13/4** To prevent **7.14/1** to use, to control, used to control, in order to bring **8.3/1** anxious to receive **8.3/2** challenged to make **8.7** used to enhance **8.8** begin to doubt their right to manage **8.11** necessary to tackle **8.12** gearing up to deliver **8.15** time to accept **8.17** useful to consult **8.21** to put **8.24** the will to implement **8.29/2** help you develop **8.30** need to bring **10.9** allow to require **10.14** to expedite **10.15** obligation to protect **10.16** hopes to increase **10.18** need to characterize **10.42** failure to account for **10.43** idea is to find, using to alter, to make **10.44**

urged to include, in an effort to instruct, how to write **10.47** plan to meet **11.9/1** try to find **11.12** To perform **143** in order to assess **14.11** method to predict **15.2/1** should not plan to use, not to discuss **B.1** helped to set up **B.2** to head

MODALITY

can: **5.8** can provide **6.9/4** can hold **8.29** can help **8.30** can't resolve **15.4/2** can't e *could:* **8.30** could give **14.3** could cause *may:* **5.15** may reflect *made possible* :**7.12** have made it possible, has made it possible *must:* **8.27** must spell . . . out **B.1** must master *should:* **8.29** should be exploring **15.2/1** should not plan would **15.4/2** would e

TRANSITIVE VERBS-PASSIVE VOICE

Note: All non-restrictive and restrictive -ed clauses are tenseless passives; see listing under these headings.

future tense: **4.3** will be provided, will be presented, will be discussed **9.5** will be financed *infinitive future tense:* **7.11/3** to be developed *present tense* **4.2** is dedicated, are outline **5.1** are designed **5.4** are coordinated **5.6** are referred to, are optimized **5.7** is simplified **5.18** are reported **5.24** is used **6.9/2** are monitored **7.5/2** are met **7.8** is supported **7.10** is used, is

known **7.13** is addressed **7.14/1** is illustrated **7.14/2** is used **7.20/2** is known, is made **8.8** is changed, are reversed **10.1** is subjected to **10.12** is used **10.23** are measured to **10.31** is made **11.2** is designed **11.5** are owned **11.8/2** is demonstrated **12.2** are established and controlled **14.9** is studied, are made, are gathered, are correlated **14.10** is described **14.11** is proposed **B.1** is relieved **B.5** is defined *present continuous tense:* **6.10** is being wasted **7.1/2** is being developed **7.14/1** is being used **8.3/2** are being challenged **10.8** are being investigated *past tense (generally in the past):* **4.2** has been . . . overlooked **5.16** have been leached . . . carried . . . and re-deposited **5.31** has been done **6.4/1** have been attributed to **6.11** have . . . been faced with **7.2** has been applied and . . . achieved **8.2** have been raised **8.9** have been achieved **10.1** has been calibrated **12.2** have been . . . improved **14.11** have been measured **15.4/2** has . . . been revised *past tense (specific time in the past):* **6.10/1** was developed **7.5/1** were submitted, was applied **7.7** was observed **7.8** was increased **8.1** were submitted **8.7** were wetted . . . and viewed, was used **8.28** were paraded **10.4** was attended **10.25** have been investigated **10.27** was digested **11.12** was ground down, were leached, were . . .

enclosed, was tumbled **12.1** was installed **14.7** was translated **14.11** was measured, was found **B.1** was troubled **B.3** was excerpted **B.4** was born *past in past tense (pluperfect):* **10.27** had been . . . reduced **10.30** had been . . . attempted *past continuous tense:* **8.28** were being taught *infinitives* **6.9/3** needing to be adjusted **7.11/2** first to be developed **B.2** seems to be changing

MODALITY

can: **4.5** can be measured, can be used **5.18** can be used **5.9/3** can be sent and transmitted **6.9/5** can be sent and received **6.9/6** can be seen **7.14/1** can be seen **7.14/2** can be illustrated **8.8** can be made **10.48** cannot be seen **12.2** can be viewed *could:* **7.21** could be operated **8.28** could . . . have occurred *may* **8.8** may be challenged *must:* **7.13/3** must be made *need:* **6.9/3** needing to be adjusted *should:* **7.20/1** should be rejected **10.44** should be urged *would:* **8.9** would be referred

MOOD

imperatives: **6.7/2** Use, Press, Remove, use **8.30** think **10.35** fill it out, send it **7.14/1** Let us assume **7.14/2** assume **8.27** say so **14.2/1** keep in mind **15.4/2** let me know

15.4/3 let me know *subjunctives* **7.18/3** requires that . . . be considered **8.9** Should . . . be passed **8.11** to ensure that we . . . take **8.14** imperative that . . . be combined

-ING FORMS

as tenses: see list of *continuous tenses; adjectives:* see lists under *adjectives; clauses:* see lists of *restrictive* and *non-restrictive clauses; nouns:* **7.4** mining **7.18/2** using **8.10** establishing **8.20** arguing **8.25** eliminating **9.5** decommissioning **10.8** crossings **10.22** reneging **12.2** modeling , . . . *-ing (effect):* **5.7** so isolating, causing **5.19** making **6.2** thus reducing **6.10/2** resulting in **7.2** enhancing . . . and contributing to **7.4** contributing **7.14/1** meaning **10.23** thus enabling **10.40** making by . . . *-ing (means):* **5.20** by standardizing **6.10/2** by providing **10.1** by keeping for . . . *-ing (purpose):* **4.2** for working **5.11** for . . . recording **7.14/1** for not using **7.14/2** for considering **10.12** for bleaching *from . . . -ing:* **7.21** from staging **9.6** from examining **10.14** from staking in . . . obtaining **8.2** *in . . . -ing:* **8.8** in managing **14.3** in correlating **14.7** in determining **B.4** in researching *of . . .-ing:* **8.30** of seeking **10.42** of using **10.43** of catalyzing *other:* **7.17** being small, not requiring a long . . . time

10.17 worth defending **10.22** close to forcing **10.24** included bleaching of catalyzing **10.46** subsequent to installing **15.4/1** having gotten

Special Index: *Adjectives*

CHARACTERISTIC

3.1 *external* energy sources **4.2** *linear dynamic* systems **4.3** *previous* research, *dynamic* analysis **5.1** *multicoil,* . . . system, *multicoil* bird and receiver, *single-component* . . . system, *commercially-available* . . . system, *new* . . . bird, *digital* receiver, *additional* components, *vertical* (component), *horizontal lateral* (component) **5.2** *northern bleached* softwood, *in-plant* modifications, *new* boiler, *environmental* compliance **5.5** *new* development, *basic* HUMMINGBIRD, *small,* "strap-down" console, *IBM compatible* 486 PC, *plug-in* processor boards, *large* volumes, *end user* **5.7** *summary* readings, *harmonic* distortions, *true* power **5.8** *step-by-step* instructions **5.10** *pre-tune* and *adaptive tuning* algorithms **5.13** *on-board* navigation computer, *current* deviation **5.14** *micritic* walls, *inner* diameters **5.15** *evolutionary* event, *environmental* change **5.16** *Base and precious* metals, *basal* redbed sandstones, *saline* brines, *regional* fault systems **5.17** *holed, coarse* screens, *high-density, light and heavy, centrifugal* cleaners, *0.008-in.* . . .*fine* screens **5.18** *vertical* derivative, *magnetic* bodies, *analytic* signal, *geological* map, *magnetic* latitude **5.19** *logistical* costs **5.21** *external* battery packs **5.24** *portable, digital* power analyzer **5.27** *one-button* . . . menu, *continuous automatic* set-ups **5.29** *ethical* duty, *intellectual* property **5.31** *preliminary* . . . testwork **6.1** *variable, high-current* output, *molded-case* circuit breakers, *thermal, magnetic or solid-state* motor overload relays **6.2** *Oily* . . . condensate **6.4** *incorrect* installation, *inadequate* lubrication, *trouble-free* operation **6.5** *different* programs **6.6** *same* lighting level, *twin, fluorescent* lamps **6.7** *close* tolerances, *confined, hard-to-get-at* space **6.9** *far* north, *continental* United States, *major* . . . networks, *same* position, *constant* communication, *different* location **6.10** *exact* location, *softer* rocks, *various* parameters **7.1** *western* end, *discordant* veining, *northeastern* part **7.2** *new* . . . grades, *recent* applications **7.3** *Russian* commercial power reactors, *noticeable* improvement, *safe* operations, *normal* power operations **7.4** *essential* component **7.5** *main* . . . masonry piers, *empirical* . . . method **7.6** *new* article, *international* . . . group **7.7** *different* behaviour, *various* turbines **7.8** *previous* kinetic data **7.9** *low* productivity **7.10** *constant* factor, *continual* changes **7.11** *new* . . . project, *Canadian* context, *Canadian* infrastructure, *largest* . . . project, *69-kilometre, multi-lane* . . . highway, *largest single* . . . contract, *Canadian* history, *first, all-electronic* toll highways, *new* jobs, *first major* infrastructure project **7.12**

new developments, *rapid* advances, *lightweight* systems, *available* aircraft **7.14** *original* level, *above* equation, *same* scenario, *constant* . . . energy **7.16** *conical* point, *tangential* touching **7.17** *long* . . . time, *high* altitude, *lower* . . . rate **7.18** *recent* popularity, *non-harsh* conditions, *recent* . . . . developments **7.19** *average* . . . salary, *associate* company **7.20** *minimal* risk, *main* conclusion, *empirical* and *theoretical* basis, *undetectably* small, *clear* evidence **7.21** *overall* . . . performance **8.1** *glulam* . . . arches, *central* . . . beam **8.2** *potential hazardous* nature, *toxic* metals, *new* sites, *stringent* . . . operations, *increasingly* unsatisfactory **8.3** *other* countries, *new* techniques **8.4** *charismatic* chairman, *new* ideas, *150-room* hotel **8.6** *heavy* . . . packs **8.7** *green* filter **8.10** *new* business **8.13** *integral* part **8.14** *high* performance, *new* . . . technologies **8.15** *Canadian* industry **8.16** *smaller* . . . projects **8.20** *environmentally friendly* process **8.21** *renewable* resources **8.22** *nominal* fee **8.28** *naked* women **8.29** *hard* place, *new* products, *competitive* edge **8.30** *independent* . . . party **9.1** *main* types, *dendriform and lamelliform* elements **9.3** *large* step, *even larger* one **9.4** *magmatic* origin **9.7** *wide* array, *key* assets, *large* mine **10.1** *steady* flow, *various* soil types, *glass* beads **10.3** *primarily* female, *young* children **10.4** *most recent* . . . annual meeting **10.7** *spill-free* connection and disconnection **10.9** *specific* approaches **10.10** *primary* function **10.12** *high-density* **10.13** *different*

specimens **10.15** *confidential* information **10.18** *new* materials **10.20** *next* part, *graphical* viewing **10.21** *resultant* rod **10.23** *Preliminary* failure **10.24** *laser* light, *ultra-violet* light, *blue* light **10.26** *world-wide* representatives **10.27** *toxic* compounds **10.28** *other* . . . programs **10.29** *socially responsible* design **10.30** *reverse* DST **10.31** *other known* solutions, *colinear* cracks, *infinite* sheet **10.32** *major* areas, *'green'* transportation **10.36** *entire* . . . campaign **10.38** *already complex* management **10.40** *diverse* profession, *scientific* discoveries **10.41** *main* difference **10.42** *depletable* resources, *essential* value **10.43** *new* ways **10.44** *Canadian* law schools **10.45** *electronic* . . . "tags" **10.46** *new* turbines **10.47** *professional* . . . salespeople **10.48** *classic* example, *present* time **11.1** *Special* regulations **11.2** *stationary* Sword-Feeder, *special* applications **11.3** *recent* budget **11.7** *negative* publicity, *good* thing, *earliest* stages **11.9** *Canadian* issue **11.11** *different* conditions, *sufficiently* accurate, *consistently* conservative **11.12** *separate* samples **11.13** *possible* backups **14.3** *conventional* interpretation, *peak* amplitude, *different* modes **14.7** *same* performance, *single-stage* unit, *same* input, *wide* range, *given* . . . input **14.9** *present* paper, *gaseous turbulent* jet, *flat and horizontal* surface, *different* conditions, *dimensionless* representation **14.11** *round* tube, *inner* pipes, *outer* pipe, *experimental* error, *simple and accurate* method **B.1** *frontier* engineer, *present* studies, *static* enrolment **B.2** *same* state **B.3** *Canadian* history

EPITHET

3.1 *clear-cut* ... distinction **4.1** *Ineffectual* Policies **4.2** *critical* ... information, *tentative* schedule **4.3** *general* structural representation, *brief* review, *powerful* ... analysis **5.1** *new* system, *powerful* tool, *next-generation* ... receiver, *more consistent* ... quality **5.4** *major* traffic system **5.7** *general* ledger, *very* accessible, *maximum* information **5.8** *unfamiliar* locales **5.13** *very* steep topography **5.14** *sudden* appearance, *abundant* ... cyanobacteria **5.15** *true* evolutionary event **5.19** *big* project, *readily* mineable, *only* 10 km, *much-needed* jobs **5.21** *heavy* battery packs **5.24** *accurate* and *user-friendly* instrument **5.25** *most comprehensive* report **5.26** *rugged* unit **5.28** *extensive* training **5.29** *faithful* agents **5.30** *excellent* diagrams, *comprehensive* nature, *extremely* useful **6.1** *proper* motor overload protection, *nuisance* tripping, *appropriate* control circuitry **6.4** *intrinsically reliable* ... components **6.5** *small* business, *helpful* tool, *sophisticated* ... designs, *complex* ... equations, *comprehensive* databases **6.6** *lower* stress level, *healthier, fatter* birds, *lower* mortality rate, *extra* bonus **6.9** *virtually any* information **6.10** *"smart"* ... system, *efficient* blasting, *significantly* less **6.11** *serious* problems **7.11** *major* ... project **7.12** *direct* result **7.13** *superior* technology **7.14** *better* choice, *better* chance **7.18** *special*

sealing **7.20** *dubious* extrapolation, *best* alternative **8.3** *top-notch* committee, *best* engineers **8.4** *opulent* Institute for Learning, *typical* ... facility **8.11** *best* way **8.14** *truly* high performance **8.23** *bad* environmental choice **8.25** *whole* range **8.28** *disgraceful* acts, *diverse* values **8.29** *competitive* edge **8.30** *creative* ways **9.7** *key* assets **10.6** *popular* method **10.22** *serious* problems **10.36** *impressive* record **10.40** *highly* diverse **10.43** *whole* idea **11.8** *Useless and misleading* **11.9** *special* ... issue **14.9** *very* different ... conditions **B.2** *significant* appointment

NOUN

3.1 *water* pump, *energy* sources **4.1** *Policy* Dilemma **4.2** *analysis* techniques *research* contributions, *process* description, *literature* review, *research* topics, *field* testing, *background* information **4.3** *time* series, *space* representations, *time series* analysis **4.4** *fuselage* skin splice **4.5** *human* needs **5.1** *electromagnetic* system, *bird and receiver* design, *time-domain* system, *exploration and resource evaluation* community, *mineral* exploration, *cost* reductions, *product* quality **5.2** *softwood* pulp mill, *modernization* program, *cogeneration* plant **5.4** *traffic* system, *traffic* signals **5.5** *survey* systems, *data* acquisition, *processor* boards **5.6** *production, transaction* systems **5.8** *route guidance* systems, *global* systems **5.10** *Process* Controller **5.11** *magnetic* recording, *tape* drive **5.13** *current* deviation, *navigation* computer, *survey* alti-

tude **5.16** *fault* systems **5.17** *process* equipment, *flotation* cells **5.18** *wavenumber* information **5.19** *inventory* costs, *ocean* shipping **5.20** *air* leaks **5.21** *battery* packs, *battery* packs **5.24** *power* analyzer **5.25** *mineral* industry, *mineral statistics* section, *Ontario Mineral Score* **5.26** *storage* oscilloscope **5.27** *measure* menu **5.28** *production* engineers, *production* employees **5.29** *PEO* members **5.31** *cobalt* recovery **6.1** *motor overload* protection , *motor overload* relays, *control* circuitry, *Circuit* Breaker, *Motor Overload Relay Test* Set, *ground-fault, trip* devices **6.2** *human* error, *oil-water* separator **6.4** *machinery* components, *design service* life, *bearing* failure **6.5** *Apple Macintosh* computer, *software* programs, *business* task **6.6** *stress* level, *light* solution, *lighting* level, *mortality* rate, *energy* costs, *electronic* ballasts **6.9** *telecommunications* coverage, *television* networks, *satellite* channels, *voice, data, image, data, and transmission* services, *business, educational and government* sectors, *ground* antennae, *Satellite* signals, *world* events, *TV* screens, *hockey* game **6.10** *muck* pile fragmentation, *drill* ... system, *New Brunswick* Coal Ltd., *Mineral Development* Agreement, *waste* rock, *performance* variables **7.1** *mylonite* zone, *Gilbert Bay* Pluton **7.2** *product* quality **7.3** *power* operations, *power* reactors **7.4** *trade* balance **7.5** *masonry* piers, *grid* line, *masonry* walls, *design* methods, *engineering* analysis **7.6** *engineering* projects, *Development* Agency **7.7** gas liquid system, *dispersion* behaviours **7.8** *sulphur to molybdenum* ratio, *molybdenum* loading **7.10** *pulp mass* flow, *chip* properties, *moisture* content **7.11** *toll* highways, *infrastructure* development, *Ontario* government, *Highway 407* project, *road construction* project, *toll* highway, *civil-engineering* contract, *toll* highways, *infrastructure* project **7.12** *exploration* strategies, *navigation* technology, *survey* platform, *ground* surveys **7.13** *information* highway **7.14** *motor* load **7.15** *automobile and air* travel **7.16** *kiss* singularity **7.17** *attitude* receiver, *data* rate **7.18** *profile* . . . technology, *rail* technology, *surface* height, *precision* machining, *maintenance* convenience **7.21** *reactor* performance, *oxygen* addition, *performance* loss **8.1** *wood* beams, *building* official, *window* arches, *building* department **8.2** *landfill* capacity, *landfill* sites, *government* regulations, *public* pressure **8.3** *admissions* process, *university* professors **8.4** *exercise* rooms, *tuck* room **8.6** *power* cord **8.7** *ink* particles **8.8** *Management* decisions, *grievance and arbitration* procedures **8.9** *decision* process **8.12** *Ontario* schools **8.13** *heat* loss **8.19** *transport* industry **8.21** *energy* sources, *power* map, *power* industry, *wind* farm, *water* heaters **8.22** *track* records **8.24** *esearch and technology* activities **8.25** *process* chemicals **8.28** *Lady Godiva* rides, *arts and humanities* courses **8.29** *Research* Council **8.30** *industry* leader **9.3** *bleach* plant **9.7** *copper-mine* gold **10.1** *soil* types, *soil* densi-

ties, *water* heads **10.3** *systems* review, *employment* practices, *breakfast* meetings **10.6** *micro-hardness* test **10.8** *border* crossings, *speed* trucks **10.12** *disc* filters **10.13** *stress/strain* distributions **10.15** *law* obligations **10.16** *rail* shipments, *transportation* costs **10.18** *development* stages **10.22** *waste* disposal, *U.S.* government, *waste* commitments, *plant* shutdowns **10.23** *material* . . . strains, *failure* theories, *failure* results, *cruciform* specimens, *strength* data, *specimen* design **10.25** *exploration* targets **10.28** *waste* management programs **10.29** *task* groups, *design* demand, *design* capability, *design* export **10.32** *ozone layer* protection, *energy* use, *resource* conservation, *site* issues **10.35** *Notice of Intention* form, *awards* gala **10.36** *northwest Europe* campaign, *repair* services **10.39** *PEO* Council **10.42** *energy* matters **10.44** *law* schools, *Bar Admission* courses, *language* course, *law* students **10.45** *"vehicle"* tags, *vehicle identification* numbers, *inspection* stations, *driver* delays **10.46** *power* station, *power* rating **11.3** *technology* strategy **11.4** *mass* balances **11.5** *circuit* topographies **11.6** *gold* exploration, *stock-market* fluctuations **11.8** *topic* sentence **11.11** *design* purposes, *design* perspective **11.13** *highway* safety, *inspection* stations **11.14** *magnetic* data **12.1** *University of Calgary* system, *heading/pitch* baseline **12.2** *materials* handling, *machine* design, *support* systems, *mine* design, *production* planning **14.3** *damage* initiation, *time*

domain, *time* models **14.7** *methane oxidation coupling* performance, *fluidised-bed* reactor, *reaction* mode, *spouted-bed, fluidised-bed* units, *oxygen* reactor, *oxygen* input, *gas phase oxygen* pressure, *hydrocarbon* yield **14.9** *size* distribution, *jet stagnation* point, *image* analysis, *particle* samples, *dispersion* parameter **14.11** *heat transfer* coefficient, *coal-water* mixture **B.1** *U.S. space* shuttle **B.2** *physics* department **B.4** *Mineral Resources* Division, *gold* metallogeny, *mineral deposit* research, *island arc* terranes **D.2** *grid* points, *stability* equations **D.3** *sound transmission loss plate/porous/plate* system

QUANTITY

3.1 *two* . . . categories **4.2** *third* section **4.3** *three* . . . model classes, *some* analysis **5.1** *several* years, *first* . . . system, *approximately 30 000* tonnes **5.2** *multiple* . . . modifications **5.4** *third* . . . traffic system, *approximately 1700* . . . signals **5.7** *all* phases **5.11** *500 Mbyte* . . . hard drive, *60, 150 or 525 Mbyte* hard drive **5.13** *most* advantageous **5.15** *some* change **5.17** *two* pulpers, *three* . . . screens, *two* . . . cleaners **5.19** *several* advantages **5.20** *three* areas, *fewer* adhesives and sealants **5.22** *further* reduction, *five* years time **5.23** *three* engineers **5.25** *two-year, first* publication **5.28** *35* production engineers **6.4** *some* bearings **6.5** *every* step, *3, 500* . . . software programs **6.6** *more* light and heat, *six week* life, *four* barns **6.7** *some* Plasticine or Duxseal **7.1** 3 km **7.2** *all* . . . operations, *154* deviations, *199* deviations 7.3 *330 000* people, *some 115* communities, *approximately 15%*, total ... exports, *12$ billion*, total production 7.5 *three* times, *18* times 7.7 *several* ... regimes 7.11 *20, 000* ... jobs 7.16 *two* ... sheets 7.17 *many* advantages 7.20 *only* fault, *all* accounts 7.21 *several* catalysts 8.1 *first* drawings, *further three* sets 8.4 *150-room* hotel 8.9 *three* resolutions 8.20 *more* ... friendly, *many* angels 8.22 *first few* occasions 8.30 *third* party 9.1 *two* ... types 10.3 *several* fronts 10.8 *second* initiative 10.11 *several* features 10.13 *every* specimen 10.14 *some* areas 10.19 *four* levels, *several* stopes, *60* metres 10.21 *several* times 10.22 *many* ... facilities 10.27 *enough* sediment 10.29 *four* areas 10.30 *two* ... solutions, *two* ... cracks 10.32 *five* areas 10.35 *first* step 10.36 *11,000* ... engineers 10.46 *928* MW 11.11 *several* airfoils 11.12 *24* hours 12.2 *three* ... components, *second* component, *third* component 14.7 *two-stage* ..., *single-stage*, *total* oxygen 14.11 *three* ... pipes, *thirteen* kinds B.2 *first* ... engineer

TYPE

3.1 *solar* ... plant, *active* ... solar plants, *passive* ... solar plants 4.2 *multivariate* ... systems, *industrial* process, *multivariate* analysis and modelling, *thermo-mechanical* process 4.3 *structural* representations, *model* classes, *time* series, *state* representations, *multivariate spectral* analysis, *multi-input, single-output*

systems,4.4 *single-shear lap* splice, *single-shear sult* splice, *double-shear* splice 4.5 *solar* energy 5.1 *airborne* ... system 5.2 *northern* bleached *kraft* ... mill 5.5 *airborne multiparameter geophysical survey* systems, *data acquisition* HDD, *processor* boards 5.6 *on-line* ... systems, *order entry* systems, 5.8 *invehicle* systems 5.9 *Legend Plus* Controller, *Red Lion* Controls 5.10 *6100 Series 1/16 DIN Universal I/O* ... Controller, *West* ... algorithms 5.11 *SCSI* interface, *hard* drive 5.13 *fixed-wing* surveys 5.15 *Precambrian-Cambrian* boundary 5.16 *redbed* sandstones, *Upper Devonian* sandstones, *Precambrian* basement 5.17 *Lamort Pulpers, Veticel* ... cells, *Gyroclean* cleaners 5.19 *open-pit* methods 5.20 *hydraulic, chemical and air* leaks. 5.24 *Electrocol Navovip digital* ... analyzer, *electrical* systems 5.25 *computer* system, *Ontario Mineral* Score 5.26 *dual channel, 50 Mhz, digital* ... oscilloscope, *3 2/3 true-rms* multimeter 5.29 *professional* engineers 5.30 *cubic* nickel 5.31 *metallurgical* testwork 6.1 *MULTI-AMP Model MS-2* ... Set 6.2 *air* condensate, *Envirosaver* ... separator, *disposal* costs, *sizing* chart 6.5 *Apple Macintosh* computer, *2D* and *3D* designs, *mathematical* equations 6.6 *Philips* Lighting, *incandescent* system, *Philips T8* ... lamps, *Advance Mark VII dimmable electronic* ballasts 6.9 *Anik* satellites, *geostationary* orbit, *solar* energy, *hydrazine* fuel 6.10 *on-line* . .. system, *Aquilina Mining* Systems 7.1 *granitic* vein, *Rexon's* Cove, *greenschist-*

facies ... zone 7.4 *National Mining* Week 7.5 *professional* Engineer 7.6 *Lending* Agencies, *environmental* group, *Third* World, *Canadian International* ... Agency 7.7 *dual impeller* ... system, *flooding, loading* ... behaviours 7.8 *bulk* properties, *15%Mo/Al$_2$O$_3$* catalyst, *pure cristalline* MoS$_2$, PPG Canada 7.10 *oven dry(OD)* ... flow 7.11 *public-private* partnership, *public-private sector* partnership 7.12 *geophysical* technology, *3-dimensional* space, *geophysical* operator, *airborne* surveys, *line/km* cost 7.13 *chief executive* officer, *Medialinx Interactive* 7.14 *transfer-screw* speed, *specific* energy 7.15 *Quebec City-Windsor* corridor, *Transport 2000* advocates, *electric* trains 7.17 *GPS* ... receiver 7.18 *linear anti-friction* technology, *servicelife, base-to-mounting* ... height 7.19 *graduate* engineers, *United* Kingdom 7.20 *ACES* report, *scientific* data, *Scientific* evidence, *social* and *economic* costs 7.21 *two-stage* reactor, *interstage* addition, *overall* ... performance, *large scale* reactor 8.2 *disposal* option 8.3 *environmental* issues 8.4 *chief executive* officer, *social* centre 8.6 *analog Nova-Scrope AB* and *digital Nova-Scrobe DB* stroboscopes, *high-performance internal rechargeable* batteries, *AC* ... cord 8.7 *10X planachromat HD* objective, *Koehler* illumination, *10X final* magnification 8.8 *collective* agreement 8.9 *Annual General* Meeting, *Executive* Committee 8.11 *catch-22* situation 8.12 *McMaster* University 8.14 *inert* gases

8.16 *capital* projects, *economic* turn-around **8.21** *independent* . . . industry, *solar* . . . heaters, *nuclear* plants, *non-renewable* technologies **8.23** *environmental* choice **8.25** *environmental* concerns **8.28** *social* graces **8.29** *international* competition, *National* . . . Council **9.1** *mesoscopic* framework **9.3** *TCF* . . . *TEF* . . . plant, *TEF* Mill **9.7** *Exall* Resources, *Mazaruni River gold-diamond* project, *Santo Thomas* . . . mine **10.3** *Tech* Ltd., *drop-off* responsibilities **10.4** *IVHS America* **10.7** *Todo-matic* . . . couplings **10.8** *Windsor/Detroit* area, *Niagara* frontier, *AVI* technologies, *commuter* vehicles **10.9** *financial* assurances **10.11** *cellular* crust **10.13** *experimental* results **10.14** *Inuit* settlements **10.15** *common* law **10.17** *Bahia Sull* Mill, *Cluster* rule **10.19** *shrinkage* stopes **10.22** *United States*, *medical* facilities **10.23** *ultimate* strains, *tubular* specimens **10.25** *IP, TEM and magnetic* techniques, *Hailal Safil* region **10.27** *toxic* compounds **10.28** *nuclear waste management* programs **10.29** *associate* officer, *Visual* Arts, *Ontario Arts* Council **10.32** *environmental* impacts, *indoor environmental* quality **10.33** *Donhue* Mills, *Maclaren* mill **10.36** *RCEME* engineers, *1st Canadian* Army **10.38** *discipline-configuration* management **10.40** *practical* problems **10.42** *environmental* news, *growth-progress-wealth* equation **10.43** *chemical* reactions, *energy-* and *yield* efficient **10.46** *low-pressure* turbines, *900 MW Gosgen nuclear* . . . station **10.47** *MRO* customers **10.48** *regional-to-*

site-specific exploration **11.2** *Sword-Feeder* **11.3** *Federal* Government **11.4** *mathematical* model, *kinetic* mechanisms **11.6** *Voisey Bay* nickel discovery **11.12** *0.1 N acetic acid* solution **11.14** *"analytical* signal," *vertical* and *horizontal* derivatives, *magnetic* data **12.2** *structural* components **14.3** *Acoustic* emission **14.5** *reproductive* structures **14.7** *two-stage* . . . reactor, *inter-stage* addition, *catalytic* reactions, *non-catalytic* . . . reactions, *plug-flow* behaviour, *partial* pressure **14.9** *experimental* study, *experimental* conditions, *Stokes* number **14.10** *DSI* instrument, *NanoMechanical* Probe **14.11** *laminar* flow, *coal-water* mixture, *Newtonian* correlation, *thermal* conductivities **B.1** *Canadian Aeronautics and Space* Institute, *Candian Space* Agency, *biomedical* engineering **B.2** *electrical* department, *Worcester Polytechnic* Institute, *Clark* University, *Queen's* faculty **B.3** *Queen's* Engineers, *Applied* Science **B.4** *BSc* degree, *Carleton* University, *MSc* degree, *Geological* Survey, *Early Proterozoic Trans-Hudson* Oregon, *massive sulphide* deposits, *Archaen and Early Proterozoic* . . . terranes, *Cretaceous ophiolite* terranes, *regional* . . . *hydrothermal* systems **D.1** *experimental* observations **D.2** *linear* . . . equations

-ED

3.1 *self-contained* . . . devices, *self-regulated* devices, *self energized* devices, *electrically-driven* pump **4.2** *proposed* contributions, *planned* . . . contri-

butions, *proposed* research topics **4.3** *well-known* model classes **5.1** *widely-used* . . . system, *towed* bird **5.2** *improved* operating capability, *increased* capacity, *bleached* softwood **5.5** *integrated* . . . systems **5.9** *full-featured* . . . controller **5.13** *planned* . . . surface, *planned* altitude, *planned* rate **5.15** *well-calcified* cyanobacteria, . . . *limited* biota **5.16** *brecciated* limestones **5.17** *slotted* . . . screens **5.21** *hand-held* instruments **5.26** *hand-held* instrument, *battery-powered* unit **5.28** *recycled* pump **6.2** *compressed* air **6.9** *hydrazine-powered* thrusters **6.10** *improved* . . . *fragmentation, computerized* . . . system **7.7** *agitated* . . . system **7.11** *estimated* 20, 000 new jobs **7.12** *reduced* costs **8.1** *wood* beams **8.3** *interested* parties **8.4** *glass-encased* structure **8.6** *hand-held* instruments **8.7** *transmitted* light **8.8** *non-unionized* environment **10.17** *proposed* . . . rule **10.47** *product and service-oriented* salespeople **11.2** *hand-held* . . . Sword-Feeder **11.3** *soon-to-be-released* . . . strategy **11.5** *integrated* . . . topographies **11.6** *renewed* interest **11.11** *predicted* and *experimentally observed* locations **11.12** *distilled* water **11.13** *reduced* . . . manoeuvres **12.2** *integrated* systems **14.3** *measured* . . . parameters **14.7** *inclined,* . . . *mechanically-agitated* . . . units **14.9** *settled* particles **14.10** *newly-developed* instrument **B.2** *U.S.-trained* engineer, *earned* PhD

-ING

3.1 *heating* plant **4.1** *Losing* Strategy, *Winning* Strategy, *pulping* process **5.2** *operating* capability **5.6** *processing* systems **5.8** *positioning* systems **5.11** *recording* system **5.16** *oxidizing* . . . brines, *reducing* agents **5.18** *following* advantages **5.27** *graphing* functions **6.9** *living* room **6.10** *monitoring* system, *drilling* system **7.2** *calending* operations **7.4** *mining* industry **7.5** *supporting* masonry piers, *engineering* analysis **7.6** *Lending* Agencies, *engineering* projects, *developing* world **7.7** *flooding, loading* . . . behaviours **7.9** *manufacturing* downturn **7.10** *feeding* system **7.11** *planning* stages **7.13** *living* dead **7.14**

incoming chips **7.15** *existing* infrastructure **7.17** *settling* time, *measuring* receiver, *operating* conditions **7.18** *operating* conditions **7.19** *starting* salary **8.1** *building* department, *building* official **8.2** *declining* . . . capacity **8.3** *changing* times, *practising* engineers **8.17** *energy-rating* standard **8.25** *driving* forces **8.28** *engineering* students **10.2** *engineering* graduates **10.7** *self-sealing* couplings **10.8** *trucking* industry **10.9** *mining* activities, *decommissioning* obligations **10.12** *bleaching* towers **10.42** *alarming* news **10.43** *drafting* course

11.8 *reading* text, *composing* exercise **12.2** *mining* methods, *mining* process **14.3** *increasing* attention **14.7** *operating* conditions, *bubbling* . . . reactor **14.9** *settling* diameters **B.1** *engineering* assistant, *teaching* assistant, *engineering* school **B.3** *engineering* history

Selected Bibliography

Books

Alred, G.J., and Oliu, W.E. and Brusaw, C.T. (1992). *The Professional Writer: A Guide for Advanced Technical Writing*, New York, New York: St. Martin's Press.

Baron, D. (1986). *Grammar and Gender*, New Haven, Connecticut: Yale University Press.

Beene, L. and White, P. (eds.) (1988). *Solving Problems in Technical Writing*, New York, New York: Oxford University Press.

Bell, J.K. and Cohn, A.A. (1976). *Rhetoric in a Modern Mode*, Beverly Hills, California: Glencoe Press.

Blicq, R.S. (1983). *Technically Write!*, Englewood Cliffs, New Jersey: Prentice Hall.

Blicq, R.S. (1985). *Administratively Write!*, Scarborough, Ontario: Prentice Hall.

Capp, G.R. (1966). *How to Communicate Orally*, Englewood Cliffs, New Jersey: Prentice Hall.

Carey, G.V. (1971). *Mind the Stop*, London: Pelican.

Corbett, E.P.J. (1977). *The Little Rhetoric and Handbook*, New York, New York: John Wiley.

Couture, B. (ed.) (1986). *Functional Approaches to Writing: Research Perspectives*, London: Francis Pinter.

Ebbitt, W.R. and Ebbitt, D.R. (1990). *Index to English*, New York, New York: Oxford University Press.

Fearing, B.E. and Sparrow, W.K. (eds) (1989). *Technical Writing: Theory and Practice*, New York, New York: Modern Language Association of America.

Godfrey, D.W.H. (1983). *Modern Technical Writing*, Toronto, Ontario: McGraw Hill Ryerson.

Hahn, H. (1999). *Hanley Hahn Teaches the Internet*, Indianapolis, Indiana: Que Corporation.

Halliday, M.A.K. and Hasan, R. (1976), *Cohesion in English*, London: Longman.

Hodges, J.C., Whitten, M.E., Brown, J. and Flick, J. (1990). *Harbrace College*

Handbook for Canadian Writers, Toronto, Ontario: Harcourt Brace Jovanovich.

Hoey, M. (1983). *On the Surface of Discourse*, London: George Allen and Unwin.
Hoey, M. (1991). *Patterns of Lexis in Texts*, Oxford: Oxford University Press.

Janis, J.H. (1977). *College Writing: A Rhetoric and Handbook*, New York, New York: Macmillan.

Jordan, M.P. (1984). *Rhetoric of Everyday English Texts*, London: George Allen and Unwin.

Jordan, M.P. (1984). *Fundamentals of Technical Description*, Malabar, Florida: Krieger.

Lannon, J.M. (1994). *Technical Writing*, New York, New York: Harper Collins.

Lay, M.M. (1982). *Strategies for Technical Writing*, New York, New York: Holt Rinehart and Winston.

Mann, W.C. and Thompson, S.A. (eds.) (1992). *Discourse Description*, Amsterdam, Holland: John Benjamins.

Martin, J.R. (1992). *English Text*, Amsterdam, Holland: John Benjamins.

Messanger, W.E. and de Bruyn, J. (1986). *The Canadian Writer's Handbook*, Scarborough, Ontario: Prentice Hall.

Miller, C. and Swift, K. (1988). *The Handbook of Non-Sexist Writing*, New York, New York: Harper and Row.

Minister of Supply and Services Canada (1982). *How to Write SI*, Ottawa, Ontario: Metric Commission Canada.

Roberts, J., Scarry, S. and Scarry J. (1994), *The Canadian Writer's Workplace*, Toronto, Ontario: Harcourt Brace.

Rodman, L. (1996). *Technical Communication*, Toronto, Ontario: Harcourt Brace Jovanovich.

Saunders, P. (1992). *Strategy: Writing at Work*, Toronto, Ontario: Harcourt Brace Jovanovich.

Strunk, W. Jr. and White, E.B. (1979). *The Elements of Style*, New York, New York: Macmillan.

Turner, R.P. (1964). *Grammar Review for Technical Writers*, San Francisco, California: Rinehart Press.

Vallins, G.H. (1953). *Better English*, London: Pan Piper.
VanAlstyne, J.S. and Maddison, G.R. (1986). *Professional and Technical Writing Strategies*, Englewood Cliffs, New Jersey: Prentice Hall.

Werlich, E. (1976). *A Text Grammar of English*, Heidelberg, Germany: Quelle and Meyer.

Wilcox, R.P. (1967). *Oral Reporting in Business and Industry*, Englewood Cliffs, New Jersey: Prentice Hall.

Williams, J.M. (1989). *Style*, Chicago, Illinois: University of Chicago Press.

Winter, E.O.O. (1976). *Fundamentals of Information Structure*, Hatfield, England: University of Hertfordshire.

Winter, E.O.O. (1977). *A Clause-Relational Approach to English Texts*, Special Monograph Issue of *Instructional Science*, Amsterdam, Holland: Elsevier.

Young, M. (1989). *The Technnical Writer's Handbook, Mill Valley, California: University Science Books*.

Young, R.E., Becker, A.L. and Pike, K.L. (1970). *Rhetoric, Discovery and Change*, New York, New York: Harcourt Brace Jovanovich.

Reference Works

A Canadian Guide to English Usage (1997). M. Fee and J. McAlpine, Toronto, Ontario: Oxford University Press.

A Dictionary of American-English Usage (1957). M. Nicholson, New York, New York: Signet.

Chambers's Technical Dictionary (1958). C. F. Tweney and L. E. C. Hughes, Eds., London: W.& R. Chambers.

McGraw-Hill Encyclopedia of Enginering, S.P. Parker, Ed., New York, New York: McGraw Hill.

Fowler's Modern English Usage (1996). Oxford: Oxford University Press.

Funk and Wagnalls Canadian College Dictionary (1989). Toronto, Ontario: Fitzhenry and Whiteside.

Modern American Usage (1966). W. Follett, New York, New York: Hill and Wang.

Pocket Oxford Dictionary (1993). Oxford: Oxford University Press.

Robert's Rules of Order (1981). Atlanta, Georgia: Scott Foresman and Company.

The Careful Writer: A Modern Guide to English Usage (1965). Bernstein, T.M. (1965), New York, New York: Atheneum.

The Chicago Manual of Style (1993). Chicago, Illinois: University of Chicago Press.

The Concise Oxford Dictionary (1984). Oxford: Oxford University Press.

The Concise Roget's International Thesaurus (1994). New York, New York: Harper Collins.

Usage and Abusage (1969). E. Partridge, London: Penguin.

Van Nostrand's Scientific Encycolpedia (1995). A. D. Concidine, Ed., New York, New York: Van Nostrand Reinhold.

Webster's Seventh New Collegiate Dictionary (1995). Toronto, Ontario: Thompson Allen and Son.

Journals

IEEE Transactions on Professional Communication

Journal of Advanced Composition

Journal of Technical Writing and Communication

Technical Communication

Technical Communication Quarterly

Technostyle

The Bulletin for the Association for Business Communication

The Journal of Business Communication